America's National Scenic Trails

By Kathleen Ann Cordes

PHOTOGRAPHS BY JANE LAMMERS

FOREWORD BY STEVEN ELKINTON

UNIVERSITY OF OKLAHOMA PRESS : NORMAN

Also by Kathleen Ann Cordes

(with Hilmi Ibrahim) *Outdoor Recreation* (Dubuque, 1993)0

(with Hilmi Ibrahim) *Applications in Recreation and Leisure,* 2d ed. (St. Louis, 1999)

America's National Historic Trails (Norman, 1999)

To our parents, Ed and Rita Cordes
and Virginia Lammers

LIBRARY OF CONGRESS CATALOGING-IN-PUBLICATION DATA

Cordes, Kathleen A.
America's national scenic trails / by Kathleen Ann Cordes ; photographs by Jane Lammers.
    p. cm.
Includes bibliographical references and index.
ISBN 0–8061–3296–5 (pbk. : alk. paper)
1. United States—Guidebooks.   2. Trails—United States—Guidebooks.   3. National parks and reserves—United States—Guidebooks.   4. Scenic byways—United States—Guidebooks.   5. Outdoor recreation—United States—Guidebooks.   6. United States—Description and travel.
I. Title.

E158.C827 2001
917.304'929—dc21
                                                    00–061597

Contents

Illustrations

Maps

Foreword

Trails have universal appeal. Early humans left a tracery of travel routes reflecting their restlessness, desire to discover what is over the horizon, to gather food, to follow game, to seek mates, to trade, and to make war. Until roads and railroads began obliterating these tracks and trails, later generations took them for granted. In our own century, however, even as trails for trade and travel largely disappeared, trails for recreation emerged. And these trails are here to stay, cherished by hikers, horseback enthusiasts, and volunteers.

Most nations have trails, but few have formally recognized them. In the United States the National Trails System Act of 1968 was passed in response to two distinct national trends: an increasing interest in outdoor recreation and a burgeoning environmental awareness. The 1960s saw passage of remarkable national legislation establishing designated wildernesses, establishing historic preservation as

national policy, and providing federal funds for the establishment of park lands and the protection of rivers. At the same time, Laurence Rockefeller's Outdoor Recreation Resources Review Commission issued a call for more federal involvement in recreation of all kinds, seeing recreation as key to national character, fitness, and health. The idea of protected national trail corridors—developed and operated in partnerships—grew out of these two trends and successfully captured Congressional attention.

As these trails have been conceived, studied, developed, and maintained for more than thirty years, public tastes and interests have changed. Many different types of trail users now vie for access to trails. Trails have been constructed in the remotest backcountry and the most urban neighborhoods. Together with the National Historic Trails and the recent coast-to-coast American Discovery Trail, the National Scenic Trails are a gift of visionaries and hard-working volunteers who believe in them so much that they want you and me to fall in love with them as they have.

As the millennium turns, Kathleen Cordes has chosen an excellent time to feature America's eight National Scenic Trails. Her ability to describe trails in all their complexity is evident—as are the skills of photographer Jane Lammers—in their earlier work, *America's National Historic Trails.* America's National Scenic Trails are a millennial gift that just might be in place for public enjoyment a thousand years from now!

STEVEN ELKINTON

Program Leader for National Trails System Programming
National Park Service

Acknowledgments

I would like to acknowledge first the thousands of dedicated, hardworking trail volunteers. Without them, there would be few trails to write about or photograph or travel. Their collective effort has fueled the identification or creation of each national scenic trail. Taken together, their efforts were, and still are, herculean.

With thousands of miles of trail to explore, help from local people was essential. Whether professionals or volunteers, these individuals helped in countless ways. They wanted even more people to know about their trails—how to reach them, how to enjoy them, how to celebrate them, and how to volunteer to maintain them—and they were willing to lend a helping hand and point the way whenever and wherever possible. Our heartfelt thanks to all of them. Special appreciation is due the leadership of the Appalachian Trail Conference, the Continental Divide Trail Alliance, the Pacific Crest Trail Association, the North Country Trail Association, the Florida Trail Association, the Potomac Heritage Trail Committee, the Natchez Trace Trail Conference, and the Ice Age Park and Trail Foundation. They are truly champions of the national trail community.

At the University of Oklahoma Press, we would like to thank John Drayton, director, for his strong, steady support and clear vision for the book; Jean Hurtado, acquisitions editor, who welcomed the manuscript with open arms; Jo Ann Reece, associate editor, and Sheila Berg, copy editor, for patiently and skillfully transforming the manuscript into a handsome book; Caroline Dwyer, publicist, for sharing her bright anticipation of the book's reception at just the right time; and Steve Rice, direct mail manager, for skillfully spreading the word. Talented researcher John Strey always found answers to the difficult questions, and the experts at each of the national trails never failed to provide contacts, references, and materials, including their valuable comprehensive plans. Steve Elkinton, program leader for the National Trails System of the National Park Service, carefully reviewed each chapter and provided thoughtful insights and suggestions that made the book better. I am most appreciative of the advice offered by the manuscript reviewers: Janice Artemel, Tim Francis, Lynna Howard, Brian King, Bill Menke, Pamela J. Schuler, and Joe Sobinovsky. Andrew Hanson of the state of Wisconsin had invaluable suggestions for the chapter on the Ice Age National Scenic Trail. Kent Wimmer reviewed the manuscript and provided answers to the tough questions on the Florida Trail, and William R. Menke did so on the North Country Trail. Jeff Schaffer of the Pacific Crest Trail generously refined the information on the volcanic formations in the Pacific Crest Trail corridor. Friends and colleagues Dave Sanderlin, Bob Bacon, Anne Rosser, Gisella Duarte-Cosman, and Colleen Beck of San Diego, Judy Elliott of Carlsbad, Mary and Eddie Vogelsang of Baltimore, and Nancy Lammers of Alexandria offered continued and meaningful support throughout the multi-year project.

Marc Magliori and Dominick Albano of Amtrak extended their support over and over as we crisscrossed the country to reach the various trailheads and access points. Others such as Rob Fennimore of Kaufman Boots, Jamie Tipton of North Face, Madeline Cassidy of Pentax Binoculars, Frank Federer of Redfeather Snowshoes, and Michael Brooks of Rocky Boots, and the people at Smartwool provided sturdy equipment for us on the trail. Lucette Brehm of the Delta Queen Steamboat Company saw to it that we could reach the Natchez Trace National Scenic Trail. Magellan helped us with their GPS navigator.

Along each national trail state and local people provided key support. For the Appalachian Scenic Trail: Cheryl Smith in Georgia and the Amicalola Falls State Park Resort near Springer Mountain; Chris Mackey of North Carolina and the towns of Cherokee, Ashville, and Boone, especially Curtis Smalling and the Linville Inn of Boone; Catherine Fox of Virginia and the Peaks of Otter Resort near Roanoke; Cindy Harrington of West Virginia and Blue Ridge Outfitters, View and Ranson Armory House in Harpers Ferry, and the Cottonwood Inn and Washington House in Charles Town; Rob Burbank of New Hampshire and Appalachian Mountain Club's Pinkham Notch Lodge; Margie Wright of Maine and the Riverview Resort in Bethel and Martha Bekny of the Piper Brook Inn of Rangeley. For the Continental Divide National Scenic Trail: in New Mexico, Mike Pitel and Gary Romero of Santa Fe, Ellen MacAndrew-Caplan of Gallup, and Armanda Ortega of the historic El Rancho Hotel in Gallup; in Colorado, Connie Burke of Grand Lake, Betty and Sue at Spirit Mountain Ranch Inn in Grand Lake, Jerry Craig, our wonderful and generous fishing guide at Grand Lake, Scott Brackett of the Delaware Hotel in Leadville, the Leadville, Colorado, and Southern Railway, David Thomas of Estes Park, Helen Brown and Debra Vallia at the Aspen Lodge of Estes Park, Patti Zink of Durango, and the Durango to Silverton Narrow Gauge Railway; in Wyoming, Christie Levitt, Stephanie Anderson of TW Service's Mineral Hot Springs Lodge and Old Faithful Lodge of Yellowstone, Nona Reid of Trails West in South Pass; and in Idaho, Georgia Smith. For the Florida National Scenic Trail: Tracy Louthain of Tallahasee, Greg Langley of Lake Buenavista, Jessup Lake Gator Alley, Chalet Suzanne in Lake Wales, and Jayne Talesca Behrle of Orlando. For the Natchez Trace National Scenic Trail: Doris Ann of the Monmouth Plantation of Natchez and the people of Natchez and Tupelo, Mississippi; in Tennessee, Barbara Parker, Amanda Fuller, and Mary Bell Grande of Nashville and John F. Currie of Thermal Sash in Trenton for his cool head in an emergency on the trail. Along the North Country National Scenic Trail: Joe Banicki of Ohio, the Shawnee Park Resort, and Cecil Childress of AMFAC. For the Pacific Crest National Scenic Trail: Mary Cochran of California, Bill Chernock of Historic Zephyr Cove Resort at Lake Tahoe, Lassen Mineral Lodge in Mineral, California, and Susan Solera and Debra Wakefields of Oregon. For the Potomac Heritage National Scenic Trail: the people of Alexandria and Mount Vernon, the Hotel Washington in the District of Columbia, and the people of Harpers Ferry.

Thanks to our wonderful parents, Rita and Ed Cordes, and Virginia Lammers who shared their support throughout the project. Finally, we would like to thank the National Park Service, the USDA Forest Service, and the Bureau of Land Management employees who have worked so diligently to develop and administer our country's national trails and all state, county, and city park personnel, private landowners, naturalists, outfitters, and others who supported our book project.

KATHLEEN ANN CORDES
JANE LAMMERS

San Diego, California

Abbreviations

The following abbreviations are used frequently in the text, especially in the Points of Interest sections.

AT	Appalachian National Scenic Trail	**National Trails**
CNHT	California National Historic Trail	
CDT	Continental Divide National Scenic Trail	
FNST	Florida National Scenic Trail	
IANST	Ice Age National Scenic Trail	
INHT	Iditarod National Historic Trail	
JBANHT	Juan Bautista de Anza National Historic Trail	
LCNHT	Lewis and Clark National Historic Trail	
MPNHT	Mormon Pioneer National Historic Trail	
NTNST	Natchez Trace National Scenic Trail	
NPNHT	Nez Perce (Nee-Me-Poo) National Historic Trails	
NCT	North Country National Scenic Trail	
ONHT	Oregon National Historic Trail	
OVNHT	Overmountain Victory National Historic Trail	
PCT	Pacific Crest National Scenic Trail	
PENHT	Pony Express National Historic Trail	
PHNST	Potomac Heritage National Scenic Trail	
SFNHT	Santa Fe National Historic Trail	
SMNHT	Selma to Montgomery National Historic Trail	
TTNHT	Trail of Tears National Historic Trail	

Other Trails, Agencies, and Sites

BLM	Bureau of Land Management
NHL	National Historic Landmark
NHS	National Historic Site
NHT	National Historic Trail
NMP	National Military Park
NM	National Monument
NNL	National Register of Natural Landmarks
NP	National Park
NPS	National Park Service
NRHP	National Register of Historic Places
NSA	National Scenic Area
NST	National Scenic Trail
NWR	National Wildlife Refuge
RA	Recreation Area
SHS	State Historic Site
SP	State Park
SR	State Route
TVA	Tennessee Valley Authority
USFS	United States Forest Service
USFWS	United States Fish and Wildlife Service
WLR	Wildlife Refuge

America's National Scenic Trails

Introduction

Happily may I walk.
May it be beautiful before me.
May it be beautiful behind me.
May it be beautiful below me.
May it be beautiful above me.
May it be beautiful all around me.
In beauty it is finished.

ANONYMOUS, NAVAJO NIGHT CHANT

Nature has time to reveal her secrets on a national scenic trail: a red hawk in flight, a blue and white columbine in bloom, a cascadubg waterfall, or a snow-clad buffalo. She has time to remind us of our natural bond with this rich expanse of land we call America, where trails have been a natural part of existence for centuries, even millennia. A vivid reminder of this fact, the Natchez Trace is so worn down by passing feet and hooves that segments are now fifteen to twenty feet below the surrounding land. The succession of bison, elk, and other wildlife, as well as explorers, American Indians, trappers, soldiers, pioneers, and many others, has left a deep impression in the soft loamy soil. Whether the trail segment is young or old, a journey on a national trail brings us close to our natural surroundings. Few know this experience better than the hearty individuals known as "through-hikers" who complete a a single journey from one end of a national trail to the other.

Inspired by the development of the Appalachian National Scenic Trail in the east and the Pacific Crest National Scenic Trail in the west, the momentous National Trails System Act of 1968 spurred the development of one of the most significant recreational endeavors of our time. A precious legacy for future generations, the national trails mark long-distance pathways through some of America's most scenic lands and commemorate epoch journeys in American history. With the passage of the 1968 legislation, the United States undertook the creation of a trail system that has already identified eight national scenic trails, twelve national historic trails, and more than eight hundred national recreation trails.

National scenic trails are defined by law as continuous, extended routes of outdoor recreation within protected corridors. They provide the trail-goer with the opportunity to experience America apart from constant reminders of our technological, fast-paced world. The first two to be recognized by Congress, the Appalachian Trail and the Pacific Crest Trail, both reach distances of well over 2,000 miles. They stretch north-south along majestic mountain ranges, the former along the crests and ridges of the ancient eastern Appalachian range and the latter along the rugged western Sierra Nevada and the volcanic Cascades. With segments still under construction, the 3,000-mile-plus Continental Divide Trail threads together remote wildlands found in the Rocky Mountains along the Continental Divide. When finished, the diverse North Country Trail—the longest of the national scenic trails—will stretch more than 4,000 miles from Lake Champlain in New York to Lake Sakakawea in North Dakota, crossing northern hardwood forest, rural farmlands, glacial terrain, and tallgrass prairie. The Ice Age Trail and the Florida Trail, each contained within the boundaries of a single state, reach lengths of 1,000 miles or more. Wisconsin's Ice Age Trail offers outstanding examples of glaciated terrain, including eskers, drumlins, potholes, and kettle moraines; along the Florida Trail one encounters subtropical, dense wildlands teeming with abundant wildlife, including the alligator and the rare Florida panther. The Potomac Heritage Trail follows the river past Mount Vernon and the U.S. capital, then joins the towpath of the C&O Canal

through historic Maryland and continues to the 70-mile Laurel Highlands on a ridge of the Alleghenies of Pennsylvania—a 700-mile corridor through the populous eastern United States. Several longer segments of trail for use by equestrians and hikers have been marked in areas along the 445-mile Natchez Trace Parkway. More trail is planned along this southern corridor that follows the route of the Choctaw and Chickasaw through cypress swamps and hardwood forests, near ancient Indian ceremonial mounds, and over rolling farmland.

The national scenic trails can be enjoyed in all four seasons. Winding past striking landscapes, recreationists may encounter bright rhododendron gardens on the Appalachian; northern hardwood forests ablaze in fall color on the North Country; and snow-clad volcanoes on the Pacific Crest. Mountain meadows sprinkled with wildflowers such as Indian paintbrush refresh the spirit on the Continental Divide, summer waterfalls impart a cool mist on the Ice Age, and cypress swamps evoke a sense of mystery on the Trace all year long. Among the contrasting scenes is a view of the Capitol across the Potomac during the April cherry blossom season or the sight in winter of a great white heron in flight over the trail in Florida.

Lands in the trail corridors provide a diverse playground for outdoor enthusiasts. The trails themselves are generally intended to be footpaths, although equestrians and pack animals are permitted in areas with a tradition of such use. The mystique of the Old Trace enlivens the imagination of a traveler on horseback pondering a nineteenth-century boatman's trek home from Natchez. Llama packers head out to thread the Divide, and equestrians complete end-to-end journeys on the Pacific Crest. Cyclists and others are permitted on several multiuse segments, such as the Little Miami River Trail in Ohio and the trailway around Lake Okeechobee. Backpackers and hikers take breaks to enjoy diverse activities along the trail corridor. Rafting enthusiasts shoot the white-water rapids of the Nantahala in the Smokies; canoeists glide through the mineral-rich Suwani waters of Florida; expert kayakers flirt with the Great Falls in Maryland. En route, snowshoers explore the markings on the land along the Ice Age, while cross-country skiers encounter elk amid the snow-laden pines of the North Country.

Five of the eight designated national scenic trails are administered by the National Park Service (NPS), three by the U.S. Forest Service (USFS). Land along the trail corridor, however, may be in public or private ownership. Certified segments on federal lands, including many stretches across Bureau of Land Management (BLM) areas, are clearly marked with each trail's logo. These logos also appear widely on connector trails. To officially recognize components of a trail on nonfederal land, segments are certified by a federal administrator. Not all points of interest shown in this book are certified segments, although they might be one day. Likewise, certified segments could lose their status if they do not continue to meet the act's criteria. For certified segments on private property, arrangements for visitation are generally clear; even so, the traveler should take care not to venture away from the established trail corridor. For segments that are not certified that lie on private property, the trail visitor should be keenly aware of trespassing laws and obtain permission to pass through. When visiting trails on public lands, care should be taken to determine if a permit is required by the local land management agency.

Trail associations, state agencies, local communities, historical societies, and hiking clubs serve vitally important roles in establishing and maintaining trails. For example, with its thirty-one volunteer trail-maintaining clubs, the Appalachian Trail Conference manages the day-to-day operations of the trail in coordination with the National Park Service. The American Hiking Society provides important stewardship as advocate for the National Trails System and is the founder and coordinator of National Trails Day, America's largest yearly celebration of trails. The Rails to Trails Conservancy has vigorously advocated the conversion of abandoned railways and canalways into trailways, a few of which have been incorporated into the national scenic and historic trails. Volksmarch and Elderhostel play dynamic roles in introducing the national trails to others. In fact, in 1999 Elderhostel offered more than six hundred courses on national trails. And without the support of thousands of volunteers organized by hundreds of trail associations, the trails would not be a reality. Advocacy at the local, state, and federal levels is critical to obtaining funding for construction and maintenance of trails. As a means to coordinate their work with Congress and federal agencies, the Partnership for the National Trails System was formed in 1991. The nation is indebted to countless dedicated hardworking individuals who have voluntarily shared their resources, talents, and energy.

First Lady Hillary Rodham Clinton infused new energy into this monumental undertaking by establishing the Millennium Trails Initiative, which will help carry the trails movement into the twenty-first century. The program selected the flagship National Millennium Trails, which include two national scenic trails—the Appalachian and North Country—and three national historic trails—the Iditarod, Juan Bautista de Anza, and Lewis and Clark. In cooperation with trail advocacy groups such as the Rails to Trails

Conservancy, American Hiking Society, and American Trails, the Department of Transportation is providing significant funding for the development of urban and rural trails in America. Some of this funding will be directed toward the enhancement of the National Trails System. Another milestone for the national trails was reached in 1998 when Congress approved funding for the National Park Service to acquire land along the last thirty miles of unprotected Appalachian Trail. As the twenty-first century dawns, the achievement of a fully protected Appalachian Trail corridor sets a new standard for national scenic trails.

This book celebrates and shares the wealth of U.S. national scenic trails with all the world's citizens. Each chapter is divided into the following sections: *The History of the Trail, The Trail Today,* and *Points of Interest.* A map accompanies each *Points of Interest* section, and photographs of sites and activities help the reader to plan a visit. Highlights of the public lands along the trail corridor and interesting sites in the area are also mentioned. For instance, historic mining operations, ghost towns, and railroad sites are included in the Continental Divide chapter. The Other Attractions sections alert the reader to nearby sites that, although not directly related to the trail, may be worth a visit.

Readers interested in joining the efforts to enhance national trail growth may contact the associations and offices listed at the beginning of each chapter. Contributing to this national legacy by joining a trail club close to home can be an especially rewarding and enjoyable volunteer experience.

America's National Historic Trails, published in 1999, is the first volume of this series. It covers the twelve national historic trails (NHT) that identify routes of exploration, migration, freedom, and military actions that are part of the fabric of America. Not necessarily continuous, the national historic trails identify historic routes, remains, and artifacts that together tell the story of past adventures and conflicts. Some trail segments are so pristine that they invite today's adventurer back into time to an environment that was experienced by earlier inhabitants, explorers, pioneers, and entrepreneurs.

Many of the national historic trails have motor tour routes marked with distinctive signs and interpretive centers along the way. Modes of travel may vary—from cars, wagons, steamboats, trains, canoes, kayaks, rafts, horses, snowshoes, cross-country skis, dogsleds, and snowmobiles to bicycles, bush planes, backpacking, hiking with llamas, or just plain walking. In any case, the anticipation and preparation for a vacation along one of these routes provides an exciting focus on a particular period in the history of the United States.

A forthcoming volume in the series, on America's National Scenic Byways and all-American Roads, will cover the nation's very best scenic byways that have been designated for the first time by the U.S. Department of

TABLE 1. NATIONAL SCENIC TRAILS

Trail Name	Authorized Mileage	Administering Agency	States
Appalachian	2,144	NPS	Conn., Ga., Md., Mass., Maine, N.H., N.J., N.Y., Pa., Tenn., Vt., Va., W.Va.
Continental Divide	3,200	USFS	Colo., Idaho, Mont., N.Mex., Wyo.
Florida	1,300	USFS	Fla.
Ice Age	1,000	NPS	Wis.
Natchez Trace	694	NPS	Ala., Miss., Tenn.
North Country	4,300	NPS	Mich., Minn., N.Y., N.Dak., Ohio, Pa., Wis.
Pacific Crest	2,638	USFS	Calif., Oreg., Wash.
Potomac	704	NPS	Md., Pa., Va., D.C.

TABLE 2. NATIONAL HISTORIC TRAILS

Trail Name	Authorized Mileage	Administering Agency	States
California	5,665	NPS	Calif., Colo., Idaho, Iowa, Kans., Mo., Nebr., Nev., Oreg., Utah, Wyo.
Iditarod	2,450	BLM	Ala.
Juan Bautista de Anza	1,200	NPS	Ariz., Calif.
Lewis and Clark	3,700	NPS	Idaho, Iowa, Ill., Kans., Mo., Mont., Nebr., N.Dak., Oreg., S.Dak., Wash.
Mormon Pioneer	1,300	NPS	Ill., Iowa, Nebr., Utah, Wyo.
Nez Perce	1,170	NPS	Idaho, Mont., Oreg., Wyo.
Oregon	2,170	NPS	Idaho, Kans., Mo., Nebr., Oreg., Wash.
Overmountain Victory	300	NPS	N.C., S.C., Tenn., Va.
Pony Express	1,966	NPS	Calif., Colo., Kans., Mo., Nebr., Nev., Utah, Wyo.
Santa Fe	1,203	NPS	Colo., Kans., Mo., N.Mex., Okla.
Selma to Montgomery	53	NPS	Ala.
Trail of Tears	2,219	NPS	Ala., Ark., Ga., Ill., Ky., Mo., N.C., Okla., Tenn.

Transportation. The volume will include information on hiking opportunities, outdoor recreation and cultural and historical activities, as well as maps and color photographs.

America's National Scenic Trails is intended to serve as a general guide to the national scenic trails. Because the trails are growing and ever changing and only general maps are included, to access and hike specific segments it will most likely be necessary to consult with trail associations for suggested topographical maps, guidebooks, map books, and highway maps and to inquire locally. Addresses, telephone numbers and Web sites listed at the beginning of each chapter and Appendixes A and B help hikers to obtain additional information on detailed routes, certified segments, required permits, and up-to-date safety precautions. Some sites and trail segments have not been developed yet or may not permit public access, so it is important to respect the rights of private property owners. Before hitting the trail, hikers should let someone know where they are going and when they are due back. And sensible precautions and common sense should always be used in the backcountry. Be forewarned: following the national trails can be so appealing that once started, you may never want to stop. Happy Trails.

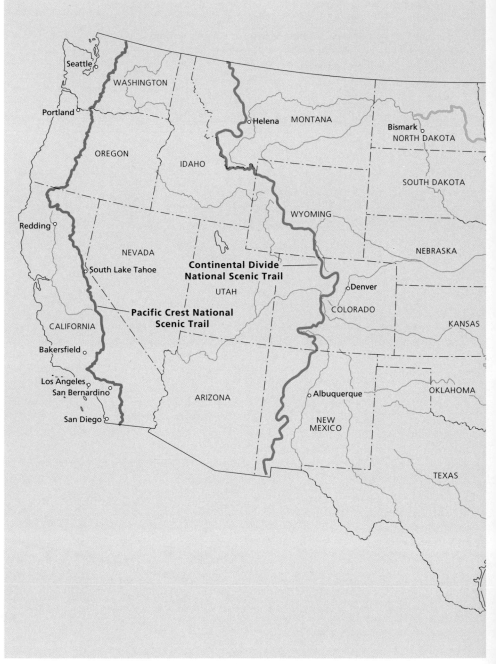

Seattle

WASHINGTON

Portland

OREGON

Redding

NEVADA

South Lake Tahoe

CALIFORNIA

Bakersfield

Los Angeles
San Bernardino

San Diego

Helena

MONTANA

Bismark
NORTH DAKOTA

SOUTH DAKOTA

IDAHO

WYOMING

**Continental Divide
National Scenic Trail**

NEBRASKA

UTAH

Denver

COLORADO

KANSAS

**Pacific Crest National
Scenic Trail**

ARIZONA

Albuquerque

NEW
MEXICO

OKLAHOMA

TEXAS

NATIONAL SCENIC TRAILS OF THE UNITED STATES

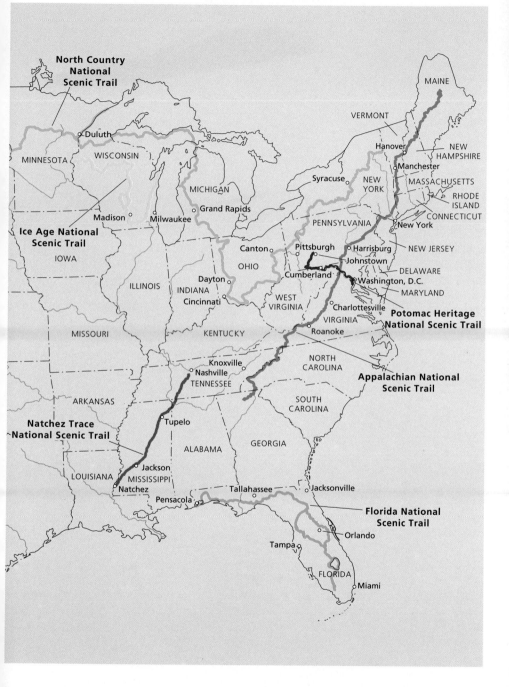

North Country National Scenic Trail

MAINE

VERMONT

Duluth

Hanover

NEW HAMPSHIRE

MINNESOTA

WISCONSIN

Manchester

Syracuse

MASSACHUSETTS

NEW YORK

RHODE ISLAND

MICHIGAN

Grand Rapids

Madison

Milwaukee

PENNSYLVANIA

CONNECTICUT

New York

Ice Age National Scenic Trail

Canton

Pittsburgh

Harrisburg

NEW JERSEY

IOWA

Johnstown

DELAWARE

OHIO

Cumberland

Washington, D.C.

Dayton

ILLINOIS

INDIANA

MARYLAND

Cincinnati

WEST VIRGINIA

Charlottesville

Potomac Heritage National Scenic Trail

VIRGINIA

MISSOURI

KENTUCKY

Roanoke

Knoxville

NORTH CAROLINA

Appalachian National Scenic Trail

Nashville

TENNESSEE

ARKANSAS

SOUTH CAROLINA

Tupelo

Natchez Trace National Scenic Trail

ALABAMA

GEORGIA

Jackson

LOUISIANA

MISSISSIPPI

Natchez

Tallahassee

Jacksonville

Pensacola

Florida National Scenic Trail

Orlando

Tampa

FLORIDA

Miami

VIEW OF HARPERS FERRY

At Weverton, Maryland, the AT merges with the C&O Canal Towpath of the Potomac Heritage National Scenic Trail before meeting a steep, blue-blazed side trail that leads to Maryland Heights. From this rocky outcrop there is a spectacular view of the confluence of the Potomac and Shenandoah Rivers and of Harpers Ferry, the headquarters of the Appalachian Trail Conference and of Harpers Ferry National Historical Park.

Appalachian National Scenic Trail

I view the existence of this pathway and the opportunity to travel it, day after day without interruption, as a distinct aspect of our American life.

MYRON H. AVERY, 1951

The granddaddy of the national scenic trails, the Appalachian Trail (AT) links the crests and ridges of the subdued Appalachian mountain range that stretches from Maine to Georgia. Those who have hiked it, and many others who have read about the epic journeys, know that it is not only one's physical nature that is challenged by this trail. A trek on the AT challenges the spirit as well. Finally reaching the summit of Katahdin at the northern terminus, the hiker's experience can be transcendent. On the way, one experiences solitude along Maine's northern bogs, beaver ponds, moose-dotted lakes, mountains, and forests. A sense of achievement follows the challenging ascent to the high peaks of New Hampshire's White Mountains. A calming gratitude arrives while crossing Vermont's bucolic valleys and the forested Green Mountains on the legendary Long Trail. Determination fuels and strengthens in Massachusetts, Connecticut, New York, and Pennsylvania as peaks, river valleys, and more peaks are mounted, traversed, and mounted in the historic countryside. As one nears the midpoint,

ADMINISTERING AGENCY
National Park Service Appalachian Trail Park Office
c/o Harpers Ferry Center
Harpers Ferry, WV 25425
304-535-6331
www.atconf.org

DESIGNATED
1968

APPROXIMATE MILEAGE
2,160 miles (3,456 kilometers)

STATES
Georgia, Tennessee, North Carolina, Virginia, West Virginia, Maryland, Pennsylvania, New Jersey, New York, Connecticut, Massachusetts, Vermont, New Hampshire, Maine

Maryland's enjoyable ridge trail leads to the confluence of two mighty rivers, the Potomac and the Shenandoah, where inspiration arrives once again at the site of historic Harpers Ferry. A mixture of strength, refreshment, and endurance enriches the body and soul on Virginia's long stretch in the Shenandoahs. Colorful wildflowers enliven the senses as the AT hiker crisscrosses the Skyline and Blue Ridge Parkways, reminded for a time of civilization left behind. Views from massive, round grassy balds in Tennessee and North Carolina sharpen a hiker's vision as the low clouds and blue haze obscure the succeeding outlines of the endless mountain ranges. Nearby in Cherokee National Forest, whitewater river running in deep river gorges exhilarate the senses. The sounds of birds chirping, the sight of delicate wildflowers in bloom, and the drama of squirrels scurrying amid the trees of the richly diverse forest is a taste of the masterpiece of nature in the Great Smoky Mountains. Each day passed on the trail in the rugged wilderness of southern North Carolina and northern Georgia gains the hiker more distance from Springer Mountain, the southern terminus, and as the miles mount the promise of an epic journey takes hold. The unfolding of an end-to-end hike on the AT in the wooded, wild, pastoral, culturally significant, and spiritually rewarding lands of the ancient Appalachian Mountains takes on a mystical quality for both the brave adventurer and for those who look on with admiration.

The History of the Trail

New England's trail movement of the late nineteenth and early twentieth century, known as the *tramping* movement, was elevated to new heights in 1921 when Emile Benton MacKaye (pronounced *Ma-Kye*) published an article in the October issue of the *Journal of the American Institute of Architects.* The forester, conservationist, and New Deal activist shared his vision of a long-distance footpath along the crests of the Appalachian chain. In an increasingly urbanized and mechanized world, he wrote, "time for true leisure of the average adult American appears . . . to be meager indeed," and he went on to urge his readers to use leisure time wisely and to pursue healthy recuperation in the open air. He wrote that the country needed to develop facilities in the mountains so that people could benefit from "oxygen in the mountain air along the Appalachian skyline." Setting leisure aside, he discussed the practical aspects of building a long-distance footpath: it would lead to the development of new jobs and serve as "a battle line against fire and flood—even against disease." His economic arguments did not receive support, but his compelling vision of a recreation resource caught on and changed the course of recreation and land conservation in the United States.

Like many transforming events, the seeds of MacKaye's article had been germinating for some time. MacKaye wrote, years later, that his vision of a north-south mountain footpath may have first occurred to him as early as 1897 while hiking in New Hampshire's White Mountains, where the Appalachian Mountain Club (AMC), founded in 1876, had built an extensive network of trails. In the first decade of the twentieth century, James P. Taylor and members of the Green Mountain Club (GMC) successfully built the Long Trail, Vermont's famous footpath that is now 265 miles. A veteran of the Long Trail, Will S. Monroe, promoted his idea to connect the Long Trail to the Delaware Water Gap in Pennsylvania and New Jersey. In 1914 Taylor discussed a plan for a "grand trunk" trail along the mountain ridges from Quebec to New York. He was the featured speaker at the first meeting of the New England Trail Conference in 1916, organized by local trail club leaders such as Taylor of the GMC, Allen Chamberlain of the AMC, and Philip Ayres, a forester. There Taylor's plan was received enthusiastically and stimulated the exchange of ideas. Sumner Hooper of Maine suggested an extension of the Long Trail to Katahdin, Maine. And William Hall, a forester, suggested a link with the southern Appalachians. The pot of simmering ideas was ready to boil when MacKaye published his inspiring vision in the prestigious journal.

BENTON MACKAYE SIGN

The Benton MacKaye Trail, named in honor of the AT's founder, may one day connect the AT with the Florida National Scenic Trail to allow a through-hike the full length of the Eastern Seaboard.

Equally significant to the formation of the Appalachian Trail was MacKaye's determination and zeal. Reaction was immediate, and implementation swift. Lessons learned from his entrepreneur father, who produced, among other things, Buffalo Bill's Wild West Show, may have helped MacKaye to promote the nationwide project. He forwarded reprints of his article to influential individuals and met with many of them. And he quickly mapped out the trail with catchy locations for the termini— from the highest point in the Northeast, Mount Washington, to the highest peak east of the Rockies, Mount Mitchell. It was a vivid image, worthy of news coverage. During the summer following publication of the article, volunteers marked and cut a segment of the Appalachian Trail in Palisades Interstate Park in

Soon extensions and branches to
Katahdin, Maine, and Lookout
Mountain, Tennessee, were developed, and a unique partnership
between the public and the
private sectors was born. MacKaye,
recognized as the father of the
Appalachian Trail, put it this way:
"The Appalachian Trail is to this
Appalachian region what the
Pacific Railway was to the Far
West—a means of 'opening up'
the country. But a very different
kind of 'opening up.' Instead of a
railway we want a 'trailway.'"

Also in 1925, an important
New Englander came onto the
scene: Myron H. Avery, maritime
attorney and one of the founders
of the Potomac Appalachian Trail
Club. Avery became the first
elected president of the ATC and
in 1926 joined the executive
committee and the board. By
1930 he began his official twenty-
one-year tenure as chair when his
predecessor, Judge Arthur
Perkins, stepped down for health
reasons. At the helm, Avery actually blazed much of the AT in
1933–34 with his own home-
made measuring wheel, and he
spurred the hardy corps of
volunteers on to the remarkable
achievement of building the
entire trail by 1937. After the
final link was in place between
Maine's Spaulding and Sugarloaf
Mountains, the AT stretched
from Katahdin all the way to
Mount Oglethorpe in Georgia, a
southern terminus destined to
change yet again.

In the years between his arrival
and the trail's completion, Avery

New York. By 1923 dedication
ceremonies for the first
completed segment were held at
Bear Mountain.

To spur growth, MacKaye
founded the Appalachian Trail
Conference (ATC) on March 3,
1925. Palisades Interstate Park
general manager, Maj. William A.
Welch, served as chair. At the
conference plans were formulated
to run the trail from New
Hampshire's Mount Washington
to a different southern terminus,
Cohutta Mountain in Georgia.

KATAHDIN FROM DAICEY POND AT
BAXTER STATE PARK

The AT's northern terminus in Maine's Baxter State Park is located atop Katahdin, a granite monolith whose name means "greatest mountain." From the banks of Daicey Pond, where two lean-tos are reserved just for through-hikers, there is a tranquil view of the legendary mountain.

left a lasting legacy. First, the official AT emblem—today's ATC trademark—was designed by the ATC's first president, Welch, and adopted by the conference. Second, Avery pressed for and won a northern terminus in his native Maine. Third, in 1935, when government officials decided to locate Virginia's Skyline Drive virtually on top of the trail, he urged the AT's relocation. The pragmatic Avery saw this as an approach that would avoid the alienation of important government allies. MacKaye saw the Skyline issue as far more profound: he believed it was a threat to the very existence of wilderness and to Shenandoah National Park in particular. He saw the AT as a wilderness sanctuary about to be invaded by Skyline Drive and the automobiles that would travel it. MacKaye held to the conviction that the move should be opposed philosophically, and a rift formed between the two men that never healed. Just one year before the AT's completion, MacKaye turned his energy to the founding of the Wilderness Society. Avery became the first person to walk all the sections of the trail.

In 1937, with the trail complete, the primary goal of the ATC became the development of a buffer zone. Authorization of the Blue Ridge Parkway the very next year usurped another 120 miles of the trail, and once again trail building was the top priority, this time for more than a decade.

HIKER ON SKYLINE TRAIL

Virginia contains more than one-fourth of the AT—about 500 miles, with about 100 miles paralleling Skyline Drive through beautiful Shenandoah National Park. In the 1930s when the parkway was built, much of the AT was relocated by the Civilian Conservation Corps. Today hikers enjoy vistas of forested slopes, jagged rocks, waterfalls, and canyons along one of the most visited sections of the AT.

Neglected during World War II and the immediate postwar years, the AT fell into disrepair. However, Earl V. Shaffer's through-hike in 1948, the first uninterrupted trek reported by the media, stirred publicity, stunned onlookers, and infused new vigor into the trail vision. Completion of the AT for a second time occurred in 1951. For the occasion, Avery sparked the volunteers to construct a string of shelters along the route that had been originally envisioned in the 1930s. Afterward, he announced he would not run for reelection and underscored the trail's need for some form of public protection. He wrote, "We enter now in Appalachian Trail history, the stage where emphasis and attention must be focused on the benefits resulting from this opportunity to travel the forests of the eastern United States, as our forefathers knew them."

In 1958, to combat commercial developments such as chicken farms at Mount Oglethorpe, the ATC moved the trail's southern terminus to Springer Mountain. Other modifications in the 1950s and 1960s enhanced the trail and made it safer to travel. But the corridor was still vulnerable. Commercialization, timber cutting, and urbanization could be held at bay only by protective federal legislation. In 1964 Sen. Gaylord Nelson of Wisconsin introduced legislation to protect the AT and its surroundings. At about that time, President Lyndon B. Johnson directed Secretary of the Interior Stewart Udall to develop recommendations for a national system of trails that would help to enhance the quality of life in the United States. Furthering the goal of the Great Society initiative, President Johnson's speech on February 8, 1965, called for a balanced system of trails that would protect and enhance the quality of the outdoor environment and provide opportunities for healthful outdoor recreation:

PIAZZA ROCK LEAN-TO

The idea of building a series of shelters along the trail was initially discussed in the 1930s and finally implemented by volunteers in 1951. The 260 three-sided structures, called lean-tos in some areas, are located approximately one day's journey apart and provide accommodations for hikers on a first-come basis. This lean-to is named Piazza Rock after a huge granite slab that juts out from the side of a cliff near Rangeley in Maine.

The forgotten outdoorsmen of today are those who like to walk, hike, ride, horseback, or bicycle. For them, we must have trails as well as highways. Nor should motor vehicles be permitted to tyrannize the more leisurely human traffic. In the backcountry, we need to copy the great Appalachian Trail in all parts of America, and to make full use of rights-of-ways and other public paths.

An ATC committee worked with the Bureau of Outdoor Recreation's 1966 nationwide trail study, "Trails for America," to provide acceptable national trails legislation. On October 2, 1968, President Johnson signed Public Law 90-543, the National Trails System Act, which named the Appalachian Trail America's first national scenic trail and the Pacific Crest Trail, the second (see PC). The secretary of the interior delegated his responsibility to preserve and protect the Appalachian National Scenic Trail to the National Park Service, which included the authority to use, as a last resort, the power of eminent domain to uphold the charge. Ten years later, in 1978, at a time when 45 percent of the AT lay on private land subject to development, additional legislation passed that strengthened the government's ability to acquire land. Acquisition increased when Congress and President Jimmy Carter authorized more than $90 million for AT lands. Since 1978 the NPS, in cooperation with the USFS and the states, has actively acquired land in the AT corridor. To augment the land purchase program, the ATC established the Trust for Appalachian Trail Lands in the 1980s, making it possible to protect more lands adjacent to the trail, including mountain meadows, fragile tundra, and rare plant and animal sanctuaries, for future generations.

In an unprecedented move in 1984, in recognition of the ATC 's long-standing tradition of volunteer construction, development, and maintenance of the AT, the NPS delegated to it much of the day-to-day management of the trail. In the delegation agreement, the ATC and its thirty-one trail-maintaining clubs were authorized to manage new federal lands in the corridor. Although partnership agreements between the ATC, the NPS, and the USFS date back to 1935, this was the first time that the NPS had entrusted a private organization with the day-to-day stewardship of large national park lands. A new era of trail corridor management had begun.

To complete the protection of the entire AT before the end of the century, the federal government, under President Bill Clinton, set aside $15.1 million in October 1998 to purchase land surrounding the last thirty miles of unprotected trail corridor. As the new millennium begins, the ATC can celebrate the achievement of its goal of a protected corridor, a goal that has been pursued since 1937. Clearly a patriarch of footpaths around the world, the ATC is a sterling role model for other trail organizations. Its achievement not only marks a milestone in AT history, it sets forth a standard of land conservation for other national scenic trails to applaud, aspire to, and achieve again and again.

FORESTS OF THE GREAT SMOKY MOUNTAINS NATIONAL PARK

Internationally renowned for its biological diversity, the Great Smoky Mountains National Park Biosphere Reserve is the subject of a unique biological project called the All Taxa Biodiversity Inventory (ATBI). Over the next ten to fifteen years, scientists and volunteers from all over the world will undertake a task that has never been accomplished before anywhere: they will compile an inventory of all species in the park. Few locations match the biological diversity of the Smokies, which has more than 4,000 identified species of plants, including more than 1,500 flowering plants, and over 450 identified vertebrate species, of which 230 are birds and 65 are mammals, including the black bear and the red wolf. Officials at the park are aware of over 2,250 species of fungi, 330 species of mosses and liverworts, and 230 species of lichens. These staggering numbers represent only the identified species; scientists estimate that there are more than 20,000 types of fungi alone and a total of over 100,000 biological species to be inventoried. With just under 10,000 identified, much work remains in this pioneering ATBI effort. To find updates on the pioneering ATBI or to get involved as a volunteer, visit the Web site at www.discoverlife.org.

The area's biological diversity is attributed to a number of factors, including a long growing season, plentiful rainfall from the Gulf of Mexico, the presence of diverse soils, and the northeast-southwest alignment of the southern Appalachian Mountains. Elevation changes foster diversity, creating a broad spectrum of life zones in a compact area. A glimpse of the variety is accessible to most visitors as they pass through the park's five life zones. For each 1,000 feet of elevation gained in the park, the change in life zones is equivalent to moving 250 miles farther north, rendering a walk in the park, from mountain base to mountain peak, comparable to traveling 1,250 miles north to the terminus of the Appalachian Trail.

Unlike most areas of North America, the forests in the southern Appalachians have been a relatively stable platform for the evolution of life for more than 230 million years. Setbacks experienced nearly everywhere else, such as the complete encroachment of ice or the inundation of the land, did not occur here. Today, the tree diversity has become so rich, with over 130 species, that it exceeds that found in all of Europe.

Natural factors, national park status, and scientific research have resulted in the identification of more old-growth virgin forests in the park than anywhere in the eastern United States. For instance, there are sixty-one old-growth oak and twenty-nine old-growth eastern hemlock stands remaining that were left undisturbed by European settlers. Researchers note that small trees are not necessarily young ones. For example, the oldest eastern hemlock, 504 years, measures less than 20 inches in diameter. It took one hemlock 157 years to add just 2 inches of diameter. The oldest tree in the park, 563 years, is a black gum, and a few eastern hemlocks have kept it company for more than five hundred years. The park holds the distinction of being home to more record-size trees than any other federal lands in the United States. One of the massive old champion trees is a red maple that has a 23-foot circumference and towers 141 feet in the air. Nine species reach a height of over 150 feet. We are just beginning to learn about this rich and diverse biosystem; many of the twenty-two national champion trees were only recently identified.

All five forest types that dominate the Great Smoky Mountains can be seen from the lookout tower at Clingmans Dome, near the Appalachian Trail. These represent the major forest types found in eastern North America and encountered along the AT.

SPRUCE-FIR FOREST. Red spruce and Fraser fir dominate this evergreen forest that is found in the park at higher elevations above 4,500 and is best developed above 5,500 feet. The climate at this elevation relates to that of sea level in Maine and Quebec, where a similar forest grows. In the park, spruce-fir is the dominant forest along the Appalachian Trail, and hikers will note that many of the Fraser fir trees have died. The cause is a non-native insect called balsam woolly adelgid, a threat throughout the eastern United States. Other standout species are yellow birch, mountain ash, hobblebush, and blackberries.

NORTHERN HARDWOOD FOREST. Although interspersed with many species, sugar maple, American beech, and yellow birch characterize this broadleaf forest. It

TABLE 3. COMMON WILDFLOWERS IN THE SMOKIES

Common Name	Scientific Name	When	Where	Appearance
Hepatica	Hepatica nobilis	March–May	below 3,000'	white
Bloodroot	Sanguinaria canadensis	March–May	below 3,000'	white with orange center
Spring beauty	Claytonia virginica	March–May	wide ranging	pink/white with dark stripe
Painted trillium	Trillium undulatum	April–May	3,000–6,600'	white with pink V
Dutchman's breeches	Dicentra cucullaria	April–May	below 5,000'	white, pantaloon shaped
Sweet white violet	Viola blanda	April–May	above 2,500'	white on reddish stalks
Creeping phlox	Phlox stolonifera	April–May	1,000-3,500'	blue/pink in large patches
Crested dwarf iris	Iris cristata	April–May	below 3,500'	violet-blue
White trillium	Trillium grandiflorum	April–May	below 3,500'	waxy white/pink with age
Showy orchis	Orchis spectabilis	April–May	below 3,000'	white, deep lavender
Smooth yellow violet	Viola pennsylvanica	April–May	below 2,500'	yellow
Trout lily, dogtooth violet	Erythronium americanum	April–May	wide ranging	yellow inside, bronzy outside
Fire pink	Silene virginica	April–June	below 5,000'	bright red
Fringed phacelia	Phacelia fimbriata	April–June	2,500–5,000'	white, light blue, lavender
Foamflower	Tiarella cordifolia	April–June	below 4,000'	white, small
Vasey's trillium	Trillium vaseyi	April–June	below 3,500'	maroon
Columbine	Aquilegia canadensis	April–June	below 2,500'	red and yellow
Flame azalea	Rhododendron calendulaceum	April–July	wide ranging	orange, red, or yellow

Source: *Forests and Wildflowers in the Great Smoky Mountains National Park* (Gatlinburg: Great Smoky Mountains Natural History Association, August 1994). With permission.

dominates the middle to upper elevations from 3,500 to 5,000 feet and resembles forests throughout much of New England, New York, and Pennsylvania. Northern hardwood forests of North America produce brilliant fall color displays that few locations in the world can match. The third week in October is usually the peak color in this area.

PINE-OAK FOREST. Major species in this forest type are red, scarlet, black, and chestnut oaks and table mountain, pitch, and white pines. Hickories appear in some areas, as do yellow poplar, dogwood, and dense thickets of rhododendron and mountain laurel. Fire, which occurs in the drier ridges of the park, is required by some species for natural propagation.

HEMLOCK FOREST. Hemlocks are often found along stream-banks and moist shady slopes where water temperatures remain cold year-round. Throughout the Appalachians, hemlocks dominate streamsides up to elevations of 4,000 feet.

COVE HARDWOOD FOREST. Found at low to midlevel elevations of 4,500 feet, this forest supports the Appalachians' most diverse ecosystem and typically lines the valleys throughout the park. Important species include tulip poplar, American basswood, red maple, sweet gum, yellow buckeye, black birch, and dogwood. This lush, diverse broadleaf forest offers warm temperatures, a long growing season, and plentiful rainfall.

The table on page 22 lists the most commonly found wildflowers of the two hundred species in the Smokies.

The Trail Today

The Appalachian National Scenic Trail is a major resource for outdoor recreation in the United States. The ATC energetically maintains and protects it from overuse through an extensive network of dedicated volunteers who are considered the backbone of the AT. To volunteer for the Appalachian Trail Conference or one of its affiliated trail-maintaining clubs, contact the ATC at www.atconf.org or call 304-535-6331.

With convenient access from large urban areas in the East, most users are day-hikers or weekend backpackers. But many hikers seeking self-discovery, self-reliance, and adventure have attempted to complete the entire journey, a grueling 2,000-plus-mile trek. Twenty-nine-year-old World War II veteran Earl V. Shaffer, seeking healing through walking from his postwar depression, was the first person known to have traveled the route from end-to-end. The number of annual end-to-enders jumped significantly in 1978 from 77 to 115, and the number has continued to climb over the years. In 1998 more than fifteen hundred backpackers aimed for the accolade "2,000 milers," and about

WHITE BLAZE AND BRONZE PLAQUE

A boulder at the southern terminus at Springer Mountain is marked with the AT's characteristic white blaze and a plaque that bears the words, "A footpath for those who seek fellowship with the wilderness." A metal drawer built into the boulder holds the hikers' register.

three hundred hearty individuals succeeded. The entire trek takes five to seven months. The majority begin the pilgrimage in March or April at Springer Mountain and trek north, hoping to reach Harpers Ferry by July 15 and Katahdin before winter sets in, or by October 15, when the park closes to overnight use.

Southbounders have a more difficult journey, and, for various reasons, few complete the trek. (Perhaps the challenge prompted Shaffer to successfully complete a north-south trek in 1965, elevating him to another record: the first to complete through-hikes in opposite directions.) Although it

is possible to start as early as June in the depths of Maine's blackfly season, most southbounders smartly opt for the recommended July start. Hikers who wish to avoid crowds flip-flop: they start somewhere in the middle of the trail, head north or south, and then flip to the other end to hike the uncovered ground. And then there are individuals like Steve "Yo-Yo" Nuckolls, who, on his journey of self-discovery, had not yet found himself when he reached Katahdin in the fall, so he turned around and trekked right back to Georgia during the lonely winter. While some suggest that Warren Doyle holds the record for spending the most time on the trail, he definitely holds the record, at seven, for the most through-hikes. Despite his lack of sight, the remarkable Bill Irwin and his guide dog Orient completed an inspiring trek in 1990. At the age of sixty-seven, three-time through-hiker and

Ohio farmer, Emma "Grandma" Gatewood, was the first woman to do a through-hike alone in 1955. Equipped with sneakers and a duffel bag, she continued to hike the AT into her seventies, perhaps inspiring many of the seniors today who hit the trail for a through-hike. Once again, Earl Shaffer, at age seventy-nine, may not have been able to resist the challenge. In 1998, wearing a tattered pith helmet and carrying an army rucksack, he became the oldest person to complete the trek. With fifty years since his first long walk, the veteran says the third time is the last. In May 1999 dancer Jacques d'Amboise danced and trekked all the way to Katahdin. In towns and cities along the way, he taught his now-famous trail dance to children to further art education and to herald the new millennium.

The amount of use by each through-hiker equals the impact of approximately two hundred day- hikers, so low-impact travel is especially important. Through-hikers and overnighters are welcome to stay in the three-sided shelters built by club volunteers who maintain the trail. Typically located about 10 to 12 miles apart the entire length of the trail, the shelters are available on a first-come, first-served basis. Fees are required for campsites in the Whites and at Maine's Baxter State Park, and the popular Appalachian Mountain Club huts in the White Mountains of New Hampshire and the AMC-operated Bascom Lodge at Mount

TWO HIKERS ON ROUND BALD

Curtis Smalling takes a break from his bird-watching tours along the AT corridor to talk with the author. With a master's degree in Appalachian history and as the director of *Horn in the West*, an outdoor musical about Daniel Boone and the overmountain men, Smalling has stories to tell about the Revolutionary War heroes of the Overmountain Victory National Historic Trail. On Roan Mountain the AT and the Overmountain Victory Trail cross.

Greylock in Massachusetts require fees and advanced reservations and may opt for trail work as payment. In Virginia, the ATC owns and operates the popular twenty-six-bed Bears Den Hostel near Bluemont. The Potomac Appalachian Trail Club has huts and cabins in Shenandoah National Park; reservations are required for the cabins. There are many other wonderful accommodations, too numerous to mention here.

For current information on campsites, shelters, post offices, and various trail conditions, consult an up-to-date *Appalachian Trail Data Book*,

APPALACHIAN TRAIL BACKPACKERS PASS CATAWBA RHODODENDRONS ON ROAN MOUNTAIN

In the southern Appalachians the AT threads the Tennessee–North Carolina border between high grassy balds. In June throngs of visitors are attracted to Roan Mountain when the Catawba rhododendrons are in bloom. Backpackers on the AT at Roan's Round Bald make their way north amid the profusion of pink blossoms that blanket entire hillsides on the mountain.

such as a turn, a shelter, or a side trail. Side trails, blazed in blue, can lead to shelters or other sites.

Mountain bikes are not allowed on the footpath at all, but there are opportunities for other recreational activities. Canoeing is possible on the many ponds and rivers, and ice-climbers are welcome in winter. Bird-watching tours are available in areas; blooms of the Catawawba rhododendron in June on Roan Mountain and on other balds in the southern Appalachians attract birds and birders alike. Although the great majority of visitors are drawn to the trail from late spring through October, use during other months is on the increase everywhere.

All motorized vehicles are specifically prohibited from the footpath, although a nearby automobile route usually parallels the pedestrian route at some distance. Jamie Jensen provides details in his book, *Road Trip USA,* a Moon Travel Handbook. It is important to note that all road crossings of the trail are not designated access points and may lack parking and informational signs. Dogs are permitted to accompany hikers on the AT except in the Smokies, in part of Bear Mountain State Park in New York, and in Baxter State Park. To keep these faithful companions out of harm's way, they must be leashed in all national park lands, which is a good practice just about everywhere along the trail. Snakes, porcupines, and playful skunks tend to leave a lasting impression

available from the ATC. The ATC also publishes a range of excellent travel guides with extensive information for the day-hiker and the through-hiker. Topographic maps are available for purchase to augment the posted trail signs and blazes. The 2-inch-wide-by-6-inch-high white rectangle blazes on trees, poles, and rocks clearly mark the well-maintained trail. Above the timberline, rock cairns lead the way. If a blaze is absent for a distance of a quarter mile, it is wise to turn back, as a change in the route has probably been missed. Two blazes, one blaze above the other, is a tip-off that a sudden shift in the trail lies ahead, at their expense. Traveling on horseback, or with the aid of pack animals, is not allowed except in one location in the Smokies, where it is recognized as a traditional use.

To prepare for a safe journey, hikers should pack clothing that will protect against dramatic changes in weather. This is especially important for those going into the higher elevations of the Great Smoky Mountains and the White Mountains and at the northern terminus, Katahdin, Maine. Extreme weather may occur year-round in Vermont, New Hampshire, and Maine, so proper gear is essential. Summer thunderstorms can bring lightning and slick conditions. Besides avoiding high places and tall or metal objects during lightning storms, hikers need to avoid wet caves, bodies of water, and low spots where water will collect. In slippery conditions, exercise caution. Ann and Myron Sutton found stepping on mulch, sand, and wet leaves was safer than stepping into mud, on wet stones, or on pine needles. First-aid techniques—such as methods to treat or resist hypothermia and hyperthermia (see CDT), hantavirus (a deadly disease that made news in the Four Corners area of the Southwest), giardia (a microscopic organism in open water), sunburn, blisters, insect stings, snakebites (although quite rare), and other animal and bug bites—are invaluable and are worth learning before beginning a journey.

Because of the spread of Lyme disease, hikers should check on the latest prevention techniques and other precautionary steps to ward off the tiny deer ticks that can carry it. Long-sleeved shirts and pants made of light-colored fabrics make it easier to spot the dark pests. For additional protection, socks should be pulled over pant legs and shirts should be tucked in. The New York State Department of Health recommends tick repellents that contain 10 to 30 percent concentrations of DEET. The repellent should be sprayed on clothes, with special attention to cuffs, the waistline, and shoes. Even with these protections, health officials recommend that hikers check their skin at least once a day for the dark-colored pinhead-size deer tick, particularly during the high-risk months of June and July. If a tick is still moving when found, it likely has not fed. Once fed, a tick can grow to the size of a small pea.

If a tick is found embedded in the skin, removal with a tweezers rather than a match, followed by antiseptic on the affected area, is recommended. Symptoms of Lyme disease are an expanding red rash that may resemble a bull's-eye, fever, headache, fatigue, stiff neck, or muscle and joint pain. It is believed that a tick must feed for at least eight to twelve hours to transmit Lyme disease. A physician can treat Lyme disease with oral antibiotics, which are most beneficial when administered shortly after

**APPALACHIAN TRAIL AND VERMONT'S
LONG TRAIL NEAR HARMON HILL**

From the Connecticut River at the
Vermont–New Hampshire border, the AT
climbs steep hills and lowland hardwood
forest to Shernburne Pass, where it joins
the Long Trail to travel the crest of the
Green Mountains to the Berkshire Hills of
Massachusetts.

less from a road. Segments of the
AT in national parks, where
hunting is prohibited, may offer a
safer bet at this time.

Finally, do not forget physical
fitness preparation. Because the
AT is set among some of the
oldest mountains on earth, hikers
sometimes underestimate the
challenge it presents. The
Appalachians lack the height of
their younger counterparts in the
West, but the trail sometimes cuts
directly up steep hills. As a rule,
elevation changes of 1,000 feet
slow down even fit hikers by
adding at least a half hour to the
trek. A little extra weight in the
pack makes a big difference in the
difficulty of the climb. Faced with
yet another hill, long-distance
hikers are known to jettison
nonessentials.

The AT travels through fourteen states, eight national forests,
six national park units, and more
than sixty state forests, parks, or
game lands. Mostly a forested
path, the trail presents encounters
with diverse terrain, plant and
animal life, and a variety of
cultural and ecological sites.*
Although generally following the
crest of the Appalachian
Mountains, the route descends
into pastoral valleys and travels
alongside or crosses great rivers of
the eastern United States such as
the Penobscot, Kennebec,
Androscoggin, Connecticut,
Housatonic, Hudson, Delaware,

the infection occurs. A new
vaccine is available but is not
expected to be 100 percent effective in preventing infection and is
recommended only for individuals who spend a good amount of
time in infected areas.

Personal safety on or near the
trail cannot be guaranteed. There
are always risks, and hikers should
take precautions against crime
just as they would do anywhere.
Traveling with companions is
highly recommended. But do not
assume safety at any time.
Although few complications have
been reported, extreme caution
must be exercised during the
hunting season, from the end of
September until the beginning of
January. Hikers should wear blaze
orange and whistle or sing when
in valleys or if one-half mile or

*Material in this section is taken from
the National Park Service's
Appalachian Trail Comprehensive Plan.

RESTING ON A ROCK OUTCROPPING

Steep trail may lead to rewarding respites and opportunities to swap hiking tales with others along the way. Through-hikers often adopt colorful trail monikers for use with their new trail companions and for signing the numerous trail registers along the route.

Lehigh, Schuylkill, Susquehanna, Potomac, James, New, Holston, Wautauga, Nolichucky, French Broad, Big Pigeon, Little Tennessee, and Nantahala. The Appalachian system is an old and complex set of mountain ranges of worn-down and subdued uplands. The White Mountains, Green Mountains, Taconic Range, Berkshire Hills, Shenandoahs, Blue Ridge Mountains, Great Smoky Mountains, and others form a belt stretching from Quebec to Alabama. Separating the Eastern Seaboard from the interior of the continent, most of the ranges run north-south and parallel to one another in strips,

separated by broad open valleys. The White and Great Smoky Mountains reach the highest elevations in the chain.

Beginning in the north at the summit of Katahdin,* the AT winds its way through the remote, lake-dotted forests of Maine, a state with more uninhabited land than any in the East. Characterized by disconnected mountains at first, then a short, rugged section, and finally steep, 4,000-foot mountains in the west, Maine's AT offers solitude in the wilderness. It then traverses mostly ridge trail along the White Mountains of New Hampshire, where fall presents striking red, orange, and yellow displays of American beech, American mountain ash, basswood, large tooth aspen, northern red oak, pin cherry, quaking aspen, red maple,

*Though most through-hikers walk northbound, the long-standing tradition of the trail is to list features north-to-south.

speckled alder, striped maple, sugar maple, sumac, tamarack, tupelo, white ash, white birch, witch hazel, and yellow birch.

After winding through the Presidential Range, the AT crosses the Connecticut River into Vermont, passing through woods and farmland before it joins 104 miles of the Long Trail along the crest of the southern Green Mountains. A succession of ridges interspersed with valleys and small towns line the trail through the Berkshires, the Housatonic Highlands of Massachusetts and Connecticut, and New York's Main Ridge and Hudson Highlands, which offer a glimpse of Manhattan. The trail then passes through New Jersey's Highlands. Near High Point, it climbs onto the Kittatinny Mountain ridge before encountering glacial Sunfish Pond. West of the Delaware River, it continues on Blue Mountain through much of Pennsylvania, where quite a few rocks are found underfoot and views of rich dairy country lead hikers to order a tasty ice-cream cone, or, if a through-hiker, a half gallon, to become an official member of the "Half-Gallon Club" at the AT's halfway point. Following South Mountain through historic southern Pennsylvania and Maryland, the AT reaches the picturesque confluence of the Potomac and Shenandoah Rivers at Harpers Ferry, the headquarters of the volunteer powerhouse Appalachian Trail Conference.

Proceeding through Virginia on the Blue Ridge south to Roanoke, the trail traverses heavily forested Shenandoah National Park where more than one hundred species of trees provide forest cover for black bears (see CDT chapter for a more detailed discussion about bears), bobcats, mountain lions, and white-tailed deer. Wildflowers are in bloom from April through October, and the sounds of more than two hundred species of birds might be heard, including the flycatcher, the barred owl, and a variety of warblers. After the Roanoke area, the AT picks its way through the complex mountain system of the southern Appalachians . Mount Rogers is the highest point in the state and home of the northernmost natural stand of Fraser fir along the trail. In June and July hillside displays of wild rhododendrons and azaleas are magnificent throughout the entire region.

After completing the Virginia stretch of the AT, the longest in any state, the trail crosses over into Tennessee and North Carolina. Here it offers crestline on Holston Mountain, the Iron Mountains, Roan Mountain, the Unaka Mountains, Bald Mountain, the Great Smoky Mountains, the Cheoah Mountains, and the Nantahala Mountains. Unusual high-elevation grassy balds grace this region of the trail, offering spectacular unobstructed views. Scientists conjecture that the harsh, windy conditions at higher elevations are responsible for these topographical features. Another unusual feature of the area is the blue, smokelike haze that hangs on the mountains and gives them the appellation "smoky." From the Lookout Tower above Clingmans Dome in Smoky Mountains National Park Biosphere Reserve, an expansive view of the forested ranges of the southern Appalachians unfolds. Following the Blue Ridge, once again, up and down in remote rugged regions of southern North Carolina and northern Georgia, the trail reaches its southern terminus at Springer Mountain.

The former Maine commissioner of conservation, Dick Anderson, and other modern visionaries are developing plans for an international connecting side trail that would depart from the AT just before it crosses Baxter State Park and proceed to the conclusion of the Appalachian Mountains at Parc Forillon and Cape Gaspé in Quebec. The proposed International Appalachian Trail (IAT) will run from Baxter State Park across the northeastern corner of Maine to the Canadian border. In Canada, the IAT will cross northern New Brunswick and into Quebec at Matapedia. In eastern Quebec, the Appalachians and the proposed IAT will finally come to an end at Forillon National Park at the eastern end of the Gaspé Peninsula, where whales are sometimes seen from atop the 300-foot cliffs. Cape Gaspé derived its name from the Micmac Indian word *Gespeg,* which appropriately means "end of the land." For information about connecting Alabama and Florida to the AT, see the FNST chapter.

MAINE (281 MILES)

1. KATAHDIN. The northern terminus of the AT lies atop a 5,267-foot solitary mountain named Katahdin by the Penobscot Indians, meaning "Greatest Mountain." The AT's 4,000-foot ascent to the summit spans a mere 5 miles, with roughly 2,500 feet of the ascent above the tree line. Here hikers and climbers are exposed to the elements in what is for most the last leg of the journey. Taking on a mythical quality for hikers long before it is in sight, the crown jewel of Baxter State Park, Katahdin, has six peaks and a network of hiking trails. Near the top, Thoreau Spring bears the name of the Transcendentalist Henry David Thoreau, who in September 1846 explored the area around the lower part of Katahdin but not the spring, which is located amid the 4,734- to 5,267-foot peaks. Baxter State Park, near Millinocket, encompasses 202,064 acres with old-growth forests, streams, ponds, and lakes; it is the largest designated wilderness in New England. The park's management policy

Points of Interest

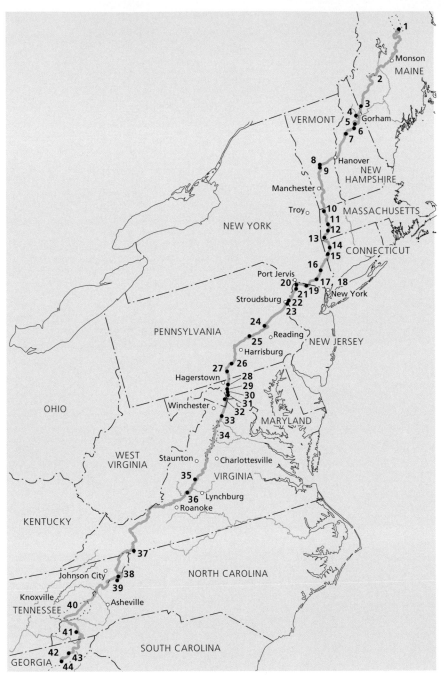

1

Monson
MAINE

2

3
4
5   Gorham
6
7

8   Hanover
9   NEW
     HAMPSHIRE
Manchester

VERMONT

Troy   10   MASSACHUSETTS
        11
        12
13   14
        15   CONNECTICUT
     16
NEW YORK

Port Jervis
20   17 18
   21 19   New York
Stroudsburg 22
         23

24

PENNSYLVANIA   25   Reading
                     Harrisburg   NEW JERSEY

            26
        27   28
Hagerstown   29
              30
              31
              32
         33
OHIO   MARYLAND
            34

WEST   Staunton   Charlottesville
VIRGINIA
        35   VIRGINIA
KENTUCKY   36   Lynchburg
               Roanoke

        37

Johnson City   38
             39
Knoxville
        40   Asheville
TENNESSEE

    41

42   43   SOUTH CAROLINA
GEORGIA 44

NORTH CAROLINA

APPALACHIAN NATIONAL SCENIC TRAIL

aggressively protects the wilderness from overuse, so black bears might be more common than accommodations. Camping by reservation is permitted at authorized campgrounds and campsites only. Activities include birdwatching, mountain climbing, fishing, canoeing, winter sports, watching for moose and caribou, and staying away from blackflies in June. The Maine Appalachian Trail Club (MATC) provides the best map for this section of the AT. *Other attractions:* In Millinocket, wilderness outfitters provide camping, fishing, canoeing, and kayaking adventures as well as white-water rafting trips on the Penobscot, Kennebec, and Dead Rivers. *Nearby:* In Caratunk, the AT crosses the dangerous 400-foot-wide Kennebec by ferry; Route 201, from Caratunk to Solon, nicknamed "moose alley," is a state scenic highway that the AT follows across the Great Bend of the Dead River, past Pierce, and East Carry and West Carry ponds. The scenic route is named the Arnold Trail, after Benedict Arnold, who, in 1775, along with his army of eleven hundred men, followed it to Quebec intending to attack the British. Along the way, the army became bogged down in the ponds, streams, and swamps. They did not have the log walkways available to them that the Maine ATC has generously built to protect the fragile bogs.

2. BIGELOW PRESERVE. Bisecting the wooded, wet, 33,000-acre wilderness preserve on Maine Public Reserve land, the AT mounts the 17-mile-long range that has six major summits. Located east of Stratton and north of Carrabassett Valley, Bigelow Mountain offers excellent sunrise and sunset views of the lakes. A section of the trail forms the northern side of a demanding 11-mile triangular Bigelow Loop hike. Activities include camping, fishing, boating, swimming, and winter sports. *Nearby:* Rangeley has the largest remaining unprotected segment of the AT, the Saddleback Ski Area; Rangeley Lake State Park, with 691 acres, has camping, boating, fishing, swimming, and snowmobiling.

3. GRAFTON NOTCH STATE PARK. Grafton Notch is a gap in the mountains, formed by river action and glacial erosive forces, that separates Maine's third highest mountain, 4,180-foot Old Speck, from Baldplate Mountain. The park is located north of Bethel. It has Moose Cave and AT with steep ascents and descents known for rugged hiking past gorges and spectacular waterfalls and over natural stone bridges. Near the AT's departure from Maine, this rocky forested scenic area is at the end of the Mahoosuc Range. Grafton has scenic driving and fishing. *Other attractions:* In Newry, the Sunday River Resort, host of the thirty-first biennial meeting of the ATC, has skiing, mountain biking, and canoeing; Sunday River Bridge (1870) is a covered bridge known as Artists' Bridge.

At historic Bethel, the Androscoggin River Trail; bicycle and canoe rental. In West Bethel, guided horseback riding, llama trekking, and canoe treks. *Nearby:* From Berlin, New Hampshire, roads lead to the AT segment for Maine's giant boulder–strewn Mahoosuc Notch, considered by many the toughest mile on the AT.

NEW HAMPSHIRE (161 MILES)

4. WHITE MOUNTAIN NATIONAL FOREST. Set aside as a national forest in 1911, the rugged White Mountains in New Hampshire and Maine draw more visitors—about six million annually—than Yellowstone and Yosemite National Parks combined. Awe-inspiring gorges, waterfalls, wooded hollows, and treeless summits highlight the 886,000-acre forest where the AT is posted as the Franconia Ridge Trail. Thought to be one of the most impressive segments of the AT, the route runs above timberline and on the edge of three federally designated wildernesses where hikers are drawn to the grand peaks of the dramatic Presidential Range. Side trails lead to the summits along the 25 miles of alpine ridge walking on the AT between Crawford Notch and Pinkham Notch, where severe weather has resulted in tragedy. Descents into notches at the lower elevations offer remarkable natural features. Activities include camping, horseback riding, scenic and four-wheel driving, canoeing, kayaking, rafting, boating, fishing, cross-country and downhill skiing, snowshoeing, and snowmobiling. Forest headquarters is in Laconia; ranger stations are in Bethlehem, Gorham, Bethel, Plymouth, and Conway.

5. MOUNT WASHINGTON STATE PARK. This 52-acre state park lies atop the Northeast's highest mountain, Mount Washington, at 6,288 feet, where grassy lawns with tundra species typically found hundreds of miles north, a bare granite summit, and a few buildings are cloaked in clouds 55 percent of the year. Despite years of meteorological studies that proved that Mount Washington has the world's worst weather and highest wind velocity, a quarter of a million people from all over the globe visit each year. Ignorance of these harsh weather conditions has led to many accidents caused by exposure. The park is reached by hiking the trails, ascending the 8-mile scenic auto road first opened in 1861 as the Carriage Road, or taking the Cog Railway from Bretton Woods (see Crawford Notch below). On top, visitors see the historic summit stage office, the Sherman Adams Summit Building, the restored hotel called the Tip Top House (1853), and Mount Washington Observatory. *Other attractions:* At the base of the mountain at Pinkham Notch, the Appalachian Mountain Club Pinkham Notch Visitor Center and Lodge offer educational displays, maps, AT guidebooks, guided trips, and free evening

lectures. Reservations can be made here for the AMC's chain of eight huts from Carter Notch (built in 1914) to Lonesome Lake or by calling the nation's oldest conservation and recreation organization at 800-262-4455. Shelters of the nearby Randolph Mountain Club (RMC) are available on the northern slope of Mount Adams.

6. CRAWFORD NOTCH STATE PARK. Views of the majestic Presidential Range are enjoyed from the AT that crosses this park near Bretton Woods, noted for Silver and Flume Cascades; Arethusa Falls, one of the highest in the state; and the Willey House, a stopover in the late 1700s for wagon passengers on their way from northern New Hampshire to the seacoast. Activities include camping, scenic driving, fishing, and touring the visitor center. *Other attractions:* At Bretton Woods, the legendary Mount Washington Hotel (1902); Mount Washington Cog Railway takes a scenic round-trip journey to the top of Mount Washington on one of the steepest tracks in the world.

7. FRANCONIA NOTCH STATE PARK. The awesome AT on the Franconia ridge crosses this park in the heart of the White Mountain National Forest in the deep, 6,640-acre valley between towering peaks of the Franconia and Kinsman mountain ranges. Side trails lead through the narrow dramatic Flume, a unique geological formation that took shape during the Ice Age, and under a covered bridge. Other features of this park near Lincoln are Old Man of the Mountain, a natural granite profile that juts out of a sheer cliff above Profile Lake; The Basin, a deep glacial pothole (see IANST); and Echo Lake. Activities include camping, rock climbing, scenic driving, fishing, swimming, cross-country and downhill skiing, snowmobiling, touring the visitor center and the New England Ski Museum, and a scenic ride on the Aerial Tramway (the site of the first passenger aerial tramway in North America). *Other attractions:* From Lincoln, the Kancamagus National Scenic Byway (Route 112), known locally as the Kanc, offers dramatic views through the White Mountains National Forest on the way to Conway. At Conway, the Conway Scenic Railroad has nostalgic excursions to Crawford Notch and Bartlett on the Notch Train; Passaconaway Historic Site has a home built by one of the earliest settlers in the area. *Nearby:* The AT passes right through town before it leaves the state at Hanover, home of Dartmouth College, the nation's ninth oldest (chartered in 1769). Dartmouth Outing Club, the oldest college outing club in the United States (1909), helps to maintain the AT. At Cornish, Saint-Gaudens National Historic Site consists of the home, gardens, and studios of one of the nation's foremost sculptors, Augustus Saint-Gaudens (1848–1907). Near Sharon, Vermont, the Mormon prophet's Birthplace Memorial

will be of special interest to those interested in the Mormon Pioneer NHT (see *America's National Historic Trails*).

8. GIFFORD WOODS STATE PARK. A short segment of the AT passes through the 114-acre park near Killington at the edge of the Green Mountain National Forest, where a virgin grove of forest—mainly old-growth sugar maples—is found. The park is located along a major migratory flyway, and birds and birders flock there in spring and fall. Activities include camping, fishing, and winter sports. *Other attractions:* At Sherburne Pass, the AT follows the famous Long Trail for 104 miles along the crest of the Green Mountains south to Massachusetts. A turn north leads to a 160-mile trek to Canada. Anyone planning such a hike would benefit from the *Guide Book of the Long Trail* and other guides and maps available from the Green Mountain Club in Waterbury Center, now 7,000 members strong, which has protected and maintained the Long Trail since 1910. At Killington, the Killington Ski and Summer Resort at Calvin Coolidge State Forest; Killington Peak, on a steep side trail in the Coolidge Range of the Green Mountains, is the second highest peak in the state and reaches 4,235 feet. *Nearby:* Plymouth, President Calvin Coolidge State Historic Site.

9. GREEN MOUNTAIN NATIONAL FOREST. The 340,000-acre forest along the main range of the Green Mountains in Vermont is traversed by the Long Trail and a segment of the AT south of Killington. It also has White Rocks National Recreation Area near Wallingford, six wilderness areas, secluded hollows, the Champlain Valley, and battlefields of the Revolutionary and French and Indian Wars. Activities include camping, horseback riding, fishing, boating, swimming, cross-country and downhill skiing, snowshoeing, ice fishing, iceboating, and snowmobiling. District offices are located in Rutland, Manchester Center, Middlebury, and Rochester. *Nearby:* In Rutland, the Norman Rockwell Museum has more than two thousand of the illustrator's reproductions. At Manchester, the American Museum of Fly Fishing; Southern Vermont Art Center; and the Georgian Revival mansion, Hildene, which belonged to Robert Todd Lincoln, Abraham Lincoln's son, and is open for tours; Mount Equinox (3,816 feet) is the highest peak in the Taconic Range. Near Bondville, Stratton Mountain (3,936 feet) is thought to be one of several spots where Benton MacKaye recalled that he first envisioned what would become the AT. At Arlington, the Norman Rockwell Exhibition is hosted by several local residents who served as his models; Daniel Webster Memorial. In Bennington, the Bennington Museum exhibits paintings by the folk artist Grandma Moses. At Old Bennington, the Bennington

Battle Monument, which can be viewed from the AT at Harmon Hill, celebrates the Revolutionary War victory of the Green Mountain Boys on August 16, 1777.

MASSACHUSETTS
(89 MILES)

10. MOUNT GREYLOCK STATE RESERVATION. Atop the state's highest point, 3,491-foot Mount Greylock near Clarksburg in the Berkshires, the AT reaches its high point in Massachusetts on a 14-mile segment where views of five states are possible. At the summit, there is a war memorial and the AMC-operated historic Bascom Lodge. Activities include camping, bicycling, horseback riding, cross-country skiing, snowshoeing, snowmobiling, interpretive programs, and AMC-guided hikes and bird-watches. *Other attractions:* At Clarksburg, Clarksburg State Park offers vistas of the forested Berkshire Hills and Green Mountains, camping, hiking, fishing, canoeing, swimming, cross-country skiing, and snowshoeing. *Nearby:* At North Adams, Natural Bridge State Park has tours of the 550-million-year-old white marble bridge that was created by glaciers during the last Ice Age and later described by Nathaniel Hawthorne; Western Gateway Heritage State Park has six wooden railroad buildings on the NRHP and narrates the construction of the Hoosic Tunnel, an undertaking that cost 196 people their lives. In Williamstown, Sterling and Francine Clark Art Institute; and the western terminus of the legendary Mohawk Trail (SR 2), America's first scenic automobile route.

11. OCTOBER MOUNTAIN STATE FOREST. The AT passes through this 14,000-acre state forest southeast of Pittsfield. Activities include camping, horseback riding, fishing, canoeing, boating, cross-country skiing, snowshoeing, and snowmobiling. *Nearby:* In Pittsfield, Arrowhead was the home of Herman Melville when he wrote *Moby-Dick;* Berkshire Atheneum, the town's public library, has the Herman Melville Memorial Room devoted to the author; the Berkshire Museum exhibits paintings; Hancock Shaker Village has craft demonstrations at the restored Shaker community founded in 1790; Canoe Meadows Wildlife Sanctuary.

12. BEARTOWN STATE FOREST. In this forest south of Stockbridge, spectacular views are available from the AT near glacial Benedict Pond. Activities include camping, bicycling, horseback riding, fishing, canoeing, boating, cross-country skiing, snowshoeing, and snowmobiling. *Nearby:* In Stockbridge, Mission House was built in 1735 to serve the Stockbridge Indians; Indian Burial Ground; Stockbridge Library displays Stockbridge Indian artifacts; Norman Rockwell Museum has the largest collection of the illustrator's original art and offers views of the Housatonic River and the surrounding Berkshires;

Berkshire Theater Festival is held during the summer; Berkshire Botanical Garden; Naumkeag is a Stanford White–designed mansion with tours; Chesterwood was the summer home and studio of Daniel Chester French, who sculpted the statue of Abraham Lincoln for the Lincoln Memorial in Washington, D.C., and the Minuteman statue in Concord. Near Sheffield, a monument commemorates the bloody 1787 farmers' rebellion against repressive state taxes led by Daniel Shays.

13. MOUNT EVERETT STATE RESERVATION. Mount Everett, the second-highest mountain on the AT in Massachusetts and the ninth highest in the state, offers views of the Housatonic River Valley, the Taconic and Berkshire Ranges, and the outlying Catskills. The 1,356-acre state reservation near Mount Washington has canoeing, fishing, cross-country skiing, and snowshoeing. *Other attractions:* Mount Washington, Bash Bish Falls State Park.

CONNECTICUT
(51 MILES)

14. HOUSATONIC MEADOWS STATE PARK. Views of the Housatonic River Valley to the east are seen from the AT as it passes through the park near Cornwall Bridge. Activities include camping, canoeing, cross-country skiing, snowshoeing, and fly fishing (permitted along a 2-mile stretch of the Housatonic River). *Other attractions:* West Cornwall has an 1837

covered bridge over a white-water section of the Housatonic River. *Nearby:* Near North Kent, Macedonia Brook State Park features two peaks with outstanding views of the Catskills and Taconics; Kent Falls State Park is located on the east side of the Housatonic River.

15. SCHAGHTICOKE INDIAN RESERVATION. A section of the AT on the reservation leads to Indian Rocks with overlooks of the Housatonic River Valley. At the confluence of the Housatonic and Ten Mile rivers, American Indian settlements date to before written history. Members of the Schaghticoke Indian tribe played a role in the Revolutionary War by signaling messages over a 100-mile stretch along the ridges between Stockbridge, Massachusetts, and Long Island Sound in New York. *Nearby:* At Kent, the Sloane-Stanley Museum, on top of the ruins of a nineteenth-century iron furnace, exhibits paintings of the artist and author Eric Sloane; Bulls Bridge, a covered bridge that spans the Housatonic River, dates to the early 1800s. George Washington and his army crossed an earlier bridge in this spot several times during the Revolutionary War.

NEW YORK (89 MILES)

16. CLARENCE FAHNESTOCK MEMORIAL STATE PARK. The AT reaches the summit of Shenandoah Mountain, where there is an excellent view of Canopus Lake. Cabins are available in the park at the Taconic

Outdoor Education Center near Mead Corners. Activities include camping, bicycling, horseback riding, cross-country skiing, snowshoeing, ice skating, snowmobiling, and performing arts programs. For more than two decades, Franciscan friars at Graymoor Christian Unity Center have extended hospitality to through-hikers. *Other attractions:* Near Beacon, Hudson Highlands State Park has scenic views, hiking, fishing, and boating. *Nearby:* In Poughkeepsie, the Post Office (NHL) has nationally recognized murals; Young-Morse Historic Site was the home of the telegraph inventor Samuel F. B. Morse; riverboat tours. At Hyde Park, the Culinary Institute of America and its four restaurants; Eleanor Roosevelt National Historic Site, her retreat and home; Franklin D. Roosevelt Museum and Library; home of Franklin D. Roosevelt National Historic Site; Franklin D. Roosevelt Museum and Library; Vanderbilt Mansion National Historic Site; Ogden Mills and Ruth Livingston Mills State Park, which features the Mills Mansion State Historic Site. The adjoining Margaret Lewis Norrie State Park has a late-nineteenth-century golf course.

17. BEAR MOUNTAIN STATE PARK. After crossing the Bear Mountain bridge, the AT passes through the park's Trailside Museum and Zoo along an original 1923 section. Although MacKaye's original concept for the AT included trailside study centers, this is the only exhibit that ever developed. The AT drops to its lowest elevation, 124 feet above sea level, at the zoo. This original 1923 section is the only spot on the AT that is traveled underground. The park's Bear Mountain Inn, along the trail, provides a rustic setting for lodge dining. Other park facilities include a swimming pool, bathhouse, ski jump, and skating rink. Bear Mountain, one of the highest points on the trail in New York at 1,305 feet, offers views of New York City's skyline at a distance of 45 miles. Farther south, Prospect Rock is the highest point on the AT in New York at 1,433 feet. Park activities include bicycling, fishing, boating, swimming, cross-country skiing, sledding, ice skating, performing arts programs, and touring the Trailside Museum and Zoo.

18. HARRIMAN STATE PARK. Along with volunteers from the New York–New Jersey Trail Conference, Maj. William A. Welch, general manager of Palisades Interstate Park from 1912 to 1940 and first chair of the ATC, completed the first section of the AT in 1923 in Harriman–Bear Mountain State Park. Mary Averill Harriman, widow of railroad magnate Edward Harriman, foiled a plan to build a prison at the the base of Bear Mountain by donating 10,000 acres for a park. As a result, Sing Sing, the prison that gives rise to the phrase, "sent up the river," was built 20 miles south on the Hudson River. Just off the Palisades Parkway, the park is 30 miles north of New York

City. Activities include camping, bicycling, fishing, boating, swimming, cross-country skiing, sledding, ice skating, snowmobiling, and recreation programs.

NEW JERSEY
(73 MILES)

19. **WAWAYANDA STATE PARK.** After passing through the Hewitt State Forest, the AT crosses this 11,736-acre state park and then descends into nearby Vernon in Vernon Valley, once a glacial lake. The park's name comes from a Lenape Indian word for "water on the mountain." Near the top of Wawayanda Mountain, a blue-blazed side trail leads a short distance to Pinwheel's Vista for a worthwhile view of the valley, the Kittatinny Ridge, and New York's Catskills. Activities include camping, fishing, boating, swimming, cross-country skiing, snowshoeing, sledding, ice fishing, ice skating, and snowmobiling.

20. **HIGH POINT STATE PARK.** Breathtaking vistas are possible on a short blue-blazed side trail up High Point Mountain, New Jersey's highest point, near Montague. At the 1,803-foot summit, a monument commemorates New Jersey's wartime heroes. Located along the crest of the Kittatinny Mountains, the state park has cabins, a visitor center, and a nature center. Activities include camping, fishing, boating, swimming, cross-country skiing, snowshoeing, sledding, ice fishing, ice skating, sledding, and a campfire program.

21. **STOKES STATE FOREST.** Cabins are available in the state forest near Branchville, which links High Point State Park with the Delaware Water Gap National Recreation Area. Activities include camping, fishing, boating, cross-country skiing, snowshoeing, sledding, ice fishing, ice skating, and snowmobiling.

22. **DELAWARE WATER GAP NATIONAL RECREATION AREA.** The Delaware River flows through the famous gap in the Kittatinny Ridge of the Appalachian Mountains to run the length of the scenic and historic recreation area, which covers 70,000 acres in New Jersey and Pennsylvania. Rugged and remote, the AT curves along the Kittatinny Ridge for 25 miles on the New Jersey side. The Kittatinny Point Visitors Center can be seen from the toll bridge that crosses the Delaware near Columbia. Activities include camping, bird-watching, fishing, canoeing (free guided trips), boating, tubing, swimming, cross-country skiing, snowshoeing, ice skating, sledding, snowmobiling, and touring visitor centers.

23. **WORTHINGTON STATE FOREST.** Containing some of the state's most rugged terrain, this forest near Columbia extends from the Delaware Water Gap north for 8 miles and has Sunfish Pond (NNL), the southernmost glacial pond on the AT. Activities include camping, boating, fishing, cross-country skiing, snowshoeing, sledding, and snowmobiling.

In Stroudsburg, Pennsylvania, the Quiet Valley Living Historical Farm is a re-created 1765 Pennsylvania German farm with costumed guides.

PENNSYLVANIA (229 MILES)

24. HAWK MOUNTAIN SANCTUARY. At Eckville, the Hawk Mountain Sanctuary has more than 2,000 acres of Allegheny mountaintop and attracts more than fourteen species of hawks, falcons, and eagles. Each year, an estimated twenty thousand birds of prey use the mountain's strong updrafts to aid their journey south. An informative visitor center near the AT's Eckville Shelter provides exhibits on the raptors and access to scenic overlooks. The migration season from late August to late November is the best time for a visit. Until Rosalie Edge founded the sanctuary in 1934, hunters frequented the area at this same time. The Keystone Trails Association and the Potomac Appalachian Trail Club offer an AT guide and maps for Pennsylvania. *Nearby:* At Hamburg, from an elevation of 1,635 feet along the rocky AT, the Pinnacle offers a panoramic view of rural Pennsylvania. Near Elverson, Hopewell Furnace National Historic Site presents one of the finest examples of a rural American nineteenth-century iron plantation.

25. SWATARA STATE PARK. Near Pine Grove in the Cumberland Valley, this 3,500-acre park is known for its marine fossil bed, from the Middle Devonian period of the Paleozoic era. *Nearby:* At Grantville, Memorial Lake State Park has an 85-acre lake surrounded by Fort Indiantown Gap Military Reservation. In Harrisburg, the State Capitol; the Capitol Preservation Committee's Civil War Flag Project has four hundred Civil War battle flags; the State Museum of Pennsylvania displays one of the world's largest paintings, *The Battle of Gettysburg: Pickett's Charge;* Dauphin County Historical Society in the Simon Cameron-Hogn Harris Mansion; River Park, located on the banks of the Susquehanna River; *Pride of the Susquehanna* river cruises. At Carlisle, Cumberland County Historical Society Library and Museum exhibits eighteenth-century iron-furnace products; Trout Art Gallery at Dickinson; Carlisle Barracks, home of the first nonreservation school for American Indians that was attended by Olympian Jim Thorpe; Kings Gap Environmental Education and Training Center. At Mount Holly, the AT meets the Mason Dixon Trail, which passes through Gifford Pinchot State Park.

26. PINE GROVE FURNACE STATE PARK. Remains of a Revolutionary War iron furnace are visible from the AT in the nearly 700-acre park. Just north of the park a sign marks the midpoint of the entire AT. With changes in the AT route, the

precise midpoint migrates each year, but for any through-hiker who has made it this far, it would be safe to start celebrating. Pine Grove Furnace has camping, hiking, fishing, boating, swimming, cross-country skiing, snowshoeing, ice fishing, ice skating, and environmental education programs. *Other attractions:* Ironmasters Mansion, built in 1827, served as a stop on the Underground Railroad and is now an American Youth Hostel (AYH).

27. CALEDONIA STATE PARK. The AT traverses the northernmost extension of the Blue Ridge through the 1,130-acre park near Fayetteville. Confederate soldiers on their way to the battle of Gettysburg burned the Caledonia Ironworks owned by Thaddeus Stevens, an outspoken abolitionist. Highlights of the park include the museum in the reconstructed Thaddeus Stevens Blacksmith Shop, the Totem Pole Playhouse, an Olympic-size swimming pool, an eighteen-hole golf course, and cabins. Activities are camping, bicycling, golf, fishing, cross-country skiing, snowshoeing, and environmental education programs. *Other attractions:* Near Fayetteville, between Quarry Gap shelter and Birch Run shelter, massive thickets of mountain laurel are in peak bloom in late June and early July. *Nearby:* At Gettysburg (14 miles east of Caledonia State Park), Gettysburg National Military Park commemorates the great battle fought on July 1–3, 1863, the turning point

of the Civil War; Gettysburg National Cemetery, where on November 19, 1863, Abraham Lincoln delivered the Gettysburg Address; Lincoln Room Museum; Lee's Headquarters and Museum; Eisenhower National Historic Site, the only home owned by President Dwight D. Eisenhower and his wife, Mamie.

MARYLAND (46 MILES)

28. SOUTH MOUNTAIN STATE PARK. The park follows the north-south ridge of South Mountain, which extends from Pen Mar to Weverton. From here the AT begins a 40-mile stretch that follows the ridge through Maryland. Activities include camping, cross-country skiing, snowshoeing, sledding, and AT weekend hikes. *Other attractions:* In Cascade, Pen Mar County Park has views of the countryside, band concerts on summer weekends, and a nearby campsite. Remains of the former amusement park that first opened here in 1878 can be seen from the AT. At Thurmont (PHNST), Catoctin Mountain Park, administered by the National Park Service and home to Camp David located on the forested ridge that forms the eastern rampart of the Appalachian Mountains, has panoramic views of the Monocacy Valley. Named for the Kittoctons, an American Indian tribe that lived at the foot of the mountains near the Potomac River, the mountain park has cabins, camping, horseback riding, scenic drives, fishing,

canoeing, cross-country skiing, and snowshoeing. A hike from the visitor center leads to a moonshine still where whiskey-making demonstrations are conducted on weekends. The adjoining Cunningham Falls State Park has a 78-foot-high cascading waterfall and ruins of the Catoctin Iron Furnace that produced iron for Revolutionary War and Civil War arms.

29. GREENBRIER STATE PARK. The AT passes by the park, which has a sandy beach on its 42-acre lake. Activities at the park near Boonsboro include camping, fishing, canoeing, boating, swimming, cross-country skiing, snowshoeing, sledding, ice skating, ice fishing, and a visitor center. *Other attractions:* At Boonsboro, Boonsborough Museum of History; Crystal Grottoes Caverns tours. In Hagerstown, the Washington County Museum of Fine Arts; Maryland Theater, a restored 1915 vaudeville house still used for concerts; Hagerstown Roundhouse Museum, with railroad memorabilia and a railroad library; Hager House (1739) and Museum, with authentic furnishings of the period (NRHP); Miller House and Historical Society exhibits Civil War and Chesapeake and Ohio Canal (C&O) artifacts; Rose Hill Cemetery contains the Statue of Hope marking the burial place of more than two thousand Confederate soldiers who died in the battles of South Mountain and Antietam.

30. WASHINGTON MONUMENT STATE PARK. In 1812 citizens of craggy mountainside Boonsboro dedicated the first monument in the country—a rugged stone tower—to George Washington. A history center at the park exhibits firearms and Civil War memorabilia. Hawk Watch is held each fall, and the park has camping, cross-country skiing, snowshoeing, and sledding. *Nearby:* Near Sharpsburg, at Antietam National Battlefield, McClellan clashed with Lee in the bloodiest single-day (September 17, 1862) battle of the Civil War; the Antietam Creek Aqueduct (see PHNST). At Frederick, Monocacy National Battlefield interprets the Confederate victory of July 9, 1864, which opened a path to Washington, D.C., but also caused such a delay that Union forces were able to marshal a successful defense of the capital.

31. GATHLAND STATE PARK. The park, located in Crampton Gap near Brownsville, was at one time the South Mountain home of the Civil War journalist George Alfred Townsend. Today, it is the site of a unique collection of ruins and restored buildings that Gath (his pen name) designed and constructed for his Gathland estate. It is also the site of a memorial arch, the country's only monument dedicated to war correspondents and artists. Some of Townsend's writings can be read at the visitor center. Activities include camping, cross-country skiing, snowshoeing, and sledding. *Other attractions:* At Weverton, the AT merges with the C&O towpath (see PHNST) at

Lock 31 for 2.8 miles before crossing the Potomac River on the Goodloe Byron Memorial Footbridge. Less than a mile after the bridge crossing, a side trail leads to Maryland Heights, a rocky rampart with spectacular views of Harpers Ferry, the confluence of the Shenandoah and Potomac Rivers, and the railroad bridge that was named for Congressman Goodloe Byron, a strong supporter of the AT. Another powerful figure, Supreme Court justice and AT 2,000 Miler, William O. Douglas, played a significant role in preserving the C&O Towpath after he participated in an awareness campaign (see PHNST). Sandy Hook has the Harpers Ferry AYH.

32. HARPERS FERRY NATIONAL HISTORICAL PARK. George Washington selected this site at the confluence of the Potomac and Shenandoah Rivers for the federal armory, the same armory that was the target of abolitionist John Brown's raid (see PHNST). Ironically, it was Col. Robert E. Lee who suppressed the 1859 raid that later captured the attention of the nation and influenced events that led to the Civil War. Harpers Ferry, with its strategic location and large arsenal, changed hands eight times during the Civil War. Information on the renovated buildings and historical themes is available at the visitor center. In

1993 ATC volunteers labored to restore the beautiful AT steps and terraces that lead to a spectacular view from a boulder in town that was stabilized in the nineteenth century. There is a myth that it replaced Jefferson Rock, which tumbled down years earlier but from which, in 1783, Thomas Jefferson was inspired as he viewed the confluence of the Shenandoah and Potomac rivers. For reasonable rates, Amtrak provides convenient access to Harpers Ferry from Washington, D.C., and other points. *Other attractions:* In Harpers Ferry, the AT passes near the busy, but very helpful, ATC Headquarters before crossing the Shenandoah into Virginia. Located at Washington Street and Storer College Place, ATC Headquarters has information on the town and the trail and sells a wide range of excellent ATC publications and products; Blue Ridge Outfitters, a few miles west, has popular rafting and canoe trips.

VIRGINIA (547 MILES)

33. SKY MEADOWS STATE PARK. On the eastern side of the Blue Ridge Mountains near Paris, this beautiful small park has rolling pastures, woodlands with bountiful spring trillium, and scenic vistas. A blue blaze from the AT leads to the visitor center, which is housed in the 1820s Mount Bleak Mansion. Activities include camping, horseback riding, fishing, and seasonal cultural programs. *Nearby:* At Bluemont, ATC-owned and

managed Bears Den Hostel can be reached from another AT blue blaze at Bears Den Rocks, where expansive views are possible from Lookout Point.

34. SHENANDOAH NATIONAL PARK. Astride a beautiful section of the Blue Ridge Mountains, the 195,000-acre park has one of the most popular segments of the AT. In the 1930s, when the 105-mile Skyline Drive displaced the old AT route, the Civilian Conservation Corps (CCC) labored to relocate and build much of this 100-mile stretch. From either the AT or the narrow, mountainous Skyline, travelers will enjoy gorgeous vistas of sheer slopes, jagged rocks, forests, waterfalls, and canyons. Diverse forests offer more than one hundred species of trees, songbirds, and lush thickets of Catawba rhododendrons, azaleas, and other wildflowers that are abundant from late spring through mid-July. Hemlock-hardwood forests offer exciting fall color displays. Running the length of the park, Skyline Drive crisscrosses the much longer AT thirty-two times as it runs from Front Royal in the north to near Waynesboro in the south. About 40 miles into the park on the AT, Hawksbill Mountain, Shenandoah's highest point at 4,051 feet, is the home base of a peregrine falcon release program designed to reintroduce the swift raptor. In September Calf Mountain, north of Beagle Gap near Waynesville, provides a five-star spot right on the AT to watch hawks migrate. AT huts and cabins along the route in the park are maintained by the Potomac Appalachian Trail Club (PATC), based in Vienna, Virginia. Reservations are required for cabins, but huts are available on a first-come, first-served basis. Each year approximately two million guests visit the national park, named for the Shenandoah River and dedicated by Franklin Roosevelt in 1936. *Shenandoah* is thought to be an American Indian word that means "Daughter of the Stars." Activities include camping, birding, horseback riding, scenic driving, fishing, swimming, cross-country skiing, snowshoeing, nature programs, and stopping by the visitor centers. *Other attractions:* At Front Royal, the Chester Street Historic District; Warren Rifles Confederate Museum; Skyline Caverns, with rare cave flower formations. In Waynesboro, the P. Buckley Moss Museum displays the internationally recognized artist's works that depict the Shenandoah Valley and the Amish and Mennonite people of the area. *Nearby:* In Charlottesville, Monticello, the home of Thomas Jefferson, which he designed; the University of Virginia offers student tours of the campus, which was founded by Jefferson; the Old Courthouse, also designed by Jefferson; Lewis and Clark Memorial, honoring the explorers who were born in this area; Memorial to George Rogers Clark, honoring the brother of William Clark for his contributions to the United States; Ash Lawn–Highland, once owned by

James Monroe, the nation's fifth president; Historic Michie Tavern, opened in 1784 and now housing the Virginia Wine Museum in its cellar; Baboursville Vineyards & Historic Ruins, which maintains the remains of a mansion designed by Jefferson. At Waynesboro, Skyline connects with the 469-mile Blue Ridge Parkway that extends southwest to the Great Smoky Mountains National Park in North Carolina and Tennessee. The Blue Ridge has received the very special designation All-American Road by the Department of Transportation Scenic Byways Program.

35. GEORGE WASHINGTON AND JEFFERSON NATIONAL FOREST (NORTHERN END). The northern end of the 1.8-million-acre George Washington and Jefferson National Forest spans an area of more than one million acres from Winchester in the north to Covington in the south. Crossing forest lands, the first 100 miles of the Blue Ridge Parkway are paralleled by the AT, where hikers encounter Humpback Mountain, Three Ridges, Hanging Rock Overlook, The Priest, Crabtree Falls, Punchbowl Mountain, Brown Mountain Creek, Bluff Mountain, the Tie River, and Apple Orchard Mountain before reaching Roanoke. Easy access points permit excellent day or weekend hikes that are written about by Victoria and Frank Logue in their *Best of the AT* series. Trailheads at wayside exhibits often lead to exhilarating AT hikes. For instance, Long Mountain Wayside on Route 60 has AT's Brown Mountain Creek area, known for prolific displays of orchis, mountain laurel, and other wildflowers. Standouts of the forest include more than 950 miles of hiking trails; five of the highest waterfalls in the Blue Ridge; Priest Mountain (4,063 feet); remnants of Elizabeth Furnace; a 100-foot-long suspension bridge used by the AT to cross the Tye River; and Highlands Scenic Tour, a 20-mile scenic drive. Activities include camping, bicycling, scenic drives, off-roading, fishing, boating, swimming, and a visitor center at Massanutten Gap near Luray. The supervisor's office is located in Harrisonburg. *Nearby:* At Lexington, the restored historic downtown district; Virginia Military Institute (VMI) offers the George C. Marshall Museum and Library, VMI Museum, Jackson Memorial Hall, and Friday afternoon full-dress parade; Washington and Lee University has Lee Chapel and the president's house that Gen. Robert E. Lee designed; the Confederate general Stonewall Jackson's House was the residence of Gen. Thomas J. Jackson; Stonewall Jackson Memorial Cemetery is the final resting place of the general, his family, and more than one hundred Confederate veterans; the Alexander Withrow House survived the town's 1796 fire; Virginia Horse Center; Lexington Carriage Company narrated tours; Ben Salem Lock, used by

canal boats in the 1800s; Theater at Lime Kiln, which offers outdoor theater and concerts; Goshen Pass Natural Area; Chessie Nature Trail. In Lynchburg, the Lynchburg Museum at the Old Court House (1855) has Monacan Indian, Quaker, and Civil War displays; Maier Museum of Art at Randolph-Macon Woman's College; Anne Spencer House and Garden, with tours of the Harlem Renaissance poet's home and restored garden; Old City Cemetery has a Confederate Section; South River Meeting House, with interpretive guided tours; Poplar Forest, designed and built by Thomas Jefferson as a personal retreat. At Natural Bridge, the Natural Bridge of Virginia is of immense size, bears the initials G.W. carved by George Washington, and offers a dramatic evening interpretive laser show; Natural Bridge Caverns.

36. GEORGE WASHINGTON AND JEFFERSON NATIONAL FOREST (SOUTHERN END). The southern end of the George Washington and Jefferson National Forest embraces 710,000 acres and contains 300 miles of the AT along the Blue Ridge Mountains, with 20 miles along the West Virginia border. The southern segment of the forest, designated Mount Rogers National Recreation Area, has 60 miles of AT, with spruce-fir forests, rock outcroppings, meadows, streams, blueberry and rhododendron thickets, and excellent views. Mount Rogers

(5,729 feet) is Virginia's highest mountain and one of the AT's highest points in the state; a blue blaze leads to the top. Other highlights along the AT in Jefferson include McAfee Knob and Tinker Ridge, with outstanding views; Peters Mountain, with views of West Virginia; Keefer Oak, the largest oak tree on the AT; and Audie Murphy Monument, near Catawba's Brush Mountain on a blue blaze that leads near the 1971 plane crash site of the war hero and actor. Highlights of the Jefferson National Forest are Cave Mountain Lake Recreation Area, Virginia Highland's Horse Trail, Big Walker Mountain Scenic Byway, Mount Rogers Scenic Byway, and Cascades National Recreation Trail, with a 70-foot waterfall. It also has the Virginia Creeper Trail, where bicycles and horses are welcome. Converted from an abandoned rail corridor, the route was once an American Indian footpath also used by pioneers, including Daniel Boone. Activities include camping, bicycling, horseback riding, scenic drives, fishing, boating, swimming, and winter sports. The supervisor's office is located in Roanoke. *Other attractions:* In Roanoke, Center in the Square, adjacent to the historic farmers' market (1874), is a restored 1914 warehouse that shelters the Art Museum of Western Virginia and other museums and organizations; the Appalachian Railroad Heritage Partnership sponsors special events; Virginia Museum of Transportation; Harrison

Museum of African American Art; Mill Mountain Zoological Park. Near Smith Mountain Lake, Booker T. Washington National Monument is the site of the birthplace and early childhood home of the black leader and educator; Smith Lake State Park is known for its excellent fishing. At Pearisburg, Holy Family Church Hostel was an old barn that church members reconstructed for backpackers; a side trip leads to West Virginia's New River Gorge National River, Gauley River National Recreation Area, and Bluestone National Scenic River near Fayetteville for some of the country's best white-water activity.

37. GRAYSON HIGHLANDS STATE PARK. Surrounded by Mount Rogers National Recreation Area, this state park near Volney provides access to the popular Rhododendron Gap (elevation 5,440 feet) on the AT. From mid-June to early July, crowds are awestruck by the profusion of bright rhododendron blossoms that decorate hundreds of acres of the surrounding area. The park offers alpine views, waterfalls, and ponies that roam freely, except when some are sold at auction during the Grayson Highlands Fall Festival. Park activities include camping, bicycling, horseback riding, fishing, interpretive programs, and a visitor center. *Nearby:* At Abingdon, Craig's (aka Dunn's) Meadow once served as the mustering point for the Virginia militia that marched to Kings Mountain (South Carolina) with other frontier militias to attack British loyalists during the American Revolutionary War. The site now serves as a starting point for the Overmountain Victory National Historic Trail (see vol. 1); and the Virginia Creeper Trail. The AT meets the Creeper at Creek Junction and again north of Damascus. Damascus is a very AT-friendly town and has a Trails Day Festival each May.

TENNESSEE AND NORTH CAROLINA (375 MILES)*

38. CHEROKEE NATIONAL FOREST. Eastern Tennessee's 633,000-acre national forest is divided in two by Great Smoky Mountains National Park. Besides accommodating almost 170 miles of the AT, the national forest has two national recreation trails (the John Muir and Warrior's Passage) and more than two hundred recreational sites. The mountainous terrain is enhanced by world-famous deep river gorges and waterfalls, streams, and a dense forest composed largely of pine, hemlock, oak, and poplar. Activities include camping, bicycling, horseback riding, scenic driving, fishing, rafting, boating, waterskiing, and swimming. The

*Because the AT runs along the border for 210 miles, the mileage noted represents the total for both states. Sites in North Carolina are distinguished by that state's name. Sites in Tennessee will stand alone.

supervisor's office is in Cleveland. *Other attractions:* Near Hampton, the AT uses Watauga Dam at Watauga Lake to cross the Watauga River. Completed in 1948, the TVA dam displaced approximately seven hundred people who lived along the river's banks in exchange for flood control, electricity, jobs, and recreation. *Other attractions:* Roan Mountain State Park features 6,285-foot Roan Mountain. The AT follows the ridgeline of Roan across the largest expanse of grassy balds in the southern Appalachians. A side trek to Roan's 600-acre rhododendron garden on top is a sheer pleasure at peak bloom in mid-June, annual festival time. At the park's visitor center, a stone monument honors the Overmountain Men, a patriot army of rugged individualists who fought in the battle of Kings Mountain (see OVNHT), and the AT joins a small portion of the OVNHT. *Nearby:* Near Elizabethton, Sycamore Shoals State Historic Park (see OVNST) on the Watauga River was the site of the first permanent American settlement (NRHP) outside the thirteen original colonies and the site of the 1775 Pennsylvania Purchase from the Cherokee Indians (see TTNHT, in *America's National Historic Trails*). At Erwin, outfitters provide white-water river running on the Nolichucky; Erwin National Fish Hatchery; Farmhouse Gallery & Gardens features the wildlife art and works of area woodcarvers; Unicoi County Heritage Museum.

In Greeneville, the site includes the seventeenth president's two homes, tailor shop, and the Andrew Johnson National Cemetery; Nathanael Greene Museum holds memorabilia associated with President Andrew Johnson.

39. PISGAH NATIONAL FOREST. The AT threads the northwestern boundary of this 500,000-acre forest with towering mountains in western North Carolina. The Cradle of Forestry, housed in a building once part of the George Washington Vanderbilt estate, has an outdoor museum and monument that commemorates the birthplace of scientific forestry in the United States. Elsewhere, Sliding Rock is a natural water slide and Looking Glass Rock is thought to be the largest granite monolith in the southern Appalachians. In the forest and near the Blue Ridge Parkway, Mount Mitchell State Park holds Mount Mitchell (6,684 feet), eastern America's highest point. Benton MacKaye had envisioned this site as the southern terminus of the AT, but it was changed to Mount Oglethorpe and then Springer Mountain. The supervisor's office is in Asheville and a ranger station is in Hot Springs, a town where hikers may want to relax in a mineral bath. White-water rafting trips on the French Broad River are available, and canoes can be rented. The Jesuit Hostel is operated by the priests at the Jesuit House of Prayer, a retreat facility. Activities include camping, bicycling, scenic

driving, fishing, boating, and swimming.

40. GREAT SMOKY MOUNTAINS NATIONAL PARK (GSMNP). With more than 70 miles of the AT on crestline trail, the nation's most visited national park preserves more than 500,000 acres of forest in Tennessee and North Carolina. The park is one of the largest protected land areas east of the Rocky Mountains and contains some of the highest peaks in the East, including Clingmans Dome (6,642 feet), the highest point in the state and the highest point on the AT. An observation tower at the top provides a 360-degree view that reaches above the Fraser firs (see *Forests of the Great Smoky Mountains* for a more detailed discussion about Fraser firs). GSMNP, headquartered in Gatlinburg, is the target of intense scientific research. It is a designated biosphere reserve because it contains an enormous variety of plant and animal life. It is also a designated World Heritage Site because it protects abandoned structures of the southern Appalachian Mountain culture. These were left behind when the resident families were moved to create the national park. Endangered red wolves and the park's infamous wild hogs may be encountered. The multitude of bears are kept out of camp at night by wire-fenced shelters (see the CDT chapter for a discussion of bears and safety). Horses may be used on about half of the AT in GSMNP. The AT

runs the length of the park and in this segment offers the highest elevations of the entire route. Lands of the AT and the Blue Ridge Parkway combine to provide a corridor of public land that connects with Shenandoah National Park. Activities are camping, bicycling, horseback riding, scenic driving, fishing, cross-country skiing, sledding, naturalist programs, and visitor centers. *Other attractions:* The AT leads to the Fontana Dam visitor center at the south end of the highest dam (480 feet) in the eastern United States. North Carolina's Fontana Village housed the TVA employees who built the dam on the Little Tennessee in 1946. The village now serves as a public recreation area and resort, with many of the original buildings still in use. *Nearby:* In North Carolina, Cherokee—for centuries the home of the Eastern Band of the Cherokees—has the Cherokee Indian Reservation Visitor Center, Museum of the Cherokee Indian, Oconaluftee Indian Village; *Unto These Hills,* a drama about the Cherokees from the arrival of Hernando de Soto (1540) through the Trail of Tears (see TTNHT). In Gatlinburg, the Great Smoky Arts & Crafts Community has more than eighty craft shops; Sky Lift, a cable chair, can be taken to Crockett Mountain (2,300 feet) for a panoramic view of the Smokies; Gatlinburg Space Needle also has views; the Smoky Mountain Jamboree and the Smoky Mountain Travelers offer bluegrass and mountain music; Gatlinburg Passion Play.

41. NANTAHALA NATIONAL FOREST. Nantahala, "land of the noonday sun," is the name the Cherokee gave the 2,000-foot Nantahala Gorge where the rays of the sun meet the bottom only at noon. Now, the entire 515,000-acre national forest, the river, the dam, and the town in North Carolina's mountainous southwestern tip have taken on the name. With flowering shrubs and spectacular views amid 4,000-foot gaps and 5,000-foot peaks, the AT is splendid. But it is not the only national trail in the forest. Trail of Tears National Historic Trail crosses the Snowbird Mountains from Andrews to Robbinsville. Other forest features include the Slickrock Wilderness, the enchanting Joyce Kilmer Memorial Forest, Dry Fall, Whitewater Falls, and Whiteside Mountain, named for its white granite face. Accessible via a blue-blazed trail at Rock Gap, Waslik Poplar—with a massive 26-foot circumference—is the second-largest poplar tree in the United States. At Standing Indian Mountain (5,498 feet), a short blue-blazed trek to the top offers expansive views of the southern Appalachians. Activities include camping, bicycling, scenic driving, fishing, boating, and swimming. The supervisor's office is in Asheville. *Other attractions:* At Nantahala, the AT passes through the Nantahala Outdoor Center, which has excellent guided white-water trips, a kayak course, a hostel,

supplies, music, and delicious barbecue.

GEORGIA (75 MILES)

42. CHATTAHOOCHEE NATIONAL FOREST (CNF): The Chattahoochee, depending on which direction a through-hiker is headed, is either the first or the last national forest to be traversed on the AT. Highways crossed by the AT in this segment are nearly a day's journey apart, imparting a feeling of rugged wilderness. The 749,000-acre national forest stretches from the wild and scenic waters of the Chattooga River on its northeastern boundary through the Blue Ridge Mountains and across the ridges and valleys of northwest Georgia. It has the state's highest mountain, Brasstown Bald (4,748 feet). An observation deck and exhibits about the mountains are available at the visitor center. Anna Ruby Falls is a double falls that comes together at the base to form Smith Creek. Activities include camping, fishing, boating, swimming, and visitor centers. The supervisor's office is located in Gainesville. *Other attractions:* Near Batesville, Moccasin Creek State Park has camping, hiking, fishing, boating, and waterskiing; Unicoi State Park offers a lodge and conference center, camping, hiking, fishing, boating, swimming, tennis, and mountain culture programs.

43. BLOOD MOUNTAIN. A Creek and Cherokee legend has it that the mountain once ran red with blood after the two nations

battled there. Thus, it received its name long before it was protected in the Chattahoochee National Forest (CNF). Today, more than forty thousand people head to the highest peak (4,461 feet) on the trail in Georgia each year, making it the most visited spot on the AT south of Clingmans Dome. Hikers will find a shelter on top, but water must be carried in or gathered from a stream about 1.3 miles away. *Other attractions:* At Blairsville in the CNF, Vogel State Park has rental cottages, camping, hiking, fishing, boating, swimming, mini-golf, square dancing, and nature programs. Two waterfalls are located on Helton Creek, just south of the park. Three miles east, at Neels Gap, white AT blazes lead hikers through the breezeway of Walasi-Yi Center, a backpacking outfitter that caters to through-hikers.

44. SPRINGER MOUNTAIN. Before 1958 the southern terminus of the AT was located at Mount Oglethorpe to the southwest, but today the trail reaches its southern terminus at 3,782-foot Springer Mountain in the Chattahoochee National Forest. A bronze plaque, made in 1934 and installed in May 1959 on Springer, marks the southern terminus with these words: "A footpath for those who seek fellowship with the wilderness." The Georgia AT Club and the Forest Service marked the trail's southernmost blaze astride a boulder with a new plaque in 1993. In that same boulder is a metal drawer with the hikers'

register. A blue-blazed approach trail from Amicalola Falls State Park reaches Springer Mountain from the south. Heading north, the trail soon meets the Benton MacKaye Trail, named for the AT's founder. *Other attractions:* Near Dawsonville, Amicalola Falls State Park, also nestled in the Chattahoochee, is named for the highest waterfall east of the Mississippi River. The Amicalola, true to its Cherokee name, meaning "tumbling waters," plunges 729 feet in a succession of seven cascades. The park has a beautiful lodge and conference center, cottages, a shelter for through-hikers, camping, fishing, an interpretive program, and a visitor center. *Nearby:* At Dahlonega, the Dahlonega Courthouse Gold Museum State Historic Site provides exhibits on the Gold Rush of 1828, America's first rush for gold. Built in 1836, the courthouse is the oldest public building in the state; Consolidated Gold Mines offers tours; Crisson Gold Mine and Blackburn Park & Campground presents gold panning opportunities; Chestatee Overlook–CNF for scenic views of Blood Mountain Cove; Holly Theatre has bluegrass music at the historic landmark. At Calhoun, New Echota State Historic Site, on Georgia's Chieftains Trail, was the capital of the Cherokee Nation from 1825 to 1838 and is the trailhead for the Trail of Tears National Historic Trail; Blue & Gray Trail. In Dalton, Confederate Cemetery, and monument to the town's hospitals for aiding Confederate soldiers; Dug Gap Battle Park, with breastworks built by Civil War soldiers; Crown Garden and Archives (1884/NRHP), a center for local history, including the bedspread tufting that led to the carpet industry; Western & Atlantic Depot (1852); Llama Treks offers tours in the CNF. Near Fort Oglethorpe, Chickamauga and Chattanooga National Military Park is the nation's oldest and largest military park; 6th Cavalry Museum, located on a former parade field (NRHP), showcases the lives of the cavalrymen.

SOUTH PASS AT THE SWEETWATER RIVER

During the westward movement, pioneers looked for a narrow passage through the Rocky Mountains. Much to their surprise, they were already in the gentle South Pass as they followed the friendly Sweetwater River up the eastern side of the Divide. Eager to see water flowing toward the Pacific Ocean, emigrants rarely stopped at South Pass. Today Trails West offers wagon trips in the area where portions of the California, Mormon, Oregon, and Pony Express National Historic Trails join as they cross the Divide.

Continental Divide National Scenic Trail

Yesterday at noon we arrived at the "culminating point" or dividing ridge between the Atlantic and Pacific. . . . Thus the great daydream of my youth and of my riper years is accomplished.

CHARLES STANTON, LETTER TO HIS BROTHER,
SIDNEY STANTON, JULY 19, 1846

The Continental Divide National Scenic Trail (CDT) lies on the ridges and high granite peaks of the Rocky Mountains primarily on public lands in New Mexico, Colorado, Wyoming, Idaho, and Montana. As it follows the great Continental Divide that parts the waters of North America, it crosses high-desert sage flats, volcanic lava flows, remote canyonlands, lush wildflower-blanketed meadows, dense conifer forests, thick prairies, and delicate tundra amid heavily glaciated terrain. With much of the trail above timberline, it offers a truly superior outdoor experience in some of America's remotest wildlands. Nature is forceful on the Divide, wildlife is plentiful, and wilderness is untamed. Whether joining a group for a hike in grizzly country, hiking long distances in spectacular alpine terrain, or traveling on horseback or with the help of a llama, the trail offers an unforgettable journey. As today's

ADMINISTERING AGENCY
U.S. Forest Service, Rocky Mountain Region
740 Simms Street
Golden, CO 80401
303-275-5045

FURTHER INFORMATION
Continental Divide Trail Alliance
P.O. Box 628
Pine, CO 80470
303-838-3760 or 888-909-CDTA (2382)
www.CDTrail.org

Continental Divide Trail Society
3704 N. Charles St., #601
Baltimore, MD 21218-2300
410-235-9610
www.gorp.com/cdts

DESIGNATED
1978

APPROXIMATE MILEAGE
3,260 miles (5,216 kilometers)

STATES
New Mexico, Colorado, Wyoming, Idaho, Montana

travelers pass along the Divide, they are reminded of others who have encountered it and left their mark: ancient cliff dwellers, American Indians, trappers, merchants, pioneers, Pony Express riders, miners, loggers, and railroad and highway workers. On the CDT, memories are imprinted that last a lifetime—memories of awe-inspiring views from rocky ridges, of brilliantly colored alpine wild-flowers, of a bright-eyed white-tailed deer or a mighty bull elk with its velvety rack, of the ephemeral and powerful forces of nature, or the equally powerful emotions that engulf and renew the spirit. It may well be impossible to travel the Continental Divide Trail without a renewed reverence for one's life, nature, America, and the earth.

The History of the Trail

The Continental Divide, which bisects the American West, seems to have a special meaning to all who encounter it. The Blackfoot of northern Montana called it the "Center of the World;" others refer to it as the "Backbone of America." When explorers, trappers, pioneers, and miners faced the Divide they saw an obstacle to surmount, cross, and leave behind. They realized that once over it their old world would fade behind them. No longer would the natural direction of the waters flow east into the Atlantic Ocean, the Gulf of Mexico, or the Arctic Ocean. Instead, the waters would drain west to the Pacific, pulling them toward a new life. Perhaps it is the mystery at this center of the world, the strength of the backbone that parts all waters, or the promise of fresh new horizons that draws the hiker to it, staying close, almost hugging it. Regardless of the Continental Divide's meaning to one's own journey, it remains one of the most prominent topographic features in the United States.

A fairly continuous ridge along the north-south–trending mountains in North America, the Continental Divide meanders through the Rocky Mountains, the largest mountain system on the continent. In Alaska the divide traverses the Seward Peninsula and the Brooks Range, then curves through Yukon Territory and British Columbia and enters the United States in western Montana. Forming part of Montana's boundary with Idaho, the Great Divide then winds through Wyoming, Colorado, and New Mexico. Continuing southward, it travels into Mexico and Central America, roughly paralleling the Sierra Madre Occidental and the Sierra Madre del Sur. Though the term *continental divide* can refer to the principal parting of the waters of any continent, this Great Divide is the only one to slash the river systems of two continents.

The Rocky Mountains, which provide the setting for so much of the Continental Divide National Scenic Trail, were formed about

CREST AT ROCKY MOUNTAIN NATIONAL
PARK IN COLORADO

The CDT follows the crests of three chains of Rocky Mountains—the Southern, Middle and Northern Rockies. In the rugged Southern Rockies, the segment in Rocky Mountain National Park passes popular destinations, including Grays Peak, Rollins Pass, and Berthoud Pass.

65 million years ago by a tremendous upheaval of the earth's crust. Further upheavals, volcanism, the erosion of wind and rain, and glaciers eventually sculpted them into their various shapes. The topography fluctuates from low prairie to high, uneven, intensely glaciated areas with treeless sawtooth crestlines that rise dramatically above timberline. Rocky gorges and broad structural valleys separate the resulting ranges that tend toward a north-northwest to south-southeast alignment, lying end to end to form mountain chains. Three chains of Rockies, the Southern, Middle, and Northern, together stretch the length of the United States along the Divide.

The Southern Rockies reach from the Sangre de Cristo range in New Mexico to central Wyoming and include the highest peaks in the Rocky Mountain system. Wheeler Peak, New Mexico's tallest, rises 13,161 feet, and in Colorado, Mount Elbert is the highest, reaching 14,433 feet. Rocky Mountain National Park lies in the Southern Rockies and offers tundra, rolling uplands, and snow-clad peaks that may not melt until August. The Middle Rockies stretch from northwestern Colorado/northern Utah to the upper Yellowstone River in Montana. They encompass the Grand Tetons, the Yellowstone, and South Pass, where grand basins filled with enormous volumes of the sedimentary waste from eroded mountains hide the gentlest passing over of the Great

CONTINENTAL DIVIDE TRAIL AT TWIN LAKES, COLORADO

Just west of Independence Pass, the golden aspens drape Collegiate Peaks near Twin Lakes, Colorado.

Divide. High peaks in this range include Wyoming's Gannett Peak (13,804 feet) and Montana's Granite Peak (12,799 feet). From southern Idaho to the Canadian border in western Montana, the Northern Rockies embrace Glacier National Park and Idaho's 12,662-foot Borah Peak. A geologically complex region,

these mountains offer the most varied landscape in the chain. Most of the Rockies in central Idaho are well below 10,000 feet and punctuate the most extensive wilderness country in the coterminous United States. Although the degree of human habitation and use varies greatly in the mountains, many areas along the Divide in the Southern, Middle, and Northern Rockies remain virtually pristine wildlands.

Needless to say, these awesome peaks hampered the journeys of the American Indians, the early explorers, mountainmen, gold-seekers, the nineteenth century pioneers (see Volume 1 of this book series), the railroad builders and highway crews. For them the Rockies represented a barrier to conquer, to cross, to survive and leave behind. What would these early travelers` think of today's outdoor pioneers who look to the magnificence of the Rockies and attempt to hug the Great Divide, to stay close to it for outdoor adventure, to experience nature, to meditate, or to reach back to America's earlier times? Perhaps, they would understand the hikers' desire to connect with those powerful moments when others surmounted the obstacle, the formidable barrier that separated them from their destiny; to step upon the same land where Meriwether Lewis and William Clark nearly perished in 1805 and handily traversed on their return in 1806; to gaze at the path of the swift young Pony Express riders, young men with a purpose and destination that was perfectly clear. Those early travelers might applaud this transformation of the American spirit, this love of the land with its limitlessness and promise of freedoms that they cherished enough to risk all to pursue.

As one of the founders of the Wilderness Society, Benton MacKaye knew the awe-inspiring beauty of the forests and wilderness lands located along the spine of the Great Divide in the Rocky Mountain region. As father of the Appalachian Trail, MacKaye had

the foresight to understand that a grand trail worthy of national scenic trail status could thread together the outstanding primitive wilderness areas. The path would loosely follow the Continental Divide as it meandered in serpentine fashion from the Canadian border in Montana to the Mexican border in New Mexico. The idea was included in the Bureau of Outdoor Recreation (BOR) 1966 report, *Trails for America,* and when Congress held hearings on the proposed National Trails System, according to Tom Lorang Jones, author of *Colorado's Continental Divide Trail, The Official Guide,* MacKaye proposed his idea of a grand Continental Divide trail. The idea captured the imagination of Congress, and two years later, when the National Trails System Act was passed, the Continental Divide Trail was listed for study for future national trail designation.

The BOR, assisted by other government agencies, private organizations, and individuals, undertook the CDT feasibility study authorized by Congress. As they evaluated the potential route, AT hiker and East Coast attorney Jim Wolf decided to take a look for himself in summer 1973. With pen in hand and pack strapped to his back, he hit the trail in Montana and scouted the proposed route. Returning home with copious notes, he published a detailed guidebook of the Montana CDT. Avid CDT supporters joined him in a relentless

ACOMA-TO-ZUNI HIKER WITH CDT SIGN

At El Malpais National Monument in New Mexico, the CDT deviates from the divide to follows an ancient trail that was used as a trade route between Zuni and Acoma Pueblos. Tall basalt rock cairns, which would be hidden from sight if it were not for the tall sticks jutting up from the center, guide the hiker through four periods of basalt lava flows.

lobbying campaign to achieve national scenic trail designation. Meanwhile, the BOR completed their feasibility study and wrote to Congress that the scenic beauty of the lands crossed by the CDT was unsurpassed by any other in the country. In their 1976 report, they recommended that existing recreational trails and primitive roads in the national forests and national parks be linked together to form the thread trail. Wolf, equipped with extensive firsthand experiences on the CDT and knowledge about hiking, botany, zoology, and history, provided

testimony to the Congressional Oversight Committee and urged official designation. Shortly thereafter, on November 10, 1978, Congress designated the Continental Divide National Scenic Trail. The United States now had a concept for a third north-south–aligned national scenic trail. Rough as it was, much cutting and polishing would be needed before the trail would take shape. The idea sparkled brilliantly, but sparse government funding, the lack of local volunteers, and the very short season in which to access the trail slowed development.

Assisted by an advisory council representing both public and private interests, the secretary of agriculture in consultation with the secretary of the interior was given the responsibility for trail development. The secretary of agriculture delegated the responsibility of coordinating trail management to the chief of the Forest Service—a natural step as about 75 percent of the trail corridor was on national forest land.

In the legislation, the CDT was intended to be a modest trail for hiking and equestrian use that would stretch approximately 3,100 miles from Mexico to Canada. This route would be located as close as possible to the Continental Divide in such a way as not to significantly mar the land or vegetation or prove incompatible with wildlife. Where this placement was not possible, the trail would be located elsewhere in the vicinity of the mountain spine. Deviations in the route were to be limited to the distance needed to accommodate these considerations. The route would permit limited motorized vehicle use on certain existing primitive roads if such use was in practice at the time of the CDT designation. Even so, the overriding idea was to keep the trail essentially nonmotorized. Some of these mandates would be modified as the trail took shape.

Like the AT and the PCT before it, the spirit, tenacity, and determination of countless individuals would be needed to make the CDT a reality. Having operated informally in the mid-1970s, the Continental Divide Trail Society (CDTS) was established officially in 1978, although it is not a nonprofit organization. Dedicated to helping to plan, develop, and sustain the trail as a silent trail, Jim Wolf served as the society's director. Each summer the attorney headed out west to hike another segment of the proposed route, publishing trail guides that contained mile-by-mile descriptions of preliminary and potential routes. Although not always the official route of the CDT, packs of maps have been made available so that members can plan a trek along the Divide. Wolf has helped CDT trekkers to follow the route's unmarked segments and to cross rough and wild terrain. Today, more than two hundred fifty backpackers and equestrian riders from nearly all fifty states and many foreign countries are members of the CDTS, which is based in Baltimore, Maryland.

The 1,480 miles of CDT that the Forest Service inventoried in 1981 consisted of well-established pack trails, 1930 footpaths built by the Civilian Conservation Corps, Forest Service roads, and park trails. During the 1980s and early 1990s, federal budget cutbacks slowed trail formation. As a result, in 1995 the Continental Divide Trail Alliance (CDTA) was formed as a nonprofit organization to help promote, build, maintain, and protect the CDT in cooperation with federal land management agencies The alliance organized volunteers and solicited resources from the private sector to help finish the trail by the year 2008, the CDT's thirtieth anniversary. Staffed by enthusiastic leadership, the alliance has developed a strong grassroots constituency. The expertise of Paula Ward, a landscape architect, and Bruce Ward, past president of the American Hiking Society, has provided a strong foundation for the alliance.

Shortly after forming, the CDTA held four state conferences and launched a Uniting Along the Divide campaign. With the help of corporate sponsors, government officials, and volunteers, this successful promotional effort resulted in a voluntary inventory of the trail's present status. The publicity attracted even more volunteers for summer work projects to build and repair the trail. To date, the CDTA has coordinated more than forty thousand hours of volunteer labor on over 644 miles of trail. To keep the momentum going, the determined CDTA initiated the Adopt-a-Trail Program, which recruits local volunteers to inspect and maintain a 3- to 25-mile segment of trail on a regular basis. Government agency cooperation is gaining momentum as well. In June 1999 representatives of the U.S. Forest Service, National Park Service, the BLM, and the CDTA signed a memorandum of understanding in the Treaty Room of the White House setting forth their mutual commitment to completing the CDT by the year 2008.

BEAR COUNTRY

The Continental Divide region in Glacier and Yellowstone National Parks and in the national forests in Montana, Idaho, and northwestern Wyoming contains most of the critical grizzly bear habitat remaining in the western United States. Only one hundred fifty years ago, about one hundred thousand grizzlies populated North America from the arctic tundra to the desert Southwest. Their distribution began to dwindle after the early 1900s due to loss of habitat and predation by humans. Bear numbers have increased as a result of protection under the Endangered Species Act, but these aggressive wanderers require large tracts of range. Clearcutting, road building, development of residential subdivisions, and increasing numbers of recreationists fragment the remaining habitat. The negative effect on the welfare of the grizzly bear is a cause of important concern among land managers, scientists, and the general public in these areas.

Black bears, also encountered in the region of the Continental Divide, are found in other mountain and forest areas throughout the United States. These bears, unlike brown bears, are shier and more secretive by nature and generally attack only when defending themselves or their cubs against humans. Their first response is usually to flee from humans by using rough terrain, trees, and cavities. On the other hand, some CDT hikers report that bears they have encountered on the trail do not run away unless they are in areas that still allow hunting. Mothers and cubs will likely try to run from perceived danger, but a grizzly mother tends to see matters quite differently. In fact, the majority of grizzly attacks involve mama bears. In either case, hikers should make every effort to avoid coming between a mother and her cub, black or brown.

When a black bear does not leave an area, the aroma of food is probably present. Bears can smell food more than two miles away. Travelers on the trail can help protect bears and themselves by learning proper food storage techniques and following the procedures of land managers, keeping in mind that "a fed bear is a dead bear." Bears quickly learn to associate food with people, making them much more aggressive. Aggressive bears must be moved or destroyed by animal control officers. Improper food care in bear country can also result in personal injury and cause unnecessary risks for other hikers and campers.

Because bears are unpredictable, there are no hard and fast rules on how to protect oneself. In general, and especially in grizzly country, travelers should be alert and travel with a large group during the middle of the day. Every effort should be made to stay odor-free by keeping clean. Scented lotions, soaps, deodorants, and cosmetics should not be used, and before the trip, it is important not to use scented water softeners, whose strong, sweet smell attracts bears. Needless to say, carrying dried or freeze-dried food in backpacks is much safer than carrying greasy and smelly food like fish and chips. Food should be eaten in one spot, and any remaining food should be stored properly, typically in a waterproof bag such as kayakers use, but follow local policies should always be followed. While on the CDT hikers should minimize time in prime bear habitat and obvious feeding areas. This, unfortunately, includes a good-looking, ripe berry patch and the less obvious avalanche chutes where bears like to graze. Because a startled bear is more inclined to attack—a good reason not to jog on the trail— travelers in bear country are advised to make noise. Singing and clapping hands is thought to be more effective than carrying bells. Making noise is especially important when approaching blind corners, in thick brush, on windy days, and near running water, where it may be more difficult for a bear to sense human presence. Noisemakers and flashlights may make handy deterrents when tent camping at night. Food should not be eaten or stored in a tent, of course, and cooking clothes should be stored like food. Sleeping in a tent is more advisable than sleeping out in the open, and tents should be placed at least 150 feet upwind from the cooking area. Local procedures rule, but typically food is placed in waterproof bags and hung at least 12 feet up and 4 feet out in a tree. Bringing a dog along is usually not recommended in bear country, and if man's or woman's best friend is going along, it should not be allowed to wander. Unleashed, dogs have led bears back to their companions.

Do not depend on color to distinguish a grizzly from a black bear. Grizzlies can be any color from almost black to white, and black bears vary from jet black to brown to cinnamon or even blond. It is best, of course, if travelers are not close enough to see that the grizzly's fur is grizzled and has long, sliver-tipped guard hairs that create an often mixed or silver-tipped, collared appearance. The grizzly's face is concave or dished, it stands 6 to 8 feet high, and it has a humped muscle over the shoulders and long claws. Black bears have fairly straight muzzles and Roman noses, with heads that are small in proportion to their bodies. They stand 5 to 6 feet high, and their claws are not as remarkable as the grizzly's. According to one old tale, it is easier to tell the two by just sneaking up behind the bear, giving it a swift kick, and climbing up a tree. If the bear knocks the tree over and eats you, it's a grizzly. If it climbs up the tree and eats you, it's a black bear. Obviously, this old tale should not be tested, and information on bear encounters should be studied before entering bear country.

The Trail Today

When complete, the Continental Divide National Scenic Trail will take hikers, backpackers, horseback riders, and llama packers through six of the seven ecological zones found in North America. The route passes through twenty-five national forests, twelve wilderness areas, three national parks, one national monument, and eight BLM resource areas. From the sands of the Chihuahuan desert in New Mexico to the tundra of the Rocky Mountains, this unique recreational resource exposes its guests to magnificent unspoiled scenery, an abundance of wildlife and vegetation, culturally diverse experiences, and historic sites through some of America's most dramatic and wild backcountry. This is not to say that the vast route is completely free of the signs of civilization.

Scattered along or near the trail are the remains of historic mining towns, mining equipment, and abandoned mines. These are from mining for gold, silver, lead, and copper that began in the 1880s in the land surrounding towns such

BLUE COLUMBINE

Typically found east of the Continental Divide, the dainty blue columbine (*Aquilegia coerulea*) grows in the foothills to the alpine zones. Colorado's state flower, a member of the buttercup family, was first discovered in 1820 on the northeast side of Pikes Peak. Wildflowers are diverse and abundant as the CDT crosses six of the seven ecological zones.

as Marysville, northwest of Helena, Montana. Also linked to the mining boom were the railroads that crossed the

Continental Divide. The station house on Marshall Pass and other early railroad features in the Gunnison and San Isabel National Forests are found in Colorado near the trail. A significant site at Cumbres Pass near the New Mexico–Colorado border could precipitate a nostalgic trip on the Cumbres and Toltec Scenic Railroad or the Durango to Silverton Narrow Gauge.

The ancient cliff dwellers left their mark too. Ruins are seen at the nearby Gila Cliff Dwelling National Monument in New Mexico. And the Zuni-to-Acoma portion of the CDT goes back at least one thousand years. American Indians who lived on the flanks of the Rocky Mountains when the Europeans arrived—such as the Blackfoot, Coeur d'Alene, Flathead, Kalispel, Kutenai, Shoshone, and Ute—left behind campsites, game-drive sites, and vision quest sites. Deep ruts and swales created by pioneer wagon trains are seen along the Oregon, California, and Mormon Pioneer Trails that crossed the Great Divide near South Pass in Wyoming. Landmarks of the Pony Express, such as remnants of station houses, remain, as do abandoned wagon roads, logging camps, sawmill sites, fire lookout towers, and reforested lands. And remnants of homesteading, ranching, and early engineering technology dot the way, making it clear that the hiker is not the first on the scene and probably won't be the last.

Meanwhile, panoramic views unfold for trail users. On the

THE DURANGO TO SILVERTON NARROW GAUGE RAILROAD

For an enjoyable journey through railroad and mining history, the authentic coal-fired, steam-operated locomotive pulls a string of bright passenger cars over southwestern Colorado's rugged Rocky Mountains in the San Juan National Forest. In continuous use since 1882, the line follows the Animas River from Durango to Silverton where the Old One Hundred Gold Mine and the Mayflower Gold Mill offer educational tours. Along the route, the conductor will make unscheduled stops to pick up CDT hikers.

Targhee Divide in Idaho, hikers enjoy views of Henry's Lake and Montana's Hebgen Lake. Unlike the Appalachian Trail, no shelters await CDT travelers. Unless in grizzly country, they may choose to camp under a charcoal sky studded with bright stars. Nearby, but not always right on the trail, exhilarating white-water river

JERRY CRAIG AND THE AUTHOR CATCH AND RELEASE

According to fishing guide Jerry Craig, one of the best trout streams in America is just off the CDT near Grand Lake, Colorado. Craig gave the author some handy fly-fishing tips on selecting a fly pattern suitable as trout food and presenting it in such a way that the natural movements of the insect are imitated. After plucking out the fly, this one darted away very quickly.

running, canoeing, kayaking, pleasure boating, and swimming abound. Some of the nation's best fly fishing is found along the trail, as in Grand Lake, Colorado. Herds of elk grazing, the lone moose feeding, the eagle departing the nest—these are just some of the sights in the early morning or late afternoon. Large mammals such as bighorn sheep, black bears, brown bears, coyotes, deer, gray wolves, javelinas, moose, mountain goats, mountain lions, North American lynx, North

American wolverines, pronghorn antelope, rocky mountain elk, and wild horses may be encountered along the journey by hikers and horseback riders. Birders look or listen for the bald eagle, black tern, blue grouse, boreal owl, Cooper's hawk, golden eagle, great horned owl, loggerhead shrike, merlin, northern goshawk, northern harrier, osprey, peregrine falcon, red-tailed hawk, roadrunner, sage grouse, turkey vulture, and white-tailed ptarmigan.

Cross-country skis and snowshoes present a means to explore portions of the serene CDT amid a winter wonderland setting. Ski communities such as Keystone, Breckenridge, Steamboat Springs, Telluride, and Winter Park offer the additional excitement of superlative downhill skiing. Searching out one of the many rustic mountain lodges open in winter along the CDT can provide a home base for snowshoe-clad adventurers. Winter visitors in Yellowstone National Park can view bubbling mudpots, aquamarine pools of steaming water that emit an otherworldly luminescence, or powerful eruptions of volatile geysers, all in a geothermal setting that is in stark contrast to the surrounding blankets of snow and ice. Two lodges with blazing fireplaces enthusiastically welcome the Yellowstone visitor in winter.

Some segments along the route allow motorized vehicles, and the CDT's special statutory language permits such use where it was

LONE ELK IN YELLOWSTONE NATIONAL PARK

Trail plans for the CDT include passing Old Faithful Geyser in Yellowstone National Park, one of the world's most successful wildlife sanctuaries. During the winter months, elk, bison, and other animals are easily seen from snowshoes. It is a responsible practice to maintain a good distance from the animals, especially in winter when they have precious little energy to spare.

CROSS-COUNTRY SKIERS

Ski touring programs present an exhilarating, relatively inexpensive way to enjoy the CDT. In this case, equipment was rented in Gallup, New Mexico. Many ski communities hug the Divide, including Telluride, Winter Park, Keystone, Breckenridge, and Steamboat.

allowed at the time that a trail segment was dedicated. This has drawn opposition, however. If the trail is to remain intact as a nonmotorized path, approved motorized sections will need to be closed or avoided and other routes developed. Complicating these matters is the impact on wildlife, which needs further study. Trail segments located in wilderness areas are not open to motorized or mechanized use of any type. Parallel to the CDT is the 2,465-mile Great Divide Mountain Bike Route, which is the longest such route in the world and presents an epic journey for cyclists. The route follows a combination of fire access roads, jeep trails, occasional paved sections, and single-track trails. More information can be obtained through the Adventure Cycling Association at www.adv-cycling.org or by calling 800-755-2453.

Vegetation along the trail corridor is influenced by elevation, latitude, exposure, and precipitation. For instance, in the Colorado and southern Wyoming region, the alpine zone, generally found above 11,500 feet, with its snowdrifts and cold temperatures in spring and winter, is characterized by grass, thistle, clover, snow buttercup, alpine sandwort, Parry's primrose, and American globe flower. Rocky slopes and cliffs support common juniper, ocean spray, brittle fern, red raspberry, Jacob's ladder, and Colorado columbine. Vegetation is often stunted on the eastern slopes exposed to strong arid winds. The cold moist subalpine zone, generally found between about 10,000 and 11,500 feet in Colorado, is composed of subalpine forest of limber, bristlecone, and lodgepole pine, spruce-fir forest, grasslands, medium to tall shrubs, and tall and short forbs (herbs other than grass). Below the subalpine forest, the cold to moderately warm montane and aspen zones, found between about 8,500 and 10,000 feet in Colorado, supports limber pine, bristlecone pine, lodgepole pine, Douglas fir, aspen, alder, willow, dogwood, blue spruce, juniper, brush honeysuckle, whitestem currant, Saskatoon serviceberry, grasses, and tall and short forbs. In the foothills zone, at approximately 8,000 to 8,500 feet in Colorado, cool to cold moist winters and hot to moderately hot, dry summers provide for such vegetation as sagebrush, shrubs, gambel oak, serviceberry and chokecherry, narrowleaf cottonwood, and Pacific willow. These life zones are found at lower elevations farther north in Idaho and Montana, where, for instance, the alpine zone drops to 6,000 feet in Glacier National Park. Correspondingly, similar life zones farther south in New Mexico are found at correspondingly higher elevations.

Portions of the trail require reconstruction, rerouting, signing, and marking, and other segments need to be built to fill gaps. Side trails to access significant cultural, historical, recreational, or scenic opportunities also await development. Much of the route that remains to be formulated and constructed is hindered by the location of private or other noncompatible lands. Although the National Trails System Act of 1968 contained language to permit a 50-mile range on either side of the geographic Continental Divide, the corridor still presents some obstacles to be surmounted. For example, privacy rights and land disputes cause stumbling blocks to completion in northern New Mexico. To avoid disrupting the Jicarilla Apache, attempts to locate the route off the reservation and to the east of the Divide have uncovered other complications: disputed land grant claims that date back to the 1848 Treaty of Guadalupe Hidalgo, the treaty that ended the war between the United States and Mexico. Most of the land grant property is held by the U.S. Forest Service or the Bureau of Land Management while the decades-old adispute is resolved. Even if settled, many of those involved wonder why these lands east of the Divide should be "invaded." Likewise, logging issues thwart trail placement in and around the Carson National Forest.

Nonetheless, the 1998 CDTA *State of the Trail Report* estimates that 70 percent of the trail is "complete," although this portion of the route may still be difficult to find and require CDT signs to guide the traveler. The Montana-Idaho segment is furthest along at 95 percent, Colorado is at 90 percent, New Mexico is at 45 percent, and Wyoming is at 25 percent. Volunteer efforts have helped to advance the CDT. For instance, in the Gila National Forest twelve students from Trinity University in San Antonio, Texas, spent a productive spring break helping to build trail in the Black Range Mountains. To learn how to help, potential volunteers are asked to check the CDTA Web site at www.cdtrail.org or call 888-909-CDTA.

Completed or not, statistics indicate that about twelve through-hikers undertake the trip from end to end each year. Advance preparations and physical conditioning for a trek of this magnitude takes months. For starters, the CDTA and CDTS offer guidebooks, maps, mailing addresses, and advice about route selection, buying supplies, choosing equipment, selecting drop sites and resupply points, and packing and shipping boxes. To follow the official route of the trail, a guidebook is essential. Westcliffe's newly released guidebooks to the CDT are very useful, both for preparations and once

LOGAN PASS BOARDWALK TRAIL AT GLACIER NATIONAL PARK

In spite of the occasional blow-down, washed-out bridge, or overgrown vegetation, the CDT in Glacier National Park in Montana is in first-rate shape and usually easy to follow. Boardwalks protect fragile tundra in the park, unlike some tundra areas on the CDT where through-hikers hopscotch from rock to rock to minimize damage.

on the trail. Up to six to eight months is usually allotted to complete the entire journey. Despite the best preparations, through-hikers must traverse open terrain that requires a good deal of care and thus a slow pace in some areas. Direct passage over alpine tundra may damage vegetation that has taken more than one hundred years to grow a mere inch, so hikers need to cross in hopscotch style, using rocks as stepping-stones where trail has not yet been laid down. When it is

OBSERVING A RAINBOW IN WYOMING

Guides lead horse- and llama-packing expeditions on the CDT. After a long ride, chow, and just before cowboy poetry readings at the campfire, this group is awed by a rainbow outside Dubois, Wyoming.

impossible to avoid stepping on the vegetation, hikers should fan out to avoid the repeated abuse caused by single-file lines. Fortunately, designated sections of the trail over fragile tundra have been cut and marked, for instance in Glacier National Park and some wilderness areas, which minimizes the impact on the land.

Montana or New Mexico is the logical starting point for a through-hike, but both present the hiker with the probability of encountering substantial snow in the mountains that renders terrain hazardous or impassable. The Continental Divide Trail Society recommends a creative

alternative to these inhospitable conditions: cover the lower elevations in New Mexico and southern Wyoming in the spring, then wait until July before attempting the snowier portions of the trail in the mountains.

Hiking conditions vary from easy to difficult, but the natural hazards in wildlands call not only for physical readiness but also for safety preparedness. For the segments where the trail is yet to be laid down, the route selected will make a big difference in safety. There are actually two lines of thinking regarding the placement of trail either near or apart from hazards along the route. One is to follow the Continental Divide as closely as possible, regardless of known hazards such as steep-sided slopes, knife-edged ridges, persistent-snow fields, large rock slides, long durations with exposure to wind and lightning, and no water. Proponents of this strict routing believe these

AMERICA'S NATIONAL SCENIC TRAILS

conditions are part of the trail experience. The other option is to select the route that provides for maximum safety. This includes relocating trail from high-altitude areas with inherent hazards to lower and safer elevations where trees, not hikers, are the obvious target for lightning strikes. The existing route in Montana-Idaho is a compromise, with much of the route on or near the Divide and with some detours around terrain that would be snowed in almost year-round or terrain that would require rock-climbing gear.

All trail users are encouraged to plan very carefully as there are few markings or blazes. Guidebooks and appropriate topographical maps, a compass or global positioning system (GPS), and the know-how to use them are essential to stay on course. This chapter should not be used alone to actually follow the trail. Up-to-date guidebooks to help plan a trek are now available from Westcliffe Publishers in Colorado. Warm protective clothing, rugged camping gear, sturdy boots, a hat, ultraviolet sunglasses, sunscreen lotion, bug repellent, first-aid supplies, and first-aid know-how are needed. Isolated segments of the trail present minimal opportunities for communications in an emergency, so taking responsibility for spotting risks inherent in backcountry travel and knowing how to handle them is a must that cannot be emphasized enough. This includes knowing how to handle high altitudes and high water, what to do when lightning

strikes, and how to protect against giardia, Colorado tick fever, Rocky Mountain spotted fever, Lyme disease, and various viruses. Caution is needed where the trail crosses roads or highways or where motorized use is allowed. Hunting season calls for dressing in hunter's orange, observing posted signs, and following recommended precautions. CDT travelers are encouraged to check in with local district ranger stations to inform the staff of plans, to inquire about trail conditions, and to check the weather forecast. In some cases, backcountry permits are required.

Frost can occur at any time of the year over much of the trail's corridor, although it would be unusual at 4,000 to 7,000 feet, where summer temperatures run an average of 70 to 100+ degrees Fahrenheit. These averages can be misleading because warm temperatures at the lower elevations of New Mexico are factored in. Winter temperatures at this elevation average 26 to 65 degrees Fahrenheit, and annual precipitation is 11 inches. At higher elevations, from 7,000 to 11,000 feet, in Colorado, Wyoming, and Montana summer temperatures average 60 to 90 degrees Fahrenheit, winter temperatures average 28 to 59 degrees Fahrenheit, and annual precipitation averages 20 inches. In the highest elevations, from 11,000 to 14,000 feet, found in Colorado's Southern Rockies, summer temperatures average a cool to comfortable 44 to 78 degrees, and thunderstorms are frequent. Winter temperatures average below 0 to 45 degrees, and average annual precipitation is 40 inches, which converts to lots of snow, for example, more than 80 inches in Glacier National Park. Snowfall typically occurs from October to May, and weather can be severe from October to July, with strong winds. As a rule of thumb, for every 1,000 feet of elevation gained, there is a corresponding drop in temperature of 5 degrees. Microclimates that create cold spots in valleys or other unusual weather conditions are common in the Colorado Rockies, and changes in weather along the trail can be swift, severe, and extremely hazardous.

The trail's southern terminus in New Mexico is at the U.S.-Mexico border near Antelope Wells. Alternative locations are under discussion. The CDT traveler begins the northward journey by crossing the Alamo Hueco and Hatchet Mountains through the arid Chihuahuan desert to the Gila National Forest and Aldo Leopold Wilderness. Other potential changes to the route may redirect the CDT to the Gila Cliff Dwellings National Monument, where ruins of the ancient Anasazi civilization whisper about the past.

As it travels from Pie Town to Cuba, the CDT enters one of its most fascinating segments. In the volcanic El Malpais National Monument, the trail joins the thousand-year-old Zuni-Acoma trade route for seven and one-half miles as it crosses four of the five porous-rock lava flows in the monument. Navigation is aided by ancient rock cairns, some piled five feet high with long sticks protruding from the top. Although the route is situated in the most hospitable terrain in the badlands, it still requires sturdy boots and long pants and takes six to seven hours to complete. Carrying a compass is recommended, and taking plenty of water is a must. After passage through the Cibola National Forest and the canyonlands near the famous Ghost Ranch, the route crosses the Santa Fe and Carson National Forests, known for brilliant wildflower displays. Nearby pueblos and Spanish-speaking villages offer significant cultural opportunities.

Breaking into Colorado near Cumbres Pass, the trail winds through the scenic alpine territory in the San Juan Mountains in the South San Juan and Weminuche Wildernesses Areas. In the remote San Juan Mountains the alert hiker may spot bighorn sheep, black bear, deer, and elk. The Weminuche has some of the most rugged and majestic peaks in the continental United States. After crossing a portion of the lesser-known La Garita Wilderness, with streams that teem with brook, brown, cutthroat, and rainbow trout, the route ascends to the Collegiate Peaks, Mount Massive, Hunter-Fryingpan, and Holy Cross Wilderness Areas, where Colorado's highest mountains are found. The route continues almost entirely on national forest land in the San Juan, Rio Grande, Gunnison, San Isabel, White River, Pike, Arapaho, and Routt National Forests. Numerous wilderness areas in these forests are linked together by the CDT, including Vasquez Peak, Indian Peaks, Never Summer, Mount Zirkel, and Huston Park. The trail reaches above tree line in Vasquez Peak, and by Indian Peaks the exceptional vistas are considered by some to be the best mountain views in the United States. Never Summer borders the western side of Rocky Mountain National Park, where it provides a spectacular mountain backdrop for the park's Trail Ridge Road. In Mount Zirkel, birders spot bald eagles, osprey, peregine falcons, and sandhill cranes, and as the route traverses Rocky Mountain National Park, hikers will find bighorn sheep, the living symbol of the park. BLM-administered lands are traversed at Muddy Pass, the lowest crossing of the Divide in Colorado at 8,772 feet and where the explorer John C. Frémont crossed in 1844. The high-elevation Southern Rockies in the western half of Colorado have 53 peaks that reach over 14,000 feet and 831 others that reach 11,000 to 14,000 feet.

After exiting Colorado about 40 miles north of Steamboat Springs, the CDT continues through the Medicine Bow portion of the Medicine Bow–Routt National Forest, south ·of Encampment. Following the eastern rim of the Great Divide Basin, the route makes its way to South Pass and the glacially carved Wind River Range. The route travels the Divide through the Bridger-Teton and Shoshone National Forests before entering Yellowstone, established as the nation's first national park in 1872. From the south the route passes geologic natural wonders, backcountry lakes, and hot springs. West of Old Faithful Geyser, the CDT route leaves the park on the Summit Lake Trail and crosses into Idaho's Targhee National Forest. En route, you can learn about ewes and targhees at the U.S. Sheep Experiment Station.

Threading the Idaho and Montana border, the CDT follows the backbone of the Rocky Mountains in the Targhee, Gallatin, Beaverhead, and Salmon National Forests of the Centennial Range and the Beaverhead Mountains of the Bitterroot Range. It passes high above the Red Rock Lakes National Wildlife Refuge and Big Hole National Battlefield. In the area of Chief Joseph Pass, the CDT bears signs for the crisscrossed route of the 1805 Lewis and Clark Expedition (see NPNHT and LCNHT in *America's National Historic Trails*). Northward from Chief Joseph Pass, the CDT travels the length of the Anaconda-Pintler Wilderness, which was named for the Anaconda Mountain Range and the early Big Hole settler Charles Ellsworth Pintler. On the way to the U.S.-Canada border, the CDT travels through Deerlodge, Lewis and Clark, Helena, and Flathead National Forests and crosses the Scapegoat and Bob Marshall Wilderness Areas, where grizzlies roam. While passing through Glacier National Park, the route exits the park and crosses the Blackfeet Reservation near the town of East Glacier and then reenters the park for a final stretch.

In Glacier National Park, named "the land of shining mountains" by the early French explorer Pierre La Verendrye, the CDT offers stunning views of high plains from the summit at Scenic Point. It passes Saint Mary's Lake, Virginia Falls, and Saint Mary's Falls on the way to Many Glacier. An official route leads to the Belly River Customs Station for entry into Canada, but the traditional route heads westward to the Granite Park Chalet and into the Waterton valley, where it reaches its northern terminus at Goat Haunt Ranger Station. The stalwart hiker can continue the expedition by following the western shore of

Waterton Lake into Waterton, Canada. For a more leisurely approach, hikers may want to take the ferry into the town site. Those entering Canada must pass through customs.

Approximate mileage for each state is indicated in the Points of Interest section below. Most of the public areas in the CDT corridor cover large expanses of land, and many locations and nearby towns have been included for those accessing a section of the trail by automobile. For the most part, it is impractical for hikers on foot or horseback to travel to the *nearby* locations unless they can afford a day or more for a departure from the trail. A reminder: the CDT passes through some of the most rugged and remotest lands in the lower forty-eight states. A trek through this country, whether for a day, a week, or even longer, requires detailed preparation and careful planning. Contact the association for detailed guidebooks and advice on ways to prepare for a trek—it might be one of the best outdoor experiences of your life.

Points of Interest

NEW MEXICO
(790 MILES)

1. ANTELOPE WELLS. This town is at the southern terminus where most of the trail is incomplete and the final route is yet to be decided. There have been suggestions to make Columbus, which is both scenic and historic, the terminus. For now, the CDT

corridor follows the U.S.-Mexico border east for 11 miles and then turns north through the Alamo Hueco Mountains. Water is scarce in the windy dry desert here. There is an abundance of man-size cholla, bright green mesquite, and pungent desert sage. Jackrabbits, cottontails, coyotes, white-tailed and mule deer, pronghorns, javelinas, rattlesnakes, and other

AMERICA'S NATIONAL SCENIC TRAILS

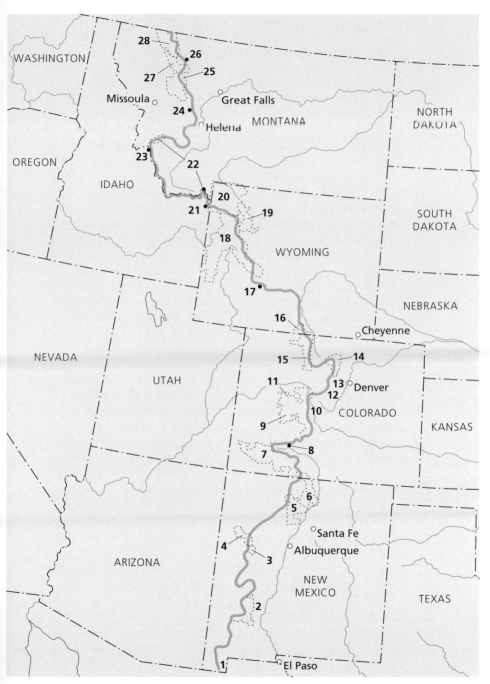

WASHINGTON

28
26
27
25

Missoula ○
24
Great Falls ○
Helena ○
MONTANA

OREGON

23
22

IDAHO
20
21
19
18

WYOMING

17

16
Cheyenne ○

NEVADA

UTAH

15
14
11
13 ○ Denver
12
10
9
COLORADO

KANSAS

7
8

6
5

4
○ Santa Fe
3
○ Albuquerque

ARIZONA
NEW
MEXICO
TEXAS

2

1
○ El Paso

CONTINENTAL DIVIDE NATIONAL SCENIC TRAIL

OREGON

NORTH
DAKOTA

SOUTH
DAKOTA

NEBRASKA

desert creatures scurry too fast to get a look. Hawks and eagles might be spotted soaring overhead, and cattle from the area's huge ranch will inevitably be heard and seen. *Nearby:** In Columbus, the Columbus Historical Museum has exhibits in the Southern Pacific Railroad depot; Pancho Villa State Park on the western slope of the Little Florida Mountains records the March 9, 1916, raid of the small border town by Gen. Francisco "Pancho" Villa and his guerrilla soldiers. At Deming, the Deming Luna Mimbres Museum has American Indian, Hispanic, cowboy, and gem and mineral displays; Rockhound State Park permits visitors to seek out and take home up to fifteen pounds of gemstones and minerals. Near Cloverdale, there are guided tours of Whipple Observatory.

2. GILA NATIONAL FOREST. Canyon country of this 3.3-million-acre forest is crossed by the CDT in both the main unit near Silver City and a smaller one along the Big Burro Mountains northeast of Lordsburg. South of Silver City, in the national forest, the CDT is complete and in good condition. North of Silver City, trail conditions improve along the rugged crest of the Black Range, where turkeys, elk, bobcats, mountain lions, and even black

*Nearby locations are provided for the traveler with a car or an abundance of time to depart from the CDT corridor. Be sure to check travel distances before departing from the trail for one of these locations.

bears might be spotted. Plans are being considered to reroute segments of the CDT that are located on roads. The mountains here—the Black, Mogollon, Tularosa, and Diablo—once served as the stronghold of Geronimo and other Apache warriors, and during the thirteenth century, lands near the corridor were occupied by the Mimbres Indians, known for their esoteric black-and-white pottery painted with geometric designs and abstract images of animals, insects, birds, and fish. Weathered remains of their ancient pithouses are hidden under land depressions and raised mounds barely detectable on the banks of the Mimbres River. Easier to spot are overturned mounds that are the dirty work left behind by the illegal pot hunters who callously bulldozed entire archaeological sites to unearth the prized Mimbres pots buried with the dead. Gold and silver mining boomed in southern New Mexico in the 1880s, and the CDT route leads to the historic mining town Pinos Altos, whose hardware and buildings were simply left behind when the strikes played out. The forest contains the headwaters of the Gila and Mimbres Rivers, part of the San Francisco River, and the first wilderness preserve in the United States: the 558,065-acre Gila Wilderness, located directly north of Silver City, which was established in 1924 at the suggestion of the conservationist Aldo Leopold. A plaque, 15 to 20 miles west of the Divide and 8 miles south of Pleasanton, marks the Leopold Vista Historical Monument. A second wilderness, the 202,016-acre Aldo Leopold, contains the most rugged and wildest portion of the Black Range, with a difficult-to-follow CDT where wild turkeys, elk, bobcats, mountain lions, and black bears might be seen. Ravaging fires that damaged the trail were probably first spotted from the Divide's 8,872-foot Lookout Mountain. For further information, contact forest headquarters in Silver City. *Other attractions:* Gila Cliff Dwellings National Monument near Gila Hot Springs offers fascinating archaeological ruins and the bonus of Lightfeather Hot Springs near the visitor center. Near Lordsburg, the ghost town at Shakespeare offers guided tours on specific weekends; Steins, another ghost town, is 19 miles southwest of Lordsburg. In and near Silver City, the Silver City Museum occupies an 1821 mansion and has mining and American Indian artifacts; Fleming Hall at Western New Mexico University contains the nation's largest permanent exhibit of Mimbres pottery; Billy the Kid sites; Old Tyrone was the home of the Phelps-Dodge Open Pit Mine and Mill; Santa Rita del Cobre Fort is a replica of Old Fort Webster; Kneeling Nun is a monolith located east of Silver City on N.M. 152; City of Rocks State Park has towering lava monoliths; Faywood Hot Springs is 2 miles from U.S. 180 next to the state park. Near Glenwood,

the Catwalk National Recreation Trail is steep and has suspended bridges crossing Whitewater Canyon. In Mogollón, the ghost town's Mogollón Museum. *Nearby:* In Hillsboro, the old historic mining town's Black Range Museum.

3. EL MALPAIS NATIONAL MONUMENT AND NATIONAL CONSERVATION AREA. Administered by the NPS and the BLM, these areas have more than 300,000 acres of volcanic landscape and wilderness. In El Malpais (Spanish for "badlands" and pronounced *mal-pie-EES*), CDT hikers encounter volcanic cinder cones, lava tubes, ice caves, sandstone bluffs, pinyon forests, archaeological sites, and historic homesteads. Following the monument's quixotic thousand-year-old trail that was used as a trade route between Zuni and Acoma Pueblos, the CDT passes through four periods of lava flows. Maps are available at the ranger station. Rattlesnakes are common in this area, especially in the hot summer months, and there is a need to carry plenty of water. Elsewhere, the CDT follows I-40 and N.M. 117 for 14 miles until private land issues are resolved. A few miles from the trail is La Ventana Natural Arch, formed from eroded sandstone approximately 65 million years ago. El Malpais has deep traditional ties with the neighboring Acoma, Laguna, Zuni, and Navajo cultures, who have pueblos and reservations nearby. There is a visitor center in Grants and another 9 miles south of I-40

on N.M. 117. *Nearby:* North of Grants, the CDT is incomplete. At Grants, the New Mexico Museum of Mining has a replica of a mine; Ice Caves and Bandera Volcano can be reached via N.M. 53; El Morro National Monument's Inscription Rock bears the carved names and dates of Spanish explorers and westbound pioneers; missions and churches in Cibola County off I-40. Near Gallup, Red Rock State Park has a museum exhibiting American Indian displays, a rodeo arena in a natural amphitheater, and the colorful Indian Inter-Tribal Ceremonial held every second week of August; Historic Route 66.

4. CIBOLA NATIONAL FOREST. In most places, dirt roads serve as the CDT on the 1.6-million-acre national forest in the west-central portion of the state. There are units near Pie Town, Gallup, and Grants—all near the Continental Divide. Mount Taylor, sacred to the region's American Indians, is the highest point in the CDT corridor in New Mexico, at 11,301 feet. Near Albuquerque, the Sandia State Game Refuge, established in 1921, offers special protection for Rocky Mountain bighorn sheep, and the Sandia Peak Aerial Tramway offers expansive views. The Kiowa (SFNHT) and Black Kettle National Grasslands are part of Cibola. For further information, contact forest headquarters in Albuquerque.

5. SANTA FE NATIONAL FOREST. Sun-baked crumbly clay hills marked by deep gullies and known as the Badland Hills stretch from north of Cuba to west of Chama over a good portion of the Santa Fe National Forest, which has more than 1.5 million acres of forest and rangeland divided into two units. The unit west of the Rio Grande— crossed by the CDT—has San Pedro Parks, Chama River Canyon, and Dome Wildernesses, Santa Clara Peak (11,561 feet), San Pedro Mountain (10,610), Chicoma Peak (10,230 feet), the Jemez Mountains and the Jemez State Monument, with ruins of the original home of the Jemez Indians. Except in San Pedro Parks Wilderness and the Chama River Canyon Wilderness where the trail is in good shape, the CDT simply follows roads. Bandelier National Monument, with its thirteenth-century cliff houses, adjoins this section of the forest. Noted for its ten thousand years of human history (see SFNHT), the Pecos National Historical Park is located between forestlands and neighboring pueblos that border portions of the Santa Fe Trail. For further information, contact the headquarters in Santa Fe. *Nearby:* In Los Alamos, the Bradbury Science Museum provides technical interpretation of the history of the Manhattan Project and the Los Alamos National Laboratory of the U.S. Department of Energy; Fuller Lodge Art Center in the Los Alamos Ranch School (NHL) displays the creative works of northern New Mexico artists; the County Historical Museum.

6. CARSON NATIONAL FOREST. Wildflowers are abundant in the 1.5-million-acre forest named for Kit Carson. Here the CDT leads to the Forest Service's Ghost Ranch Living Museum near Abiquiu Reservoir, with geology and animal displays and exhibits about the region's cultural history. A few miles north of the reservoir is the mystical Ghost Ranch conference center where Georgia O'Keefe painted and other artists, philosophers, and archaeologists have gathered over the years. North of the ranch, Spanish land grant, private land, and cattle grazing issues have stalled the designation of the CDT route. Other forest attractions are the San Juan and Sangre de Cristo Mountains, northern portions of the Chama and Pecos Wildernesses, Wheeler Peak with the state's highest point at 13,161 feet, Latier Peak, and Cruces Basin Wilderness, alpine lakes, and high green valleys with Spanish-speaking villages. Pueblo Indian villages and the Rio Grande Wild River National Recreation Area border the forest. The high country provides a panoramic view of the Southern Rockies from remote areas as well as from the Enchanted Circle Byway on the way to Taos. For further information, contact forest headquarters in Taos. *Nearby:* At Tierra Amarilla in the state's northern mountains, El Vado Lake State Park and Heron Lake State Park. In Chama, trout fishing begins in June, and the Cumbres and Toltec Scenic Railroad offers fabulous views of the jagged San Juan and Sangre de Cristo ranges on its way to Osier, Colorado. In Osier, a connection to Antonito is possible on the Colorado Limited.

COLORADO
(770 MILES)

7. SAN JUAN NATIONAL FOREST. The nearly 2-million-acre national forest west of the Divide received its name (Spanish for Saint John) from the San Juan River and the San Juan Mountains. Hikers comment that this segment of the CDT has a dramatic mystical quality. From Cumbres Pass (elevation 10,022 feet), the CDT reaches the 127,000-acre South San Juan Wilderness, where the trail reaches its first true high country, with stunning waterfalls and luminescent lakes. High plateaus above timberline and volcanic peaks that exceed elevations of 13,000 feet have snowfields, windy conditions, and stretches of trail along exposed ridges where it may snow even in August. The pristine 490,000-acre Weminuche Wilderness offers superlative CDT that is rugged and remote in the higher elevations and presents low wet areas that will probably be rerouted. The Weminuche, named for the Ute Indians, is for many Colorado backcountry lovers the most spectacular of wilderness lands, offering sunbathed peaks, tundra, lakes, tarns, rugged cliffs, rock outcroppings, creeks teeming with trout, and wildflowers such as white bitter cress, yellow paint-

brush, and purple columbine. It is Colorado's largest wilderness area and features La Ventana (Spanish for "window"), a rock formation with a breathtaking view of the Needle Mountains, a mecca for mountain climbers. La Ventana is located on a ledge at an elevation of 12,857 feet. The climb up to the narrow 150-foot-high geometric notch is very steep. From famed Wolf Pass (elevation 10,857 feet), where annual snowfall averages 460 inches, the CDT's route leads to the Silverton area. Thousands of North American elk summer along the Divide, so caution is appropriate in September's rutting season and during the hunting season. Areas of the forest away from the CDT include the San Juan Lizard Head Wilderness, 14,246-foot Mount Wilson, Treasure Falls, and Anasazi ruins in the Chimney Rock Archaeology Area. If driving to the trail, the San Juan Skyway, selected as an All-American Road, snakes through the San Juan and Uncompahgre National Forests through Old West towns, picturesque Telluride, and Mesa Verde National Park. The historic coal-burning Durango and Silverton Narrow Gauge Railroad offers exceptional views of portions of the Needle Mountains and takes passengers through the gorgeous deep canyon of the Río de Las Animas. For further information, contact forest headquarters in Durango. *Nearby:* In Durango, the Victorian downtown, called Main Street, is a National Historic District; Third Avenue National Historic District, also known as The Boulevard, offers one of the best examples of Victorian residential houses and mansions in the United States; outfitters arrange river trips and jeep tours. In Silverton, the entire town is a National Historic Landmark District; San Juan County Museum has early mining and railroad displays; the terminus of the Durango and Silverton Narrow Gauge Railroad; One Hundred Gold Mine Tour takes visitors on an electric mine train for a look at early mining; outfitters offer tours; the Million Dollar Highway is a famous section of the Skyway (US 550) from Silverton to Ouray (you-RAY). The mining town of Ouray, named for the Southern Ute chief and called the "Switzerland of America," has a National Historic Landmark District; Bachelor-Syracuse Mine provides a mine train into Gold Hill; jeep tours to ghost towns and mining areas; dog-sledding; and snowmobile tours through the Uncompahgre National Forest. The Uncompahgre National Forest is known for Dry Mesa Dinosaur Quarry. The Southern Ute Indian Reservation holds its Bear Dance in late May, its Sun Dance in early July, and the Southern Ute Fair in early September. The Ute Mountain Indian Reservation generally holds its Bear Dance in June; Ute Mountain Pottery Factory; Ute Mountain Tribal Park has Anasazi ruins. Telluride and Purgatory are known for their ski areas.

8. RIO GRANDE NATIONAL FOREST. The 1.8-million-acre Rio Grande slopes to the east of the Continental Divide. The CDT is somewhat difficult to follow here as it runs through the spectacular 104,000-acre La Garita Wilderness and the remote South San Juan and Weminuche Wilderness Areas shared with the San Juan National Forest. Horse packers offer trips in the CDT backcountry, where it is possible to see magnificent herds of elk several hundred individuals strong. With spectacular views in all directions, 5 miles of CDT lie on Snow Mesa, a massive flat grassy tundra covering 30 square miles where rugged 13,334-foot Coney Summit and Red Mountain rise up in the west; flat-topped Uncompahgre and rugged Wetterhorn rise to the north, and La Garita rises to the east. In La Garita, the CDT follows the Colorado trail's high-elevation ridges with bone-chilling precipitous drops amid magnificent windswept terrain. The last 10 miles in La Garita descend into lower elevations. Away from the CDT, the forest holds a part of the Sangre de Cristo Wilderness near Great Sand Dunes National Monument, with some of the largest and highest sand dunes in the nation; a portion of the San Juan and Sangre de Cristo Mountains; the San Luis Valley with the headwaters of the Rio Grande, the third longest river in the United States. A dilapidated sawmill and cabin are two of the historic sites. The Wheeler Geologic Area has a haunting landscape in the La Garita range with barren, pale gray, brittle-looking vertical rock formations. For further information, contact forest headquarters in Monte Vista. *Nearby:* At Monte Vista, the Monte Vista National Wildlife Refuge attracts sandhill cranes, whooping cranes, and bald eagles in season.

9. GUNNISON NATIONAL FOREST. The nearly 1.8-million-acre national forest contains twenty-seven peaks that reach over 12,000 feet, two of which reach elevations of over 14,000 feet ("fourteeners"). High-elevation CDT runs through two of the forest's wilderness areas, La Garita and Collegiate Peaks, between which is located Cochetopa Pass (elevation 10,032).

Efforts are under way to improve the trail markings so that the above-timberline route is less difficult to follow. When Juan Bautista de Anza was governor of the Spanish colony of New Mexico (see JBANHT in *America's National Historic Trails*), the Utes showed him Cochetopa Pass, which he used to pursue a band of Comanches who had exasperated his colonists. Other historic sites include abandoned sawmills, a homestead, a cabin, a mining town and mill, and historic transportation. For further information, contact forest headquarters in Delta. *Nearby:* At Montrose, the Montrose Historical Museum is located in the Denver and Rio Grande Railroad (D&RG) depot; the Ute Indian Museum with Ute

Indian artifacts and exhibits of the travels of Franciscan padres Serrano y Dominquez and Silvestre Vélez de Escalante and a botanical garden of medicinal plants commemorating the peaceful chief Ouray; Black Canyon of the Gunnison National Monument, carved by the Gunnison River; Curecanti National Recreation Area, named for a Ute chief, has three reservoirs along the Gunnison River; Grand Mesa and Uncompahgre National Forests; the BLM's Gunnison Basin Resource Area.

10. SAN ISABEL NATIONAL FOREST. Seventeen fourteeners tower over this four-unit, 1.1-million-acre national forest. Colorado's highest, 14,433-foot Mount Elbert, located just east of the Divide at accessible Independence Pass, attracts thousands of climbers each year. CDT hikers will be awed by this high-mountain scenery with alpine wildflowers in summer and quaking aspen that drape entire hillsides in gold, yellow, light green, and orange in September in the Collegiate Peaks, Mount Massive, Hunter-Fryingpan, and Holy Cross Wildernesses. Collegiate Peaks has a concentrated array of clustered fourteeners on the CDT just north of Silverton. Among them, Mount Yale near Lake Rebecca and the Three Apostles create reflections at sunset. Portions of the steep route descend to the Colorado trail, which may be completely snow covered in July. Near Holy Cross, the route will probably change

because it is heavily used by motorcycles. Wildlife is plentiful in the forest, and there are many species of birds, such as grouse, ptarmigan, and wild turkey. Historic sites include wagon roads at Old Monarch Pass, Tincup Pass Road, and French Pass Road; town sites and cemeteries from the nineteenth-century mining boom at Twin Lakes, Hancock, Winfield and Rockdale; railroad sites at Boreas Pass railroad grade and station, the Alpine Tunnel, and the former grades of the Denver, South Park and Pacific, Midland, and Denver & Rio Grande Railroads; and several abandoned high-country ranches. There are excellent fishing and white-water opportunities. For further information, contact forest headquarters in Pueblo. *Nearby:* Leadville, the nation's highest incorporated town is half circled by the Divide and offers the National Mining Hall of Fame and Museum; Healy House and Dexter Cabin, with mining displays from the late 1800s; the Heritage Museum, with exhibits of life in Leadville during the bonanza; the Tabor Home on 5th Street, which belonged to the flamboyant Horace Tabor who made his fortune there; Tabor Opera House; the Leadville, Colorado and Southern Railroad Company, with trips through mining country; Mount Massive, with a visitor center, hiking, and cross-country skiing; Arkansas Headwaters Recreation Area, with one of the west's foremost recreation rivers.

At Buena Vista, outfitters provide river trips.

11. **WHITE RIVER NATIONAL FOREST.** Located on both sides of Interstate 70, the national forest has views of awe-inspiring peaks—Grays, Torreys, Bierstadt, and Evans—and offers up Rocky Mountain scenery that is breathtaking and readily accessible. The CDT crosses the Collegiate Peaks, Hunter-Fryingpan, and Holy Cross Wildernesses. From Rollins Pass to I-70, the route follows barren rocky ridges and bald summits that remain snow-clad into August. The White River Wilderness has more than 2 million acres with eleven peaks over 14,000 feet, more than fifty caves tucked in the mountains, one of the world's largest elk herds, and the world-famous ski areas Vail and Aspen. Other favorite spots include Maroon Bells, Mount of the Holy Cross (14,005 feet); Glenwood Canyon, with cliffs that rise 1,000 feet above an 18-mile stretch of the Colorado River; Trappers Lake; and Green Mountain reservoirs. Historic sites include the Mitchell town site (a historic charcoal-processing location); old mines; Denver & Rio Grande Railroad grade; mountain passes used by early pioneers; and homestead cabins of prospectors and trappers. For further information, contact forest headquarters at Glenwood Springs.

12. **PIKE NATIONAL FOREST.** The CDT route passes near the ghost town of Alma and along bristlecone pines below Mount Bross. A large expanse of land stretches a good distance from the CDT and has the popular 14,264-foot Mount Evans by the town of Echo Lake (shared with Arapaho National Forest) and the distant 14,110-foot Pikes Peak near Manitou Springs. Much of this busy 1.1-million-acre forest is situated east of the Divide near Colorado Springs and Denver. The forest has Windy-Ridge Bristlecone Pine Scenic Area and historic sites such as the remains of early mining operations, railroads, stage routes, and one of the last operational lookout towers. The latter can be reached by taking the Devil's Head National Recreation Trail. For further information, contact forest headquarters in Pueblo. *Nearby:* In Salida, near Monarch Pass (elevation 11,312 feet), Salida Museum has American Indian, pioneer, and railroad displays; outfitters offer white-water rafting and jeep tours; Monarch Scenic Tram provides views of Pikes Peak. Cripple Creek is a National Historic District; Cripple Creek District Museum is located in an original railroad depot; Mollie Kathleen Gold Mine has underground tours; Cripple Creek and Victor Narrow Gauge Railroad offers mine tours in the coal-burning steam locomotive; and Florissant Fossil Beds National Monument has a visitor center, a wealth of fossils, and petrified redwoods.

13. **ARAPAHO NATIONAL FOREST.** The 1-million-acre forest, named for the Plains Indians who hunted in the region,

is located on both sides of the Divide, which separates the watersheds of the Platte and Colorado Rivers. The CDT route crosses three wilderness areas. Vásquez offers expansive views of the Great Plains to the east, views of alpine lakes far below the trail, and some of the most challenging ascents and descents of the entire CDT. Indian Peaks, the magnificent showcase wilderness and one of the most visited in Colorado, has marshy meadows, picture-perfect Jasper Creek, Devil's Thumb, dwarf spruce, and gentle grades of tundra that burst into miniature fall color displays in late summer. Never Summer Mountains Wilderness offers accessible rugged tundra dotted with light gray boulders with bright pumpkin orange and pale green lichen. Historic sites include pack trails; wagon roads; narrow- and standard-gauge railroad routes; prospector, trapper, and homestead cabins; and mining sites. For further information, contact forest headquarters in Fort Collins. *Nearby:* At Breckenridge, the downtown is one of the state's largest National Historic Districts, with 254 buildings on the NRHP. In Winter Park, the Moffat Tunnel is a historic railroad tunnel and major route through the Continental Divide; Cozen's Ranch Restoration Museum interprets local history. In Hot Sulphur Springs, the Grand County Museum has displays on the Moffat Tunnel. At Grandby, Arapaho National Recreation Area. La Poudre Pass is

a convenient resupply point for through-hikers and was used in the 1870s and 1880s by stagecoach riders headed for Lulu City.

14. ROCKY MOUNTAIN NATIONAL PARK. The 265,753-acre high-country park between Grand Lake and Estes Park has swooping green valleys, plentiful and varied wildlife, the deep shade of lodgepole pines and spruce, trail with crashing streams on one side and steep rock walls on the other, and fourteeners made of hard granites and gneisses. At about 12,000 feet the trail reaches the broad back of the Divide and expansive fields of bright pink, red, and yellow wildflowers in boulder-strewn meadows. Alpine tundra in the one-third of the park that lies above timberline has miniature plant life with profuse displays of wildflowers such as alpine columbine, saxifrage, alpine forget-me-nots, and others with vivid color that their lower-elevation cousins only approach in intensity. In these higher elevations, more than one through-hiker has reported such a blinding deep fog that he reverted to crawling the trail on hands and knees for fear of stepping off a precipitous ledge. Outstanding examples of moraines and glacial deposits are found in Moraine Park (see IANST), where the museum interprets the area's environmental history. On the park's west side, mining boomtowns such as Lulu City, Dutchtown, Gaskill, and Grand Lake grew up in the 1880s. Lulu City is a ghost town

in a 5-mile-wide bowl where the Divide can be viewed on three sides. Grand Lake and Estes Park are connected by scenic Trail Ridge and Beaver Meadow Roads, which pass through the park. At Milner Pass (elevation 10,758 feet), the road opens to a view of the sky-scraping Never Summer Mountains. A permit is required for overnight stays. For further information contact the superintendent at Estes Park. *Other attractions:* The CDT passes through the town of Grand Lake, the western gateway to the national park. Beautiful glacial Grand Lake, the largest natural lake in the state, is surrounded by snowcapped peaks. There is excellent fishing from the well-equipped Beacon Landing Marina, Jerry J. Craig offers guided fishing trips to streams along the CDT. Historic Grand Lake Lodge (NHL) opened in 1920; Spirit Mountain Lodge opened more recently.

15. ROUTT NATIONAL FOREST. Mountain ridges and wildlife such as bear, deer, elk, and moose are found in this high-elevation forest with over a million acres. The CDT doubles back on itself in the stark Never Summer range, where volcanic eruptions created rocky terrain that makes for a strenuous hike. East of I-40 from Muddy Pass to Arapaho Pass, the progress of the CDT route is thwarted by private land disputes. Pressing on through the Mount Zirkel Wilderness northwest of Steamboat Springs, the CDT

offers pleasant tundra walking amid large volcanic boulders, tarns, aspen-dominated woods, and fields of wildflowers, including yellow daisylike arnicas. Most of the CDT route is at about 11,000 feet in elevation on the way to Wyoming. Sites in the forest include Rabbit Ears Pass (9,426 feet), Mount Zirkel (12,180 feet), historic Parkview Mountain Fire Lookout, Pipas Camp, the Wyoming Trail, Fireline Stock Driveway, Old Rabbit Ears Pass Monument, the Central Stock Driveway, and the Ellis Trail—listed on the NRHP. (The Routt was combined with Wyoming's Medicine Bow National Forest and the Thunder Basin National Grassland in Wyoming to form the Medicine Bow–Routt National Forests and Thunder Basin National Grassland.) Forest headquarters is located in Laramie, Wyoming, but there is an administrative worksite in Steamboat Springs. *Other attractions:* Near Walden, Arapaho NWR has waterfowl, sage grouse, golden eagles, prairie falcons, Sora and Virginia rails, and sandpipers. In Steamboat Springs, Fish Creek Falls, a popular ice-climbing spot in winter, tumbles 283 feet through a geologic fault; rafting trips on the North Platte River; the Yampa River Trail leads from downtown to the mountains; Steamboat Springs Hot Springs; Strawberry Park Natural Hot Springs; Tread of Pioneers Museum; Steamboat Springs Ski Gondola; Steamboat Lake State Recreation Area.

16. MEDICINE BOW NATIONAL FOREST.

The forest's three districts comprise more than one million acres. The Brush Creek/Hayden District straddles the Continental Divide in the Sierra Madre. Here, the CDT proceeds toward the Huston Park Wilderness and on to Battle Pass, at an elevation of 9,915 feet. North of Huston, the final route of the CDT has not yet been selected. Historic mining sites for the wealth of natural resources—gold, coal, oil, gas, and uranium—are found at Bridger, Gold Creeks, and Savery Creek Mines, the Battle Mining District, and the Portland Mine and town site. The historic Savery Stock Driveway and the Hahns Peak and Laramie Wagon transportation sites are in the forest. For further information, contact forest headquarters in Laramie. *Nearby:* Bridger Pass, south of Rawlins, is the where the Continental Divide splits to form the Great Divide Basin, also known as the Red Desert of Wyoming. Two-thirds of the Red Desert is located on public land administered by the BLM. Here, waters flow neither to the Atlantic nor to the Pacific but into the vast sunbaked oval and seep into the ground. When complete, the CDT route will follow the higher-elevation ridges that form the eastern side of the basin. Areas like Young's Pass on the rim of the Great Divide Basin have high grassy meadows with pine stands, cold springs, and good views of mountains, buttes, sage flats, and wildlife, including mule deer, coyotes, sage grouse, and prairie dogs. Permission is required to pass over the patchwork of private land below the trail where vast ranches, oil and natural gas wells, and coal and uranium mines are located. Down below, the basin is nearly treeless and can be very cold, hot, dry, and windy. The desert area near the eastern CDT corridor, inundated by ancient seas long ago, has Ferris Dune Field with Indian rice grass blown by winds that reach some of the highest speeds recorded in the continental United States, horses that escaped ranches and now run wild, and thousands of pronghorn antelope. Mountains in this area have cores of Precambrian granite that are 2.5 billion years old; Ferris Mountain has streaked white arches visible from great distances. *Nearby:* At Encampment, the Grand Encampment Museum interprets the American Indian encampment that gave the town its name. Rawlins, just east of the Divide, has tours of the Wyoming Frontier Prison that operated from 1901 to 1981, and prison memorabilia is exhibited at its museum; the Carbon County Museum interprets life in the West; Seminole State Park has a reservoir surrounded by giant white sand dunes.

17. SOUTH PASS.

The selection of the CDT route is still under study in this rocky, sage-covered flat that provides an unusually gentle pass over the Continental Divide. Large animals, American Indian hunters, Astorian fur traders, and the military used the pass before wagons first rolled over it in 1824. Between 1841 and 1866, a massive wave of immigrants, some three hundred thousand strong, made their way through the gap on their way to settle the West (see ONHT, CNHT, and MPNHT in *America's National Historic Trails*). So gradual is the incline at the relatively mild elevation of 7,750 feet that some pioneers did not even realize they were crossing the great Continental Divide. Pony Express riders rushed through in the 1860s before train and highway crews diminished the importance of the mild crossing by blasting more convenient routes elsewhere through the formidable Rockies. Even then a conglomeration of stark hills to the south, known as the Oregon Buttes, dominated the view from the CDT corridor. The land is managed by the BLM, which has posted interpretive markers about the Divide on backcountry roads and on State Highway 28 about 4 miles west of the Sweetwater Bridge. Contact the Rock Springs, Wyoming, BLM office about their summer tours of South Pass. *Nearby:* At South Pass City, Trails West offers excellent covered wagon excursions through Divide territory crossed by the Oregon, California, Mormon, and Pony Express National Historic Trails (see *America's National Historic Trails*). At the once-thriving gold

camp of South Pass City, the State Historic Site has twenty-four restored buildings with period furniture, authentic artifacts, and guides in period costume on summer weekends. Duncan Mine and the famous Carissa Mine are en route to Atlantic City, the old gold town where the main attractions are the Atlantic City Mercantile (1893), Gratrix Cabin (late 1860s), and Miner's Delight Inn. To the south about 7 miles is a monument dedicated to the Willie Handcart Company, those pioneers who perished when they were caught in deadly winter storms on their way to Salt Lake City.

18. BRIDGER-TETON NATIONAL FOREST. Northwest of South Pass City, the CDT resumes with completed trail in the Wind River Range. The remote, rugged, glaciated alpine terrain has 70-million-year-old mountains made of granite and gneiss that locals call "the Winds." Despite the many annoying mosquitoes, the area is a favorite for climbers. The nearly 3.5-million-acre Bridger-Teton has approximately 1 million acres dedicated to wilderness, one of the largest areas of undeveloped lands in the continental United States. The Bridger Wilderness, on the western slope of the Divide in the Winds, gained wilderness status with the original Wilderness Act of 1964. It has Gannett Peak, the state's highest mountain at 13,804 feet, 27 active glaciers, and 1,300 alpine lakes. Just south of Yellowstone

National Park at Two Ocean Pass, CDT travelers see the waters abruptly divide at a rock in Two Ocean Creek, forming Atlantic Creek, which flows east, and Pacific Creek, which flows west. This remote Thorofare Country abutting Yellowstone National Park is prime grizzly habitat. East of Jackson, the Gros Ventre Wilderness is known for the Gros Ventre Slide Geological Area where a massive 1925 landslide created a dam and Lower Slide Lake. Excellent views of the Grand Tetons are possible from the high-elevation mountains in the Teton Wilderness, another of the nation's first wilderness areas. In the forest, the snowbound Gros Ventre, Salt River, Teton, Wind River, and Wyoming ranges give birth to the headwaters of the Green, Snake, and Yellowstone Rivers. For further information, contact forest headquarters in Jackson. *Other attractions:* In Pinedale, the Museum of the Mountain Men offers excellent interpretation; the Upper Green River Rendezvous National Historic Landmark commemorates the gathering site of mountain men and American Indians; Father DeSmet Monument marks the location of the state's first Catholic Mass. At Jackson, Jackson Hole Museum has American Indian, trapper, pioneer, and cattleman exhibits and offers tours of the historic Town Square; the Jackson Hole Historical Society has American Indian and pioneer artifacts; outfitters supply float, wagon, and sled-dog trips; the National Museum of Wildlife Art has the largest collection of western wildlife art in the world, including works by Bierstadt, Bodmer, Catlin, and Russell; Jackson National Fish Hatchery; National Elk Refuge, created in 1912; Grand Teton National Park, with the most impressive portion of the Teton range; John D. Rockefeller, Jr., Memorial Parkway, a scenic 82-mile corridor that links Grand Teton and Yellowstone National Parks.

19. SHOSHONE NATIONAL FOREST. Reaching to the state's border with Montana, America's oldest national forest covers 2.5 million acres east of the Continental Divide. In addition to the Wind River Range, the forest includes portions of the Beartooth and Absaroka ranges. More than half of that acreage lies within the boundaries of five wildernesses. Two, Popo Agie, and Fitzpatrick, in the southern part of the forest, are crossed by the CDT and divided by the Wind River Indian Reservation. The Popo Agie, named for a Crow word meaning "Beginning of the Waters," is an alpine wilderness that has more than three hundred lakes and ponds and twenty peaks over 13,000 feet. The CDT passes through its northwest corner. The Fitzpatrick, named for mountain man Tom Fitzpatrick, has forty-four active glaciers that lie on Wyoming's highest mountain and is also crossed by the CDT. Grizzlies are found in the remote North Absaroka and the

Absaroka-Beartooth Wilderness Areas, and the Washakie Wilderness, known for its steplike buttes and petrified forest, was named for a Shoshone chief. More than 1,500 miles of scenic roads include Chief Joseph Scenic Highway and the popular Buffalo Bill Cody Scenic Byway, which leads to Yellowstone National Park. *Nearby:* At the Wind River Indian Reservation, the Arapahoe tribe has educational tours that provide insight into Arapahoe and Shoshone history and culture; powwows are held at various times; and the Sun Dance is held in July. In Dubois, the Dubois Museum interprets local history and geology; National Bighorn Sheep Interpretive Center. Cody, founded by Col. William F. "Buffalo Bill" Cody, has the famous Whitney Gallery of Western Art and outstanding western activities.

20. YELLOWSTONE NATIONAL PARK. Final designation of the CDT has not yet been determined in America's first national park, founded in 1872. The Divide corridor crosses the southern portion of Yellowstone's caldera, and for now, 80 miles of backcountry CDT follow existing trails on high forested plateaus that pass lakes, thermal basins, and portions of fire-damaged terrain. The route stays below timberline among lodgepole pines and passes two of the park's three backcountry thermal areas where ethereal aquamarine hot springs camouflage the danger of the scalding-hot, deadly mineral water. Trail plans for the CDT include passing the famous Old Faithful Geyser. Covering 3,472 square miles, the park is mainly in Wyoming, but its boundary spills over into Idaho and Montana. Yellowstone's immense caldera covers an area of 50 by 30 miles and was formed by a volcanic explosion more than half a million years ago. Today, molten rock is found only 3 miles below the Yellowstone's surface, and it gives rise to the most varied and largest hydrothermal features on earth, including eruptions of steaming hot geysers, bubbling mudpots, and lava rock flows. Mount Sheridan, at 10,308 feet, offers views that richly reward those who make the 2,800-foot climb to its summit. Roaming the multimillion-acre sanctuary are bison, black bears, bighorn sheep, coyotes, deer, elk, grizzly bears, moose, pronghorn antelopes, and wolves. Though bison tend to warm up in the thermal areas, tired backpackers should not. This point is made poignantly clear in Lee Whittlesey's book, *Death in Yellowstone.* Park headquarters are located at Mammoth Hot Springs.

IDAHO (180 MILES)- MONTANA BORDER

21. TARGHEE NATIONAL FOREST. The Continental Divide forms the eastern and northern boundary of the 1.8 million-acre forest that lies mostly in Idaho and the 12-million-acre Greater Yellowstone ecosystem. The difficult-to-follow CDT crosses

from the western boundary of Yellowstone National Park, stretches across the plateau along the ridges of the massive Island Park caldera, and continues with climbs and descents for nearly 100 miles before reaching the Beaverhead National Forest. This is grizzly bear country, and human traffic is light in the summer. Other wildlife are moose, elk, black bears, antelope, deer, and close to three hundred species of nesting birds; at the forest's western end in the Divide corridor, wolves have been sighted. Meandering over the Idaho-Montana border all the way to Chief Joseph Pass, CDT hikers may need to fend off strong headwinds while standing with one foot in Idaho and the other in Montana. From atop the alpine ridge of the Centennial Mountains at Targhee Pass and Raynolds Pass, CDT hikers can gaze down at snowmelt-fed Henry's Lake in Idaho and Hebgen Lake in Montana (NPNHT in *America's National Historic Trails*). In 1877 the Nez Perce crossed the Divide several times in this area with the U.S. Army in pursuit—at least once at Chief Joseph Pass and at Bannock Pass. The forest, named for the Bannock Indian chief Tygee, who signed the Fort Bridger Treaty of 1868, has semidesert lands, 10,000-foot peaks, high-mountain lakes, springs, waterfalls, alpine meadows, and trail that was once used by Bannock and Shoshone hunters. Historic sites include Johnny Sack Cabin at Big

Springs and Old Nicholia Mine in Smelter Canyon, northeast of State Highway 28. A float trip on the Big Spring National Recreation Water Trail or a visit to the opal mine in the Dubois Ranger District are standouts. Unfortunately, the bark beetle has destroyed a huge percentage of the area's lodgepole pine, and to combat future infestations, foresters have planted a variety of aged trees in a mixed forest. For further information, contact forest headquarters in Anthony.

22. BEAVERHEAD-DEERLODGE NATIONAL FOREST. Together, the Beaverhead and Deerlodge form one 3.3-million-acre forest that gives rise to the Ruby, Big Hole, and Beaverhead Rivers in heavily glaciated terrain that offers CDT hikers steep climbs and rewarding vistas. Visible to the north and far below the trail near Lakeview is 40,000-acre Red Rock Lakes National Wildlife Refuge, which was established in 1935 to protect trumpeter swans. Today it has many nesting pairs as well as sandhill cranes, ducks, geese, deer, coyotes, elk, moose, pronghorns, muskrats, beavers, badgers, and red fox. In two places along the Centennial Mountains, the CDT crosses the U.S. Sheep Experiment Station. The Divide follows the crest of the craggy Centennial and Beaverhead Mountains of the Bitterroot Range that flank the southern and western boundaries of the Beaverhead in Montana. The Madison Range fills in the Beaverhead's eastern border to

create a bowl of open valleys divided by mountain ranges. The CDT ascends and descends over the full length of the Anaconda-Pintler Wilderness, where waterfalls and wildlife are abundant and switchbacks lead to groves of graceful larch trees that cover north-facing slopes. Brilliant wildflower displays blanket the lake-dotted and stream-crossed lands. CDT hikers and horseback riders enjoy views of the Mission Mountains to the northwest and the Beaverhead Mountains of the Bitterroot Range on the Idaho-Montana border to the southwest. In addition, historic mining sites, remnants of old cattle ranches, and parts of the area crossed by Lewis and Clark (see LCNHT in *America's National Historic Trails*) and the Nez Perce Indians (see NPNHT) are of interest. In southwestern Montana, the Deerlodge straddles the Divide in the midst of ghost towns and scattered historic mines with forest that shows signs of clear-cutting. Eventually the CDT east of Butte will be routed near the 90-foot statue, *Our Lady of the Rockies,* situated on the Continental Divide at 8,500 feet above sea level. For further information, contact forest headquarters in Dillon. *Nearby in Montana:* Virginia City and Nevada City, located 1.5 miles apart, are two authentically preserved and restored mining camps from the gold rush era. At Bannack, Bannack Historic State Park offers a walking tour of the ghost town that served as the state's first territorial capital and

was the site of the first major gold strike in Montana in 1862. Near Wisdom, Nez Perce National Historical Park at Big Hole National Battlefield is the location of the tragic battle between Col. John Gibbon's troops and the Nez Perce in 1877 (NPNHT; see *America's National Historic Trails*). In west-central Montana's copper country near Butte, gold and silver were mined in the 1860s, and copper was brought out starting in about 1900. Anselmo Mine Yard interprets Butte's mining history on a seasonal basis; the Mineral Museum has more than one thousand five hundred specimens on display; the World Museum of Mining unveils an 1899 mining camp; the Neversweat and Washoe Railroad carries passengers from the World Museum of Mining to Kelley Mine; Berkeley Pit, formerly the largest truck-operated open pit copper mine in the United States, is open for viewing at select times; the historic Wah Chong Tai Company Building is in the heart of former Chinatown. In Anaconda, sites include the Historic District and the now derelict 585-foot smokestack from a copper smelter; the Copper Village Museum and Arts Center has a copper smelter on display; Lost Creek State Park is home to mountain goats and bighorn sheep. At Philipsburg, the 1890s mining town has a renovated national historic business district and the Ghost Town Hall of Fame.

23. SALMON NATIONAL FOREST. The CDT passes

through this 1.8-million-acre forest in Idaho along the Continental Divide in the Bitterroot Range. The forest has a portion of the largest wilderness outside of Alaska—Frank Church–River of No Return, the Salmon Wild and Scenic River, historic mining towns, and the Lewis & Clark and Nez Perce National Historic Trails. For further information, contact the forest headquarters in Salmon. *Nearby:* In Salmon, the Lemhi County Historical Museum has American Indian and pioneer artifacts; west of the town, the Salmon River, enjoyed by whitewater enthusiasts, is known as the "River of No Return" because of its strong rapids.

MONTANA (750 MILES)

24. HELENA NATIONAL FOREST. From east of Deer Lodge, the western portion of the nearly 1-million-acre national forest straddles the Continental Divide. The CDT here crosses MacDonald Pass (elevation 6,325 feet) and Rogers Pass (elevation 5,610 feet) on its way to Scapegoat Wilderness. The Scapegoat, also in the Lewis & Clark and Lolo National Forests, straddles the Divide and has massive limestone cliffs that are an extension of the Chinese Wall (in the adjacent Bob Marshall Wilderness). Sites include ghost towns, old sapphire mines, and fire lookouts. For further information, contact forest headquarters in Helena. *Nearby:* Just 3 miles off the CDT near Blossburg, the once-thriving gold camp of Marysville has nearly forty buildings, many listed on the National Register; the post office kindly holds hikers' resupply packages. At Deer Lodge, the Grant–Kohrs Ranch National Historic Site was the headquarters of an 1800s cattle empire; the Old Montana Prison as well as area museums can be toured. Near Boulder, Elkhorn Ghost Town stands as a reminder of Montana's 1880s silver boom. In Helena, the state capitol with Charles M. Russell's largest painting, *Lewis and Clark Meeting Indians at Ross' Hole;* the Montana Historical Society Museum has a Russell collection and an 1864 pioneer cabin; Holter Museum of Art; Canyon Ferry and Holter Lake Recreation Areas.

25. LEWIS AND CLARK NATIONAL FOREST. Rugged mountain peaks reach 8,000 feet in the forest along the Continental Divide. With some segments on roads, the CDT traverses along the Divide in the shared Scapegoat Wilderness and continues north to the Bob Marshall Wilderness, "the Bob," where grizzlies, black bears, cougars, wolves, and wolverines roam freely. Named for the tireless forester and persistent advocate of wilderness, the Bob also lies in the Lolo and Flathead National Forests and offers the CDT traveler impressive views of the massive 1,000-foot limestone escarpment. Resembling the Great Wall of China and referred to as the "Chinese Wall," the escarpment is the longest contin-

uous cliff formation in the Rockies and follows the Divide in the Bob for 12 miles. The CDT route leaves the wilderness at Muskrat Pass, crosses forest lands to Marias Pass, and then enters Glacier National Park from the southeast. In the forest's eastern division, mountains are domelike and there are no rivers or lakes. For further information, contact the supervisor in Great Falls. *Other attractions:* Lolo National Forest; Wolf Creek Bridge Recreation Area at Rogers Pass. *Nearby:* In Choteau, the Old Trail Museum offers paleontology programs, tours of Pine Butte Swamp, and a Nature Conservancy preserve. In Great Falls, the Lewis & Clark National Historic Trail Sites and Interpretive Center; C. M. Russell Museum Complex, with the most complete collection of his original art and memorabilia, his home, and his studio; Giant Springs Fish, Wildlife and Parks Visitor Center and Fish Hatchery; upper Missouri National Wild and Scenic River; Benton Lake National Wildlife Refuge.

26. BLACKFEET INDIAN RESERVATION. Near the town of East Glacier, 5 miles of the CDT route enter the scenic 1.5-million-acre Blackfeet Indian Reservation, the home of Montana's largest tribe. The Lewis and Clark route also crosses the reservation, which serves as the eastern gateway to Glacier National Park and as a destination in its right. Eight major lakes and numerous rivers and streams present excellent fishing opportunities. Far from the CDT, Browning, the reservation's headquarters since 1895, holds Indian Days outside the Museum of the Plains Indian during the second week of July.

27. FLATHEAD NATIONAL FOREST. The second-largest national forest outside of Alaska encompasses more than 2.3 million acres. Almost half of this area lies in the Bob Marshall Wilderness Complex, which is composed of the Bob, the Scapegoat, and the nearly 286,000-acre Great Bear Wilderness. The CDT route crosses the first two (described above in #25, Lewis & Clark National Forest). The forest is also known for the Flathead Wild and Scenic River, Hungry Horse Reservoir, Jewel Basin Hiking Area in the Bigfork region, and Mission Mountain Wilderness near Condon. For further information, contact the supervisor in Kalispell. *Nearby:* At Swan River, Swan River National Wildlife Refuge; Swan River State Forest. From Polson, boat excursions on Flathead Lake. At Pablo, the Flathead Indian Reservation is the home of the Confederated Salish and Kootenai tribes; Ninepipe and Pablo National Wildlife Refuges; the Mission Mountains Tribal Wilderness Arlee Powwow in early July and the Elmo Powwow in mid-July. In Saint Ignatius, Flathead Indian Museum and Trading Post; Four Winds Historic Village and Trading Post; Saint Ignatius Mission, constructed in the early 1890s, has fifty-eight original murals. At Moiese, the

National Bison Range, established in 1908, protects one of the most important remaining herds of American bison.

28. GLACIER NATIONAL PARK. Straddling the Continental Divide in a rugged section of the Northern Rockies, the 1-million-acre Glacier National Park, founded in 1910, has spectacular mountain scenery. Many of the park's forty glaciers are clustered near the Divide, but the large ones that shaped the park's valleys and geologic features have been gone for ten thousand years. Grinnell Glacier is the largest remaining today and spans an impressive 300 acres. Glaciation has left us with rugged mountains, timberline views, sapphire lakes, crystal-clear streams, and cascading waterfalls. Dense forests contrast with mountain wildflowers that brighten the terrain with the orange of Saint John's wort, the yellows of arnica, the pinks and purples of monkey flowers, and the purples of asters. No wonder John Muir wrote, "Give a month at least to this precious reserve. The time will not be taken from the sum of your life. Instead of shortening, it will indefinitely lengthen it and make you truly immortal." More than 700 miles of trails await the visitor for day hikes, backpacking, and horse packing. Several trails have been linked to form the CDT, which is in excellent condition, although there are some precipitous dropoffs. For instance, at Iceberg Notch there is a 1,600-foot drop to Iceberg Lake. CDT enters the park at mile-high Marias Pass on U.S. 2, then stretches along Two Medicine Lake, across Pitamakan Pass, near Triple Divide Peak, to its official terminus at Belly River Customs Station. (In practice, the traditional northern terminus is at Goat Haunt Ranger Station.) Triple Divide Peak—the climbable 8,011-foot ridge of Norris Mountain—is the only place in North America where waters flow to three oceans: the Atlantic, the Pacific, and the Arctic via Hudson Bay. It has an overlook of Split Mountain and the valley below. Atop Norris Summit there is an awe-inspiring 360-degree view. Reynolds Mountain, at 9,147 feet, offers a rewarding four-hour climb with a memorable view. Glacier has nearly every large mammal species that is native to the United States, including some two hundred grizzlies (there are about five hundred in the northern Continental Divide area), mountain goats, ptarmigan, and marmots. Supplementing the park's outstanding natural features are Granite Park and Sperry Chalets (NHLs) for backcountry hikers, Many Glacier Hotel and Cabins, and rustic Lake McDonald Lodge. Amtrak stops at East Glacier and at West Glacier, where outfitters offer expeditions of all kinds. The park's exceptional Going-to-the-Sun Road permits most travelers to visit 6,664-foot Logan Pass on the Continental Divide, with access to outstanding CDT with glaciated terrain. *Other*

attractions: At Waterton Park in Alberta, Canada's Waterton Lakes National Park adjoins Glacier National Park. Together they form the Waterton-Glacier International Peace Park, established in 1932. Waterton Lakes National Park was established in 1895 and has lush green tallgrass prairies laced with wildflowers with nearby mountains to the west. The park has the 1926 landmark wooden chateau, the Prince of Wales Hotel.

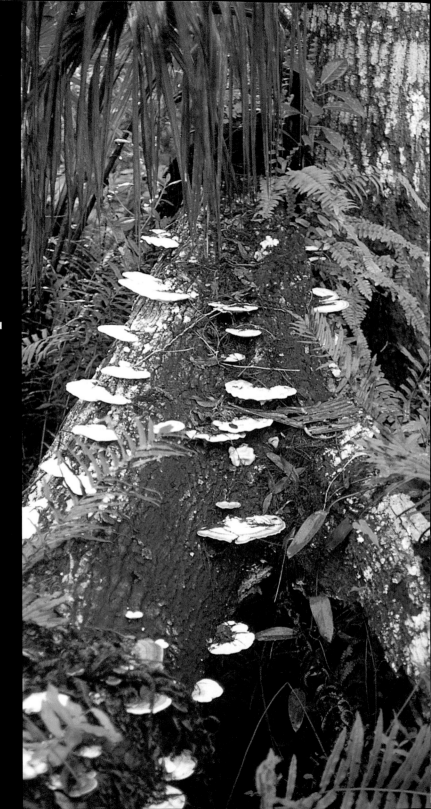

LOG WITH WHITE MORELS

The sub-tropical Florida National Scenic Trail provides outstanding opportuni- ties to appreciate and enjoy Florida's wetlands, abundant wildlife, and star-filled skies.

Florida National Scenic Trail

From high in a plane . . . the Big Cypress seems an undulating misted surface full of peaks and gray valleys changing to feathering green. East of it, sharply defined as a river from it banks, move the vast reaches of the saw grass.

MARJORY STONEMAN DOUGLAS,
THE EVERGLADES (1947)

Sweeping through the heart of Florida from Big Cypress National Preserve in the south to the Gulf Islands National Seashore in the western panhandle, the semitropical Florida National Scenic Trail (FNST) will extend some 1,300 miles through many of Florida's most breathtaking natural areas. Cypress swamps, sawgrass marshes, and tropical hammocks in the Big Cypress Preserve punctuate the southern portion of the trail's terrain. Along the central section, the trail passes piney wilderness and clearwater springs in the Ocala National Forest, longleaf pine flatwoods in the Osceola National Forest, and high sand hills and limestone bluffs along the Suwannee River. Rich ecosystems teem with life: saltwater marshes in Saint Marks National Wildlife Refuge, native hardwood titi thicket in the Apalachicola National Forest, wiregrass forests in the unspoiled wild country at Eglin Air Force Base, and windswept sand dunes and beaches along Gulf Islands National Seashore.

ADMINISTERING AGENCY
USDA Forest Service
National Forests in Florida
325 John Knox Road, Suite F-100
Tallahassee, FL 32303-4160
850-942-9300

FURTHER INFORMATION
Florida Trail Association
P.O. Box 13708
Gainesville, FL 32604
352-378-8823
www.florida-trail.org/~fta
1-800-343-1882

Florida Department of Environmental
   Protection
Office of Greenways and Trails
2600 Blair Stone Parkway
Tallahassee, FL 32399-2400
850-488-3701

DESIGNATED
1983

APPROXIMATE MILEAGE
1,300 miles (2,090 kilometers)

STATE
Florida

With machete in hand, Jim Kern cut his way through Big Cypress Swamp to Highlands Hammock State Park in central Florida. Amid shoulder-high grass and waste-deep swamp water, this real estate agent, nature photographer, and writer kept going because he was inspired. Traveling the Appalachian Trail two years earlier, in 1964, he envisioned a long-distance trail through Florida's diverse scenic and wild areas. Ultimately, he dreamed it would connect with the Appalachian Trail (see AT) for a through-hike all the way to Katahdin, Maine. This vision drove him on as he hacked his way through snake and alligator habitat to reach his destination.

Jim Kern's trail blazing was not in vain. A newspaper article about the episode caught the attention of readers, who responded to Kern's invitation to form a trail association. With twenty-four founding members, the Florida Trail Association (FTA) has now grown to six thousand members in fifteen chapters. Machetes and other tools have enabled trail volunteers to develop more than 1,000 miles of trail in the Sunshine State, including the main trail and numerous side and loop trails. The Florida Trail System is the result of thousands of hours of volunteer trail building and maintenance, of which the FNST is the centerpiece of success. A remarkable effort, the trail provides many opportunities to appreciate the state's wetlands and wildlife and at the same time

safeguard these precious areas. The continuous subtropical Florida National Scenic Trail, the focal point of the Florida Trail System, is the subject of this chapter.

Congress established the Florida National Scenic Trail (FNST) in 1983 and directed the secretary of agriculture to administer it. Through delegated authority, the U.S. Forest Service provides guidelines for development and management and certifies portions of the trail that are open to the public. This designation affords various degrees of trail protection, and to date, approximately 550 miles of the 1,300-mile route are certified. Florida Trail Association volunteers and local, state, and federal agencies work to build and maintain the trail and bridge the gaps between existing segments. As the FNST becomes a reality, one might ask what happened to the man with the machete in hand and a dream in his heart. Jim Kern's leadership in Florida propelled him to another dream; he became the founding president of the American Hiking Society, a nonprofit organization that now has more than one hundred thirty member organizations and ten thousand individual members dedicated to establishing, protecting, and maintaining foot trails in America. Again and again, he continues to blaze new trails. He has also founded another nonprofit organization called Big City Mountaineers, which pairs disadvantaged and desirous young people with adult mentors for a life-altering backpacking experience. Kern has demonstrated that which is most inspirational about long-distance hiking: by taking that first step toward a goal and by putting one foot ahead of the other over and over, a dream can be transformed into a reality, and the enjoyment is in the journey.

THANK YOU FOR PRESERVING OUR WETLANDS

That the vitality of the land is dependent on the health of the entire watershed is perhaps nowhere more apparent in the National Trail System than along the FNST. In southern Florida, the vital water system consists of three essential elements: the Kissimmee River, Lake Okeechobee, and the Everglades. Although the FNST does not pass directly through the Everglades, its southern terminus is located just north in an area known as Big Cypress. It then encircles Lake Okeechobee, follows a portion of the Kissimmee River, and continues to points north and west.

About a century ago, this freshwater system nurtured an ecosystem unique to the earth. Water flowing from a chain of lakes traveled into the Kissimmee River. It carried the water downstream through the savanna to Lake Okeechobee, an area higher than the area to the south. Because the lake is shallow and has low banks, the water would periodically overflow. The overflow would move south across the saw-grass marshes, over the then-undrawn boundaries of Big Cypress National Preserve and Everglades National Park. This flowing water in part evaporated, which in turn contributed moisture for rain in a constantly renewing cycle. But after the Civil War, an environmental onslaught began and efforts were undertaken to contain the flood-prone lake.

By the turn of the twentieth century, a network of locks, dams, and canals were established for flood control. Farming was tried, but the topsoil dried to a powder or decomposed. Nutrients that were released flowed south. To tame the flooding system, the U.S. Army Corps of Engineers strengthened dikes and dug more channels. Finally, plumbing projects of the 1940s changed the water wilderness. As the population grew, water was further tapped for human needs, greatly affecting nesting and wading birds, whose numbers declined dramatically. High concentrations of mercury were found in fish, egrets, and Florida panthers. Cattails began to take over thousands of acres of former saw-grass marsh. Alligator nests flooded when excess summer water could no longer spread over larger areas. During dry periods, the region was parched. Indicator species—the Florida panther and the alligator—almost became extinct as a result of the environmental degradation.

The 1970s brought recognition of the need to protect the entire water system, but the damage from earlier practices lingered. By the 1980s polluted Lake Okeechobee burst into blooms of blue-green algae, perhaps nature's desperate call for help. The situation threatened other forms of life in the lake. To save the unusual ecosystem, a commitment to restore a more natural flow of water was necessary. Water managers responded to requests for help, and a computer program was designed to imitate seasonal rainfall conditions. Annual water deliveries were made for the appropriate distribution of water allotments. A levee was breached to assist the restoration of natural water flow. Successful rehabilitation of the Kissimmee was effected by engineers, and waterfowl began to return.

New ordinances and laws were designed to protect Florida's water. For example, landfills had to be lined, and gas storage tanks were banned to prevent the contamination of groundwater. Dairy pastures had to be drained into special holding ponds so that manure nutrients would not reach Lake Okeechobee. In 1987 the Florida legislature passed the Surface Water Improvement and Management Act, which required the state to detail plans for pollution reduction and environmental restoration. In July 1991 the state settled a lawsuit by agreeing to acquire 37,000 acres of farmland that released phosphorus and could serve as a natural filter to remove contaminants from farms. The project to return the Kissimmee River to its former course is scheduled for completion in the early 2000s.

Not only in Florida, but across the United States, no part of the landscape provides as many benefits as America's wetlands. These benefits include waterfowl breeding; habitat for waterfowl and other birds, threatened and endangered species, shellfish, and freshwater fish; timber production; flood control; water quality; saltwater intrusion control; shoreline stabilization; reduction of coastal storm damage; and recreational opportunities such as fishing, hunting, photography, and wildlife observation. Wetlands serve as breeding ground for more than 50 percent of waterfowl. Sixty to 90 percent of U.S. commercial fisheries depend on wetlands.

The term *wetlands* encompasses a variety of wet environments, including coastal and inland marshes, wet meadows, mudflats, ponds, peat lands, bogs, bottomland hardwood forests, wooded swamps, and fens. Wetlands can be described as transitional areas between land and water where soils are soaked with water for an extended or indefinite period. A wide variety of wetlands have formed across the country that can be divided into two broad categories: nontidal and tidal.

Swamps, marshes, peat lands and riparian wetlands are types of nontidal wetlands. A swamp tends to be saturated with water on a permanent basis or at least for a prolonged period. Its vegetation is dominated by trees, such as the bald cypress, tupelo gum, and water oak. The FNST passes through an extensive swamp in the western portion of the Bradwell Bay Wilderness Area in the Apalachicola National Forest. A marsh is similar, but it is open and dominated by grasses or sedges. Plants in marshes tend to be soft-stemmed or herbaceous, such as rushes, cattails, and water lilies. Hikers on the FNST pass many marshes in the Big Cypress National Preserve and the Ocala National Forest. A bog has a much drier appearance, but it is acidic and quite mushy when touched. The surface material of a bog is composed largely of sphagnum moss or other organic matter rather than mineral soil. Bogs may evolve in former glacial lakes (IANST). When northern bogs support trees, they are known as muskegs. Atlantic white cedar is the characteristic plant of southern bogs. The floating vegetation mat is often composed of sedges in which bog orchids appear. These areas are called quaking bog, because they quake when jumped on. The Okefenokee National Wildlife Refuge, north of the FNST in the Osceola National Forest, is an example of a quaking bog. A bog is one of the two types of peat lands; the other is known as a fen. Fens are richer than bogs in nutrients and are less acidic. Plants in fens typically include sedges, willows, grasses, and

reeds. Riparian wetlands form in the floodplains of rivers, streams, and creeks. The presence of water has a pronounced impact on the type of vegetation that an area supports. In the arid west, the wetland vegetation is in striking contrast to that of the uplands. In the southern United States, bottomland hardwood forests are considered riparian. During parts of the growing season, some of these types of wetlands are dry. The FNST passes through many bottomland hardwood forests, including those along the Suwannee, Withlacoochee, Aucilla, and Little-Big Econ Rivers.

Tidal salt marshes, mangrove swamps, and tidal freshwater marshes are types of tidal wetlands that are found along the coastlines and located within reach of saltwater tidal action. Tidal salt marshes develop near river mouths, behind barrier islands, in bays, on coastal plains, and in other areas affected by tides. They can range from narrow fringes on steep shorelines to nearly flat expanses several miles wide, and typically include grasses and plants adapted to salt water. The FNST crosses extensive salt marshes on top of dikes in the Saint Marks National Wildlife Refuge. Mangrove swamps replace tidal salt marshes in subtropical and tropical regions. "Mangrove" refers to the salt-tolerant trees that dominate these wetlands. Tidal freshwater marshes form farther inland along bays, inlets, and tidal rivers that are still affected by ocean tides. Grasses and floating-leafed aquatic plants dominate these wetlands. The Florida Everglades, for example, are dominated by saw grass, which is actually a sedge. Anhingas (snake birds), blue herons, and egrets are attracted to these marshes.

The terminology used for wetlands is not exact. What one locality calls a bog, for instance, might very well be referred to elsewhere as a swamp or a marsh. In all cases, though, the plant growth in wetlands is restricted to species whose roots can take the water. Wetlands are also widely recognized for their high productivity of waterfowl and wildlife, and in many areas they filter the pollution from faulty sewage systems. Still, agricultural and commercial development have eliminated many of these valuable areas over the years.

To study the problem, in 1979 the U.S. Fish and Wildlife Service launched a massive pioneer study, the National Wetlands Trends Analysis.* The twenty-year study used aerial photographs of wetlands that had been taken between the mid-1950s and the mid-1970s. Analysts found that in the mid-1970s there were a total of 99 million acres of wetlands left in the lower forty-eight states.

*Material in this section is used with permission from *America's Endangered Wetlands,* by the U.S. Fish and Wildlife Service; *Wetlands in the National Parks,* by the National Park Service; and *Outdoor Recreation,* by Hilmi Ibrahim and Kathleen A. Cordes (p. 384).

This represented about 5 percent of the nation's land surface. The overwhelming portion of these existing wetlands—93.7 million acres—consisted of inland fresh-water marshes, swamps, bogs, and ponds. The remaining 5.2 million acres consisted of coastal saltwater marshes. Over the twenty-year period under study, net annual wetland losses averaged 458,000 acres, with the inland marshes and swamps being the most affected. Yet these vegetated wetlands are considered the most valuable. During these two decades, 6 million acres of forested wetlands, 400,000 acres of shrub swamps, 4.7 million acres of inland marshes, and 400,000 acres of coastal marshes and mangrove swamps were destroyed. More than 11 million acres of wetlands disappeared, an area twice the size of New Jersey.

One important aspect not measured by the study was the deterioration of many wetlands. Reduced quality of wetlands stems from many sources, including pollution from rivers, streams, and adjunct fields; urban encroachment; the building of highways and railroad beds; the construction of ditches for mosquito control; and oil and gas development canals that allowed saltwater intrusion into fresh-water marshes. In Florida, for example, the inland marshes provide both feeding areas for wading birds and wintering grounds for waterfowl. They also supply breeding habitat for such species as the rail, the mottled duck, and the endangered Everglade kite. In addition, they serve as prime habitat for furbearers, alligators, and various other kinds of wildlife. As a result, the conversion of these marshes to agricultural land significantly affected both waterfowl and other wildlife populations.

Our critical and precious wetlands can be preserved. The nation's coastal marshes, for instance, are faring better than other types of wetlands because of protective laws enacted by the federal government and a number of states during the 1960s and 1970s. However, as the space needed for cropland continues to grow and as urban areas expand, America's wetlands will inevitably be under further pressure. It is therefore more important than ever to monitor wetlands and proposed alterations of them so that wise decisions can be made. In the words of Marjory Stoneman Douglas in her 1947 book, *The Everglades.*

All is not lost. The future for South Florida, as for all once-beautiful and despoiled areas of our country, lies in aroused and informed public opinion and citizen action. If more and more of us continue forcefully and untiringly to demand a balanced development of land, of salt and fresh water, of people and wilderness, farms, cities, appropriate industries, wildlife and recreation such as the region can intelligently be expected to support, we can still bring back much usefulness and beauty to a changed and recreated earth.

The Trail Today

Lined with palms, pines, cypress, and moss-draped live oaks, leading past salt- and freshwater marshes, hammocks, swamps, springs, rivers, lakes, prairies, sand hills, and ocean beaches, the FNST offers an exceptional hiking experience through many of Florida's most scenic natural areas and diverse ecological regions. Approximately 550 miles of certified trail that sport orange blazes are open to the public. Marked with posts that display the official Florida National Scenic Trail logo, often accompanied by wooden signs displaying distance and directions, the FNST is user-friendly. Many other segments of trail are signed, marked, and passable but are not yet certified and thus do not display the official trail logo. To hike some portions of the Florida trail that cross private land, hikers must be members of the Florida Trail Association, which has excellent resources for planning a long-distance hike. For instance, the association has developed a new guidebook and a set of maps. Interpretive centers at Big Cypress National Preserve, Saint Marks National Wildlife Refuge, Gulf Islands National Seashore, and many of the national forests and state parks along the trail are helpful in planning a trek and also have informative displays and

FLORIDA NATIONAL SCENIC TRAIL, SIGN, AND HIKER

Certified trail segments are posted with the official trail sign and often marked with orange blazes and mileage signs.

exhibits on natural history, flora and fauna, and the history that enrich the outdoor experience.

Birding and wildlife observation on the FNST is phenomenal. More than four hundred species and subspecies of birds have been identified in the state, and many can be seen along the trail. A remarkable three hundred bird species fly in to Saint Marks National Wildlife Refuge alone. Florida's distinctive tropical and subtropical ecosystem is also inhabited by alligators, armadillos, black bears, boars, bobcats, lizards, frogs, gray fox, mink, otters, panthers, and turtles. Nature's sounds at night make camp along the trail an otherworldly experience, and the sight of a rare manatee in coastal or warm inland waters makes the

daytime magical too. (Manatee habitat is aggressively protected by strict regulations. If you are interested in observing these gentle creatures, inquire at the Florida Department of Environmental Protection for suggestions.)

The Florida landmass that provides the setting for the FNST is relatively young in geological terms. A low-lying peninsula, largely fashioned by water, waves, ocean currents, winds, and changes in sea level, the land creates a partition between the Atlantic Ocean in the east and the Gulf of Mexico in the west. In the north, the narrow panhandle stretches west along the Gulf of Mexico. Natural land changes separate the state into five regions: coastal lowlands, Everglades, central highlands, northwestern highlands (west of the Suwannee River), and the Marianna lowlands.

Climatically, Florida is divided into two regions, tropical and subtropical. The tropical zone, found south of Lake Okeechobee, is mostly covered by the Everglades, a watery expanse of saw-grass (*Cladium jamaicense*) prairie speckled with Sabal palms (the state tree) and cypress known to the Seminole Indians as *Pa-hay okee,* or Grassy Water. The southern portion of the trail passes through this terrain. North into the subtropical zone, the terrain has gentle hills in the interior that are dotted with lakes and prairies. The highest elevation in Florida, in the panhandle's Walton County, is a mere 345 feet above sea level.

Northern Florida is more temperate than other areas along the trail. Tallahassee averages 53 degrees Fahrenheit in January to 81 degrees Fahrenheit in July. In contrast, near the southern terminus of the trail at Big Cypress Swamp, temperatures average 74 degrees in the winter and 88 degrees during the summer. Shivering out-of-staters flock to Florida during the dry winter, a time when the Florida National Scenic Trail is at its best. Around October, when the rains start to taper off, the dry season begins and more of the trail is passable. There is plenty of crisp cool air to breathe, fewer insects to annoy, and a bounty of migratory wildlife to observe. At this time, hiking can still present some unique challenges. Thunderstorms begin in May. They can flood cypress stands, prairies, and other areas, leaving hikers standing waist-deep in water along many segments of the trail. Destructive hurricanes have

A SHY TURTLE GREETING HIKERS AND VEGETATION AT BIG CYPRESS

In Big Cypress National Preserve, the FNST weaves through shadowy swamp with pools of algae-laden water surrounding stands of cypress trees and a variety of plant life that is the habitat of alligators, bobcats, deer, the few remaining black bears, and the rare Florida panther.

hit the state from June to November, with September being prime hurricane season. Suffice it to say, if you are planning a hike on the FNST, stay informed about the weather no matter what the season.

MANGROVE

Spidery mangroves with intertwined roots are found at Big Cypress National Preserve and at Saint Marks National Wildlife Refuge along the trail corridor.

The trail's southern terminus at Big Cypress National Preserve is located in swamp laced with saw-grass marsh, hardwood hammocks,* estuarine mangrove forests, and sandy islands of slash pine. Habitats there support alligators, black bears, feral hogs, endangered Florida panthers, white-tailed deer, otters, snakes,

*Hammock, the early American Indian term for "shady place," denotes a cluster of broadleaf trees further classified into upland, coastal, and live oak–cabbage palm, found in hydric (wet), mesic (moderately wet), and xeric (dry) areas. Hydric hammocks supported by poorly drained soils consist of dense stands of cabbage palm, Florida elm, loblolly bay, swamp bay, sweetgum, and water oak. Mesic hammocks support hickory, laurel oak, magnolia, red bay, and scrub holly. Xeric hammocks are characterized by bluejack oak, cabbage palm, laurel oak, live oak, and some loblolly and longleaf pines. All hammocks support a high degree of plant diversity and several species of wildlife.

egrets, bald eagles, hawks, herons, kites, quail, red-cockaded wood-peckers, wild turkeys, and wood-storks. The traveler goes north past the preserve's Oasis visitor center on the Tamiami Trail (U.S. 41), amid marsh and swamp teeming with life. At the fourth-largest natural lake in the United States, Lake Okeechobee, the trail is multiuse. It forms a ribbon around both sides of the lake atop U.S. Army Corps of Engineer levees and water control structures. Past the north shore, a beautiful section of trail runs along the banks of the south-flowing Kissimmee River through open prairies, sand pine forests, live oaks, and Sabal palm hammocks. The trail winds past the U.S. Air Force Avon Park Bombing Range and through several state wildlife management areas and passes through the Tosohatchee State Reserve, bypassing Orlando on the east and north. The western loop of the FNST heads north and west through the Green Swamp, Withlacoochee State Forest, and the Cross Florida Greenway.

The FNST winds through Florida's most visited national forest, the Ocala, giving hikers a glimpse of rolling hill country as it passes sixty natural ponds, cypress and gum swamps, open longleaf pine forests, and scattered clumps of dwarf live oaks. A blue-blazed side trail leads to Alexander Springs where snorkel or scuba gear permits a closer look at the underwater vegetation. More than twenty boardwalks at Osceola National Forest reach into the swamps and wetlands that are common to the flatwoods. Rosebud orchid, pondspice, and spoonflower along the trail refresh the hiker's senses. On the third weekend in February, hikers may be surprised to run into Civil War reenactors at Olustee Battlefield State Historic Site on the anniversary of Florida's largest battle of the War between the States. In springtime, with the sounds of woodpeckers above, hikers move through the ever-present and prolific green slash and longleaf pines, amid bright huckleberry bushes in full bloom.

Near the tea-colored Suwannee River, much of the trail crosses private and public lands, including Stephen Foster State Folk Culture Center, the Suwannee River State Park, and Twin Rivers State Forest. The trail along the Suwannee River presents spectacular scenery among limestone bluffs that rise from the river's edge. From the Suwannee, the trail swings across Florida's panhandle and the northern reaches of San Pedro Bay by way of logging roads that cross private lands owned by timber companies.*

MICCOSUKEE INDIAN RESERVATION HOUSE NEAR BIG CYPRESS

Lands of the Miccosukee Indian Reservation adjoin the Big Cypress National Preserve near the FNST. Traditional dwellings use thatched roofs that shield the homes from the strong rays of the Florida sun.

Sinkholes and the disappearing Aucilla River are unusual geologic features along the trail before it begins a 43-mile stretch through Saint Marks National Wildlife Refuge, a birders' paradise.

More than any other area in North Florida, a greater variety of forest types and wildlife zones thrive along the Saint Marks segment. A 2-mile section follows the Tallahassee–Saint Marks Historic Railroad State Trail, the site of Florida's fist rail line. At the picturesque Apalachicola National Forest, more than 60 miles of the trail pass through a remote area alive with alligators, bald eagles, bears, indigo snakes, ospreys, red-cockaded woodpeckers, and sandhill cranes. Here hikers need to carry a compass and prepare for waste-deep water

*Some sections of the Florida trail are located on private land. The FTA has arranged permission in advance for only its members to enter these sections. Others should not pass without obtaining permission in advance directly from the owners. It is important to obey all posted signs. Trespassers are subject to prosecution under to Florida's strict trespassing laws. The FTA offers additional information about hiking on private lands to its membership, and status reports on other trail conditions.

OLUSTEE MARCHING CONTINGENT AND
GENERALS CONSULT AT OLUSTEE

FNST travelers might find participants
reenacting the largest Civil War battle in
Florida at the Olustee Battlefield in
February.

hikers through the Blackwater
State Forest into Alabama to link
with the 230-mile multiuse
Pinhoti Trail under construction
in northeastern Alabama and
Georgia. The Pinhoti Trail leads
to the Benton MacKaye Trail,
which connects with the
Appalachian Trail. In the meantime, the Jackson Red Ground
Trail in the state forest offers
nearly 22 miles of hiking. From
Eglin Air Force Base, the route
proceeds to Navarre and across
the bay bridge to Navarre Beach
and the Santa Rosa area of the
Gulf Islands National Seashore.
Near Pensacola Beach, a variety of
shorebirds scurry around hikers
on their way to dune grasses and
sand pines that typify the national
seashore at the FNST's northern
terminus.

Although primarily a footpath,
opportunities exist along some
segments of the trail for cycling,
horseback riding, roller-blading,
canoeing, and kayaking. The FTA
provides current information
about locations open to diverse
uses, and the Florida Department
of Environmental Protection's
Office of Greenways and Trails
has information on cycling on the
rim trail atop the levee around
Lake Okeechobee. The Office of
Greenways and Trails also has
information about the 327-mile
Florida Springs Bicycle Tour in
north central Florida, which is
routed to a few spots on the
FNST. Officially, the FNST is
classified as multiuse along Lake
Okeechobee, in the Tosohatchee
State Preserve and the Cross

in the Bradwell Bay Wilderness
Area, which features a dense
native titi thicket known to some
as buckwheat trees. (The term *bay*
in this case means a stretch of low
land between hills.)

Continuing west, the route
leads to Pine Log State Forest, and
with permit in hand, a hiker will
soon be able to traverse Eglin Air
Force Base where unspoiled wild
country protects stands of stately
300-year-old longleaf pine. A
northern spur may one day lead

Seminole greenway, on the old tram roads of the Saint Marks National Wildlife Area, and the Tallahassee–Saint Marks Historic Railroad State Trail.

Water-oriented recreation is plentiful near the trail. Lake Okeechobee is a popular fishing spot for catfish, bass, bluegill, and speckled perch. Typical for most lakes and streams along the trail corridor, a state fishing permit is required. Boating, swimming, scuba diving, and snorkeling are popular along the Gulf and in some of the inland lakes, rivers, and springs. Airboats and swamp buggies ply some of the wetlands near the trail; for instance, Big Cypress National Preserve allows them with a permit. On the Gulf Coast, sailboarding, kayaking, and shell hunting are just some of the water activities available. The opportunity to cast a line off a fishing pier or charter a boat to troll in deep saltwater is never too distant from the trail. Florida's three national forests are home to more than seven hundred lakes and ponds and four major rivers, where canoeing is especially popular. The Office of Greenways and Trails, headquartered in Tallahassee, provides information on Florida's canoe trails, and the office of the USFS in Tallahassee will provide, on request, a free moisture-resistant map of canoeing opportunities in Florida's national forests. The state's relatively flat topography renders most rivers slow moving. Streams offer canoeists the biggest challenge, but there is not much

TREE AT SAINT MARKS NATIONAL WILDLIFE REFUGE

Cyclists and roller-bladers from Tallahassee can reach Saint Marks National Wildlife Refuge on the multiuse Tallahassee–Saint Marks Historic Railroad Trail. The birders' paradise has more than 40 additional miles of FNST available for use by hikers.

white-water or exhilarating river running as in mountainous areas near other national scenic trails. The FNST passes the Big Shoals of the Suwannee River upstream from White Springs, which is one of the state's most challenging and popular canoe runs.

Near Orlando, the FNST is not far from Walt Disney World, Cypress Gardens, and numerous amusement parks. A trip to Orlando can be enriched by taking a day hike to explore the natural terrain of Florida along segments of the national scenic trail in Little-Big Econ State Forest in Seminole County or in Tosohatchee State Reserve in Orange County.

Hikers may be tempted to feed alligators along the trail, but this is illegal. Alligators that are fed

FISHING AT LAKE OKEECHOBEE

Lake Okeechobee, the fourth-largest natural lake in the United States and the largest on the trail, has a multiuse trail that forms a ribbon around both sides of the lake on top of U.S. Army Corps of Engineers' levees and water-control structures. Okeechobee is a productive fishing spot for catfish, bass, bluegill, and speckled perch.

learn to associate people with food, which creates the potential for serious injury. An alligator's jaw muscles are exceptionally strong, although once the gator's mouth is closed a person's bare hands can hold it shut—a feat difficult to accomplish if one's hand is already in its clutch. Fortunately, these agile creatures rarely attack humans. However, hikers should never test the odds by standing between an alligator and its water escape or by handling young alligators or eggs. If you are in a canoe, keep a distance of at least 10 feet. An alligator* will not ordinarily bother a canoe, but its powerful tail is used for defense as well as swimming. With that in mind, swimming in unfamiliar waters is not recommended. In general, take precautions when encountering wildlife along the Trail.

Camping facilities and camp regulations vary along the trail: some parks allow backpack camping anywhere, whereas others allow camping only at designated sites. The managing agency should be contacted for detailed information about facilities and guidelines. Rangers recommend that hikers drink at least three quarts of water each

*Alligators, often confused with crocodiles, have a much broader snout. The fourth tooth in the lower jaw fits into a pocket of the upper jaw, unlike a crocodile's fourth tooth, which remains exposed. The habitat of the more aggressive and active crocodile is marshes at the southern tip of Florida, which are not along the FNST.

day, and none of it should come from natural sources without first being treated. Even the most crystal-clear water needs to be treated, filtered, or boiled. Though volunteers routinely wade through swamps to build bridges, cut back vegetation, and paint trail blazes, a hiker can still get lost if a blaze fades or if it is missed. When a hiker loses track of the trail, a detailed map, compass, and whistle may save the day.

Florida is the nation's lightning capital. During storms, hikers should stay out of open areas and away from isolated trees and aluminum-framed backpacks. Lightning occasionally touches off wildfires, which can be especially dangerous in the drier winter and spring months. Hunting presents another dangerous hazard from September through April. Many segments of the FNST remain open at this time, although dress in hunter's orange is required or strongly suggested. Only a few segments close, but it is best to check ahead of time.

Overexposure to the sun, insect bites, and dehydration probably present the greatest hazards on the trail. Pants, long-sleeved shirts, and large hats provide sun protection and minimize scrapes from brush. Insect repellent will help ward off chiggers and ticks, although tired hikers should not entice parasites by sitting on the ground. Rangers and volunteers at visitor centers will usually offer suggestions for

TWO ALLIGATORS IN A SWAMP

The largest reptile in America can grow to 16 feet or longer. Although they may look slow, alligators can move with lightning speed when food is near.

identifying poisonous snakes and plants along the trail. Fortunately, most of the snakes hanging on tree limbs are nonpoisonous. Even so, snakes should not be approached, and with this in mind, walking at night is not recommended.

To plan a long-distance hike on the FNST, membership in the Florida Trail Association is highly recommended. Membership affords advance permission to cross certain private lands and access to long-distance trail planning tools. For instance, the Gainesville-based association has developed a new guidebook and set of maps, and other books and materials can be ordered on its Web site.

Points of Interest

1. BIG CYPRESS NATIONAL PRESERVE. The preserve near Ochopee, between Miami and Naples, is part of Big Cypress Swamp, which encompasses more than 729,000 acres in South Florida. For 31 miles, the FNST runs north-south through this semitropical ecosystem that features natural grasslands with cypress trees draped in orchids and bromeliads (air plants), amid a panoply of birds. The young cypress stands, mixed-hardwood swamps, and pine lands are still recovering from earlier logging in the preserve, named for its expanse rather than the size of its trees. Bald cypresses grow to heights of over 100 feet, while the more common variety rarely reaches 40 feet. Activities include camping, bicycling, fishing, canoeing, boating, birding, and wildlife viewing. A permit is needed for off-road vehicles, swamp buggies, and airboats. The park's visitor center has wildlife exhibits and a film about the preserve. *Nearby:* Fakahatchee Stand State Preserve near Copeland has an old-growth cypress stand, the largest stand of native royal palms, the largest concentration and variety of orchids in North America, and other rare species of plants. At the Shark Valley (north entrance to Everglades National Park), there is a visitor center and a tram tour through saw-grass prairie that includes a stop at a 65-foot tower that affords spectacular views. The Miccosukee Indian Village, west of Shark Valley, offers crafts and airboat tours. The Big Cypress Seminole Reservation has the Ah-Tah-Thi-Ki Museum and Billie Swamp Safari; the Miccosukee Indian Reservation surrounds the northeast corner of the preserve. *Nearby:* On the Atlantic coast but apart from the national trail is Biscayne National Park, composed of a chain of subtropical islands that lie between Biscayne Bay and the Atlantic Ocean.

2. LAKE OKEECHOBEE. Okeechobee, the Seminole Indian word for "plenty big water," aptly describes the state's largest fresh-water lake. Sections of national scenic trail encircle the lake atop the 35-foot Herbert Hoover Dike constructed by the Army Corps of Engineers in the 1940s. Either side has views of the lake, sugar-cane, and vegetable crops. The area abounds with wildlife including alligators, armadillos, deer, foxes, opossums, otters, raccoons, and wild boar. An occasional endangered Florida panther and Everglades kite can also be found there. Habitat includes lakes, rivers, and springs; prairies; hardwood forests, hammocks; and flatwoods. *Nearby:* The Cypress Knee Museum is outside Moore Haven. The Brighton Seminole Indian Reservation maintains one of the region's largest ranches. Downtown Okeechobee has a Mediterranean Revival county courthouse. On the east side of the lake at Pahokee, the Pahokee Bank has a series of Everglades murals; Pahokee Historical

Museum explains the region's sugar industry; Pahokee State Park offers camping and water activities.

3. HIGHLANDS OKEECHOBEE. North of Lake Okeechobee, a 9-mile section of FNST begins at the Okee-tantie Recreation Area, southeast of Okeechobee City. The trail along the east side of the heavily chan-neled Kissimmee River passes wading birds on its way to the S.R. 70 bridge at the Kissimmee River. The recreation area has a public campground.

4. KISSIMMEE RIVER TRAIL. More than 30 miles of FNST follows the Kissimmee River and river channel to the S.R. 60 bridge. Following the eastern border of the Avon Park Bombing and Gunnery Range, the trail passes the Kicco Wildlife Manage-ment Area. Popular activities include camping at designated areas, hiking, and horseback riding. Habitats include flat-woods, freshwater marshes, and swamps; lakes, rivers, and springs; hardwood forests and hammocks; scrub; and prairies. A rare vulture, Audubon's caracara, has been seen in the area. It is impor-tant to remain on the trail and not to explore beyond the blazed trail in the Avon Park Air Force Range. Details and restrictions can be obtained from the range. *Nearby:* Near Kenansville, in Three Lakes Wildlife Management Area and Prairie Lakes State Preserve, two loops of trail pass through marshlands, prairie, hardwood hammocks,

and pine forests; Lake Kissimmee State Park, named for the state's third-largest lake, has an 1876 cow camp with living history demonstrations, camping (rustic/electrical hookup), hiking, fishing, canoeing, boating, and bird-watching. In Orlando and the surrounding area, there are numerous theme parks, gardens, and museums.

5. BULL CREEK WILDLIFE MANAGEMENT AREA. Much of this 17.8-mile section of the FNST follows the west side of Bull Creek along an old railroad grade past cabbage palms, scrub oak, hardwood swamp, and cypress. Spring wildflowers adorn the area near Saint Cloud.

6. TOSOHATCHEE STATE RESERVE. More than 30 miles of FNST meander through swamps, pine flatwoods, hammocks, and marshlands bordering the Saint Johns River near Christmas. Wild irises and other wildflowers fill the woods in spring. The state reserve contains numerous American Indian mounds. Popular activities include camp-ing (rustic), hiking, bicycling, horseback riding, fishing, and nature study. *Nearby:* At Titusville, Valiant Air Command Warbird Air Museum exhibits aviation memorabilia; Merritt Island National Wildlife Refuge has a wide variety of habitats, a visitor center, and American Indian burial mounds. The refuge shares a common boundary with the John F. Kennedy Space Center and adjoins Canaveral National Seashore.

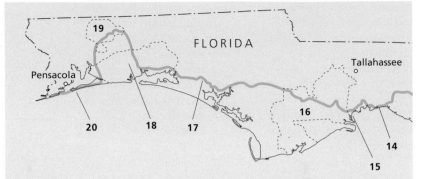

FLORIDA

Pensacola

Tallahassee

20   18   17   16   14   15

GULF OF MEXICO

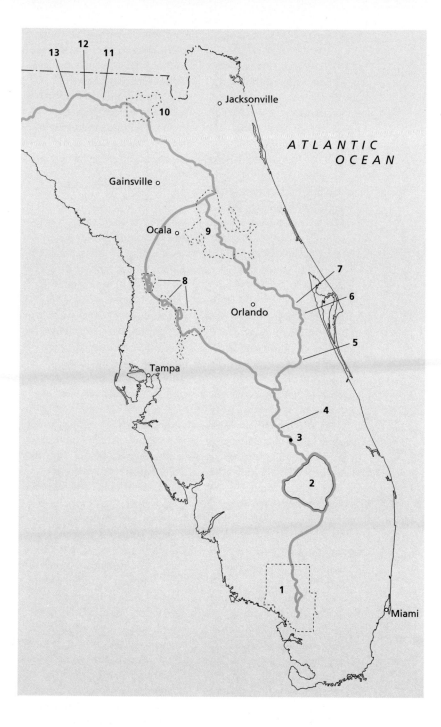

13 12 11

10

Jacksonville

ATLANTIC
OCEAN

Gainsville

Ocala   9

7

8   6

Orlando

5

4

3

2

Tampa

1

Miami

7. Seminole Ranch Conservation Area/ Orlando Wilderness Park. This 4-mile section of trail north of Tosohatchee State Reserve provides access to the periphery of the Saint Johns River flood-plain, an ideal area for wildlife viewing. The Orlando Wilderness Park is popular with birders. Bicycling, horseback riding, canoeing, and boating are also popular activities. *Other activities:* Wekiwa Springs State Park at the headwaters of the Wekiva River has boardwalks, nature trails, horseback riding, fishing, swimming, and canoe rentals. *Nearby:* The FNST follows the Cross Seminole Trail for 6 miles between Oviedo and Winter Springs. North of Oviedo, Black Hammock offers airboat rides in Lake Jesup, which boasts the largest concentration of alligators per acre of any lake in the United States. In Sanford, Amtrak station; historic Main Street; Central Florida Zoological Park; Saint Johns River cruises; Wekiva River canoe rentals and tours. Between Orange City and DeLand, Blue Springs State Park, a winter home for endangered manatees, has cabins, camping, hiking, fishing, canoeing (rentals), boat tours on the Saint Johns River, swimming, snorkeling, and cave diving; Hontoon Island State Park, accessible by boat or ferry, has Timucuan Indian mounds, cabins, camping, hiking, bicycling, fishing, boating, and nature study. At Daytona Beach, Daytona International Speedway; Daytona USA contains interactive racing displays; Mark Martin's Klassix Auto Attraction; Halifax Historical Society Museum; Museum of Arts and Science in Tuscawilla Nature Preserve; Southeast Museum of Photography; and Ponce de León Lighthouse at Ponce Inlet.

WESTERN ALTERNATE ROUTE

8. Withlacoochee State Forest. This 144,000-acre state forest is divided into separate units that have the best hiking in the Richloam, Croom, and Citrus Tracts. Seven miles of the FNST pass through the Hog Island Area of the Croom Trail. The hilly vegetation includes bald and pond cypress, longleaf and slash pine, and a mixture of hickory, gum, maple, oak, and southern magnolia. Wildflowers bloom from March to November. Sites of early homesteads and pioneer development from the 1890s are often marked by fruit trees, mines, or rock pits. The forest's main feature, the Withlacoochee River, was named by American Indians. Meaning "crooked river," it describes the twists that the river takes throughout its journey from Polk County to the Gulf of Mexico. The 83-mile Withlacoochee River (South) Canoe Trail begins in the Coulter Hammock Recreation Area of the state forest, and portions of the Withlacoochee State Trail run close to the river. Popular activities include camping, hiking, bicycling, horseback riding, fishing, and birding. In some areas, motorcycles and all-terrain cycles are permitted. The forest headquarters are located north of Brooksville. *Nearby:* Fort Cooper State Park, near Inverness, has a sparkling, spring-fed lake and offers camping, hiking, fishing, swimming, canoe and paddleboat rentals, wildlife viewing, and an observation tower.

MAIN TRAIL

9. OCALA NATIONAL FOREST. The oldest national forest east of the Mississippi River contains more than 380,000 acres of some of central Florida's last remaining traces of sand hill forests. The vegetation lives up to its name—a derivative of the Timucuan Indian word for "fair land" or "big hammock." Large live oaks, towering palms, and scrubby sand pines dominate the region, the world's most extensive scrub community. The national forest has nearly 67 miles of FNST, known as the Ocala Trail, dubbed the crown jewel of the Florida Trail System. In 1966 it became the first segment of the Florida trail to be developed. A side trail in the Juniper Wilderness leads to Pat's Island, the community Marjorie Kinnan Rawlings wrote about in *The Yearling*. The Ocala also has more than 130 miles of horse trails, and canoe rentals are available for exploration of the spring runs and wet floodplain forests. The Oklawaha River along the western and northern borders of the forest provides some of the finest

canoeing in the state. Other popular activities are camping, bicycling, fishing, boating, water-skiing, snorkeling, and scuba diving. Forest wildlife includes the bald eagle, black bear, scrub jay, and sandhill crane. The visitor center is located west of Ocala. *Other activities:* In Ocala, the Appleton Museum of Art; Don Garlits's Museum of Drag Racing; tours of area horse farms. Silver Springs has the world's largest collection of artesian springs and is listed on the National Register of Historic Places. At McRae, Gold Head Branch State Park, located on rolling sand hills, has a section of Florida Trail, lakefront cabins, camping, fishing, canoeing, boating, and swimming. *Nearby:* Saint Augustine, founded in 1565, is perhaps the oldest city in the United States. Historic landmarks from the sixteenth, seventeenth, and eighteenth centuries can be visited: Nombre de Dios Mission is the site of the celebration of America's first Christian Mass; Ponce de León's Fountain of Youth; Castillo de San Marcos National Monument, the oldest masonry fortification in the continental United States; Anastasia State Recreation Area, with good sailboarding; Fort Matanzas National Monument, a Spanish fort (1740–42), is on Rattlesnake Island and has a visitor center on Anastasia Island. East of downtown Jacksonville, Fort Caroline National Memorial commemorates the first major French attempt at settlement in the present United States;

Timucuan Ecological and Historic Preserve protects the Saint Johns River and Nassau River aquatic systems while preserving the history of the Timucuan Indian culture.

10. OSCEOLA NATIONAL FOREST. This 187,000-acre national forest, named for a famous Seminole chief, contains over 20 miles of FNST. The trail's boardwalk sections provide a means to traverse the gum swamps and cypress ponds. The Olustee Battlefield Historical Memorial at the trail's eastern terminus in the forest commemorates the largest Civil War battle fought in Florida. The Battle of Olustee is reenacted at Olustee Battlefield on the weekend closest to the February 20, 1864, anniversary date. This is a crowded but fantastic time to visit the trail. There is a small museum at the site. Ocean Pond Campground, located in the pine forest along the northern shores of Ocean Pond, is accessible from the trail. A favorite natural draw along the route is Big Shoals, Florida's only white-water rapids. The Olustee Beach Recreation Area, the Big Gum Swamp Wilderness Area, and a 373-acre research natural area (NNL) provide additional recreational opportunities. Popular activities are hiking, horseback riding, fishing, canoeing, boating, waterskiing, swimming, and wildlife viewing. Sightings of the endangered red-cockaded woodpecker are possible. The Osceola Ranger District Office is located in Olustee.

11. STEPHEN FOSTER STATE FOLK CULTURE CENTER. At White Springs, this section of trail runs almost continuously on the banks of the scenic Suwannee River. Close to the path, azaleas, dogwoods, lilies, sparleberries, and redbuds grow. The 247-acre center commemorates Stephen Foster whose song, "Old Folks at Home," brought worldwide recognition to the Suwannee River, which takes its name from a Creek word meaning "echo." The Culture Center is dedicated to preserving and celebrating the folk culture of Florida. On Memorial Day weekend, the park hosts the annual Florida Folk Festival. About ten thousand people come to the event each year to see craft demonstrations, taste traditional foods, and hear live folk music ranging from bluegrass to spirituals. Canoeing is another excellent way to enjoy the Suwannee. Other activities at the park are camping and boating. Guided tours of the Stephen Foster Museum and Carillon Tower exhibits are available daily.

12. SUWANNEE RIVER STATE PARK. A section of the trail near Ellaville follows the north Suwannee River. In the park the Withlacoochee River joins the Suwannee. South of this junction, there are Civil War earthenworks and a boat landing once used by steamboats that plied these waters. The Suwannee River (Upper) Canoe Trail and the Withlacoochee River Canoe Trail begin in Georgia and end here. The Suwannee River (Lower)

Canoe Trail begins at the park and ends at the Gulf of Mexico. Other activities include camping, fishing, boating, and nature study.

13. TWIN RIVERS STATE FOREST. The 14,713-acre state forest is composed of fourteen tracts of land located along the Withlacoochee and Suwannee Rivers. The tracts provide an array of activities, including camping (rustic), hiking, bicycling, horseback riding, fishing, and canoeing. The FNST traverses the Ellaville and Black Rivers, Mill Creek North, and Mill Creek South. Diverse natural communities in the state forest are bottomland, floodplain, sand hill, upland, swamp, and sinkhole. The Division of Forestry at the Live Oak Work Center in Live Oak can provide additional information.

14. AUCILLA RIVER WILDLIFE MANAGEMENT AREA. Dark, clear river water passes between high limestone bands and dense hardwood forests as well as swampy areas of cypress and gums. Hikers are advised to avoid the 17 miles of trail through the Aucilla Wildlife Management Area during periods of high water. The 8-mile southern portion of the trail passes pools of dark brown water, known as the Aucilla Sinks, which form when the river travels underground, emerging and disappearing in a succession of rises and sinks. The trail eventually leads to Saint Marks National Wildlife Refuge. Activities include bicycling, swimming in the nearby Wacissa River, and canoeing. The 19-mile

Aucilla River Canoe Trail begins south of Lamont; it has rocky shoals and white water that make the trip moderately strenuous.

15. SAINT MARKS NATIONAL WILDLIFE REFUGE. The 65,000-acre refuge along the Gulf of Mexico at Saint Marks is a favorite destination for birders and wildlife observers. Thousands of birds migrate to the area in winter. Impoundments offer approximately 75 miles of marked trail through the brackish marshes, hardwood swamps, pine flatwoods, and pine-oak uplands that border Apalachee Bay. Canoeing is possible in the impoundments and the bay. A 43-mile section of the FNST, which is open to bicycles, crosses the refuge. Other activities include fishing, crabbing near the shore along the 1829 Saint Marks Lighthouse (NHS), boating, and photography. The refuge has American Indian mounds from the Swift Creek period (300 B.C. to A.D. 500). *Other activities:* At Saint Marks, San Marcos de Apalache State Park has a museum and a walking tour of the grounds where the original seventeenth-century Spanish fort stood; the Tallahasee–Saint Marks Historic Railroad State Trail, designed for walkers, joggers, skaters, and bicyclists, travels 16 miles south to the Capital Circle South in Tallahassee. There is also an adjacent trail for horseback riders. *Nearby:* Near Wakulla Springs, Wakulla Springs State Park has a lodge, hiking, swimming, snorkeling, glass-bottom boat and river-

boat tours, and wildlife viewing at the home of one of the largest and deepest freshwater springs in the world. At Natural Bridge, Natural Bridge Historic Site serves as a monument to a famous Civil War battle that took place there; a reenactment is held in early March. In Tallahassee, the Capitol Complex; Governor's Mansion; Downtown Historic Trail; Museum of Florida History; Museum of History and Natural Science; Black Archives, Research Center and Museum; historical buildings and sites; Alfred Maclay State Gardens; De Soto Archaeological and Historical Site; Lake Jackson State Archaeological Site, with American Indian mounds and a ceremonial site.

16. APALACHICOLA NATIONAL FOREST. Florida's largest national forest offers 564,000 acres of wet flatwoods, low wetlands, hardwood forests and hammocks, lakes, ponds, rivers, and springs. Bradwell Bay and Mud Swamp/New River are the Apalachicola's two wildernesses. Bradwell Bay is one of two wilderness areas the FNST passes through (Juniper Prairie in the Ocala is the other). Leon Sinks Geological Area has dry and wet sinkholes and other features such as swales, caverns, natural bridges, circular depressions, and water table ponds. Hikers in the Apalachicola—a Hitchiti Indian word meaning "people on the other side"—can follow a 60-mile segment of the FNST. Other popular activities include camping,

roller-blading, bicycling, horse-back riding, fishing, swimming, canoeing, boating, wildlife viewing, and oyster hunting. District headquarter offices are located in Bristol and Crawfordsville. *Other activities:* South of Sopchoppy, Ochlockonee River State Park has camping, hiking, fishing, swimming, canoeing, and boating. Near Sumatra, Fort Gadsden Historic Site has an interpretive center with information about events that were pivotal in the First Seminole War and one of North America's first free African American settlements. North of Wewahitchka, Dead Lakes State Recreation has camping, hiking, fishing, boating, and nature study. North of Bristol, Torreya State Park, named for the rare tree that grows along the Apalachicola River bluffs, has camping, hiking, and tours of historic Gregory House (1849).

17. PINE LOG STATE FOREST. Florida's first state forest, near Ebro, was established in 1936. Nearly 7,000 acres of flatwoods and sand hills provide hikers on the FNST with excellent opportunities for wildlife viewing. Other activities include camping (rustic/electric hookup), fishing, swimming, canoeing, and boating. *Nearby:* At Panama City Beach, Museum of Man in the Sea; Captain Anderson Cruises; Miracle Strip Amusement Park; Saint Andrews State Recreation Area, a great spot for shell collecting, fishing, swimming, and boating.

18. EGLIN AIR FORCE BASE. The FNST is under development

on this 400,000-acre base, where distinct habitats include hardwood forest and hammocks, flatwoods, high pine, salt marshes, marine habitat, coastal areas, lakes, rivers, and springs. For a permit and an outdoor recreation map, contact the Eglin Air Force Base Natural Resources Office. The Air Force Armament Museum, just outside the main gate, has more than five thousand air force armaments and a movie about Eglin's history. *Other activities:* At Niceland, Fred Gannon Rocky Bayou State Park has a mature sand pine forest, camping, fishing, swimming, and boating. In Fort Walton Beach, Indian Temple Museum and Temple Mound (A.D. 1400) built over saltwater (NHL); Gulfarium, with marine exhibits and performances; John Beasley State Park on Okaloosa Island, with a boardwalk and a beach.

19. BLACKWATER RIVER STATE FOREST. This hiking trail follows Gen. Andrew Jackson's military route in the state forest. In the future, Jackson Red Ground Trail may link the FNST with the AT via the Georgia-Pinhoti Trail in Alabama. Florida's largest forest, named for the Blackwater River, has more than 180,000 acres of woodlands, lakes, and streams. It is also known for its longleaf pine/wire grass ecosystem. When combined with the Conecuh National Forest to the north, it contains the largest contiguous ecological community of this type in the world. Popular activities are camping (rustic and electric hookup), hiking, bicycling, horseback riding, fishing, swimming, canoeing, boating, and nature study. The Blackwater Forest Center is located in Munson. *Other activities:* At Holt, Blackwater River State Park also features the Blackwater River, one of the purest sand-bottom rivers in the world, and offers camping, hiking, fishing, canoeing, and, boating. The Blackwater Heritage Trail is a 9-mile-long paved railtrail linking Whiting Field to the town of Milton.

20. GULF ISLANDS NATIONAL SEASHORE. The seashore extends along 150 miles of northern Gulf Coast from Destin, Florida, to Gulfport, Mississippi. Mainland features of the Gulf Islands National Seashore near Pensacola include the beaches, military fortifications built between 1829 and 1834, and the Naval Live Oaks Reservation. Offshore islands have sparkling white sandy beaches, nature trails, and historic forts. The visitor center in the Naval Live Oaks Reservation has a nature trail and exhibits. *Other activities:* Destin, Destin Fishing Museum has lighting and sound effects that create the sensation of being underwater; Fishing Rodeo in October. Near Pensacola Beach, Fort Pickens is a strategic Civil War site where the famous Apache leader, Geronimo, was held captive from 1886 to 1888. Fort Pickens is the western terminus of the FNST.

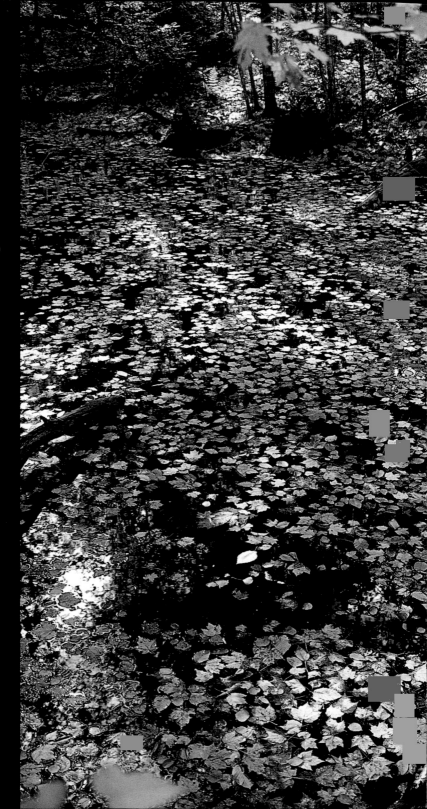

FLOATING LEAVES

Perhaps most striking amid the splendor of fall color, the unique Ice Age National Scenic Trail in Wisconsin winds its way from Sturgeon Bay in the eastern part of the state to the Saint Croix River in the western portion.

Ice Age National Scenic Trail

I think we may believe that God did not shroud the world He made in snow and ice without purpose, and that this, like many other operations of His Providence, seemingly destructive and chaotic in its first effect, is nevertheless a work of beneficence and order.

LOUIS AGASSIZ, *ETUDES SUR LES GLACIERS* (1846)

About two million years ago a tremendous ice cap formed in present-day Canada. In a series of advances, it reached into the northern part of what is today the United States. The last in the series, the Wisconsinan Glaciation, blanketed the continent from the Atlantic coast to the Rocky Mountains before it retreated some ten thousand years ago. This glaciation encroached on two-thirds of Wisconsin and left behind significant landforms and the finest ice age topography in the country. The mysteries of Wisconsin's drumlins, eskers, kettle holes, and kames unfold for the traveler along the unique Ice Age National Scenic Trail (IANST). For much of its 1,000 miles, the route follows an irregular ridge of terminal moraine marking the greatest extent of the

ADMINISTERING AGENCY
National Park Service
Ice Age National Scenic Trail
700 Rayovac Drive, Suite 100
Madison, WI 53711-2476
608-264-5610
www.aqd.nps.gov/grd/parks/icag/
www.nps.gov/iatr/

FURTHER INFORMATION
Ice Age Park and Trail Foundation
207 Buffalo Street, #515
Milwaukee, WI 52203-5712
414-278-8518
800-227-0046
www.iceagetrail.org

Wisconsin Department of Natural Resources
Box 7921
Madison, WI 53707-7921
www.dnr.state.wi.us/org/at/et/geo/iceage/

DESIGNATED
1980

APPROXIMATE MILEAGE
1,000 miles (1,600 kilometers)

STATES
Wisconsin

last major ice episode. Perhaps most strikingly beautiful amid the splendor of fall color, the trail winds its way from Sturgeon Bay in the east to the Saint Croix River in the west. Along the way the traveler passes through ice-sculpted countryside, forests and prairies, waterways, and wetlands. These legacies of a glacial age invite the traveler to enjoy the present and explore the past, to imagine the colossal movement of ice and torrential meltwater that shaped the land long ago.

The History of the Trail

Greek philosophers pondered geologic phenomena, the Roman poet Ovid wrote about the erosion of mountains and the evolution of volcanoes, and the Neo-Confucian Chinese scholar Shen Kua brought stone to life when he recognized fossilized bamboo. But it was not until the Renaissance that the first systematic geologic work of importance was set down on paper. While living in Italy, the Danish priest Nicholaus Steno's 1669 treatise on the history of the earth was published. Later, adding to Steno's study of rock strata, three Scots—James Hutton, John Playfair, and Sir Charles Lyel—established the principle of uniformity, which states that geologic processes that shape and affect the earth today are simply continuations of the past. The theory was first formalized in Hutton's revolutionary book, *Theory of the Earth,* published in 1785. His work was followed in 1802 by Playfair's more finished and readable *Illustrations of the Huttonian Theory of the Earth.* Then Lyell contributed his three-volume *Principles of Geology* between 1830 and 1833 and in 1838, *Elements of Geology.* This formulation of the fundamental principles of modern geology provided scientists with the tools to decipher the earth's history. Later in the nineteenth century, geologists began to piece together the stratigraphic record and divide geologic time into specific periods.

In the United States, serious geologic studies were spurred with the 1848 discovery of gold and the resulting call for economic surveys (see CNHT in *America's National Historic Trails*). The first Wisconsin Geological Survey was founded in 1853. Previously the study of the continent's geology had tended to be more of a hobby than a science. Nonetheless, geologists were always sensitive to the origin of the drift, a huge layer of debris, pebbles, and boulders that covered eastern Canada and much of the northern United States. Common belief held that a torrent of water and ice had caused it. This theory tied in nicely with Noah's biblical flood. It was similar thinking at the 1834 meeting of the Swiss Society of Natural Science in Lucerne that caused Johann von Charpentier's contemporaries to mock him. His paper on the extensive movement of glaciers and a colder recent climate contradicted the older explanation. Eventually, Charpentier's theory caught the attention of his friend J. L. R. Agassiz.

Agassiz, a young, successful Swiss professor, initially opposed his friend's theory but later embraced it. As circumstances would have it, while vacationing in the Alps, he went to visit Charpentier who was director of the salt mines in the area. Charpentier and Igance Venetz, a highway engineer and glacial pioneer, took Agassiz on one of their expeditions. Agassiz went on to establish similar data on glacial characteristics in the Jura Mountains. Like his colleagues, he was now convinced that there had been a fairly recent climatic change. Another friend, Karl Schimpler, would coin the term Eiszeit, or Ice Age. Agassiz's major 1840 publication, *Studies on Glaciers,* was dedicated to his companions in the Alps, and just a few months later Charpentier's own "Essay on Glaciers" was published.

Agassiz sought additional tests of his belief that the earth had passed through an ice age during which a sheet of ice had flowed southward from the North Pole. He heard of two Americans who had already found an example of glacial action in eastern North America, and in 1846 he left the debate he had created in Europe and delivered a series of lectures in the United States. The next year he joined the faculty at Harvard University. He later theorized that the Great Lakes were actually glacially carved basins. Agassiz's reputation attracted students and teachers from across the United States, and his glacial theory spread. Professor Ezra Slocum Carr brought Agassiz's theory and manner of teaching to the University of Wisconsin, where he taught in outdoor laboratories in the hills and on the lakeshores around Madison. Carr's student John Muir would later make his own explorations, theorizing about a glacial carving of the mountains of the Pacific coast (see PCT).

Perhaps the most prominent geologist from Wisconsin was Thomas Chamberlin. As the State Geologist from 1873 to 1882, Chamberlin performed a detailed inventory of the state's natural resources. He published the findings in a three-volume work, the *Geology of Wisconsin* (1877, 1880, and 1882). During his inventory, he became particularly interested in the moraines and related glacial features of the state. He went on to become president of the University of Wisconsin, chair of the geology department at the University of Chicago, and head of the glacial division of the U.S. Geological Survey. In 1894 he published the first map showing the area of North America that had been covered by glaciers during the Ice Age. The following year, he coined the names for the glacial periods, including the most recent one, the "Wisconsin Stage." He is regarded as the

KETTLE LAKE WITH FALL COLOR AT CHIPPEWA MORAINE

Basinlike depressions formed when glacial ice receded and chunks of ice were left behind and either buried or partially buried in the glacial drift. As the ice melted, water either drained, leaving a depression known as a kettle hole, or stayed in the depression, forming a kettle lake. Kettles contribute to Wisconsin's 15,000-plus glacial lakes.

premier American glacial geologist of his time.

While modern scientists accept Agassiz's theory of the erosive powers of glaciers, the present-day concept departs from his universal polar ice sheet theory. Today we know that a number of major ice ages occurred throughout the earth's history. The earliest of these took place during the Precambrian, more than 570 million years ago, and it is theorized that virtually the entire surface of the globe froze. Unfortunately, little is known about the earlier glaciations because later ones during the relatively recent Pleistocene epoch removed much of the record.

Although the Pleistocene epoch is known as the Great Ice Age, the actual extent of the glacial age reaches back even farther to the Pliocene, some 2.5 million years ago, when a sharp climatic cooling period began. Later, during the Pleistocene epoch, which began about 2 million years ago, major periods of great glaciation occurred, each followed by a warmer interglacial stage in which ice melted and retreated. Named for the states of their most southerly advance, the most recent period is known as the Wisconsinan Glaciation. It started about 35,000 years ago and ended a mere 10,000 to 12,000 years ago. The latter denotes the last time that sizable continental ice sheets advanced on the North American continent.

During the height of the Pleistocene glacial ages, ice covered more than 30 percent of the earth's land surface, including much of northern North America, Greenland, northern Europe, northern Asia, and the southernmost part of South America, as well as the ice cap Antarctica. The Great Ice Age had a profound impact on the landscape of North America. This included shaping the Great Lakes and the placement of great rivers such as the Ohio, Missouri, and Saint Lawrence. Traces of the most recent Wisconsinan provide most of the available field evidence of this glaciation on North American land surfaces, evidence that is perhaps best preserved and protected in the state of Wisconsin. Wisconsin's nearly fifteen thousand glacial lakes, abundance of ponds, streams, forested hills and ridges, and fertile farmlands are testimony to the irrepressible force that scraped over two-thirds of the state.

Although it is difficult to determine what the state may have looked like before glaciers traveled over its surface, it is assumed that much of the terrain was similar to the rocky, hilly southwestern portion. This 15,000-square-mile "driftless area," never touched by glaciers, has been evolving for hundreds of millions of years. In contrast, the rest of the state's ice-formed topography was created more recently. Great mile-thick flows of ice wore away hills, cut bluffs to bedrock, and carved broad valleys. When the ice melted back, the debris filled depressions and left behind the invaded land as it is today—weirdly drained and rolling.

During the glacial period, the rate of snowfall and the topography of the land affected the glacier's flow. While the glacier could readily travel down ancient valleys and drainages, resistant bedrock hills tended to slow progress. These ancient landforms divided the ice into tongues, or lobes. Several main lobes of the Late Wisconsinan Glaciation traveled into the state. The Des Moines, Superior, Chippewa, Wisconsin Valley, Langlade, Green Bay, and Lake Michigan lobes reached their southern limits about fifteen thousand years ago. Each lobe, up to a mile thick, contained ice that almost always drifted toward the edges of the glacier. As the ice moved, it froze around grains of sand, pebbles, and even huge boulders, picking them up and transporting them for short distances or for hundreds of miles. Rock fragments and boulders that traveled greater distances were generally more resistant to the shattering and grinding effects of glacial transports. Scraping the land along the way, they created scratches in the bedrock. These striations served nineteenth-century geologists who used them to study the direction of the ice flow. Another aid to geologists in this regard are drumlins, oval- shaped hills, created by glacial material. They aptly received their name from the Gallic word *druim,* which means "rounded hill" or "mound." Because drumlins orient parallel to the direction of the glacial flow and are steeper on their north sides, they are used to determine the direction of ice flow and the origin of glaciers. Drumlins range from approximately one-half mile to one mile in length and reach heights of 50 to 100 feet. When arranged in belts, drumlins can disturb drainage and cause small lakes and swamps to form between them.

As a glacier melts, it deposits a glacial drift, which is debris collected en route. The two types of drift are called till and outwash. Material deposited

POTHOLE

Passing through ice-sculpted countryside, travelers see drumlins, kames, snakelike eskers, and other legacies of a glacial age. This pothole, at Interstate State Park at the Wisconsin—Minnesota state line, was formed when silt and sand, carried by meltwater, was caught in whirlpools and drilled circular depressions in the bedrock of a streambed.

directly by and underneath the ice, with little transportation or sorting by the meltwater, is called glacial till. The large boulders carried by the glaciers are examples. Some of these are carried for long distances and end up in totally new surroundings. Their foreignness to the bedrock or soil on which they rest cause them to be called erratics. When composed of distinctive or unique rock types, erratics can be traced to their place of origin. They thus provide valuable information about the movement of a glacier. Moraines vary greatly and are formed when a glacier pauses long enough for ice to melt at the edges of the lobes. Rock fragments and other sediments are deposited and form sand and

gravel ridges. Ground moraines are simply let down like a blanket after stationary ice melts, or as irregularly shaped deposits when the ice is still moving. End moraines are dumps at the outer edge of the moving ice. These elongated ridges trend perpendicular to the glacier's direction of flow. Terminal moraines mark the greatest extent of a former glacier's reach. Interlobate moraines form when two lobes converge. Recessional moraines form when glacial ice retreats in a series of short bursts. Moraines that build up along the sides of glaciers are known as lateral moraines.

In Wisconsin, after glacial ice retreated, moraines blocked the flow of the Saint Croix River, which today runs along the boundary of Wisconsin and Minnesota to the Mississippi River. For many years, the course of the Saint Croix was farther east, and it shaped a valley still visible near Dresser, Wisconsin. When the ice melted around the Taylors Falls area, the Saint Croix invaded this once-shallow valley. Today's deep gorge there is a result of the glacial meltwater that cut through basalt and sandstone. Glacial meltwater also left behind large holes in the valley floor called potholes. These formed when silt and sand, carried by the meltwater, caught in whirlpools and drilled circular depressions in the bedrock of the streambed.

Outwash, or stratified drift, is composed of material that was sorted and deposited in layers by the action of glacial meltwater and streams. Outwash deposits from the Wisconsinan Glaciation can be traced to the mouth of the Mississippi, 700 miles from the nearest glacial terminus. As debris washed through holes in the ice, kames, or conical hills of stratified sand and gravel, formed. In this case, the name was derived from a Scottish word, *coomb,* which means "steep hill." Eskers are often associated with kames and consist of stratified accumulations of sand and gravel that flowed through channels in and below the ice. When laid down during the retreat, long serpentine ridges formed that range in length from a few hundred feet to several miles. Most eskers are of the smaller variety. Outwash plains are stratified drift deposited by streams beyond the glacier. These deposits often lie on unglaciated terrain past the terminal moraine, but they can be deposited on preexistent ground moraine or banked high between morainal ridges. Kettle moraines are dotted with kettle holes, basinlike depressions formed when the glacial ice receded and chunks of ice were left behind and either buried or partially buried in the glacial drift. As the ice melted the water drained or stayed in the depression, forming a dry empty kettle hole or a lake. Other areas formed in this way are now bogs or marshes. Lakes on top of glaciers acted as sediment traps for meltwater flowing on the ice from the north. After the surrounding glacier had melted, this sediment often

KETTLE LAKE AT CHIPPEWA MORAINE RECREATION AREA

A certified section of trail meanders through heavily forested, hilly terrain dotted with blue kettle lakes and ponds at the Chippewa Ice Age Reserve unit of the Ice Age National Scientific Reserve. Other geologic features are crevasse fills, ice-walled lake plains, inwash and outwash plains, end moraine, eskers, and kames.

formed mesalike hills, known as ice-walled lake plains, of various shapes and sizes. Huge lakes also formed in front of the glacier when the ice gouged rock basins or dammed streams. During the glacial retreat, many lakes drained, and the receding meltwater deposited a blanket of fertile soil in the broad lakebeds, creating fertile farmland in Wisconsin's Langlade, Rock , and Portage Counties.

By the end of the Wisconsinan Glaciation many of North America's large mammals—the camel, giant armadillo, horse, mammoth, mastodon, and saber-toothed cats—were extinct. The remaining plants and animals began to move northward. And by the Late Wisconsinan Glaciation, the first clear traces of humans in North America were evident. As the ice retreated, nomadic hunters followed the game to this area and hunted and foraged for plants. The oldest-known human site in Wisconsin is a shelter that was used for protection approximately eleven thousand years ago when the glacier was receding. This site can be seen today at Natural Bridge State Park, just west of Devil's Lake. As the ice disappeared from the area, the human population grew and tribes formed.

Much later, European explorers, traders, and missionaries arrived in the inviting Wisconsin environment as they traveled along the far-reaching waterways gouged by the glaciers. In 1673 the French Jesuit Jacques Marquette became the first European to reach the upper Mississippi River basin when he traveled from the Great Lakes up the Fox River, over a short portage to the Wisconsin River. Settlements formed along the waterways and served as ports for the shipment of the plentiful supply of lumber. Farmers tilled the fertile soils of flat outwash plains, and builders used concrete made from the rich glacial deposits to construct highways, bridges, and buildings. The state capitol was built atop a drumlin.

By the 1930s the state began to take steps to conserve its ice age legacy. A 1937 State Planning Board report, prepared with the assistance of the National Park Service, called for the protection of a 100-mile belt of moraines near the most heavily populated part of the state. This area is known as the Kettle Moraine. With the help of the Izaak Walton League (IWL), acquisitions for the new Kettle Moraine State Forest along this area commenced.

But the land acquisition process was slow. Some, including the IWL, thought it was progressing too slowly. In response, a Milwaukee attorney, Ray Zillmer, pressed for greater protection of

EAST LAKE SEGMENT, CHEQUAMEGON NATIONAL FOREST

Aspen, balsam, birch, maple, oak, and pine present a profusion of fall color along the Ice Age National Scenic Trail at Chequamegon National Forest, where visitors to the trail encounter scenic vistas of drumlins, eskers, kames, kettle holes, lakes, bogs, and marshes—the type of trail Ray Zellmer dreamed of not so long ago.

the Kettle Moraine as well as a long-distance hiking trail along the terminal moraine for hundreds of miles. With the dream of a national park marking the farthest extent of Wisconsin glaciation, Zillmer led a group of enthusiasts on a historic 1957 trek through Wisconsin's glacial country. His passionate vision played a key role in the state's conservation efforts. The following year, a group of private citizens organized the Ice Age Park and Trail Foundation (IAPTF) to support this vision. On October 13, 1964, a bill sponsored by Rep. Henry Reuss to establish the Ice Age National Scientific Reserve (IANSR) was enacted. Its purpose was to protect, preserve, and interpret the state's outstanding ice age resources. By 1971 the reserve was recognized by Congress as a part of the National Park System, although its nine separate units would be administered by the Wisconsin Department of Natural Resources (WDNR). The IANSR was officially dedicated in August 1973. Advocates also continued to promote the continuous greenway and trail first proposed by Zillmer. In 1975 the Ice Age Trail Council was formed to advance this concept. Largely through the efforts of these two organizations, segments of the trail were established and the Ice Age National Scenic Trail (IANST) came into existence. Congress recognized the trail's national significance in October 1980 by designating it a national scenic trail. In 1987 it was declared Wisconsin's first state scenic trail and additional funds were made available to acquire trail corridor.

The Trail Today

Ray Zillmer's vision in the 1950s of a trail that would follow Wisconsin's dramatic ice age terminal moraine is becoming a reality through the efforts of the IAPTF, the National Park Service, the WDNR, and countless individuals. In the early 1990s, the IAPTF merged with the Ice Age Trail Council to form a combined association that today has more than four thousand members in thirty-eight states. (How to become a member is explained on their Web site at www.iceagetrail.org.) Other partners include the USFS; county and municipal park and forestry departments; conservation, civic, and youth organizations; and individual volunteers, businesses, and private landowners. Together, they develop and manage segments of the national scenic trail.

More than 535 miles are complete, and approximately half are certified by the National Park Service, which allows them to be marked with the trail's official symbol. Yellow blazes and wooden signs with directions and distances mark the rest of the route. Innovative volunteer programs such as Project RELIANT (Restoring, Exploring, and Learning on the Ice Age National Trail) allow at-risk teens

WINDING TRAIL IN THE CHEQUAMEGON
NATIONAL FOREST

In the early 1990s, the Ice Age Park and Trail Foundation merged with the Ice Age Trail Council to form a combined association that today has over four thousand members in thirty-eight states. Many of these members volunteer to help build and maintain segments of the Ice Age.

Register of Historic Places. Of primary significance along the trail is the glacial history and geology, which is interpreted by naturalist programs and visitor centers at several of the units of the IANSR. Six of the reserve units are crossed by the trail, with three other units within driving distance.

All certified segments of the trail are open for overnight back-packing with restrictions on the location of campsites. A new set of maps available from the IAPTF focus on developed segments of the IANST and include activities and support facilities along the way. To order maps and books, contact the IAPTF at their toll-free number or access the foundation's Web site. A new book that will guide hikers on long-distance treks is in development. Naturally, it is important to respect the rights and generosity of private property owners by staying on the trail.

The Ice Age Trail is one of Wisconsin's most popular outdoor recreational resources. With the trail within 10 miles of nearly one-fourth of the state's residents, access is convenient. Most common are day hikes to experience the state's dramatic natural landforms, scenic vistas, lakes, and forests. Wheelchair-accessible areas have been developed by volunteers, and where the trail overlaps recreation rail/trails, the trail is open for cycling. A cycling itinerary that departs from the IANST is included in *On the Trail of the Ice Age,* written in

to work off required hours of community service under the guidance of IAPTF staff and trail volunteers. Together they have not only built miles upon miles of new trail but also mentoring relationships.

The visitor on the Ice Age Trail comes into contact with natural, historic, and cultural resources that include state and national park facilities, national natural landmarks, natural historic land-marks, American Indian mounds and battlegrounds, museums, and structures listed in the National

the 1980s by retired Wisconsin
congressman Reuss. Certain
sections of the trail, such as those
in parts of Taylor County, are
groomed in winter for cross-
country skiing; others are open
for snowshoeing, mushing, or
snowmobiling. A few segments
are open for summer horseback
riding. Sections of the trail on
private lands and state wildlife
areas are generally closed in late
November during deer hunting
season.

Fees, permits, and familiarity
with regulations are necessary in
some areas. For example, bikers
will need to purchase a State Trail
permit from the Wisconsin
Department of Natural Resources
for the Ahnapee, Glacial Drumlin,
Sugar River, and Tuscobia state
trails. And *hunter's blaze orange* is
recommended or required for
safety during the hunting season.
Camping arrangements should be
made in advance. Fees may be
required for camping in developed
campgrounds. A Wisconsin fishing
license is needed to fish the lakes
and streams along the route. Camp
and cycling guides, cycling maps,
and outdoor adventure guides are
available from the Wisconsin
Department of Tourism.

Primarily a hiking trail, the Ice
Age Trail is only occasionally
paralleled by highway tour routes
(see Reuss's *On the Trail of the Ice
Age*). Several scenic auto tours
through glacier country are
marked by the state highway
department. These are included
on a state map and an automobile
guide that are available from the

MUSHING

With the trail within 10 miles of nearly
one-fourth of the state's residents, access
is convenient. Most common are day
outings. During winter, certain segments
of the trail are open to cross-country
skiers, mushers, snowmobilers, and snowshoers. Winter tours are available.

WDT. Many communities along
or near the trail celebrate their
ethnic origins with traditional
festivals, foods, and parades.
Dates of regional festivities and
information about the state's
cultural heritage and museums
are available from the Wisconsin
Department of Tourism.

In establishing a trail route,
trail managers selected public
lands wherever possible to
enhance opportunities for wildlife
viewing and outdoor recreation.
The IAPTF, with the help of state
and federal grants and donations,
has accelerated the purchase of
additional tracts of private land

ROCK CLIMBING

Opportunities to imagine the colossal movement of ice and torrential meltwater that shaped the land can be enjoyed on the Ice Age Trail. Some of the Midwest's best rock climbing is found at Devils Lake State Park in Baraboo, and the rocky outcrops of Interstate State Park present challenges that guides and lessons help to overcome.

along the trail corridor. Because of the encroachment of urbanized areas, time is of the essence for land acquisitions. In protected corridor, wildlife may include deer, raccoons, minks, weasels, rabbits, squirrels, foxes, woodchucks, skunks, badgers, beavers, and porcupines. Isolated areas of central Wisconsin are home to the bobcat, and remote, northern sections of the trail are used by black bears and the endangered eastern timber wolf. Waterfowl are abundant around marshes and lakes, particularly during

migrations in the spring and fall, and bald eagles can be observed soaring high above many areas, including Interstate State Park. Even in winter snow, tracking of wildlife near the trail can be an adventure.

Recreational facilities are available at the parks and forests along the trail, and local outfitters provide adventure tours at various rivers, lakes, streams, and geologic sites nearby. Tours include canoeing, kayaking, rock climbing, horseback riding, birding, and fishing. Lessons are available in fly fishing, rock climbing, sailing, scuba diving, skydiving, waterskiing, water surfing, and parasailing. Tours offered by Paul Herr of Time Travel Geologic Tours (800-328-0995) have an exciting focus on geologic features, including those of the ice age. As an energetic professional geologist, Herr has made the exploration of Wisconsin's glacial terrain a dynamic adventure for more than twelve hundred visitors a year. His Web site (http://naturesafari.com/) has virtual tours of glacial terrain and links to geology sites.

The IANST generally follows the terminal moraine left by the last glacial advance. The trail stretches from Door County on Lake Michigan in the east, through the Kettle Moraine, south to Rock County, north through Devil's Lake and Hartman Creek State Parks, and west through the Chequamegon National Forest and the Chippewa Moraine Scientific

Reserve Unit, to Interstate State Park in Polk County at Saint Croix Falls. In general, the rolling terrain of the IANST provides a less strenuous journey than the mountainous routes of certain other National Scenic Trails such as the Appalachian and the Pacific Crest. For instance, from the shores of Lake Michigan to the highest point along the trail in Lincoln County, there is about a 1,200-foot elevation change, whereas in some segments the elevation change is a mild 200 to 300 feet.

Starting at the eastern terminus at Potawatomi State Park on Sturgeon Bay, the trail moves south and traverses a glacial spill-way. This broad, flat valley was once created by overflow from Lake Winnebago. Through Door County, the route follows the Anaphee Trail, a recreation rail/trail. Hardwood maples along this portion of the route are especially beautiful in the fall. Dune grasses and creeping junipers grow along Lake Michigan's shore. Limestone terraces that withstood the glacier's punishment show water ridges that indicate the size of Lake Nipissing, Lake Michigan's ancestor. Two Creeks Buried Forest, the smallest of the nine Ice Age National Scientific Reserve units, located on the shores of Lake Michigan, is yet to open. Nearby, facilities at Point Beach State Forest offer a 6-mile beach and various recreational activities and camping.

At the town of Two Rivers, the trail turns west, weaving its way

FAMILIES TAKE TO THE TRAIL

Primarily a hiking trail, a few segments are open for bicycling and horseback riding. Occasionally, highway tour routes parallel the trail, and scenic auto tours through glacial country are marked by the state highway department. Relatively mild elevation changes of 200 to 300 feet are enjoyed by trail-goers of all ages.

through oak prairies, hardwood forests, and white pines. Woodland flowers are abundant in season. This is where the hiker begins to encounter moraines, drumlins, and bogs. Erratics cleared from farmers' fields provided building material for the handy stone fences that are still in place today. Excellent examples of kettle lakes, eskers, and interlobate moraine are seen at Northern Kettle Moraine State Forest, a unit of the IANSR with a National Park Service visitor center. Perhaps the most notable feature of the Northern Kettle

Moraine is what many geologists consider to be the best kame field in North America. The state forest contains a dense northern mesic forest of maple, oak, red cedar; and sumac covers the rolling hills. Nearby, the Cambellsport Drumlins and Horicon Marsh units of the IANSR offer interpretation of a large drumlin field and an extinct glacial lake. After crossing the Oconomowoc River, the trail continues to the Southern Kettle Moraine State Forest, where prairie flowers brighten the woods in late spring and summer and wildlife is interpreted at the Kettle Moraine Nature Center.

At Janesville, the trail becomes a popular part of the city's park system. Farther west, the trail curves toward the north as it follows a segment of the Sugar River State Trail through stands of oak, maple, and elm. Heading north, the trail passes through areas that afford long vistas through prairie and oak savanna landscapes. Here it reaches another unit of the scientific reserve, Cross Plains, which presents opportunities to compare glaciated and unglaciated terrain. After traveling through the Johnstown End Moraine of the Green Bay Lobe, the trail crosses the Wisconsin River at a historic ferry. Beyond the river, the trail reaches a clifftop 700 feet above the surrounding landscape in the Baraboo Range, a National Natural Landmark. Devil's Lake State Park, a unit of the IANSR on the trail, provides an escape on a hot summer day. The 360-acre

lake, surrounded by oak and hickory woods, is a mecca for outdoor activity. In 1974 the geologist Robert Black said in an address about the Devil's Lake area, "No better moraine or combination of moraine and other features exists along this front from the Great Plains to the Atlantic Ocean."

North of Devil's Lake, the trail splits and then rejoins in the Chaffee Creek State Fishery Area. The eastern segment follows the historic Portage Canal segment of the trail, where Father Marquette first reached the upper Mississippi basin. This route also passes the site of John Muir's boyhood home, where a county park and national waterfowl area attract sandhill cranes and other wildlife. The western alternative passes the Dells of the Wisconsin River State Natural Area, where meltwater from the now-extinct glacial Lake Wisconsin carved high cliffs and wondrous sandstone formations. Mirror Lake, Rocky Arbor, and Roche-A-Cri State Parks offer campground facilities and unique interpretive trails. Another unit of the IANSR is located nearby at Mill Bluff State Park near Camp Douglas. Both routes pass through several of the sand counties of Aldo Leopold's *Sand County Almanac* before rejoining in Waushara County. Continuing north along a series of moraines, the trail passes several excellent trout streams, Hartman Creek State Park, the Farmington Drumlin Field, and Marathon County's scenic Dells of the Eau Claire Park.

In Langlade County, the trail turns west above a broad outwash plain known as the Antigo Flats. It crosses isolated backcountry in an area that was once heavily logged. Reforestation by the Civilian Conservation Corps and others have made this portion of the trail a gratifying wilderness experience. Hills in the area formed when glaciers crushed mountains. The trail reaches its highest point at an elevation of 1,920 feet at Lookout Mountain in the Harrison Hills segment. In central Lincoln County, the trail crosses a series of parallel ice-marginal ridges. Deposited during the glacial retreat, these ridges are similar to the growth rings of a tree in showing how far the glacier melted each summer. Following the edge of the Chippewa lobe and end moraine, the trail passes through the Chequamegon National Forest and a section of northwoods where the mix of aspen, balsam, birch, maple, oak, pine, and spruce presents a fall spectacle. (For a discussion of what causes fall color, see the chapter on the North Country National Scenic Trail). Birders can watch for bluejays, chickadees, ducks, eagles, grouse, hawks, nuthatches, and warblers. Other wildlife are common to the area: beavers, deer, muskrats, otters, squirrels, snowshoe hares, and the more elusive fisher, pine marten, and fox. The scenic glacial terrain includes eskers, kames, kettles, drumlins, swamps, and lakes.

More than 20 miles of Ice Age Trail winds through Chippewa County's heavily forested, hilly terrain past kettles and lakes. Near Bloomer, the Chippewa Moraine unit of the IANSR has an inter-pretive center situated on top of a hill that was at one time part of a glacial lake bottom. After emerging from the Blue Hills, one of the wildest sections of the trail, the route proceeds to the new Wild Rivers Rail Trail. The Ice Age Trail works its way through a mix of dense forests and dairy country. In Polk County it passes through a beautiful valley where a river flowing under the glacier carved a tunnel channel—today coursed by the Straight River. Farther west, the trail follows the Saint Croix National Scenic Riverway, an initial component of the National Wild and Scenic Rivers System, to its western terminus. The trail ends at the glacially formed spec-tacular rock gorges called the Dalles of the Saint Croix River at Interstate State Park, a unit of the IANSR. The park has more than four hundred species of ferns and flowering plants, and the forest is composed of large white pine, aspen, maple, paper birch, and other conifers. Deer, foxes, raccoons, and other small animals live in the uplands; and otters, mink, and muskrats live along the Saint Croix River and Lake O' the Dalles. There are more than two hundred species of birds, including the bald eagle, osprey, and great horned owl. An interpretive center has exhibits that explain the impact of the ice age on the forma-tion of the gorge and what caused the area's large glacial potholes.

TABLE 4. GEOLOGIC TIME CHART

Eras	Periods	Epochs	Millions of Years	Life Events	Ice Ages
Cenozoic	Quaternary	Holocene	.01		
		Pleistocene	2	Modern humans	Great Ice Age
	Tertiary	Pliocene	5	Hominids	Earlier Ice Age
		Miocene	24	Abundant grasses	
		Oligocene	37	Monkeys	
		Eocene	58	Rhinoceroses/mammoths/ elephants	
		Paleocene	66	Horses, grasses	
Mesozoic	Cretaceous		144	Last dinosaurs, flowering plants	
	Jurassic		205	Birds	
	Triassic		240	Dinosaurs and mammals	
Paleozoic	Permian		290	Extinction of trilobites, gingkos	
	Pennsylvanian		330	Coniferous plants	
	Mississippian		360	Reptiles	
	Devonian		410	Amphibians, club mosses, ferns	
	Silurian		435	Confirmed land plants	
	Ordovician		500	Land animals	
	Cambrian		570	Fishes, animals with shells	
Precambrian			570+ 2,500 4,600		Earth mostly covered with ice

Sources: Lucy E. Edwards and John Pojeta, Jr., *Fossils, Rocks, and Time,* U.S. Geological Survey, USGPO 1996-421-280; William L. Newman, *Geologic Time Online Edition,* U.S. Geological Survey, USGPO (July 28, 1997); Louis L. Ray, *The Great Ice Age* U.S. Geological Survey, USGPO 1992-307-568.

Points of Interest

1. POTAWATOMI STATE PARK. The National Trail begins with views of Green Bay and Sturgeon Bay from the observation tower of this state park in eastern Wisconsin on the Door Peninsula. This 1,200-acre woodland area, whose name means "keeper of the fire," has 2 miles of shoreline trail along Sturgeon Bay peppered with erratic boulders carried by glaciers from Canada. Hikers view pleasure boats and huge freighters on the ship canal in Sturgeon Bay that allows passage from Green Bay to Lake Michigan. Activities include camping (rustic/electrical hookups), hiking, bicycling, fishing, boating, waterskiing, canoeing, cross-country skiing, snowshoeing, snowmobiling, winter camping, and seasonal naturalist programs. The park has an accessible cabin. *Other attractions:* The Door Peninsula has more than 250 miles of Lake Michigan shoreline with historic lighthouses, cherry orchards that bloom profusely in spring, and towns with

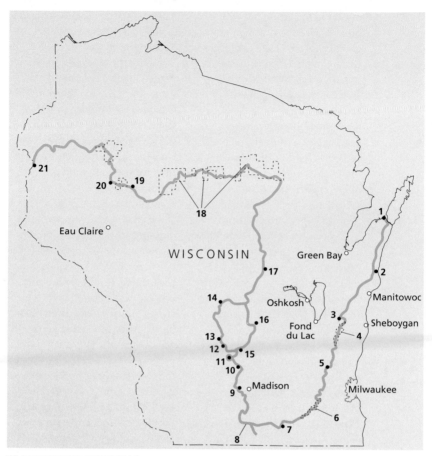

ICE AGE NATIONAL SCENIC TRAIL

Scandinavian-style fish boils. On the peninsula but away from the scenic trail are several state parks, including Whitefish Dunes, Peninsula, Newport, and Rock Island. *Nearby:* The Ahnapee Trail, a multiuse state rail trail, is a segment of the IANST that runs from the town of Sturgeon Bay to Algoma on Lake Michigan. Along the way the Ahnapee crosses wetlands, rural farmlands, and the Ahnapee River via a historic wooden bridge. Sturgeon Bay,

Cave Point, and Robert La Salle County Parks; Door County Maritime Museum; the Residential and Third Avenue Downtown Historic District; Door County Historical Museum, with a wildlife diorama; U.S. Coast Guard Canal Station, with a lighthouse tour; The Farm, a pioneer homestead; boating, sailing, and fishing charters.

2. TWO CREEKS BURIED FOREST. This national scientific reserve unit near Two Rivers is

not yet in operation but will provide access to a section of glacially formed Lake Michigan with remnants of an ancient buried forest. Gradually uncovered by Lake Michigan wave action, the ancient forest flourished more than eleven thousand years ago. Scientists throughout the world use bits of its forest materials for glacial dating. *Other attractions:* In Two Rivers, Woodland Dunes Nature Center; historic Rogers Street Fishing Village, with a restored lighthouse (1886); Great Lakes Coast Guard Museum; Neshotah Park; and Point Beach Energy Center, with nature trail and observation tower. Point Beach State Forest has campsites (rustic/electric hookups), a lakefront beach, and a northern pine forest.

3. WADE HOUSE STAGECOACH INN AND WESLEY JUNG CARRIAGE MUSEUM. At the northern end of Kettle Moraine State Forest in Greenbush, this restored inn and carriage museum is operated by the State Historical Society. Interpreters clad in period costume demonstrate life in the mid-1800s. Walking tours and carriage rides bring visitors to the sites.

4. NORTHERN KETTLE MORAINE STATE FOREST. This unit of the National Scientific Reserve located 20 miles west of Sheboygan has a 200-foot-high kettle moraine, an interlobate moraine with a ridge that runs for miles paralleling the shoreline of ancient Lake Michigan. The moraine formed when the Green Bay lobe and the Lake Michigan lobe met. The reserve offers outstanding glacial topography, including the famous serpentine Parnell Esker. The very first segments of the Ice Age Trail were laid down in this area in the 1960s and sparked the creation of the Ice Age Reserve in 1971. Near Dundee, the Henry Reuss Ice Age Interpretive Center offers excellent information on the area's dramatic glacial features. Activities at the 28,000-acre northern unit of Kettle Moraine State Forest include camping (rustic/electrical hookups), hiking, bicycling, horseback riding, fishing, swimming, boating, waterskiing, canoeing, cross-country skiing, snowshoeing, snowmobiling, the Kettle Moraine Scenic Drive, naturalist programs, and scenic views from the observation tower. The IANST continues south following the Kettle Moraine, alternating with marshy lands, towns and villages, and oak, hickory, and maple forests. *Nearby:* In Cambellsport, the Cambellsport Drumlins Ice Age Reserve Unit has an impressive concentration of drumlin hillsides and a scenic drive. Near Horicon and away from the IANST, another unit of the reserve—31,000-acre Horicon Marsh—interprets the glacial marsh of the extinct glacial Lake Oshkosh. The state-run wildlife area comprises the southern third of the unit, and the federally managed NWR comprises the northern two-thirds. Canoes can be rented to explore the marsh, where viewing wildlife, especially

during the fall geese and duck migration, is a favorite activity. A 34-mile state trail is open for hiking, biking, cross-country skiing, and snowmobiling. Blue Heron Tours offers group excursions. Interpretation is available at the national wildlife refuge visitor center. South in Washington County, land acquisition facilitated by the IAPTF in 1988 has resulted in the construction of the Kewaskum segment of the trail atop the interlobate moraine. The trail offers panoramic views of pastoral countryside, including the distant glacial kame Dundee Mountain to the north at Kettle Moraine. Trail in deep forest amid towering oaks affords enchanting hikes even in winter. Beech trees reach their northern limit here. *Nearby:* Lizard Mound County Park has effigy mounds built between A.D. 500 and 1000.

5. PIKE LAKE STATE PARK. Completed IANST offers panoramic views of the park's glacial topography from atop Powder Hill, a 1,350-foot kame. Activities at the park include rustic camping, hiking, swimming, fishing, cross-country skiing, snowshoeing, snowmobiling, and seasonal naturalist programs. *Nearby:* Holy Hill is a large kame on top of a moraine that is one of the highest points in southern Wisconsin. Holy Hill has breathtaking views of the glacial countryside, and there are also beautiful gardens and the Holy Hill National Shrine of Mary. The Loew Lake unit of the Kettle Moraine State Forest

and Monches County Forest protect a scenic stretch of the Oconomowoc River and several rare aquatic species.

6. SOUTHERN KETTLE MORAINE STATE FOREST. Certified IANST in the southern unit of Kettle Moraine stretches from Wales to the Whitewater Lake recreation area. Covering more than 20,000 acres, the rugged scenic area has a series of moraines, with some rising to heights of 250 to 300 feet. Activities include camping (rustic/electric hookups), hiking, bicycling, horseback riding, swimming, fishing, boating, waterskiing, canoeing, cross-country skiing, snowshoeing, snowmobiling, winter camping, and naturalist programs. The Kettle Moraine Nature Center and Eagle Hostel are near Eagle, and the forest has a wheelchair-accessible cabin. *Other attractions:* Eagle, Old World Wisconsin, is a seasonal outdoor museum that interprets the lifestyle of early-nineteenth-century immigrants and settlers. *Nearby:* The Lapham Peak unit of the Kettle Moraine State Forest protects one of the other high points in southern Wisconsin and showcases excellent cross-country skiing in winter. Near Milford, Aztalan State Park is an important archaeological site that features a reconstructed twelfth-century Indian village. Stretching due west from Waukesha to Cottage Grove, the non-IANST Glacial Drumlin State Trail is open to hikers, bicyclists, cross-country skiers, and snowmobilers.

7. Janesville. The town's system of parks and greenways, with notable Rotary Gardens, comprise this stretch of the IANST. With little to stop its movement, the Green Bay lobe penetrated this far south. *Other attractions:* Rock River, which begins at Horicon Marsh, is a popular spot for fishing, boating, waterskiing, and ice skating; Lincoln Tallman House (1855–57) and Milton House (1844) were stops on the Underground Railroad; Rock County Historical Society Museum; Trexler Park has waterskiing shows.

8. Sugar River State Trail. Seventeen miles of certified IANST are open to hikers, bicyclists, snowshoers, and cross-country skiers on the 23-mile Sugar River State Trail, a rail trail that continues to Brodhead in the south and New Glarus—called "America's Little Switzerland"— in the north. Along the way, the abandoned railroad bed rail trail takes outdoor enthusiasts through a covered bridge, across streams, and past eroded geologic formations originating from glaciers that preceded the Wisconsinan Glaciation. *Nearby:* New Glarus Woods State Park, with rustic campsites; Swiss Historical Village Museum; Chalet of the Golden Fleece Museum. The trail through the Brooklyn State Wildlife Area has prairies and scenic vistas.

9. Cross Plains. The Cross Plains Reserve unit, located 3 miles east of Madison, contains meltwater gorges and a terminal moraine bounded by glaciated landscape on one side and unglaciated landscape on the other. The driftless area was largely untouched by glaciers. *Nearby:* In Madison, the state capitol and other prominent buildings are located on area drumlins. The University of Wisconsin Geology Museum contains a woolly mammoth skeleton and other ice age artifacts. Chamberlin Rock commemorates the first geologist to map the terminal moraines of North America and name the glacial periods. The State Historical Museum has a unique clock designed and built by the naturalist John Muir when he was in college. Madison's First Unitarian Society Meeting House (1950), designed by Frank Lloyd Wright; Olbrich Botanical Gardens and Tropical Conservatory; University of Wisconsin Arboretum; Yahara Park, with effigy mounds. From Verona, leading west from the IANST, the Military Ridge State Trail follows an old military road built in 1855 that leads to Dodgeville. Mount Horeb, Wisconsin Folk Museum. Blue Mounds, Little Norway, a museum with cabins (1856); Cave of the Mounds (National Natural Landmark); Blue Mound State Park, with campsites (rustic/electrical hookups) and a fine place to view the driftless area.

10. Lodi Marsh State Wildlife Area. Most of this scenic valley is part of a state wildlife area that is fed by gushing springs. The area benefits from perhaps the most significant

restoration ecology efforts of the trail. Large tracts of wetlands, prairies, and oak savanna have been carefully restored to conditions predating mechanized agriculture and fire suppression. From Daves Overlook, hikers can see Gibraltar Rock and the talus slopes of the Baraboo Range to the north. *Nearby:* Lovely downtown Lodi has the first Ice Age Trail visitor center. Gibraltar Rock affords a bucolic scene of family farm–studded valleys and the lower Wisconsin River valley. The base of the prominence conceals another interglacial buried forest. When the Wisconsin River is ice-free, the historic Merrimac Ferry provides free service to the Devil's Lake area.

11. DEVIL'S LAKE STATE PARK. This unit of the scientific reserve located south of Baraboo is the largest park in the state system. The IANST winds through a 25-mile-long, 1.7-billion-year-old ridge formation made of super-hard purple quartzite, among the hardest rocks in the world. The ridge is an anomaly for the Midwest. Encircling the town of Baraboo, it reaches a height of 800 feet and extends nearly a mile below ground level. Scenic Devil's Lake formed when the Green Bay lobe deposited a moraine that blocked both ends of the gorge. Thirteen effigy mounds built by the Hopewell Indians can be found along the lakeshore. Potholes, kettles, and end moraines are there to explore. Huge quartzite and sandstone erratics have names like Elephant Rock. An area east of 360-acre Devil's Lake has glacial striations that are visible. Activities include camping (rustic/electrical hookups), hiking, bicycling, horseback riding, fishing, swimming, scuba diving, nonmotorized boating, canoeing, some of the Midwest's best rock climbing, cross-country skiing, snowshoeing, snowmobiling, geology tours, naturalist programs, an interpretive center, and a nature center. *Other attractions:* In Baraboo, Circus World Museum is located at the birthplace of the Ringling Brothers Circus. Sauk County Historical Museum is housed in a fourteen-room mansion built in 1906. The International Crane Foundation has tours of the area. Sauk City, Honey Creek Swiss Rural Historic District; canoe trips on the lower Wisconsin River; Natural Bridge State Park, with a rock shelter inhabited by humans more than eleven thousand years ago. In Greenfield, Man Mound Effigy is the largest human-shaped effigy in North America.

12. MIRROR LAKE STATE PARK. Surrounded by sandstone bluffs, this park is located three miles from the glacially formed Dells of the Wisconsin River, which are followed by the IANST. Amid scrub oaks and jack pines, the route proceeds across the flat bed of the extinct glacial Lake Wisconsin. Activities include camping (rustic/electrical hookups), hiking, bicycling, fishing, swimming, boating, canoeing, cross-country skiing, snowshoeing, and seasonal naturalist

programs. The park has a wheel-chair-accessible cabin. *Other activities:* Wisconsin Dells, Winnebago (Ho-Chunk Nation) Indian Museum; Seth Peterson Cottage (1958), designed by Frank Lloyd Wright; Wisconsin Deer Park; Beaver Springs Fishing Park; the Upper and Lower Dells and Lost Canyon sightseeing tours; parasailing lessons.

13. ROCKY ARBOR STATE PARK. The park's pines and sandstone bluffs offer an inviting spot for hiking near the Wisconsin Dells. *Nearby:* To the northwest near Camp Douglas on I-94 and away from the IANST, Mill Bluff State Park is a unit of the Ice Age Scientific Reserve. Its wave-carved sandstone bluffs were once islands in the extinct glacial Lake Wisconsin. Other features include ice-rafted boulders, evidence of wave action, sands, and marshes. Activities include rustic camping, hiking, swimming, and seasonal naturalist programs. Near Necedah, 30-plus miles northwest, the Necedah National Wildlife Refuge and Buckhorn State Park offer additional park facilities.

14. ROCHE-A-CRI STATE PARK. The French Roche-A-Cri refers to the 300-foot sandstone rock outcrop that provides exceptional views of the bed of the extinct glacial Lake Wisconsin, accessible from the IANST in this small park near Friendship. Activities include rustic camping, hiking, petroglyph hunting, cross-country skiing, snowshoeing, and seasonal naturalist programs. *Other activities:* Friendship, Quad "D" Ranch with trail, hayrides, and sleigh rides.

15. PORTAGE. The Portage Canal Segment of the IANST follows the canal that once served as an important water link between the Mississippi and Great Lakes basins. Today, the canal is open to limited canoe travel. The Portage Canal Industrial Historic District is on the National Register. *Other attractions:* Social Hill Historic District and Portage Retail Historic District are listed on the National Register of Historic Places; 1921 Pulitzer Prize-winning suffragette Zona Gale constructed the Zona Gale House for her parents in 1906. Also noted in the area is the Indian Agency House (1832) and Fort Winnebago Surgeon's Quarters (1828). John Muir County Park, on the trail, is the farm site where John Muir spent his childhood. *Nearby:* The legendary environmentalist and author of *A Sand County Almanac,* Aldo Leopold, lived in the area. His Shack is not open to the public, but the countryside that he wrote about can be seen by taking Levee Road (also called Rustic Road 49) along the south side of the Wisconsin River, west of Portage.

16. MONTELLO. A waterfall in the heart of town marks the quarry from which world-famous red granite was taken for use in monuments such as Grant's Tomb. *Other activities:* Wisconsin State Strings Museum. *Nearby:* Germania Marsh presents a

chance to see sandhill cranes, great blue herons, and bald eagles.

17. HARTMAN CREEK STATE PARK. Located on the Chain O'Lakes near Waupaca, certified IANST heads north for more than 12 miles in the park and Emmons Creek State Fishery Area. Here it passes through woods and moraine with glacial features such as kettles and erratics, one as big as a truck. This is the habitat of the endangered Karner blue butterfly. Activities include rustic camping, hiking, bicycling, horseback riding, fishing, swimming, canoeing, cross-country skiing, snowmobiling, and seasonal naturalist programs. *Other attractions:* Crystal River, for canoe adventures and trout fishing; Clearwater Harbor, with boat tours. Iola, Iola Mills Museum of Pioneer History (NRHP) has exhibits on the area's Norwegian heritage. *Nearby:* Farmington Drumlins in Waupaca County, Dells of the Eau Claire County Park in Marathon County, and Mecan Springs State Fishery Area in Waushara County.

18. CHEQUAMEGON NATIONAL FOREST. The IANST passes through a unit of this national forest whose name derives from an Ojibway (Chippewa) word thought to mean "long point" or "strip of land." Hikers, snowshoers, and cross-country skiers encounter scenic vistas, drumlins, eskers, kames, kettle holes, lakes, bogs, and marshes. Maple, aspen, pine, spruce, balsam, oak, and birch provide a profusion of fall color

along the IANST. A 42-mile segment of the trail follows the edge of the Chippewa lobe and end moraine through the Medford district of the forest (see NCNST). The Chippewa Lobe Interpretive Loop, adjoining the National Trail, has signs that explain the land formations. Mondeaux Flowage has a large sinuous esker and is an excellent location for viewing wildlife, including soaring eagles and ospreys. Campgrounds are located near the IANST. Waterproof and mud-resistant boots and a walking stick are recommended in the spring, especially along the boggy southern part of the trail, as is bug repellent in the spring and summer. Camping is permitted at least 50 feet from the trail and 75 feet from any water source. Remnants of the once-great white pine and hemlock forests that were heavily lumbered in the nineteenth century are found along the IANST in Lincoln and Taylor Counties. *Nearby:* As the IANST passes through county and private forests in Langlade and Lincoln counties, it crosses land dotted with lakes and bogs that are surrounded by spruce, fir, maple, and birch. An elevation of 1,920 feet, the high point of the IANST, is reached on the shoulder of Lookout Mountain in the Harrison Hills. Tomahawk, Tomahawk Area Historical Center; Sara Park, with the Hiawatha Trail; Council Grounds State Park, near Merrill, with camping (rustic/ electrical hookups) and a mature white and red pine forest natural area. Camp New Wood County Park in Lincoln County offers rustic campsites along the Wisconsin River. Ten miles of side trails head north to Timm's Hill with the highest elevation in the state at 1,952 feet. In 1990 Timm's Hill Trail was the first side trail to be named in the National Trail System.

19. BRUNET ISLAND STATE PARK. Just north of Cornell, the IANST reaches this island park named for an early settler who ran a trading post here. Bounded by the Chippewa and Fisher Rivers, the park has camping (rustic/electrical hookups), hiking, fishing, swimming, boating, canoeing, cross-country skiing, snowshoeing, and naturalist programs in season.

20. CHIPPEWA MORAINE RECREATION AREA. Located 6 miles north of Bloomer, the Chippewa Moraine Ice Age Reserve is a unit of the IANSR with a well-marked and exceptionally scenic certified section of the IANST. It meanders through heavily forested, hilly terrain dotted with blue kettle lakes and ponds. Special features are end moraines, kames, eskers, crevasse fills, ice-walled lake plains, inwash and outwash plains, kettle lakes, and ponds. Activities include hiking, bird-watching, a scenic drive, fishing, canoeing, and naturalist programs. Bug and tick repellent are recommended in the spring and summer. *Nearby:* Chippewa Falls, Bridge Street Commercial District (NRHP); Jacob Leinenkugel Brewing

Company (1867) offers tours; Irvine Park offers camping. Cadott, Cabin Ridge Rides on horse-drawn wagons or sleighs along Paint Creek; Lake Wissota State Park is a popular spot for camping (rustic/electrical hookups) and fishing. The trail through the Blue Hills passes scenic Hemlock and Moose Ear Creeks and near an ancient American Indian pipestone quarry. Near Birchwood, just north of Red Cedar Lake, the IANST reaches the Tuscobia State Trail. The IANST may some day be rerouted away from the Tuscobia, which runs for 74 miles from Park Falls to Rice Lake and passes through the Chequamegon National Forest to allow ATVs and snowmobilers access to the full length of the state recreation trail. West of Rice Lake, the IANST is mostly uncertified as it stretches west through the dense forests, fishery areas, and dairy lands of Barron, Washburn, Burnett, and Polk Counties to the terminus.

21. INTERSTATE STATE PARK. Above a deep gorge cut by glacial meltwaters, a rocky outcrop in Wisconsin's oldest state park is the western terminus of the IANST. Located near the town of Saint Croix Falls, the park has bedrock with potholes formed by the drilling action of rocky debris in the powerful swirling glacial meltwaters. The scientific reserve interpretive center has exhibits and displays about the Great Ice Age. Seven miles of trail offer views of the Saint Croix National

Scenic Riverway (see NCNST), which serves as the Wisconsin-Minnesota boundary north of the Mississippi. On the Minnesota side of the Saint Croix, near Taylors Falls, the companion Interstate State Park has another interpretive center and larger potholes and is definitely worth a visit. The region's geologic features include the Dalles of the Saint Croix and Lake O' the Dalles, a giant river whirlpool in the Saint Croix, and one of the world's best collections of glacial potholes. Activities include rock climbing, camping (rustic/electrical hookup), hiking, fishing, boating, boat tours, canoeing, cross-country skiing, snowshoeing, and naturalist programs. *Other activities:* Saint Croix Falls, Saint Croix Falls Fish Hatchery; Osceola Fish Hatchery; Quest Recreation offers canoes and shuttles to the upper and lower Saint Croix River.

SUNKEN TRACE WITH HIKER

Along the Old Trace, there are some areas where the loose topsoil was deeply eroded by the continual passage of animals and people. These segments, called the Sunken Trace, present beautifully shaded walking sections of trail.

Natchez Trace National Scenic Trail

Sixty-two miles of Natchez Trace National Scenic Trail have been constructed along the 450-mile corridor of the Natchez Trace Parkway, one of the busiest units of the National Park Service. The white-blazed trail segments that exist today lead hikers and horseback riders along portions an ancient footpath that has been in use for nearly ten thousand years. The Old Trace, first trampled by buffalo, elk, wolf, and cougar, is so eroded with age that in some areas trail depressions sink 15 to 20 feet below ground level. The trail holds memories of an earlier day when American Indians, explorers, post riders, "Kaintucks," land pirates, gamblers, slaves, missionaries, and military troops traversed the Trace, which was dotted with a few small inns often operated by strong pioneer women who had brought civilization to the frontier. Not yet complete, the segments of the scenic trail are found along the parkway that stretches from Natchez, Mississippi, to Nashville, Tennessee, passing through the wooded forests of Mississippi, the rolling hills of the northwest corner of Alabama, and the hills of Tennessee.

ADMINISTERING AGENCY
National Park Service
Natchez Trace Parkway
2680 Natchez Trace Parkway
Tupelo, MS 38801
601-680-4025
800-305-7417

FURTHER INFORMATION
Natchez Trace Trail Conference, Inc.
P.O. Box 1236
Jackson, MS 39215

DESIGNATED
1983

PROPOSED MILEAGE
110 miles (176 kilometers)

PARKWAY ESTABLISHED
1938

PARKWAY MILEAGE
445 miles (712 kilometers)

STATES
Mississippi, Alabama, Tennessee

149

The historic city of Natchez, Mississippi, is one of the oldest settlements in North America. It was built on the site of an ancient village of the Natchez Indians, a sun-worshiping tribe considered the closest descendants of the mound-building Mississippian cultures. The Spanish explorer Hernando de Soto encountered Indians in this area around 1541, and the Natchez's direct ancestors, known to archaeologists as the Plaquemine culture, can be traced to about 1200.

Mound building was part of a complex tribal religion that used mounds for important ritualistic temples. The Plaquemine people constructed several ceremonial mound centers, including the Grand Village mounds in the Natchez area. Construction of this complex was completed in stages, probably beginning about the thirteenth century. At the time of the arrival of the French explorers in the late 1600s Grand Village was the primary ceremonial center for the Natchez people. Emerald Mound, the second-largest ceremonial mound in the nation, located 11 miles northeast of Natchez along the Natchez Trace Parkway, may have been their ceremonial center previously. During the de Soto expedition of 1539–41 the Emerald Mound complex was thriving, but following contact with Europeans, the culture suffered a rapid decline, probably as a result of disease introduced by the explorers.

Although the Spanish passed through the Natchez area as early as 1541, it was the French who finally took possession of the land in 1716. Retracing the 1673 voyage of Father Jacques Marquette and Louis Joliet (see NCNST), the explorer René-Robert Cavelier, sieur de La Salle, and his devoted Italian lieutenant, Henri de Tonti (also spelled Tonty), paddled down the Mississippi River in 1682. After traveling 300 miles farther than previous explorers had, they arrived at the river's mouth on the Gulf. Along the way, they passed American Indian mounds, including the home of the Natchez on the high bluffs formed long ago during the ice age. Massive amounts of rich soil from the western plains were carried by strong winds and deposited on the eastern banks of the Mississippi. Subsequent to La Salle's exploration, the entire Mississippi Basin was claimed for France and named Louisiana. The French settled at Natchez on July 26, 1716, when Jean-Baptiste Le Moyne, sieur de Bienville, founder of New Orleans, established Fort Rosalie on the bluff near the site of a Natchez village. A settlement sprang up around the fort and became known as Nathez.

From the beginning, there was trouble between the French settlers and the Natchez Indians. Trade with English merchants brought the tribe better and cheaper trade items than the French offered, and the Natchez were dissatisfied with the French for demanding large land cessions without compensation. These tensions led to a rebellion on November 28, 1729, in which the Natchez destroyed Fort Rosalie and surrounding plantations. Nearly one-third of the colonists—men, women, and children—were killed, and another four hundred fifty were taken prisoner. Angry French forces, aided by the Choctaw, who traveled down the Old Trace, waged a punitive war that resulted in the complete annihilation of the Natchez, except for a few who escaped up the Trace to join the Chickasaws.

In 1763 the Treaty of Paris granted the British possession of all French lands east of the Mississippi, including Natchez. While the British were engaged along the Atlantic seaboard during the Revolutionary War, an expedition led by Don Bernardo de Gálvez, Spanish governor of Louisiana Territory, captured the city in 1779. In 1795 the Stars and Stripes first flew over Natchez at Connelly's Tavern when a Quaker surveyor, Maj. Andrew Ellicot, under orders from George Washington, waved it in defiance of Spanish rule. That October, under the terms of Pinchney's Treaty, Spain surrendered all lands north of the thirty-first parallel. Finally on March 30, 1798, the Spanish evacuated the Natchez District, and U.S. forces took possession. Natchez served as the seat of the newly organized Mississippi Territory, and by December 10, 1817, Mississippi gained statehood.

EMERALD MOUND

From the parkway at milepost 10.3, a trail leads to the top of the nation's second-largest temple mound, built by ancestors of the Natchez Indians called Mississippians. Hernando de Soto's expedition and early French explorers encountered Emerald Mound.

From the early days of settlement until it became part of the United States, Natchez was the seat of a vast empire. As the only port on the Mississippi River between the Ohio River and New Orleans, Natchez became a central link with the rest of the world. For the European explorers, knowledge of the great river first came with de Soto's 1541 exploration. Although he named the river that he was eventually buried in Espiritu Santo, or Holy Spirit, it came to be known as the Mississippi, meaning "big river." French adventurers had brought this Algonkian Indian name with them as they traveled south from the river's headwaters in today's Minnesota. The southwestern frontier and later the state were named after this vital waterway.

NATCHEZ BRIDGE WITH THE *AMERICAN QUEEN* PADDLE WHEELER

Overlooking the Mississippi River, Under-the-Hill recaptures the town's rustic pioneer flavor. Once the most notorious waterfront in America, Natchez Under-the-Hill was prominent during the days of flatboats and luxury steamboats, which still dock there today. Steamboating vacationers with the Delta Queen Steamboat Company who climb to the top of the bluff will find quaint shops and restaurants.

As the number of pioneers on the frontier burgeoned, Natchez was strategically located for commerce. As early as 1785, settlers in the Ohio Valley, shut off from the Atlantic coast by the Appalachian Mountains, began floating their extra produce downriver to markets in Natchez and beyond (see PHNST). In the early years farmers deployed hired hands downriver to Natchez or New Orleans, but after 1800 professional boatmen moved most cargo. Flatboats and keelboats were commonly employed. The flatboat was by far more popular. Constructed of massive timbers and thick planks, it was at

least 80 feet long and 25 feet wide. The sides were 5 or 6 feet high, with a portion decked over for the living quarters. This one-way downriver vessel was steered by three long oars—one on each side and one in the back. The sturdier keelboat was curved at both ends, had a cabin, and reached an overall length of about 50 to 75 feet and a width of 15 to 25 feet. Unlike the flatboat, it could be returned upriver by poling or other means, but the grueling trip required the labor of twenty men and could take as long as three months.

Boats originating in Kentucky carried whiskey, hemp, and tobacco, while the Tennessee flat boats transported mostly cotton. Those from north of the Ohio River and west of the Mississippi brought furs, lead, cattle, and horses. Myriad other goods, from furniture to apples, were brought to market. When the weather was fair, a boatman could fiddle while covering 30 miles a day; in poor conditions, however, no music was heard and the hazardous river travel slowed to a crawl. The journey typically took four to six weeks, although depending on the weather and currents, it could take much longer.

"Kentucky Arcs," as they were sometimes called, could wreck, run aground, get stuck on snags, caught in a night fog, or spin out of control in giant eddies. Hurricanes and earthquakes posed further hazards as boatmen navigated the already swift and dangerous currents. No one knows how many on the river were lost in a series of aftershocks that occurred over a two-year period following the New Madrid (Missouri) earthquake that hit on December 16, 1811. The quake itself caused the flow of the Mississippi to temporarily reverse, created a vast lake, destroyed villages, caused bluffs along the Mississippi to collapse, and opened ravines as far south as Natchez. On that very day, Nicholas Roosevelt was pioneering steamboat travel on the *New Orleans* near western Tennessee. Just as the earthquake changed the land, the steamboat would forever alter river travel, but until it gained acceptance, boatmen would continue to transport goods down the river for the next two decades.

If boatmen traveled as a group, the journey could be safer. They would moor their boats together to provide greater stability, help each other in emergencies, and thwart attempted robberies. They traded goods together and, of course, told the grandest of tall tales while on the river. Keelboater Mike Fink became a legend on the river, partly due to his own boasting—a common characteristic of boatmen as it helped to pass the time. Not only could the rough-and-tumble fighter tell a good joke, Fink declared he could shoot tin cups right off the heads of friends and their womenfolk! In later years, when he worked as a fur trapper, he supposedly tried the stunt and missed. Legend has it that the dead man's friend shot Fink dead.

After delivering the goods to market the flatboats were dismantled and sold for lumber. The boatmen would continue their camaraderie and form groups to walk or ride home together by way of the "Road to Nashville," which would later become known as the Natchez Trace. Travel on the road compared favorably to the back-breaking alternative of poling a keelboat upriver. On foot a boatman could reach Kentucky in about one month. Gradual improvements made the trip more bearable. Ferries shuttled travelers at deep-water crossings, bridges were constructed, and a chain of lackluster wilderness inns, referred to locally as stands, provided meals, entertainment, and shelter.

The Trace was composed of a series of American Indian paths between the southern and central area of North America. These paths, "traced out" by buffalo more than eight thousand years ago, were later connected by tribes such as the Natchez, Choctaw, and Chickasaw who used them for hunting and to facilitate communication. Sections of the Trace gradually took on local names, for example, the Chickasaw Trace. Residents of Fort Nashborough used this name for the section leading from northern Mississippi to their town, which in 1784 became known as Nashville. A southern section that ended in Natchez was referred to as the Path to the Choctaw Nation on eighteenth-century British maps. As the number of boatmen on the path increased, the many sections of the Trace became known collectively as the Boatman's Trail. Others who traveled it appear to have been more impressed by the ominous swamps and wilderness, and dubbed it the Devil's Backbone. By 1800 the entire route was known as the Natchez Road or the Nashville Road, depending on the traveler's destination. It was not until the 1830s, when the path fell into disuse, that the route took on a mystique and became known as the Natchez Trace. This appellation acknowledged the prominence of the Mississippi terminus and adapted the French term, *trace,* meaning "footprints." This term was attached to the earlier buffalo paths and the later American Indian routes.

From 1800 to 1820 the Trace evolved into the most vital highway in the Old Southwest—militarily, economically, and politically.* President Thomas Jefferson decided that the old 450-mile Indian trail that stretched from Nashville to Natchez should become a national road for the protection and safety of the fledgling nation. Because the route crossed wilderness lands that belonged to the Choctaw and the Chickasaw, he requested negotia-

*For comparative purposes, in 1790 Spanish authorities reported 240 passports to boatmen who were taking the northeastern Indian trails home as opposed to the 10,000 who were using the Trace by 1810, its year of heaviest use.

tions that would permit improvements to the road. On October 24, 1801, Gen. James Wilkinson, commander at Fort Adams and of all American troops in the Old Southwest, concluded a treaty that granted the United States the right to lay out a wagon road between the settlements of the Mero District in Tennessee and Natchez in Mississippi Territory. This road, called as the Post Road, was used to deliver mail, to transport troops and slaves, and for pioneer travel. With appropriation for improvement, the work of widening the road was done by soldiers.

In the War of 1812 Gen. Andrew Jackson used the Trace to good advantage. He sent 670 mounted troops down the Trace to Natchez while he loaded the remaining 1,830 men on boats and headed down the Cumberland, Ohio, and finally the Mississippi River to rendezvous with the others. After the mission was aborted in 1813, he marched his entire command up the Trace. Jackson won the hearts of his men by enduring hardships right along with them and allowing the sick to use his horse. In 1815, Old Hickory marched his troops south on the Trace to the Battle of New Orleans, and the victorious men returned via the same route. Though war and victory over the Creeks (TTNHT) and the British marked Jackson's later treks on the Trace, it was courtship that brought Jackson to it in 1791, when he walked it from Natchez to Nashville with his beloved but controversial bride, Rachel. Other notables who traveled the route included were de Soto, the Marquis de Lafayette, David Crockett, John James Audubon, Henry Clay, Jefferson Davis, Abraham Lincoln, and Aaron Burr. Meriwether Lewis tragically died on the Trace of controversial gunshot wounds only three years after returning from his tour as co-commander of the Corps of Discovery (see LCNHT in *America's National Historic Trails*).

Traveling the Trace had its dangers. Horses, known to spook on the trail, could leave the thrown rider behind with a broken leg and no provisions. This meant starvation for some. Like the American Indians, travelers learned to carry a pint of lightweight powdered Indian corn on their person to keep them alive in such emergencies. Land pirates were known to set traps, such as a fallen tree, to stall a money-carrying northbound rider long enough to rob and kill him without mercy. Boatmen were warned to travel in caravans, and rewards were offered for the apprehension of highwaymen. Included on the wanted list was the leader of the infamous Samuel Mason gang, which operated between 1801 and 1803. Hearing of the hefty reward on Mason's head, two members of his gang decided to put a tomahawk in it. After severing their slain leader's head from his body, they preserved it in a ball of clay for identification purposes and took it to the authorities in a sack. Subsequent to spilling out their proof, the recognized villains (a scar gave one of them away) were tried and hanged. Afterward, the more brutal crimes decreased on the Trace, but robbery continued, with some bandits even posing as Methodist ministers. When the traveler was in need of refuge from criminals, the American Indians—with the exception of the Creeks—generally provided sanctuary, and often helped to locate the perpetrators and turn them over to the authorities.

Not all who floated down the river would return north on the Trace. Many settled in the region, which during the first half of the nineteenth century became the heart of a vast slaveholding "cotton kingdom." Farms, located on fertile soil crossed by creeks, grew into settlements. For instance, when Anne Gooch Benton, mother of Sen. Thomas Hart Benton, arrived at Leipers Fork along the Harpeth River she brought civilization with her, including books on law, history, poetry, and religion. And she sold many of her three thousand acres to settlers. For her growing community, which would become known as Widow Benton's Settlement, she built a meeting house, a schoolhouse, and a mill. The route of the Trace was gradually altered to accommodate postal service to settlements like Widow Benton's.

Still other boatmen, who had every intention of following the Trace home, did not return for

STAND ON THE TRACE

In Tennessee at the Meriwether Lewis Monument and Pioneer Cemetery, the great explorer died from gunshot wounds on the Natchez Trace at Grinder's Stand. A broken column over his gravesite symbolizes his untimely and violent end on October 11, 1809.

NATCHEZ UNDER-THE-HILL

Natchez Under-the-Hill was a booming town once consisting of five streets with shops, houses, and businesses, until the mighty Mississippi River washed most of it away, leaving only one street. Under-the-Hill Saloon offers the ambience of riverboat days. Visitors sit inside under authentic ceiling fans or lounge in a rocking chair on the porch ovelooking the Mississippi. Across the street a DAR marker commemorates the Natchez Trace, and downtown is a walk up the hill.

reasons not of their own making. After trading goods and selling the boat lumber, the boatmen's pockets were jingling. Not bothering to visit the civilized upper Natchez on the bluff, many Kaintucks,* sojourned to the boisterous "dens of vice" or the saloons, bordellos, and gaming tables found among legitimate business establishments in the Natchez enclave Under-the-Hill. Consisting of three main streets forming tiers or terraces that ran parallel to the river, the area was bounded on the inner side by a towering bluff. Tales are still told of secret cavernous chambers found behind many of these buildings. Designed to conceal contraband goods, the caves later figured in many bloody crimes. They also destabilized the bluffs and caused several landslides. While the truth may never come to light, Natchez newspapers contained notices of the intoxicated who "broke their necks" when falling off their horses after visits to Under-the-Hill.

In 1811 the *New Orleans* steamboat was built expressly to pass over the lower Mississippi River, and the next year regular service began between New Orleans and Natchez. Five years later, Henry Miller Shreve of Shreveport, Louisiana, launched the steamboat *Washington*. Before long it made its way upriver from New Orleans to Kentucky in

*No matter where the boatmen were from, the downriver people referred to them as "Kaintucks."

twenty-five days. As designs improved, so did speed. By 1820 some steamboats could make the trip in fifteen days. For convenience, boatmen began to turn to the steamboat for their homeward journeys. This included Abraham Lincoln who made a flatboat trip in 1828 and took the steamboat home. By 1830 the return trip could be accomplished in ten days. Mail service moved to the river, the steamboats rendered the Kaintucks obsolete, and the Natchez Trace was nearly forgotten.

The golden age of the steamboat was eventually eclipsed by the railroad, but in its day steamboat travel provided the most reliable service available. Steamboats not only transported cargos of cotton and sugarcane but took on passengers who were given luxurious lounges. Some steamboats boasted of great chefs and orchestras. Fortunes were made by many citizens of Natchez who served as brokers of the goods pouring in. The lavishness and wealth of the period is reflected in the antebellum homes built throughout Natchez, many of which are extremely well preserved and open for tours.

Perhaps one of the last migrations over the Trace was the sad passage of the Cherokees and other American Indians in the 1830s. Their forced migration to Oklahoma began on the Natchez Trace to the Tennessee River and then continued on the extensive route that would later become known as the Trail of Tears (see TTNHT in *America's National*

MONMOUTH

Natchez is well known for the gorgeous refurbished antebellum homes that are available for public viewing throughout the year or during special Natchez Pilgrimage Tours. A fully narrated historic city tour takes visitors past more than fifty of the pre-1861 mansions and churches that are studied by architects and enjoyed by participants in special Elderhostel programs. Monmouth is listed on the National Register of Historic Places and is a national historic landmark.

Historic Trails). Only a faint memory of the Trace remained by the 1860s, when the Civil War brought it renewed prominence. Both Union and Confederate troops marched along the old path. After the war the Trace again fell into disuse, and the railroad became the dominant means of transportation.

By 1908 efforts to memorialize the Trace began to surface. The Mississippi Daughters of the American Revolution (DAR) made marking the trail an official project, and they invited patriotic societies in Alabama and Tennessee to do the same.

MONMOUTH SLAVE QUARTERS

At one time, slaves walked the Natchez Trace. At Monmouth, their quarters and cabins, along with the main house and the carriage house, have been restored, rebuilt, and enhanced to provide overnight lodging for tourists. Although slave auctions took place at Under-the-Hill and in downtown Natchez, most of the commercial marketing of slaves took place about a mile east of the downtown at the Forks of the Road. An informative brochure on African American heritage is available at the Natchez Convention and Visitors Bureau.

SUNKEN TRACE SIGN

Hikers and horseback riders share opened segments of the Natchez Trace National Scenic Trail. Along the Natchez Trace Parkway, milepost markers and interpretive signs indicate sections of Sunken Trace and Old Trace.

Although money was scarce, the next year the first stone marker was erected on a bluff in Natchez above the Mississippi River. By the 1930s the DAR, the Daughters of 1812, and other such societies had marked the Trace in all three states.

In 1934 Congress commissioned the National Park Service to survey the old road for possible construction of the Natchez Trace Parkway. Planned as an elongated corridor park from the bluffs and bayous of Natchez to the green hills of Nashville (at Pasquo, Tennessee), the parkway was intended to serve as a much-needed link between the two cities. To accommodate the automobile, the parkway would not follow the Old Trace in its entirety; in fact, only about 50 percent of the original Trace would lie within the actual corridor. The remainder of the original Trace would lie to either side of the parkway on country roads. By 1939 the first sections of the 450-mile parkway were built. The entire route is scheduled for completion in the first decade of the twenty-first century. Sections at the Natchez terminus and the segment by Jackson in Mississippi are included in these plans.

During parkway development, the National Trails System Act of 1968 designated the Natchez Trace one of the first trails to be studied for potential inclusion in the National Trails System. This resulted in the establishment by Congress of the Natchez Trace National Scenic Trail (NTNST) on March 28, 1983. The National Park Service was assigned to manage and coordinate the development of the trail. In 1989 the Natchez Trace Trail Conference was formed to reclaim the original Trace and establish a path that would follow it as it loosely follows the length of the parkway.

THE NATCHEZ INDIANS

French traders who lived among the Natchez Indians from 1698 to the tribe's near-demise described the Natchez, their mounds, and their social system in detailed writings. They provide important information about the Natchez and all Temple Mound people, if, as it is thought, the Natchez are the last representatives of Mississippian culture. At the time they were discovered, the Natchez lived on scattered family farms near several sprawling villages. Their crops were corn, beans, and squash. The people, described as handsome, with dark copper skin, practiced head flattening, tattooing, and teeth blackening with a mixture of tobacco and wood ashes.

The tribe was ruled by a hereditary chief-priest called the Great Sun and was divided into elite and common classes. The upper class was composed of suns, nobles, and the honored people. Suns, at the top of the hierarchy, consisted of the chief and his relatives. Set apart from the rest of the population, they held important tribal offices. Their jewelry, clothing, and food denoted this elevated status, and they were buried in public buildings or mounds. All suns, including the Great Sun, were required to marry commoners, called "Stinkards." Within this unique lineage system, the children of the female suns retained the status of a sun, but the children of male suns were reduced to nobles. This meant that the son of the Great Sun could never succeed his father, as the Great Sun's rank descended through the female line. The next Great Sun, as a result, was generally one of his sister's sons.

This unique lineage system ensured that new blood would flow into each class. For instance, the elite nobles and the honored people were required marry commoners. In a like manner, the children of male nobles were lowered to honored people and the children of male honored people became commoners. The children of female members of each class retained their mother's status. Commoners marrying commoners had nowhere to go, but children of those who married into the upper classes were able to rise to a higher level. In a departure from birthright, some commoners were elevated by acts of bravery or for sacrificing an infant at the time of a Great Sun's death. When a Great Sun died, his wife, slaves, and anyone else who wished to join him in the afterlife were strangled.

The Great Sun was an absolute monarch who held the power of life and death over his subjects. His slightest whim was to be obeyed. The journal of a French explorer included the passage, "When he gives the leavings of his dinner to his brothers or any of his relatives he pushes the dishes to them with his feet." And because his feet never touched the bare earth, he was carried on a litter wherever he went. If he did need to walk, mats were spread before each step was taken.

Only the Great Sun and a few selected priests were allowed to enter the rectangular temple on top of an earth mound. Bones of previous Great Suns were stored in the temple, where an eternal fire burned throughout the year. Once a year, on the eve of their midsummer festival, during the Green Corn Ceremony, the fire was allowed to die. At dawn on festival day, the fire was relit, and from it all village fires were begun anew.

After the French drove the Natchez from their villages, approximately four hundred of them were captured and sold into the West Indian slave trade. The refugees, driven from their homeland, soon joined other tribes, including the Chickasaws and later the Upper Creeks and Cherokees. A century later, when the U.S. government transferred these tribes to reservation lands in Oklahoma, the Natchez descendants moved with them (see TTNHT, vol. 1). Tribal ancestors held on to their language until the early twentieth century. In 1720 Stung Serpent, brother of the Great Sun, blamed trade for altering the lives of his people. Perhaps his words helped stir the revolt that would scatter the people:

Why . . . did the French come into our country? We did not go to seek them: they asked for land of us because their country was too little for all the men that were in it. We told them they might take land where they pleased, there was enough for them and for us; that it was good the same sun should enlighten us both, and that we would give them of our provisions, assist them to build, and to labor in their fields. We have done so; is this not true? What occasion then did we have for Frenchmen? Before they came, did we not live better than we do, see we deprive ourselves of a part of our corn, our game, and fish to give a part to them? In what respect, then, had we occasion for them? Was it for their guns? The bows and arrows which we used, were sufficient to make us live well.

Was it for their white, blue, and red blankets? We can do well enough with buffalo skins, which are warmer; our women wrought feather blankets for the winter, and mulberry mantles for the summer; which were not so beautiful; but our women were more laborious and less vain than they are now. In fine, before the arrival of the French, we lived like men who can be satisfied with what they have; whereas that this day we are like slaves, who are not suffered to do as they please.

The Trail Today

The Natchez Trace Parkway includes a right-of-way that averages 825 feet in width. Along this green corridor, there are 62 miles of Natchez National Scenic Trail open for hiking and horseback riding. These nature paths are primarily the result of the efforts of members of the Natchez Trace Trail Conference, Natchez Trace Trail Blazers, Vicksburg Trail Dusters, Mississippi Endurance Riders, Student Conservation Association, Eagle Scouts, Boy Scouts, Girl Scouts, and other interested volunteers who help build and maintain the trail.

Of the proposed 694-mile NTNST, these 62 miles are complete but not linked together. Portions travel the original historic Natchez Trace, leading travelers through rolling hills, meadows, pine and hardwood forests, steep ravines, and some creek crossings. These sections are marked with white blazes; spurs are blazed in blue. The southernmost section of the NTNST, near Port Gibson, Mississippi, has 10 miles of trail extending from the Russell Road Trailhead (milepost 50.8) to the Regantown Road Trailhead (milepost 59). Tent and RV camping is available at the Rocky Springs Campground and horse camping is permitted at Grand Gulf State Park. Near Ridgeland, Mississippi, there is a 20.5-mile section with a southern terminus at the West Florida Boundary Trailhead (milepost 108) and a northern terminus at the Upper Choctaw Boundary Parking Area (milepost 128.5). Ratliff Ferry and Goshen Springs Campground have tent and RV camping, and Goshen Springs Campground allows horse camping. Seven miles of trail are open in the Tupelo District in Mississippi from the West Jackson Street Trailhead (milepost 260.8) to the Beech Springs Parking Area and Visitor Center (milepost 266). Tent and RV camping possibilities include Davis Lake, Tombigbee State Park, Barnes Crossing, Whip-Poor-Will, Piney Grove/Bay Springs Lake, and Tishomingo State Park. The Natchez Trace RV Park and Trace State Park are recommended for horse camping. The northernmost section of the NTNST lies in the Leipers Fork District, located near Franklin, Tennessee. This section covers 24 miles of trail from the Highway 50 Trailhead (milepost 408) to the Garrison

Creek Trailhead (milepost 427.6). The Meriwether Lewis Campground offers tent and RV camping.

Although bicycles are prohibited on the national scenic trail, they are used on the parkway as a mode of travel to reach the NTNST segments. Other points of interest along the parkway include more than 180 sections of Old Trace, 12 major archaeological sites, 2 historic houses, 2 Civil War battlefields, 36 cemeteries, and 20 DAR markers. Mileposts and references to points of interest are located on the east side of the parkway. Old Trace segments are marked within the present-day parkway corridor. Some of the Old Trace sections have been worn down more than 20 feet deep by travelers over the centuries. This erosion is in part caused by the loose soil, referred to as loess soil, that was deposited in the region during the last ice age. Sections of the Trace that have been deeply eroded are called sunken trace. Other sections, such as the Dogwood Mudhole, show how the Trace was modified to avoid obstacles such as swampy muddy areas. Sections of the Trace within the parkway are being considered for nomination to the National Register of Historic Places, and a nomination for the parkway is also under way. In 1996, the same year that the last 5 miles of parkway in Tennessee were officially opened in a ceremony conducted by Vice President Al Gore, the Department of Transportation designated the Natchez Trace Parkway one of the nation's first All-American Roads. This distinction has been given to only 15 byways in the country, and distinguishes it as one of the nation's finest. In addition, a 14-mile segment of the parkway that bisects a unit of the Tombigbee National Forest has been designated a National Forest Scenic Byway by the U.S. Forest Service.

Commercial vehicles are not permitted on America's oldest national scenic highway, but tour buses and motor homes are allowed as long as they follow the the 50-mile-per-hour speed limit. Pulling recreational boats, bikes, horse trailers, and camping trailers is also permitted. Because bicyclists share the paved roadway with motorists, extreme caution is advised. Cyclists should be well marked in bright clothing, and bikes should have safety flags. A map of the Natchez Trace Parkway Bicycle Route developed by Adventure Cycling Association is available from the Eastern National Park and Monument Association in cooperation with the National Park Service.

Hiking on the actual parkway is not advised, but there are twenty-two separate hiking, nature, and bridle trails that lead into swamps along the route. Water tupelos and bald cypress trees, some draped with Spanish moss, grow in the swampy wetlands, while waterfalls, cool springs, and hardwood forests are found in slightly higher elevations. The best weather conditions for hiking are generally in the fall; summers are muggy. In spring, flowers add color to the surroundings, but heavy rain showers can produce muddy and wet trail conditions. Throughout the year, early mornings are the best times to spot deer and wild turkeys. Hikers should watch for copperheads, cottonmouths, and rattlesnakes.

Various opportunities for birding, fishing, canoeing, and boating are available in the region. The Delta Queen Steamboat Company offers steamboat cruises on the Mississippi and Tennessee Rivers at either end of the Trace: Natchez and Nashville. The real flavor of the steamboat era comes alive on these cruises. On-board specialists in river lore answer questions and share steamboat stories of bygone days. Camping is available at several parkway locations and at other sites near the Trace. Horseback riders using the scenic trail are asked to stay on the path; cutting across switchbacks tramples plants and creates parallel paths that erode the loose soil. Hikers are expected to yield to stock traffic. Children should be prevented from succumbing to the temptation to chase the horses, which is dangerous for everyone.

There are nine ranger stations along the parkway, and the park's headquarters and main visitor center are located in Tupelo. The Craftsman Guild of Mississippi has demonstrations and a gallery at Ridgeland, and the Kosciusko Welcome Center has a small museum and information center

TOBACCO AND BARN

Many early settlers in Natchez and later along the lower Trace, tried tobacco as their first cash crop. By 1792 annual production in the Natchez district came to half a million pounds. When Spanish merchants turned to better and cheaper tobacco from Kentucky, the business diminished overnight. Today, tobacco farms with leaves hanging in sheds to dry are not uncommon sights along the Trace in Tennessee.

near the Mississippi town that grew up with the Trace. There are additional visitor facilities and recreational opportunities in Mississippi at the Tombigbee National Forest and the Tishomingo State Park, and at the U.S. Army Corps of Engineers–administered Tennessee-Tombigbee waterway. The Corps also operates the Jamie L. Whitten Historical Center near Fulton. There is access from the parkway to state parks in Mississippi and

BELLE MEADE

In 1807 Virginian John Harding bought a 1790 log cabin, known as Dunham Station, a trading post along the Natchez Trace. Its owner, Daniel Durham, had been killed by American Indians, but his wife and children continued to live there until 1792, when the American Indians forced them out. Belle Meade's reputation as a stud farm began in 1816, and the mansion was completed in 1853. The log cabin is one of the oldest houses in Tennessee, and the plantation site is listed on the National Register of Historic Places. Tours with guides in period costume are available.

Tennessee. Major recreational sites have been developed at Rocky Springs, Jeff Busby, and Meriwether Lewis points of interest. The Colbert Ferry site is under development. Rangers conduct on-site programs for visitors.

In addition to its rich cultural history, the Parkway offers diverse natural and regional terrain.* Beginning east of Natchez, the route runs through a beech and

*Material in this section is taken from the National Park's *Natchez Trace Comprehensive Trail Plan.*

oak forest of the Loess Bluffs province with Spanish moss–draped live oak along the deeply eroded sunken portions of the Old Trace. The trace enters the Southern Pine Hills near Raymond, Mississippi, and passes through the Jackson Prairie, now occupied by the Jackson metropolitan area and Ross Barnett Reservoir. From the northeastern top of the reservoir, the road crosses pine and dry oak forests in Mississippi's North Central Hills, Flatwoods, and Pontotoc Ridge provinces. The alluvial agricultural soils around Tupelo are part of the rich agricultural Black Belt Prairie (see SMNHT) and were an important resource to the Chickasaw and other early American Indians. North of Tupelo, the parkway cuts through a mixture of pine and hardwood forests in the hills above the Tombigbee and Tennessee Rivers and traverses primarily oak- and hickory-dominated forests on the Highland Rim in Tennessee. The parkway terminus at Pasquo is on the western edge of the Nashville basin. This region is historically similar to the open bluegrass region of Kentucky.

Flowering trees, shrubs, and wildflowers along the Natchez Trace Parkway include the magnolia, mimosa, elderberry, Japanese honeysuckle, mountain ash, multiflora rose, oak-leaf hydrangea, trumpet creeper, black-eyed susan, butterfly weed, daisy fleabane, oxeye daisy, Queen Anne's lace, meadow rue, ragwort, vetch, and white clover.

Some of the many points of interest along the parkway and information on the four segments of national scenic trail that exist today are discussed in more detail below.

1. NATCHEZ. Under-the-Hill, once the most notorious waterfront in America, can be easily reached by passengers who approach Natchez on the *Delta, Mississippi,* or *American Queen* steamboat. Only Silver Street remains today; the mighty Mississippi washed away the other streets in the district. A climb to the top of the bluff takes steamboat passengers to the first DAR marker to commemorate the Natchez Trace as well as overlooks of the Mississippi River. Parkway visitors enter Natchez on U.S. 61. The city has more than six hundred historic structures, eighty of which are on the NRHP. Historic sites include the refurbished antebellum homes for which Natchez is well known. Monmouth (NHL, 1818) serves as a bed and breakfast; Stanton Hall (1857), one of America's most visited National Historic Landmarks, has the famous Carriage House Restaurant; and The House on Ellicott Hill (NHL, 1798), formerly Connelly's Tavern, on the terminus of the Natchez Trace, was where Andrew Ellicott raised the American flag for the first time in the lower Mississippi Valley. The historic mansions are open to the public during special spring, fall, and winter Pilgrimage Tours; some

are open for tours year-round. Natchez National Historical Park, established in 1988, will have its headquarters at the site of Fort Rosalie, which was established by French colonists in 1716. Other National Park Service properties include Melrose (1845), a planter's estate, and the William Johnson House (1841), the home of a prominent free African American. Grand Village (NHL), the center of activities for the Natchez Indians between 1682 and 1729, has ceremonial mounds, reconstructed dwellings, and a visitor center. Natchez Historic City Tours offers tours on a double-decker tour bus. *Other activities:* In Natchez, the Black Heritage Tour; Natchez Museum of African-American History and Culture; Natchez in Historic Photographs; and Saint Catherine Creek National Wildlife Refuge located on the Mississippi River, south of Natchez. Nearby: At Washington, Jefferson College (NRHP), the first educational institution in Mississippi Territory, was also the site of Aaron Burr's trial; Homochitto National Forest, named after the river, is rich with deer and turkey and offers camping, hiking, bicycling, horseback riding, an auto tour route, swimming, fishing, boating, waterskiing, bird-watching, and rock collecting.

Points of Interest

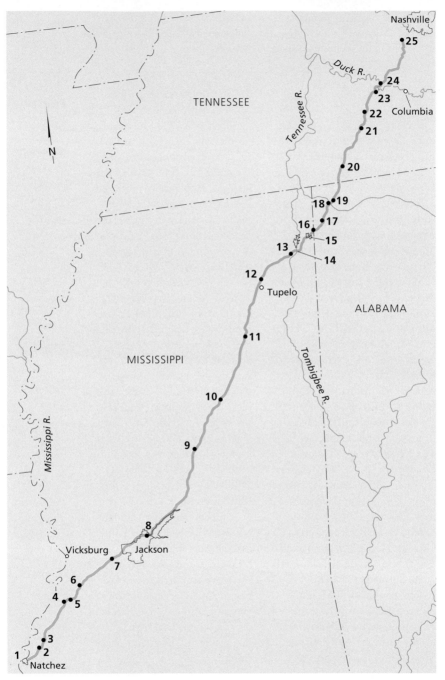

Nashville
● 25

Duck R.

● 24
23
● 22
● 21

● 20

18 ● ● 19
16 ● ● 17
● 15
13 ●
14

12 ●
○ Tupelo

TENNESSEE

Tennessee R.

Columbia ○

ALABAMA

MISSISSIPPI

N

● 11

● 10

9 ●

Tombigbee R.

Mississippi R.

8 ●
Vicksburg ○   Jackson
7 ●
6 ●
4 ●   ● 5
3 ●
1 ● ● 2
Natchez

NATCHEZ TRACE NATIONAL SCENIC TRAIL

2. EMERALD MOUND. A trail leads to the top of the nation's second-largest American Indian temple mound, located just west of the parkway (milepost 10.3). The flat-topped mound is 35 feet high and has a base that measures 770 feet by 435 feet, covering an area of about nine football fields. The mound was built by ancestors of the Natchez for ceremonial purposes between 1250 and 1600 and was still in use when de Soto visited the area in the 1540s. A thirty-foot-high secondary mound at the west end supported a third mound that is no longer extant. More than a dozen mound groups are located within 25 miles of the area. *Other activities:* West of the parkway, Natchez State Park has cabins and camp-grounds and opportunities for hiking, biking, horseback riding, fishing (the largest bass in Mississippi history was caught in Natchez Lake), and boating.

3. MOUNT LOCUST. Mount Locust, also known as Ferguson's Tavern, is one of the oldest structures in Mississippi and may date to 1779. It became one of the best-known stands on the Trace after the British owner was imprisoned by the Spanish and his land was confiscated for leading an unsuccessful rebellion against the government. This is the sole remaining stand of the more than fifty that thrived along the old National Road from 1800 to 1820. Interpretive programs are available at the restored site (milepost 15.5) from February to November. *Other activities:* One mile west of the parkway on MS 553, Springfield (1791) is the home where Andrew Jackson married Rachel Robards in a civil ceremony before returning to Nashville with his bride on the Natchez Trace.

4. SUNKEN TRACE. The loose topsoil has been deeply eroded by the continual passage of animals and people along this segment (milepost 41.5) that presents a beautiful walking section of the Old Trace near Port Gibson, the town Gen. Ulysses S. Grant called "too beautiful to burn." *Other activities:* At Port Gibson, the restored City Hall (1840); First Presbyterian Church (1859); Gemiluth Chassed, Mississippi's oldest synagogue; Oak Square (1850), a thirty-room mansion; Ruins of Windsor (1859–61), once the largest antebellum mansion in Mississippi, now twenty-three huge Corinthian columns remain; Wintergreen Cemetery, which dates to 1807 and is considered one of the more beautiful cemeteries in the state; and Port Gibson ranger station (milepost 39.2). *Nearby:* North of Port Gibson, Grand Gulf Military Monument Park, with two historic forts; Grand Gulf Cemetery; Grand Gulf Nuclear Station, with tours of the largest boiling water reactor plant in the United States. At Vicksburg, Vicksburg National Military Park; USS *Cairo* Museum, a restored Union gunboat containing artifacts; the U.S. Army Corps of Engineers Waterways Experiment Station, with free guided tours of

this major research, testing, and development facility; museums and historic homes; Mississippi River Adventures, with hydro-jet boat sightseeing tours to historic landmarks.

5. MAGNUM MOUND. This natural hill burial mound (milepost 45.7) was used as a cemetery by Mississippi period Indians before de Soto's explorations. Multiple burials in the area suggest that sacrifices were made here, as observed later among the Natchez Indians. A close relationship probably existed between these people and those who built Emerald Mound. *Other activities:* The crossing of Bayou Pierre at Grindstone Ford (milepost 45.7) marked the beginning of the lands of the Choctaw Nation. Up to this point, boatmen had been traveling in the Old Natchez District.

6. ROCKY SPRINGS. This once-prosperous town dates to the 1790s. The population that once reached 2,600 was decimated by a series of calamities: the Civil War, yellow fever, the boll weevil, and land erosion. Only a Methodist church (1837), which still holds services, and a cemetery remain (milepost 54.8). It is said that the Mason gang and other trail criminals had a hideout nearby. A campground and a section of the NTNST are also located in the vicinity between milepost 50.8 and milepost 59.

7. BATTLE OF RAYMOND. On May 8, 1863, as General Grant and his army marched up a section of Trace (milepost 78.3), a Confederate brigade fired on them. This Civil War battle was part of the Vicksburg campaign and ended when the Confederates were forced to retreat to Jackson. The small town of Raymond is just east of the Trace. *Nearby:* In Jackson, the State Capitol Building (1903); the Governor's Mansion; the Dizzy Dean Museum; museums, galleries, and historic homes; Lefleur's Bluff State Park, with camping (rustic/electric hookup), hiking, fishing, canoeing, boating (rental), tennis, golf, and an American Indian festival each spring.

8. MISSISSIPPI CRAFTS CENTER. The pioneer-style dogtrot cabin at Ridgeland (milepost 102.4) has demonstrations of traditional crafts and sells baskets, pottery, weavings, quilts, and jewelry created by members of the Choctaw tribe. A section of NTNST in this area runs between mileposts 108 and 128.5. Other activities: Ross Barnett Reservoir, a 50-square-mile body of water, parallels the parkway for 8 miles and has an overlook (milepost 105.6). The site of another of the fifty or so inns along the old road, Brashear's Stand, was advertised as "a house of entertainment in the wilderness." Sunken trace with a short loop-trail is located at the site at milepost 104.5; Boyd Mounds (milepost 106.9), the burial mound, was built between about 1300 and 1500 near the site of an earlier village constructed in about 500 by Woodland period Indians just before the decline of their culture. Archaeologists have

located at least forty-one burials at the 5-foot-high, 100-foot-long mound; Cypress Swamp (milepost 122) has a nature trail through the water tupelo and bald cypress trees. *Nearby:* In Vaughan, Casey Jones Museum State Park honors the folk hero and engineer Jonathan Luther "Casey" Jones. Near Morton, Roosevelt State Park has a visitor center, cabins, camping, hiking, fishing, canoeing, boating, water-skiing, swimming, tennis, and miniature golf.

9. KOSCIUSKO MUSEUM– INFORMATION CENTER. Kosciusko is one of the oldest remaining settlements on the trace. It was originally known as Red Bud Spring, an Indian camp-site. The museum (milepost 160) provides information about the trace and the area locals call the "Treasure of the Trace." The town, named after the Polish general and engineer Tadeusz Kosciusko, who offered his services to George Washington during the Revolutionary War, is the birthplace of Oprah Winfrey, who has a street named after her. *Other activities:* In Kosciusko, Hammond-Routt House is a restored Greek Revival house on the original Natchez Trace in the downtown area; Redbud Inn (1884) is one of the finest examples of Queen Anne architecture in the South; Kosciusko–Attala County Cultural Center is located in the former Presbyterian church building (1898); Kosciusko City Cemetery has late-nineteenth-century markers; the Natchez

Trace Festival is held the last Saturday in April; Kosciusko Ranger Station (milepost 159.7); Hurricane Creek (milepost 164), just north of town, offers a 15-minute nature walk through bottomlands with American beech, white oaks, and ferns, hills with hickory trees, and southern pine and hardwood forest at the top.

10. JEFF BUSBY SITE. This campsite is named for Rep. Thomas Jefferson Busby from Mississippi who introduced the bill that resulted in the May 21, 1934, act to survey the Old Natchez Trace for possible construction of the Natchez Trace Parkway. The campground includes an overlook on one of the parkway's higher points in Mississippi at Little Mountain (603 feet), where a large nature and history exhibit explains the great eastern hardwood forest that extended from the Gulf Coast to Canada. A 15-minute nature trail near camp identifies two dozen food plants that grow in the area. *Nearby:* Near Grenada, Hugh White State Park on Grenada Lake has a visitor center, lodge, cabins, camping, hiking, fishing, boating, water-skiing, and swimming.

11. BYNUM MOUNDS. The site (milepost 232.4) was first occupied in about 100 b.c., and the mounds were built over the next three hundred years during the Woodland Indian period. In the early 1800s the Chickasaws occupied the site. Artifacts from the site are displayed at the Parkway Visitors Center near

Tupelo. *Other activities:* Witch Dance (milepost 233.2), a picnic area, provides horseback riders with access to the Tombigbee Horse Trail, which is in the Tombigbee National Forest, adjacent to the parkway; the Tombigbee National Forest unit that bisects the parkway offers 66,341 acres of dogwood-filled forests and popular historic sites. The Tombigbee, the Choctaw word for "coffin makers," has camping, hiking, horseback riding, canoeing, boating, and swimming at Davis Lake (milepost 243.1).

12. TUPELO VISITOR CENTER AND PARK HEADQUARTERS. The center (milepost 266) has an audiovisual history program, a scale model of a flatboat and other exhibits, a half-mile loop nature trail, and parkway information. The center serves as the northern terminus for a 7-mile stretch of NTNST that leads south to the West Jackson Street Trailhead (milepost 260.8). Parkway sites in the area include the Tupelo National Battlefield (milepost 259.7), which commemorates the Confederates' unsuccessful attempt on July 14 to cut the railroad supply line for the Union Army's march on Atlanta; Chickasaw Village (milepost 261.8) has foundation markers, interpretive panels, an exhibit shelter, and nature trail; thirteen Confederate unknown soldier grave sites (269.4) are found on the Old Trace. *Other activities:* At Tupelo, Elvis Presley Birthplace; Elvis Presley Museum: Times and Things Remembered; Elvis Presley Driving Tour; the Oren Dunn Museum of Tupelo, which includes Chickasaw Indian exhibits, Elvis Presley memorabilia, Apollo mission displays; Mississippi Museum of Art (1909, NRHP); De Soto Monument, on the corner of Main and Church Streets, observes the explorer's stay in northeastern Mississippi during the winter of 1540–41; Ackia Battlefield Monument, at the intersection of President and Pierce Streets, marks the May 26, 1736, battle when the French and Choctaw, under Bienville, were repulsed by the Chickasaw; Elvis Presley Lake and Campground; Private John Allen National Fish Hatchery; Tombigbee State Park has cabins, camping, hiking, fishing, boating (rental), swimming, archery, and tennis; Brices Cross Roads National Battlefield Site recognizes the brilliant tactical victory of the Confederates who faced a much larger Union army on June 10, 1864. At Belden, Trace State Park offers cabins, camping, hiking, horseback riding, fishing, boating, waterskiing, and swimming. *Nearby:* In Fulton, the Army Corps' Jamie L. Whitten Historical Center offers guided tours and contains displays from seven federal agencies and examines waterways and Appalachian region programs. Near New Albany, Holly Springs National Forest, with rolling hills, hardwoods, and numerous lakes, offers opportunities for camping, hiking, fishing, boating, and swimming.

13. **PHARR MOUNDS.** This important archaeological site (milepost 286.7) was intermittently inhabited from approximately 2500 B.C. to A.D. 1400. Eight large dome-shaped mounds are scattered throughout the 90-acre complex. *Other activities:* Donivan Slough (milepost 283.3) has a nature trail.

14. **TENNESSEE-TOMBIGBEE WATERWAY.** The Tennessee-Tombigbee Waterway (milepost 293.2), designed to be an alternate route to the Gulf of Mexico, forms a 234-mile-long transportation artery connecting northeastern Mississippi and west-central Alabama. With its ten locks, it provides a lift of 341 feet and connects to the 16,000-mile inland waterway system. Festivals, boat races, and fishing tournaments are held along the waterway. Camping, hiking, and water sports are available. The waterway and visitor center are administered by the Army Corps of Engineers, which, in 1827, conducted the first survey of the area at the direction of Congress to determine the feasibility of connecting the two rivers.

15. **TISHOMINGO STATE PARK.** The park (milepost 302.8) near Dennis at the Alabama border has a visitor center, cabins, a swinging bridge, fields, a pool, and a 13-mile Bear Creek float trip in season. Popular activities include camping, hiking, fishing, canoeing, boating, and swimming.

16. **BEAR CREEK MOUND.** The site (milepost 308.8) was occupied by migratory hunters as early as 7,000 to 8,000 B.C. The Mississippian period flat-topped temple mound that stands ten feet high was built in stages between 1000 and 1300. The site may have served as a ceremonial center for other villages or farmsteads in the vicinity. This area is the oldest major prehistoric site on the Natchez Trace.

ALABAMA

17. **FREEDOM HILLS OVERLOOK.** A steep trail leads to Alabama's highest point (800 feet) on the parkway (milepost 317), with overlooks to the east of the foothills of the Appalachian Mountains. *Other activities:* The exhibit at milepost 320.3 gives information about stand owner and Chickasaw chief Levi Colbert, and a trail leads to Buzzard Roost Spring, the former site of the stand. Near Luka, Mississippi, J. P. Coleman State Park on the Tennessee River at Pickwick Lake has a marina, cabins, suites, camping, fishing, boating (rental), waterskiing, swimming, and miniature golf. Near Counce, Tennessee, Pickwick Landing State Park on the shores of Pickwick Reservoir has a visitor center, marina, resort inn, cabins, camping (electrical hookup/rustic), hiking, fishing, boating (rental), swimming, golf, and tennis. Boats can lock through Pickwick Dam for a scenic cruise down the Tennessee River, passing Shiloh National Military Park, historic Savannah, and the Tennessee National Wildlife Refuge.

18. COLBERT FERRY. James Colbert, the chief negotiator for the Chickasaw Indians, established a ferry at the mouth of Bear Creek. When the new road was established, he suggested a site about 20 miles upstream as a crossing for the Tennessee River. For his services, Gen. James Wilkinson agreed to erect cabins for him and build a new ferryboat (milepost 327.3). After the Chickasaw Treaty of 1801, which allowed the United States the right to lay out the road to Natchez, the U.S. government began to acquire the Chickasaw lands. In 1832 the Chickasaws sold their remaining lands and moved west. Colbert, perhaps the richest man in the Chickasaw Nation, died a year after his removal to Indian Territory in Oklahoma at the age of seventy-five. He reportedly charged Andrew Jackson $75,000 to ferry his army across the river. The stand built for him by the government in 1801 was destroyed in a 1929 fire, but its foundation can be seen near a section of Old Trace leading to Pickwick Lake. The original ferry was lost as a result of water backup behind Tennessee's Pickwick Landing Dam. *Other activities:* John Coffee Memorial Bridge (milepost 328.6–327.8) crosses Pickwick Lake, formed by Pickwick Landing Dam on the Tennessee River.

19. ROCK SPRING. A 20-minute loop trail (milepost 330.2) along Colbert Creek leads to a small natural bubbling spring. Nearby beaver have built a dam in whose backwater visitors can see fish and turtles. *Nearby:* At Florence, Indian Mound and Museum; Pope's Tavern Museum, an early stagecoach stop and inn (early 1800s), used as a hospital during the Civil War; Forks of Cypress Plantation Site, the former home of the Alex Haley family; Peter Cemetery Fieldstone Monument honors slaves buried here and references the Fourteenth Amendment; William C. Handy Home and Museum has memorabilia of the famous blues composer; Renaissance Tower has a wildflower garden, Alabama Shoals Aquarium, TVA exhibits, and views of the Tennessee River and Wilson Dam; Wilson Dam, operated by the TVA, has one of the highest single-lift navigation locks in the world; Joe Wheeler State Park, named for the Confederate general, is divided into Wheeler Dam, First Creek, and Elk River and offers resort lodges, cottages, marina, camping (rustic/electrical hookup), hiking, fishing, boating, swimming, tennis, golf, and nature programs; Wheeler National Wildlife Refuge has a visitor center, hiking trails, archaeological sites, and wildlife viewing. In Tuscumbia, Helen Keller Birthplace (1820) and Shrine offers live performances of "The Miracle Worker" in late June and July and the Helen Keller Festival in late June; Alabama Music Hall of Fame; Colbert Fossil Plant has a visitor center with photos of the construction of the TVA system.

20. SUNKEN TRACE. Progress was painfully slow when frontier travelers had to cut new trail to bypass impassable sections during the rainy season (milepost 350.5). Three distinct cuts through the woods are evident here. *Other activities:* McGlamery Stand, a village (milepost 352.9) named for John McGlamery, who built a stand at this site in 1849.

21. OLD TRACE DRIVE. Automobiles, but not travel trailers, may take the 2.5-mile road that follows the original trace route. Nearby: At Waynesboro, Natural Bridge, the only double-span natural bridge in the United States, was the site of David Crockett's first political address and served as a hideout for Natchez Trace bandits; Buffalo Trail Rides offers organized horseback trail rides twice a year; Crazy Horse Canoes provides trips on the scenic Buffalo River; Laurel Hill Wildlife Management Area; Lewis State Forest. Lawrenceburg, David Crockett's Cabin, a replica of the original; David Crockett Statue; Mexican Monument, devoted to the men who battled and lost their lives in the Mexican American War; Old Jail Museum, with local historic exhibits; an Amish community to the north; David Crockett State Park, located on the banks of Shoal Creek, where the legendary frontiersman operated a grist mill and distillery. Popular activities include camping hiking, bicycling (rental), fishing, boating (rental),

and swimming. In the summer, outdoor dramas are presented. A visitor center and a museum are also open during the summer.

22. MERIWETHER LEWIS MONUMENT AND PIONEER CEMETERY. At age thirty five, on October 11, 1809, the great explorer Meriwether Lewis died at Grinder's Inn on the Natchez Trace. Lewis had been the personal secretary of President Thomas Jefferson. On his return from his expedition with Clark, Jefferson appointed him governor of Louisiana Territory. Lewis found himself embroiled in political and financial difficulties. Headed to Washington, D.C., to resolve questions and obtain reimbursements for expenditures, Lewis departed Saint Louis and traveled down the Mississippi to Pickering, where he was joined by James Neely, the U.S. Agent to the Chickasaws. Together they proceeded up a portion of the Old Trace. Lewis stopped at Grinder's Inn to rest and there suffered fatal gunshot wounds. The circumstances of his death are still in question. A broken column, erected by the state of Tennessee in 1848, stands over his grave site (milepost 385.9) symbolizing the untimely and violent death of this young man. A pioneer cemetery, campground, ranger station, foot trail, and overlooks are also at this location. *Other activities:* Metal Ford Steele's Ironworks (milepost 382.8) was established in about 1820; Napier Mine (milepost 38.1) provided ore for the iron-

making operation; Phosphate Mine is located at milepost 390.7. *Nearby:* Hohenwald, a German and Swiss settlement, has the Lewis County Museum with the fourth-largest collection of international animal mounts in the Western Hemisphere; Buffalo River Canoeing offers tours of the river.

23. TOBACCO FARM. A 2-mile section of Old Trace begins at this early 1900s tobacco farm (milepost 401.4).

24. GORDON HOUSE AND FERRY SITE. Capt. John Gordon, who led a company of scouts under General Jackson's command during the Creek Indian Campaign, ran a ferry on the Duck River with his wife, Dolly Gordon. After the captain's death in 1819, his wife—a proud descendant of Pocahontas—managed the plantation for forty years. Their two-story home (milepost 407.7), originally constructed in 1817–18, the first brick house for 30 miles, was acquired by the National Park Service in 1977. *Other activities:* A segment of NTNST has its southern terminus at the Highway 50 Trailhead (milepost 408) and its northern terminus at Garrison Creek (milepost 427.6). *Nearby:* In Columbia, James K. Polk Ancestral Home (1816); Atheneum, a restored antebellum girl's school that became headquarters for two Union generals during the Civil War; Monsanto Ponds, a world-renowned bird sanctuary and wetlands; the National Tennessee Walking

Horse Jubilee, held in late May and early June. At Franklin, the Carter House (1830), a National Landmark, has a museum and a video about the Battle of Franklin, a Civil War engagement that took place on November 30, 1864; Carnton Plantation and McGavock Confederate Cemetery has an antebellum plantation house (1826) and the largest private Confederate cemetery in the nation; Franklin Main Street, the entire fifteen-block downtown area is listed on the NRHP; Heritage Trail is a scenic drive through an area that was plantation country in the mid-1800s. Near Murfreesboro, Stones River National Battlefield, the site of the bloody encounter that took place in late December and early January 1862–63. In early August, the International Grand Championship Walking Horse Show is held on the property.

25. TERMINUS. The parkway terminus (milepost 442.3) at Pasquo was completed in 1996. To celebrate the opening, a parade of antique cars, one for each year the parkway has been under construction, traveled the highway. *Nearby:* In Nashville, Fort Nashborough, a reconstruction of the original settlement; Travellers Rest Historic House (1799) and Grounds, Belmont Mansion (1850), Belle Meade Plantation (1853), and other area mansions; Tennessee State Capitol (1859) and Governor's Residence (1929-31); Fort Donelson National Battlefield, the site of the first major victory for the Union Army

in the Civil War (February 1862); many museums, including the Tennessee State Museum, the Museum of Tobacco Art and History, Centennial Park's Parthenon, which contains the tallest indoor sculpture in the Western world, Cheekwood Tennessee Botanical Gardens and Museum of Art, Winston-Derek's African Heritage Museum, Ryman Auditorium and Museum, which served as the former home of the Grand Ole Opry, the Country Music Hall of Fame and Museum; the Grand Ole Opry; Nashville's Breakfast Theater; Broadway Dinner Train, which travels past the Cumberland River over Civil War grounds to Andrew Jackson's home, the Hermitage; Chaffin's Barn Dinner Theatre; Opry Mills, a mega-mall under construction on the grounds of the former Opryland USA theme park; Nashville Black Heritage Tours; City Walk, a self-guided tour from Fort Nashborough to Music City USA; Belle Carol Riverboat Company, with cruises on the Cumberland River; Cheatham Wildlife Management Area. At Hermitage, The Hermitage: Home of Andrew Jackson (NHL) is the most popular historic attraction in Tennessee. The mansion was built in three phases between 1819 and 1836. From late May to late July, the annual Tennessee Jazz and Blues Society Concert Series is held on Sundays at the site and at Belle Meade.

HIKERS NEAR DRUMMOND

Stretching from Lake Champlain in New York to Lake Sakakawea in North Dakota, the longest national scenic trail beckons hikers to enjoy both adventure and solitude in a diverse setting steeped in the north country's natural beauty—lakes, streams, hardwood forests, prairies, and rolling farmlands.

North Country National Scenic Trail

Leaves is changin' overhead
Back from green to gray and red,
Brown and yeller, with their stems
Loosenin' on the oaks and e'ms

JAMES WHITCOMB RILEY, "OLD OCTOBER" (1883)

The North Country Trail corridor stretches through seven midwestern and northeastern states, from Lake Champlain in New York to Lake Sakakawea in North Dakota. Adventure as well as solitude are found amid scenes of a developing America and the undeveloped natural resources from which it grew. With 4,195 miles of trail planned, the North Country will eventually be the longest of all the national scenic trails.* Today, it is a work in progress, with more than 1,560 miles already certified. Diversity is its most alluring quality: hikers experience the Adirondack and Allegheny Mountains, rural countryside and farmlands, boreal forests, prehistoric Indian

*When Congress authorized the trail, its length was estimated at approximately 3,200 miles. However, as work progresses, it appears that it will stretch over 4,000 miles when completed.

ADMINISTRATING AGENCY
National Park Service
North Country National Scenic Trail
700 Rayovac Drive, Suite 100
Madison, WI 53711
608-264-5610
www.nps.gov/noco

FURTHER INFORMATION
North Country Trail Association
49 Monroe Center, NW, Suite 200B
Grand Rapids, MI 49503
888-454-NCTA (6282)
www.northcountrytrail.org

DESIGNATED
1980

APPROXIMATE MILEAGE
4,195 miles (6,712 km)*

STATES
New York, Pennsylvania, Ohio, Michigan, Wisconsin, Minnesota, North Dakota

mounds, windswept dunes, lake-studded glacial terrain, and the boundless expanse of the northern tall and shortgrass prairies. There are historic canal towpaths, massive rivers and playful streams, finger lakes and glacial bogs, and freshwater lakes with strong, proud, romantic names like Champlain, Michigan, Superior, and Sakakawea. Blankets of newly fallen snow in winter, gushing waterfalls and the delicate branches of white dogwood in spring, cool shade under the canopy of the lush broadleaf forests in summer, and the brilliant reds, oranges, and yellows of the northern hardwoods in the fall are some of the sublime natural experiences of a North Country trekker.

Backpack trips, day hikes, and short walks may lead to historic sites such as nineteenth-century canals, abandoned mining towns, or logging communities that tell a story of America's early settlement and growth as a nation. And the hills, valleys, lakes, and streams along the trail are the mark of the advancing and retreating glaciers that scraped the landscape a mere ten thousand to fifteen thousand years ago. The chance of a sighting of the ethereal northern lights brings a sense of mystery and calm to any North Country camping experience, while trout streams, beaches, lakes, and snow-blanketed terrain provide a rich natural playground for daytime trail adventures.

The History of the Trail

The concept of the Northern Country Trail originated in 1965 with the U.S. Forest Service's *Nationwide System of Trails Study.** The trail proposal was then included in the Department of the Interior's 1966, publication *Trails for America.* This publication set the stage for the congressional passage of the National Trails System Act of 1968, which designated the nation's first two national scenic trails and proposed fourteen other routes for feasibility studies as national trails. The North Country was one of the fourteen.

*Material in this section is taken from the National Park Service's *North Country Trail Comprehensive Plan for Management and Use* (September 1982).

Committees composed of representatives from the federal, state, local, and private sectors in each state formed to recommend a route. Their conceptual report, published in June 1975, concluded that Congress should authorize the trail with the provision that some portions were to be designated "scenic," which excludes motorized use, and some portions were to be designated national recreation trails, permitting possible motorized use, particularly snowmobiling. The report also recommended a 10-mile-wide planning corridor through which the final trail route would be located. Between 1975 and 1980 several bills were unsuccessfully introduced into Congress. Finally, on March 5, 1980, the entire trail was designated a national scenic trail when it was included in a package of amendments to the National Parks and Recreation Act of 1978. The secretary of the interior was named administrator of the North Country National Scenic Trail (NCT), a responsibility that was delegated to the National Park Service.

As originally authorized for study, the North Country Trail was to extend "from the Appalachian Trail in Vermont . . . to the Lewis and Clark Trail in North Dakota." However, Vermont expressed opposition to the connection with the Appalachian Trail because of the already heavy concentration of hikers on the Long and Appalachian Trails. As a result, this portion of the trail was not included in the trail definition as authorized in 1980. Since the earlier intention of Congress continues to have merit, the connection could be reconsidered in the future. Even without the extension, on completion the trail will be the longest continuous footpath in the country, stretching from the Vermont-New York border in the east to the North Dakota terminus of the Lewis and Clark National Historic Trail in the west.

Because the National Park Service collaborates with agencies at all levels of government and with various private sector interests, most of the responsibilities for managing the NCT are actually in the hands of state and local governments and private trail interests. In effect, this means that the NCT is actually a linear collection of new and existing federal, state, local, and private trails. A major benefit of national scenic trail designation, then, is the impetus it gives to the development of future links between these already existing trails. To provide leadership and support for trail development, the North Country Trail Association was formed in 1980.

AUTUMN COLOR

One fall day Great Bear was searching for a den, but celestial hunters were forced to slay their respected brother for food and winter clothing. When Great Bear's blood dripped down into the forest, it turned many of the leaves red, and others yellowed from the fat that splashed from the hunters' pan as they cooked the meat. Every fall since, the leaves in bear country display themselves in these spectacular colors to honor Great Bear. This story and many other legends explain why leaves change color each fall. Scientists also have an explanation that is just as interesting.

By late August or early September, a hint of color is seen in many trees, and long before the first frost, leaves start to display vibrant color. Research has shown that the coloring of leaves across the northern tier of states is a chemical reaction that occurs in broadleaf deciduous trees as the days shorten into winter. The process begins just after the longest day of the year, June 21, when the earth begins to tilt. As the sun retreats to the south, the days grow shorter, and the less direct sunlight causes cooler temperatures. This cooling sparks internal changes in trees that are manifested as changes in the color of the leaves.

All during spring and summer, the leaves have served as factories where most of the foods necessary for the trees' growth are manufactured.* This food-making process takes place in numerous cells in the leaf containing the pigment chlorophyll, which at other times of the year gives the leaf its green color. The chlorophyll absorbs energy from sunlight and uses it to transform carbon dioxide and water into carbohydrates, such as starch and simple sugars. This process, photosynthesis, goes on all summer as daylight hours lengthen. Toward the end of August, the shortened days and cooler weather cause hormonal changes that restrict the flow of nutrients to the leaves. This causes the chlorophyll to break down, and the green pigment is no longer visible in the leaf. What becomes visible are the pigments that were masked by the

*Some material in this section is taken from the U.S. Forest Service's brochure, *Why Leaves Change Color*.

stronger green color. Among these are the carotenes and xanthophyll pigments, which create the yellow and orange appearance.

At the same time, other chemical changes may occur that cause the formation of additional pigments that vary from yellow to red to blue. Some give rise to the reddish and purplish fall colors of sumacs. These colors are created by the mixing of varying amounts of the chlorophyll with other pigments in the leaf during the fall season. When warm sunny days are followed by nights below 45 degrees Fahrenheit, favorable conditions have been created for the formation of radiant red autumn colors. The warm days cause the food factories to start an on-again, off-again food-making process. During the day, sugars are made during photosynthesis, but the sugars cannot be carried from the leaves to other parts of the tree because of the cool nights. As a result, the sugar is trapped in the leaves, forming a vibrant red pigment, anthocyanin, which is found in red and sugar maples. Under favorable conditions, maples produce large amounts of anthocyanins. Although yellow can occur in predominantly red-leafed trees, yellow-leafed trees such as aspens cannot turn red because they do not produce anthocyanins. When the pigments fade, only brownish tannins remain.

The degree of fall color varies from tree to tree and year to year, depending on sun exposure and weather conditions. Leaves directly exposed to the sun may turn quite red, while those on the shady side of the same tree, or on other trees in the shade, may be yellow. Meanwhile, the foliage of some tree species may turn dull brown from death and decay. Contrary to popular belief, early frosts do not create the best colors. Sunny, warm days and cool nights create the best conditions. When there is much warm, cloudy, rainy weather in the fall, the leaves tend to have less red coloration, because the smaller amount of sugar made in the reduced sunlight moves out of the leaves during the warm nights. Only a few regions of the world are fortunate enough to have weather that produces dramatic fall color.

As the colorful display appears, other changes are also taking place that cause most of the broadleaf trees in the north to shed their leaves in the fall. At the base of the leafstalk, or petiole, where the leaf is attached to the twig, a special layer of cells develop. This abscission layer gradually severs the tissues that support the leaf, causing it to fall from its own weight or to come cascading down as a group with the first breeze. This action gives the season its name. Trees lose their leaves as a defense against the evaporation of precious liquids when food making becomes impossible because of the colder temperatures. There are only a few species, such as the oak, that hang on to their dead brown leaves until growth begins in the spring when their abscission layer grows.

The cycle of nourishment continues as the scar left behind by nature eventually heals the break on the twig, and the fallen leaves, which contain valuable elements taken from the soil, return to the ground and replenish it. As the leaves decompose, they enrich the top layers of the soil by returning part of the elements borrowed by the tree and simultaneously provide for more water-absorbing humus. Finally, North Country Trail hikers receive another kind of nourishment: a quiet cushion for weary feet and a breathtaking out-of-doors nature experience. Naturalists—young and old—can look for the perfect leaf specimen; families may practice their leaf and tree identification skills; and artists can trek to an awe-inspiring spot to splash an unbelievable spectrum of color onto the canvas.

The North Country National Scenic Trail, with its forested pathways, wetlands, waterfalls, sand dunes, gorges, tallgrass prairies, historic forts, museums, lighthouses, canals and locks, old logging routes, abandoned railroad grades, small rural communities, and wildernesses, has appeal for everyone. Both the pleasure walker and the experienced backpacker will enjoy the diversity that

The Trail Today

DRUMMOND WOODS

In northern Wisconsin, a 60-mile segment of certified trail helped to give birth to the concept of the North Country Trail. In Drummond Woods a stand of virgin pine and hemlock represent the timber that once covered all of the northern portion of the state before the logging era of the late 1800s.

the trail has to offer. In spring, the waterfalls are at their best and colorful wildflowers decorate forest floors. Sandy beaches persuade summer hikers to throw off their boots and splash and play in the waves. In fall, the green hardwood forest converts to a brilliant display of reds and golds. In winter, snow brings snowshoers and cross-country skiers to frozen falls after passing ice-glazed trees.

Diversity is rich on the North Country. Travelers can stop by Fort Stanwix National Monument in New York or visit a primeval forest in Pennsylvania's Allegheny National Forest. A cyclist can take a ride on the Little Miami Scenic Trail in Ohio or navigate a kayak around the sea arch that perforates the cliff at Grand Portal Point in Michigan. Primitive

camping in Wisconsin's North Woods provides an opportunity for relaxation and reflection. At Minnesota's Itasca State Park, a look at the headwaters of the continent's mightiest river, the Mississippi, is in order. And in season, above North Dakota's prairie, the open skies fill with millions of waterfowl as they travel the most extensive migratory bird flyway in North America.

Volunteers make the experience possible. The North Country Trail Association coordinates the volunteer effort and is the primary partner of the National Park Service. The association works closely with its chapters and affiliates, for example, the Finger Lakes Trail Conference, the Buckeye Trail Association, the Northwest Ohio Rails-to-Trails Association, the Superior Hiking Trail Association, and the American Youth Hostel Pittsburgh Conference. Each organization maintains its trail segments. The certified sections of the NCNST are marked with the trail's logo, an eight-pointed star, and supplemented by other types of markings, such as paint blazes and wooden signs that provide information on distance and direction.

To date, one-third of the NCT is complete and open for hiking. A limited number of segments allow bicycling, mountain biking, horseback riding, cross-country skiing, snowshoeing, and even sled-dog travel, but the intent of the NPS is to create a premier hiking experience. Local management officials should be contacted for trail-use restrictions. Camping is popular along the trail, but it is worth noting that regulations vary. It is wise to check with local managers in advance. Permission to pitch a tent on private property requires the approval of the property owner. Every attempt should be made to respect the rights of landowners. An additional caution to note is that the woods can be dangerous during hunting season. If one is venturing into the woodlands at this time of the year, chances of coming out improve dramatically if hunter's orange or bright yellow is worn, as opposed to brown and white. Other precautions, such as the use of bug repellents, is advisable, especially from May to late September when the mosquitoes and blackflies are out.

NCT PATCHES

After traveling the Glacier Ridge Trail and passing a restored grist mill at McConnell's Mill State Park, the NCT enters Ohio, where it follows a U-shaped pattern that makes use of much of the Buckeye Trail.

Because the NCT is more than 4,000 miles long, few individuals have attempted to complete it from end to end in one season. Opinions vary about whether it is better to start from the eastern or western terminus, because winter hits both ends before the hike can be completed. To accomplish the feat in 1978, Carolyn Hoffman snowshoed the first six weeks in New York, cycled several hundred miles in Ohio, and hiked the remainder of the trail to Lake Sakakawea, arriving 222 days later. Ed Talone took a novel approach in March 1994 when he bisected the trail in Cincinnati, started there and headed to Crown Point in New York, returned via Amtrak to Cincinnati, and trekked the other half to North Dakota the same year. Sue Lockwood, diabetic and blind, completed 2,800 miles with Talone, although hospitalization interrupted her eastern segment. Lockwood rejoined Talone in Michigan to complete the remainder of the trek. Her brother, Gordon Smith, followed behind in a van to permit Lockwood's daily dialysis treatments. Chet Fromm took another approach; he completed the trail end to end over four summers. Most of these treks are described at Web sites linked to the North Country Trail Association site. Byron and Margaret Hutchins have written

CROWN POINT STATE HISTORIC SITE AND
CHAMPLAIN BRIDGE

At the NCT'S eastern terminus near
Champlain Bridge, New York's Crown
Point State Historic Site holds the original ruins of one of the largest fortifications in colonial America. The national
historic landmark, strategically located
on a peninsula that forms the northernmost narrows of Lake Champlain, was
occupied during the French and Indian
and Revolutionary Wars.

the best single guidebook on the
trail. It is available from the
North Country Trail Store at
www.northcountrytrail.org.

Potential new segments of the
North Country will make the trail
even more difficult through-
hikers to complete before winter
sets in. One of the most exciting
alterations is in Minnesota, where
a new route will head north to the
Boundary Waters Canoe Area
Wilderness. Updates can be found
on www.northcountrytrail.org,
where Wes Boyd posts excellent

trail descriptions, and a detailed
set of maps can be obtained from
the North Country Trail Store.
Other maps can be obtained free
or for a nominal fee from the
National Park Service, the U.S.
Forest Service, local managing
authorities, and North Country
Trail Association affiliates.
County maps are usually available
from the chamber of commerce
of the appropriate county.

The North Country Trail's eastern terminus is located at Crown
Point State Historic Site in New
York, where the bridge across Lake
Champlain leads in the opposite
direction to Vermont for a possible future connection to that
state's famous Long Trail. At this
historic military fort, interpretive
trails and cross-country ski trails
traverse the park to its southern
boundary. From this point, there
is no segment leading to central
New York, but discussions are
under way to connect the North
Country with a proposed trail in

the 6-million-acre Adirondack Park. It would pass through old-growth forest, skirt waterfalls, and reward the hiker with scenic vistas from hilltops. West of the Adirondacks, the trail is composed of discontinuous segments. The Black River Feeder Canal heads west from Forestport to the community of Boonville. Turning southward, the trail meanders along the Old Black River Canal through and beyond Pixley Falls State Park where the Five Combine Locks can be explored. A potential route leads through wooded hills to the city of Rome where, in the center of town, Fort Stanwix National Monument is located. At Rome's western edge, the Old Erie Canal Village re-creates an 1840s canal village.

From Rome, the national recreation trail in the linear Old Erie Canal State Park can be taken as far as Syracuse. At Canastota, the route leaves the canal to follow state-owned portions of an abandoned railroad past Chittenango Falls State Park to Cazenovia. Near Fabius, a route connects with the Onondaga portion of the Finger Lakes Trail (FLT)*

ON A GLACIAL LAKE

The NCT leaves New York through Allegany State Park, heading into Allegheny National Forest in Pennsylvania above.

*The FLT, developed and maintained by the Finger Lakes Trail Conference, is an east-west trail running 552 miles from the Catskill Mountains in the east to the Allegheny Mountains in the west, with forests, lakes, glacial topography, secluded glens, and waterfalls set among rolling hills and farmland in the remote areas of the southern tier of New York. Maps can be purchased from the Finger Lakes Trail Conference in Rochester, New York.

where cross-country skiers and snowshoers use the footpath in the winter. The NCT follows 363 miles of the 552-mile FLT through intermittent certified segments as it passes glens, gorges, and seven of the eleven glacier-carved Finger Lakes. There are hundreds of recreation spots in the area with opportunities for a variety of outdoor activities. Bicycle tours are especially popular. After Cortland, the trail pushes on toward state parks near Ithaca. Before reaching Allegany State Park, the traveler is treated to the colorful gorge and waterfalls of Watkins Glen State Park and the canyons of the Genesee River in Letchworth State Park. At Allegany State Park, the NCT travels through nearly 20 miles of northern hardwood forest to the Pennsylvania border.

The initial 87-mile certified segment of the NCT in

Pennsylvania follows an existing trail past much of the large Allegheny Reservoir and through the rolling hills and stream valleys of the Allegheny National Forest. A number of campgrounds are located along this segment, and the scenery is outstanding. In spring, dogwood, rhododendrons, and Pennsylvania's state flower, mountain laurel, provide a colorful appearance. The forest provides habitat for a variety of wildlife, including black bears, deer, wild turkey, grouse, and pheasants. Bass, muskie, northern pike, and trout inhabit the streams and reservoir. Historic points of interest include remnants of a once-booming oil industry. At Dunham Siding, the trail to Heart's Content leads to a tract of old-growth beech and hemlock. After reaching the forest's southern boundary, the trail follows the Baker Trail through Clear Creek State Forest lands and Cook Forest State Park to the Clarion River. At the river, the national trail leaves the Baker Trail, and moves southwest to certified segments of Moraine State Park's Glacier Ridge Trail and on to McConnell's Mill State Park through the gorge of Slippery Rock Creek and over an old covered bridge.

Entering Ohio, the route parallels Little Beaver Creek, a certified segment along the national scenic river, and passes the historic communal settlement of Zoar. At Bolivar, it joins the Buckeye Trail, established by the volunteer efforts of the Buckeye Trail Association.* For nearly 600 miles, the NCT moves on and off the horseshoe-shaped Buckeye Trail that is always open to hikers, and in selected areas, it is also open to bicyclists and horseback riders primarily on the leg from Cincinnati northward. It is important to check with local authorities for the NCT trail-use restrictions. A host of recreation areas, reservoirs, nature areas, prehistoric archaeological sites, and many historic sites are found along the trail. Near Seneca Lake, the NCT leaves the Buckeye Trail to follow the scenic Little Muskingham River through the eastern unit of the Wayne National Forest. Near Stockport, the trails connect once again and push on through some of Ohio's most outstanding scenery. The middle unit of the Wayne National Forest presents stunning fall color and comes alive with redbud and dogwood blooms in spring. Along the way, state memorials commemorate prehistoric Indian cultures and the route travels near the bluffs and caves of the scenic Hocking Hills region. Side trips to archaeological mound sites should not be missed. In the Shawnee State Forest, the NCT uses a portion of the Shawnee Backpack Trail, which passes through steep hills, tall trees, and clear streams.

Before reaching Cincinnati, the NCT turns northward to follow a

*Maps on the Buckeye Trail can be purchased from the Buckeye Trail Association in Worthington, Ohio.

MARTIN HOUSE

After traveling through forests past rivers and lakes, the NCT crosses the Mississippi River to enter the northern prairies of North Dakota.

OHIO PIONEER VILLAGE

On Ohio's western side, the NCT passes near Pioneer Village at Caesar Creek State Park near Waynesville. Pioneer Village contains numerous restored log structures of early Ohio pioneers with period furnishings, a blacksmith shop, and a Quaker meetinghouse that had ties to the Underground Railroad.

certified segment of rail trail at Little Miami Scenic State Park near Milford. This portion of the Buckeye Trail parallels the Little Miami National Scenic River and is one of the longest paved recreational trails in the country. Cycling is popular along this portion of the trail, and the river presents opportunities for canoeing and kayaking. John Bryan State Park's limestone gorge contrasts with the rich, flat farmlands in the western portion of the state. Side trips lead to Caesar Creek State Park and Antioch University's Glen Helen Nature Preserve. The Buckeye Trail enters Dayton, the birthplace of aviation, which has a network of city and county parks, but the route of

the NCT bypasses it and continues to Troy. From here, the route makes use of off-road sections of the Buckeye Trail through Piqua and Lockington, past the remains and locks of the old Miami and Erie Canal, an abandoned railroad, certified segments at Lake Loramie, Grand Lake, St. Marys, and Independence Dam before crossing into Michigan.

The trail meanders northwestward across southern Michigan through local farmlands, state and local recreation areas, an abandoned railroad grade, and greenways. Southeast of Grand

Rapids, the route follows potential and existing certified segments through Battle Creek, the University of Michigan's Kellogg Biological Station, and Yankee Springs Recreation Area. The trail route skirts east of Grand Rapids, Michigan's second-largest city. A certified section at Rogue River State Game Area precedes the Manistee National Forest, where over 125 miles of trail, almost all certified, pass over sandy soil through open woodlands and rolling hills and along several beautiful rivers. The trail then passes over numerous certified segments, such as the 24-mile segment of the Shore-to-Shore Riding-Hiking Trail, developed and maintained by the Michigan Trail Riders Association in cooperation with the Michigan Department of Natural Resources and the National Forest Service. East of Kalkaska, the trail swings northward through Pere Marquette and Mackinaw State Forests into the Jordan River valley. The Jordan River Pathway, a national recreation trail, passes scenic and historical points of interest. Short stretches of existing state forest pathways continue northward through Mackinaw State Forest to Wilderness State Park past the Lake Michigan shore near excellent fishing spots for smallmouth bass. Continuing northward, the route reaches the Straits of Mackinac and the Mackinac Bridge. Reconstructed Fort Michilimackinac provides excellent historic interpretation of the pre–Revolutionary War and fur trade eras. A ferry ride to Mackinac Island offers an opportunity to visit Fort Mackinac and the island's other historic and scenic sites. One can shuttle across the five-mile Mackinac Bridge. The bridge can only be walked southbound (with thousands of others) during the Labor Day Bridge Walk.

In Michigan's Upper Peninsula, approximately 12,000 miles of streams work their way through forests, along with more than 150 waterfalls. Most of the trail segments are certified here. Starting at the Father Marquette National Memorial and Museum in Saint Ignace, the traveler has an opportunity to learn about Marquette, the early explorer. Reaching all the way to Ironwood, long segments of the national trail are in place. Entering the Hiawatha National Forest, the NCT follows existing trail to a complex of campgrounds at Brevort Lake and proceeds through stands of hardwoods and pines past lakes, wetlands, and vestiges of old logging camps and homesteads to the south shore of Lake Superior—the largest fresh-water lake in the world. From here the trail takes a turn west to Tahquamenon Falls State Park, which contains the Upper and Lower Falls of the Tahquamenon River. The Upper Tahquamenon Falls, the second-largest cataract east of the Mississippi River (sometimes called Little Niagara), gained fame in Henry Wadsworth Longfellow's *Song of Hiawatha*. Continuing beyond the park,

RUNNER ON THE BEACH AT LAKE
SUPERIOR

At Pictured Rocks National Lakeshore,
the NCT travels along the shores of
beautiful Lake Superior, the world's
largest freshwater lake, while falcons
soar above the towering sandstone cliffs.

through Lake Superior State
Forest, Muskallonge Lake State
Park, and Pictured Rocks
National Lakeshore, the hiker
experiences miles of Lake
Superior's outstanding scenic
shoreline with its dunes, intrigu-
ing rock formations, multicolored
sandstone cliffs, and dramatic
views.

At Pictured Rocks National
Lakeshore, falcons fly above the
cliffs as waves pound against the
formidable shoreline and caress
the towering sandstone walls.
This 43-mile segment of the trail,
which alternates between beach
level and cliff level, is considered
by some to be the most beautiful
along the entire NCNST. Campgrounds along this dramatic trail

are found at convenient distances,
and visitor centers are available
for backpackers, who need a
permit to hike through Pictured
Rocks. The Fox River Pathway
provides a side trip to Seney
National Wildlife Refuge, the
largest refuge east of the
Mississippi River. Leaving
Pictured Rocks National
Lakeshore, the trail enters the
western unit of the Hiawatha
National Forest past Bay De
Noc–Grand Island National
Recreation Trail. The NCT route
continues through exceptional
scenery to beautiful Laughing
Whitefish Falls on its way to
Marquette, Little Presque Isle
State Recreation Area, and the
very pretty 7-mile segment at
Craig Lake State Park. One of the
wildest sections of the trail
follows in the Ottawa National
Forest and the Porcupine
Mountains Wilderness State Park.
The park is one of the few
remaining large wilderness areas

in the Midwest. It has an outstanding trail system, untouched forest, wild rivers, and waterfalls. For several miles, the route lies just inside the park's southern boundary before it reenters the national forest and makes its way south to Ironwood.

The route enters Wisconsin through the Gabbro-Penokee-Gogebic Iron Range. Memorabilia of the area's rich mining, logging, and farming heritage is displayed in Hurley at the Iron County Historical Museum. Iron County is home to some of the state's most beautiful waterfalls. At Copper Falls State Park, where Tyler Forks River joins the Bad River, the waterfalls, canyons, streams, and stands of aspen, basswood, birch, conifer maple, and red oak are enchanting, particularly in fall. The certified segment follows existing trails through the park and into Mellen, called the "Black Bear Capital of the World," gateway to the Chequamegon National Forest. The NCT soon begins to follow the 60-mile certified segment in the Chequamegon National Forest that bears the name "North Country Trail." This was the first authorized segment of the NCT and essentially gave the longer trail its name. From the east, this portion proceeds through the Penokee Range. There are magnificent overlooks and opportunities for excellent fly fishing on the Marengo River. The western reaches of the trail cross through glaciated terrain and a mix of hardwoods and conifers in the more secluded Porcupine Lake Wilderness. At scenic Lake Owen, the trail winds through stands of large white pines and hemlocks. Near Drummond, in Drummond Woods, there is an interpretive loop that explains the history of the area's white pines. In the Rainbow Lake Wilderness, travelers pass glaciated lake terrain enhanced by mixed hardwoods, aspen, and conifers. Leaving the national forest, the trail passes through county forest lands, then enters the Brule River State Forest certified segment, a place to experience the solitude of wilderness, spectacular vistas of the Brule River valley, or exciting whitewater canoeing or kayaking. The trail parallels the south side of the river and then follows a historic portage for 2 miles to connect with the Saint Croix River. This 2.2-mile segment has been used for hundreds of years by Indians, explorers, and traders. South of Solon Springs, the NCT proceeds through the Douglas County Wildlife Area—managed for sharptail grouse and other prairie species—before it reaches the upper end of the beautiful Saint Croix River. After paralleling the national scenic riverway for a few miles, the planned route turns north along the Moose River. After reaching the Black River, the trail passes through Pattison State Park—home of Wisconsin's highest waterfall. Here Big Manitou Falls has water that crashes 165 feet as the trail reaches the Wisconsin-Minnesota state line southeast of Jay Cooke State Park.

FALL COLOR IN MICHIGAN

From the southern farmlands in Michigan, across the Mackinac Bridge, through strands of hardwoods in the state's Upper Peninsula, the NCT route in Michigan totals nearly 900 miles—the most in any state.

In Minnesota, the trail moves north by way of the Saint Croix and Nemadji State Forests and one of the state's wildest parks, Saint Croix, to the forests and vistas of Jay Cooke State Park near Duluth. At Jay Cooke a suspension bridge permits the hiker to cross the rock-lined rapids of the Saint Louis River. Several public and private camping areas are located in this area.

A study of a major new route in Minnesota is under way. This new route would turn north from Jay Cooke to follow the outstanding Superior Hiking Trail along the ridge of the Sawtooth Mountains. After following the western shore of Lake Superior to near Grand Portage National Monument, the planned route will turn west through Superior National Forest and follow the Border Route Trail and the Kekekabic Trail and then rejoin the present route at the eastern edge of Chippewa National Forest.

In Chippewa National Forest, home of the largest concentrations of bald eagles* in the coterminous United States, the certified segment extends for 68 miles through stands of pine and past Leech Lake. Near the forest's western edge, the route intersects the Heartland Trail, an abandoned railroad right-of-way that runs from Walker to Park Rapids. The NCT continues westward from Chippewa National Forest along a route through Paul Bunyan State Forest and into a

*If an eagle is spotted, the viewer should break his or her body outline by sitting down. Repeated motion caused by trying to get closer constitutes harassment.

During spring and early summer, NCT trekkers experience fields of wildflowers. Black-eyed susans (*Rudbeckia hirta*) are seen in prairies, fields, and open woods.

certified segment at Itasca State Park and the headwaters of the mighty Mississippi. A short certified segment on Clearwater County Forest lands extends to Gardiner Lake. The route enters the White Earth State Forest and the 43,000-acre Tamarack National Wildlife Refuge. The forest and wetlands provide habitat for many animals and birds, including bald eagles, loons, and trumpeter swans. From the refuge, the trail proceeds to and through the rolling wooded hills of Maplewood State Park. A view of the area from Hallaway Hill is especially lovely in the fall when the foliage of the maples and other hardwoods takes on a brilliant hue. Just beyond Maplewood State Park, the route turns due west toward North Dakota, exiting Minnesota at Breckenridge.

In North Dakota the route enters the northern reaches of the Great Plains, where rolling, fertile farmland and vast prairies are punctuated with patchy burr-oak savannas, quaking aspen, elm, and cottonwood. Past the Minnesota border, the route passes Fort Abercrombie State Historic Site. The fort, which once served as the gateway for several major travel routes to the Dakota frontier, now serves as the NCT's gateway into the state and the Red River Valley. In the Sheyenne National Grassland, a 25-mile certified segment takes hikers and horseback riders past tallgrass prairie with native grasses and forbs and cattle grazing areas. Overhead, millions of waterfowl travel the biggest migratory bird flyway in North America every spring and fall. After a certified segment in the Sheyenne State Forest, the route reaches another at Fort Ransom State Park in the scenic Sheyenne River valley. Continuing northward toward North Dakota's lakes country, the trail reaches Sully's Hill National Game Preserve, where buffalo, elk, deer, and other wildlife enjoy the native habitat and geese, ducks, and sandhill cranes fill the skies during migratory seasons. After passing Fort Totten State Historic Site on the Devil's Lake Sioux Indian Reservation, the route recrosses the Sheyenne River and reaches a 147-mile certified segment along the New Rockford and McCluskey Canals, including a segment through Lonetree National Wildlife Area in eastern Sheridan County. Cattle are not allowed here, and the prairie can be experienced much as it was when the pioneers passed through. Booming grounds for prairie chickens and sharptail grouse offer a unique bird-watching experience. Hikers need to exercise care during the mating season. At the west end of the McCluskey Canal, the route passes through Audubon National Wildlife Refuge before reaching the western terminus at Lake Sakakawea State Park, near Pick City. From here, the energetic traveler can follow the Lewis and Clark National Historic Trail (see *America's National Historic Trails*).

NEW YORK (625 MILES)

1. CROWN POINT STATE HISTORIC SITE. Located near Champlain Bridge at Crown Point, the ruins (NHL) of the French fort Saint Frederic (1734) and the British fort Crown Point (1759) comprise the remains of one of the largest fortifications in colonial America. Its strategic location on a peninsula at the northernmost narrows of Lake Champlain gave it importance during the French and Indian and Revolutionary Wars. A visitor center offers exhibits and interpretation. *Other attractions:* Crown Point Reservation State Campground offers hiking, boating, fishing, and cross-country skiing; Champlain Memorial Lighthouse, with a sculpture by Auguste Rodin, offers a view; Champlain Trail, a lakeside scenic byway; Champlain Canal; Penfield Homestead Museum in the Ironwood District of Crown Point has summer tours. *Nearby:* In Ticonderoga, the restored colonial Fort Ticonderoga (NHL), also called "Carillon," was built by the French in 1755. MV *Carillon* offers history cruises on Lake Champlain; Fort Ticonderoga Ferry travels to Vermont; Ticonderoga Heritage Museum; Boston Hancock House, for displays of local art. "Champ," a legendary serpentine monster said to have first been sighted by American Indians and Samuel de Champlain (1609), is still seen by some today.

2. ADIRONDACK PARK. In 1885 the New York legislature created a forest preserve to protect the Adirondack Mountains and the Catskill wilderness to the south. Seven years later, in 1892, a three-million-acre park was formed that has grown to 6.2 million acres of protected lands, about 40 percent of which is state owned. It is the largest park in the lower forty-eight states, including both state and national parks, and has two visitor centers. Paul Smiths has nature exhibits and information on regional ecosystems, and Newcomb Center near Long Lake has exhibits on Adirondack natural history and rents snowshoes, and the Adirondack Museum at Blue Mountain provides comprehensive information about the park, which has 46

Points of Interest

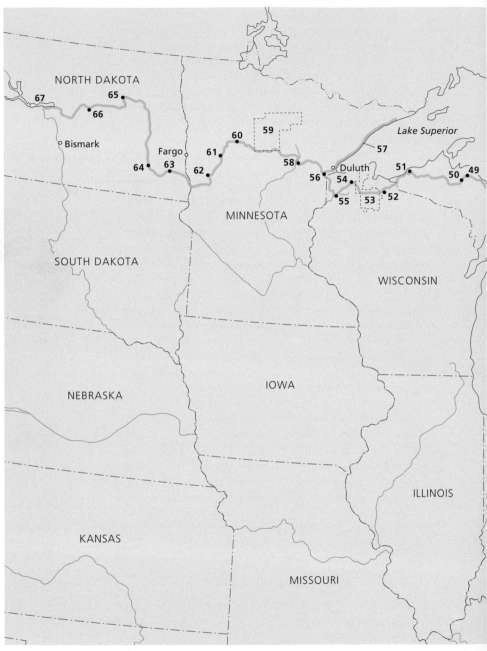

NORTH COUNTRY NATIONAL SCENIC TRAIL

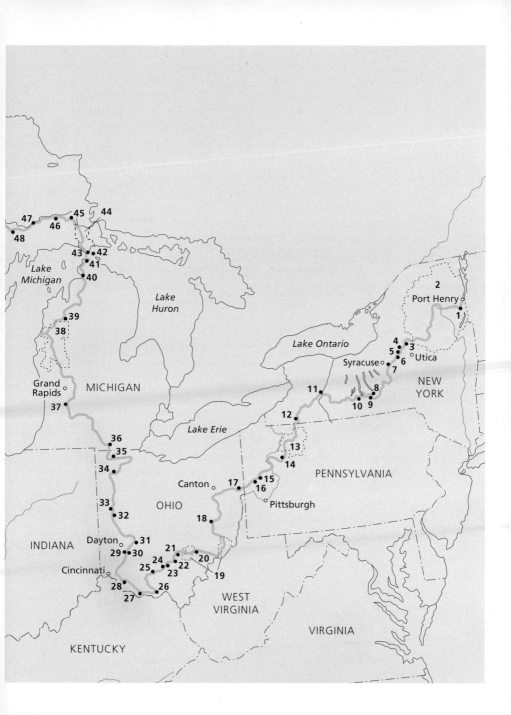

Lake Michigan

47
46
45
44
48

43 42
41
40

Lake Huron

39
38

Grand Rapids
37

MICHIGAN

36
35
34

Lake Erie

33
32

INDIANA

Dayton
31
29 30

Cincinnati

Canton
17 15
16

OHIO

Pittsburgh

18

21
24 22 20
25 23
19
28 26
27

WEST VIRGINIA

KENTUCKY

Lake Ontario

Port Henry
2
1

4 3
5 6 Utica
Syracuse 7

11
8
10 9

NEW YORK

12

13
14

PENNSYLVANIA

VIRGINIA

mountain peaks, 42 campgrounds, 750 miles of trail, and a 125-mile canoe route. The Adirondack Mountain Club is a new partner of the NCT and can be very helpful in planning a hike. Activities include hiking, bicycling, horseback riding, scenic driving, bird-watching, fishing and ice-fishing, boating, canoeing, rafting, cross-country and downhill skiing, snowshoeing, dogsled racing, snowmobiling, and naturalist programs. The Adirondack Scenic Railroad operates out of Thendara Station, just south of Old Forge.

3. PIXLEY FALLS STATE PARK. Five Combine Locks of the Black River Canal, part of the feeder system for the Erie Canal, can be visited at the park near Boonville. Activities include camping, fishing, hiking, and cross-country skiing. *Other activities:* In Boonville, the Black River Trail scenic drive; the glacial Rome-Boonville Gorge; the canal towpath, for hiking and cross-country skiing.

4. DELTA LAKE STATE PARK. The park, northeast of Rome, offers camping, hiking, bicycling, fishing, swimming, boating, cross-country skiing, snowshoeing, snowmobiling, performing arts, and recreation programs.

5. FORT STANWIX NATIONAL MONUMENT. Located in Rome, the fort was originally built during the French and Indian War and repaired later by American rebels. The American stand (1777) here was a major factor in repulsing a large army of British regulars, American loyalists, and Iroquois Indians during the Revolutionary War. The fort was also the site of the treaty of Fort Stanwix with the Iroquois (1768). The current star-shaped earth-and-log reconstruction has a museum and costumed guides. *Other attractions:* Erie Canal Village, a restored canal town, has trips aboard an 1840 horse-drawn packetboat along a restored part of the canal; State Fish Hatchery.

6. OLD ERIE CANAL STATE PARK. This linear park from Rome to DeWitt, near Syracuse, contains 36 miles of original canal that passes through Oneida, Chittenango, and Fayetteville. The NCT follows the trail for 20 miles. The Erie Canal once linked Albany on the Hudson River with Buffalo on the Great Lakes. Plans are in progress for the Canal Way Trail System to connect segments of the canal so that it can be followed for its entire length. Historic sites of Old Erie Canal State Park include the remains of lime kilns, canal era buildings, and a museum. Activities include hiking, bicycling, fishing, canoeing, cross-country skiing, snowmobiling, and ice skating.

7. CHITTENANGO FALLS STATE PARK. The main feature of this state park is the 167-foot waterfall. Located 4 miles from Cazenovia, the park offers tent and trailer sites, hiking, fishing, and performing arts and recreational programs. *Other activities:* In Cazenovia, the Lorenzo State Historic Site is composed of a federal period mansion and

garden. *Nearby:* In Syracuse, the Erie Canal Museum and canal cruises; Everson Museum of Art; Lowe Art Gallery at Syracuse University; Landmark Theatre (1928); Onondaga Historical Association Museum; Onondaga Lake Park, with the Salt Museum and Sainte Marie among the Iroquois, a re-created seventeenth-century mission with costumed interpreters; Beaver Lake Nature Center, a 600-acre preserve; and Green Lakes State Park, with a swimming beach.

8. BUTTERMILK FALLS STATE PARK. Near Ithaca, the falls descend more than 500 feet to a natural pool in the gorge, where swimming is permitted. A steep trail by the falls leads to Pinnacle Rock, a spirelike rock formation that towers 40 feet in the air. There are six other falls, cabins, and bathhouses. Activities include camping, hiking, bird-watching, fishing, boating, cross-country skiing, and snowshoeing. *Other activities:* In Ithaca, the Dewitt Historical Society makes available Finger Lakes history; Herbert F. Johnson Museum of Art; Cornell Plantations, along the Cascadilla and Fall Creek gorges, has trails and botanical gardens; Sapsucker Woods, the home of the Cornell Laboratory of Ornithology, has sanctuary trails and migrating birds; Stewart Park, on Cayuga Lake, adjoins the Fuertes Wild Fowl Preserve and the Renwick Bird Sanctuary; Cayuga Nature Center offers hiking and nature study. *Nearby:* In Jacksonville, Taughannock Falls State Park,

features a 215-foot vertical falls that is higher than Niagara Falls, trails on the edge of the gorge, camping, hiking, swimming, tennis, cross-country skiing, snowshoeing, a summer recreation program, and a summer concert series.

9. ROBERT H. TREMAN STATE PARK. The NCT runs through the length of the park, near Ithaca, which features twelve waterfalls, including the 115-foot Lucifer Falls. Near the upper entrance are the upper falls, a four-story grist mill (1839), and the Gorge Trail, which leads to the waterfalls and rectangular pools in Devil's Kitchen. Facilities include cabins, a beach with a bathhouse, and a waterfall with a swimming area. Activities include camping, camper recreation, hiking, fishing, swimming, cross-country skiing, and snowshoeing. *Nearby:* Allen H. Treman State Marine Park provides access to Cayuga Lake, the longest of the eleven Finger Lakes. Activities include fishing and boating. Finger Lakes National Forest has 2.4 miles of NCT, camping, horseback riding, fishing, cross-country skiing, snowshoeing, and nature study. Finger Lakes National Forest, between Seneca and Cayuga Lakes, has 4 miles of the Finger Lakes Trail.

10. WATKINS GLEN STATE PARK. The park, near Trumansburg, has a spectacular gorge and nineteen waterfalls. Stone steps and bridges on the Gorge Trail pass waterfalls and pools, while a staircase called

Jacob's Ladder leads to the north rim where the NCNST is routed. Activities include camping, camper recreation, hiking, fishing, swimming, boating, cross-country skiing, snowshoeing, and an evening laser show that takes the viewer back through natural and human history at the gorge. *Other activities:* Near Watkins Glen, the Farm Sanctuary offers tours of a working farm and a visitor center; boat tours of Seneca Lake; bird-watching in Queen Catherine Marsh in Montour Falls. *Nearby:* Elmira, Sullivan's Monument at Newton Battlefield has occasional reenactments of the Revolutionary War battle, camping, hiking, and bicycling; grave of Mark Twain is located at Woodlawn Cemetery; *Mark Twain* the Musical.

11. LETCHWORTH STATE PARK. The 14,340-acre park has an impressive 17-mile, 600-foot gorge known as the "Grand Canyon of the East." Other features include three waterfalls, the William Pryor Letchworth Pioneer and Indian Museum, and a restored Seneca Indian council house. Facilities include the Glen Iris Inn (1914), cabins, and a swimming pool with bathhouse. Activities include camping, hiking, bicycling, fishing, swimming, rafting, tubing, cross-country skiing, ice skating, snowmobiling, recreation programs, and a summer concert series. The park, near Castile, is only 30 miles south of Rochester and the Seaway Trail National Scenic Byway.

12. ALLEGANY STATE PARK. Nearly 20 miles of NCT pass through New York's largest state park (over 67,000 acres) near Salamanca. The park is divided into two distinct recreation areas named for the two large lakes: Quaker and Red House. It has cabins, beaches with bathhouse, a boat launch, and bicycle, boat, and ski rental. Activities include camping, hiking, bicycling, horseback riding, fishing, swimming, boating, cross-country skiing, snowshoeing, and snowmobiling. *Other activities:* In Salamanca, Seneca-Iroquois National Museum on the Allegany Indian Reservation exhibits the history and contemporary culture of the Seneca Nation. *Nearby:* In Jamestown, the Audubon Nature Center has a 600-acre wildlife sanctuary and the Roger Tory Peterson Nature Building; Panorama Rocks Park is a massive rock outcrop of a primeval seashore formation.

PENNSYLVANIA (300 MILES)

13. ALLEGHENY NATIONAL FOREST. Pennsylvania's only national forest covers 513,000 acres and includes nearly 87 miles of the NCT. Headquarters is located in Warren, and ranger stations are located near Bradford, Marienville, and Ridgeway. Kinzua Dam has a visitor center with displays, six boat launches, and a marina on the Allegheny Reservoir. Five of the forest's sixteen campgrounds are approachable only by foot or

boat. Hickory Creek Wilderness provides primitive camping and wildlife viewing, and Allegheny Islands Wilderness on the Allegheny River is the smallest federally designated wilderness. Canoeing is popular on the Allegheny Wild and Scenic River, the Clarion River, and Tionesta Creek. Buckaloons Recreation Area, site of a former Indian village on the banks of the Allegheny River, has a boat launch and the Seneca Interpretive Trail. A highlight along the NCT is a section of old-growth forest in the Tionesta Scenic Area. Activities include camping, hiking, bicycling, fishing, swimming, boating, waterskiing, canoeing, cross-country skiing, snowshoeing, and naturalist programs. *Other attractions:* Chapman State Park, located in the Allegheny National Forest and state game lands, has 7 miles of trail that connect with the NCT. There is a lake on the West Branch of Tionesta Creek, a boat launch, rentals, and a warming hut. Activities include camping (rustic/electrical hookups), hiking, fishing, swimming, boating, cross-country skiing, snowshoeing, ice fishing, ice skating, snowmobiling, sledding, tobogganing, Winter Carnival, and environmental education.

14. COOK FOREST STATE PARK. The park, near Cooksburg, accommodates 8 miles of the NCT in an impressive stand of virgin white pine and hemlock that has been designated a national natural landmark. The NCT links with certified trail in neighboring Clear Creek State Forest. Linked with the Allegheny National Forest segment, the three segments combine to form a 97-mile continuous trail. Facilities in the state park include cabins, Green Acres Stable, a swimming pool, and a visitor and historical center. Activities include camping, hiking, horseback riding, fishing, swimming, canoeing, tubing, water-sliding, cross-country skiing, ice skating, snowmobiling, sledding, tobogganing, and environmental education. Clarion River Country Days are held in June. *Nearby:* In Clarion, the Clarion County Historical Society Museum exhibits area artifacts in the mid-nineteenth-century Sutton-Ditz house; the Autumn Leaf Festival and Parade is held in October.

15. MORAINE STATE PARK. The park, near Portersville, is named for the ground moraine deposited by the Wisconsin Ice Sheet. The NCT travels for almost 15 miles on the Glacier Ridge Trail. The park's Lake Arthur is a restoration of an extinct glacial lake (see IANST). Facilities include cabins, a marina, beaches and bathhouse, and boat and bicycle rentals. Activities include camping, horseback riding, bicycling, fishing, swimming, cross-country skiing, ice fishing, ice boating, ice skating, snowmobiling, sledding, tobogganing, and environmental education.

16. MCCONNELL'S MILL STATE PARK. Near Portersville, this national landmark park

offers free guided tours of the restored grist mill in summer. Nearly 10 miles of NCT link with the Moraine State Park and the Jennings area trail segments. Picnic areas, hiking trails, and a historical center are available. Activities include hiking, fishing, white-water rafting, canoeing, kayaking, climbing and rappeling, sledding, and environmental education.

OHIO (1,050 MILES)

17. BEAVER CREEK STATE PARK. Over 6 miles of NCT pass through the park in the foothills of the Appalachians near East Liverpool. The area features forestland, streams, ruins of the Sandy and Beaver Canal, a well-preserved lock, and the restored Gaston's Mill (1837). Little Beaver Creek was an initial component of the National Wild and Scenic Rivers System. Activities include camping, hiking, horseback riding, fishing, canoeing (rentals), and ice skating. *Nearby:* In Canton, McKinley National Memorial and the adjacent McKinley Museum of History, Science, and Industry. The Cuyahoga Valley National Recreation Area, north of Akron, has a visitor center for the Ohio and Erie Canal (see Lake Loramie, Grand Lake Saint Marys, and Independence Dam below). At Zoar, the Zoar Garden and State Memorial is a quaint village that served as a refuge from religious persecution for German Separatists in 1817. In New Philadelphia, Schoenbrunn

Village State Memorial displays a partial reconstruction of Ohio's first settlement; "Trumpet of the Land" is a seasonal outdoor drama about the Christianizing of the Delaware Indians; Muskingum Watershed Conservancy District is a Muskingum River flood control and recreation project with a lake, marinas, and campgrounds. At Gnadenhutten, the Gnadenhutten Historical Park and Museum has an Indian burial mound and monument to Christian American Indians who were massacred in 1782; Tappan Lake Park.

18. SALT FORK STATE PARK. Ohio's largest state park, near Cambridge, has 3 miles of the NCT along with miles of shoreline on Salt Fort Lake. Activities include camping, hiking, horseback riding, fishing, swimming, boating, cross-country skiing, snowmobiling, sledding, ice skating, golf, and summer programs. *Other activities:* At Cambridge, the Hopalong Cassidy Festival held each April, honors hometown star, William Boyd. *Nearby:* Senecaville Lake near Buffalo and Wolf Lake State Park.

19. WAYNE NATIONAL FOREST. Approximately 35 miles of the NCT run through this national forest, named for Revolutionary War hero Maj. Gen. "Mad Anthony" Wayne. Three components near the cities of Marietta, Athens, and Portsmouth have rivers, streams, lakes, rock shelters, covered bridges, campgrounds, and trails. Canoeing, fishing, and wildlife viewing on the Little Muskingum River is especially popular in the Marietta unit in the foothills of the Appalachian Mountains, with rugged hills covered with hardwoods, pine, and cedar. *Other activities:* In Marietta, the Ohio River Museum State Memorial illustrates the history of inland waterways and presents guided tours on the 1918 steamboat *W. P. Snyder, Jr.*; *Valley Gem* sternwheeler offers excursions on the Ohio and Muskingum Rivers; Campus Marius Museum of the Northwest Territory houses the restored Ohio Company Land Office (1788) and the Rufus Putnam home, a part of the original Campus Marius Fort (1788); Muskingum Park, a riverfront common, has a monument to westward migration.

20. BURR OAK STATE PARK. Located near Glouster on the border of Wayne National Forest, Burr Oak is one of Ohio's seven resort parks. Facilities include a lodge, cabins, a beach, boat ramps, boat rentals, and more than 11 miles of the NCT. Activities include camping, hiking, horseback riding, boating, fishing, swimming, cross-country skiing, sledding, ice skating, ice fishing, and summer programs.

21. LAKE LOGAN STATE PARK. The park, near Logan, offers a swimming beach, boat rentals, and one of the best fishing lakes in the state. Activities include hiking, sledding, and ice skating. *Nearby:* At Nelsonville, the Rocking Valley Scenic Railway, with its Baldwin steam

locomotive (1916) and diesel locomotive (1950), offers round-trips to Logan.

22. HOCKING HILLS STATE PARK. Ten miles of NCT pass by a wide variety of tree species in this park near Logan. The park and forest provide a home for over one hundred species of birds as well as wildlife native to the Midwest. The park, which covers some of the most diverse terrain in the state, is divided into six areas. Special features include Ash Cave, a natural rock shelter with a spring and winter waterfall; Rock House, a formation in the sandstone cliff; and Old Man's Cave, with gorges, a waterfall, and caves. Activities include camping and cabins, birding, fishing, swimming, boating, and special events at the visitor center.

23. TAR HOLLOW STATE PARK. East of Chillicothe amid the craggy foothills of the Appalachian plateau, the park is surrounded by state forest, all crossed by the NCT. Facilities include cabins, a beach, and boat ramps. Activities include camping, horseback riding, fishing, swimming, and boating. *Other activities:* In Chillicothe, the Hopewell Culture National Historical Park provides insight into the social, ceremonial, political, and economic life of the Hopewell Culture (200 B.C. to A.D. 500); Adena State Memorial; Ross County Historical Society Museum; Knoles Log Home (1800–25), with seasonal demonstrations; and Franklin House, a 1907 prairie-style home with

museum. At Chillicothe from mid-June through early August, visitors can enjoy "Tecumseh," an outdoor drama about the great Shawnee leader.

24. SCIOTO TRAIL STATE PARK. This park is located south of Chillicothe in the Scioto Trail State Forest. The trail corridor is dotted with expansive vistas of the Scioto River valley from the ridgetops. Activities include camping, horseback riding, fishing, boating, cross-country skiing, snowshoeing, ice skating, and ice fishing. *Nearby:* Lake White State Park, near Waverly, has rustic camping and a July Fourth boat parade.

25. PIKE LAKE STATE PARK. This park and state forest near Bainbridge has cabins, a beach, boat rentals, and an outdoor wildlife display. Activities include camping, hiking, horseback riding, birding, fishing, swimming, boating, sledding, ice fishing, and summer programs. *Other activities:* Near Bainbridge, Seip Mound State Memorial has one of the largest Hopewell burial mounds and an interpretive center; Seven Caves has trails to caves and other natural attractions; Paint Creek State Park has the Paint Creek Pioneer Farm; Fort Hill State Memorial has an unrestored Hopewell earthwork, a museum, and significant natural history; Serpent Mound State Memorial has a museum and the famous Adena mound (800 B.C.–A.D. 1), the largest known serpent effigy in the world (one quarter mile long).

26. SHAWNEE STATE PARK. The park and the 60,000-acre Shawnee State Forest located in the Appalachian foothills near Portsmouth have rugged hills, tall trees, clear streams, and the breaks of the Ohio River. Together, the park and forest offer close to 16 miles of NCT, a beautiful lodge, cabins, a swimming beach, an amphitheater, a golf course, and a boat launch and boat rentals. Activities include camping, horseback riding, mound exploring, swimming, fishing, boating, golf, cross-country skiing, snowshoeing, sledding, ice skating, ice fishing, and summer interpretive programs. *Other activities:* At Portsmouth, the Boneyfiddle Historic District; Southern Ohio Museum and Cultural Center; Floodwall Murals Project, with impressive murals that depict life along the Ohio River; 1810 House, an original hand-built homestead; Greenup Locks and Dam Complex on the Ohio River; Roy Rogers Festival in June and River Days during Labor Day weekend.

27. ADAMS LAKE STATE PARK. The park near Dunkinsville offers hiking, fishing, and boating. *Other activities:* The Edwin H. Davis State Memorial, northeast of Dunkinsville, has an 88-acre nature preserve with arrowwood, black walnut, linden, redbud, red cedar, tulip, and witch hazel trees.

28. EAST FORK STATE PARK. The large park near Bethel has 8 miles of NCT, a public beach, and a separate beach for camping. Other activities include horseback

riding, fishing, swimming, boating, sledding, ice skating, ice fishing, and summer programs. *Nearby:* At Point Pleasant, Grant's Birthplace. In Cincinnati, William Howard Taft National Historic Site; Taft Museum; Harriet Beecher Stowe Memorial; Bicentennial Commons at Sawyer Point, with the 4-mile Riverwalk; Mount Airy Forest and Arboretum, the first municipal reforestation project in the United States; Burnet Woods, with hiking and a nature center; Cincinnati Nature Center; Riverfest, held along the city's waterfront during Labor Day weekend.

29. LITTLE MIAMI SCENIC STATE PARK. More than 45 miles of abandoned railroad right-of-way from Milford to south of Xenia extends through the Little Miami River valley. This wheelchair-accessible greenway serves as a segment of the Buckeye Trail and the NCT. Activities include hiking, jogging, rollerblading, bicycling, horseback riding, cross-country skiing, and canoeing on the Little Miami River (designated a state and national scenic river). The Little Miami Scenic Trail is an 80-mile multipurpose trail network that extends to Springfield near Buck Creek State Park. *Nearby:* Near Mulberry, Stonelick State Park has campsites. Near Morrow, Fort Ancient State Memorial may be a Hopewell defense dating to 100 B.C. to A.D. 500. At Lebanon, Warren County Museum has a Shaker gallery. The Golden Lamb Inn (with a Shaker museum),

established in 1803, is the oldest inn in Ohio. Ten U.S. presidents have been guests there.

30. CAESAR CREEK STATE PARK. This park, near Waynesville, serves as a nature preserve and wildlife area. Nearby Pioneer Village contains restored log structures, including the 1807 Levi Luken home and a Quaker meetinghouse with ties to the Underground Railroad. Caesar Creek Lake Visitor Center provides information about the Army Corps of Engineers water resource management and flood control and displays American Indian artifacts and trilobite (extinct marine arthropods) fossils. Activities include camping, hiking, horseback riding, fishing, swimming, boating, cross-country skiing, snowmobiling, ice fishing, and summer programs. *Nearby:* At Miamisburg, the Miamisburg Mound State Memorial displays an Adena mound, one of the largest conical burial mounds in the eastern North America. Near Spring Valley, the Spring Valley Wildlife Area is one of the state's best spots for bird-watching. Xenia, the birthplace of Tecumseh, was the site of one of the largest Shawnee Indian settlements. In 1997 the American Hiking Society named Xenia "Trail Town, USA"; it serves as a junction for several rail-trail conversions. Near Xenia at Caesar's Ford Park, the outdoor drama "Blue Jacket" is staged each summer.

31. JOHN BRYAN STATE PARK. The park, near Yellow Springs, has a limestone gorge cut

by the Little Miami River. A large segment, known as Clifton Gorge, has been designated a state nature preserve. Activities include camping, hiking, fishing, cross-country skiing, snowshoeing, sledding, and summer programs. *Nearby:* Dayton, the birthplace of aviation and former home of aviation pioneers Orville and Wilbur Wright, has the newly established NPS Dayton Aviation Heritage National Historical Park with four components: Wright Cycle Shop, the official visitor center; Huffman Prairie Flying Field; Carillon Historical Park with the Wright Flyer III, pioneer displays, transportation exhibits, and Newcom Tavern (1913); and Paul Laurence Dunbar House State Memorial, the home of the African American poet, novelist, and boyhood friend of Orville Wright. Also in Dayton, the Old Courthouse with Wright Brothers display; Wright Brothers Memorial; Woodland Cemetery and Arboretum, with the graves of Orville and Wilbur Wright; U.S. Air Force Museum at Wright-Patterson Air Force Base, the largest museum of its kind; Dayton Art Institute; Dayton Museum of Discovery; Cox Arboretum; Sun Watch Prehistoric Indian Village, a twelfth-century reconstructed Hopewell village; Aullwood Audubon Center and Farm, with museum and trails; Benjamin Wegerzyn Horticultural Center, composed of gardens and wetland woods; Charleston Falls Preserve. At Piqua, the Piqua Historical

Area offers mule-drawn rides on the Miami and Erie Canal (1825–45), which was used to transport goods from Cincinnati to Lake Erie; the Piqua Historical Museum; Garby's Big Woods Reserve, with the state's longest boardwalk.

32. LAKE LORAMIE STATE PARK. Loramie Lake near Fort Loramie is one of five feeder lakes built as part of the Miami-Erie canal system. A short canal connected the lake to the main canal. Activities include camping, hiking, fishing, swimming, boating, snowmobiling, ice skating, ice fishing, and summer programs.

33. GRAND LAKE SAINT MARYS STATE PARK. The lake near Saint Marys, also designed as a feeder reservoir for the Ohio canal system, was the largest human-made lake in the world until construction of Hoover Dam in Nevada. Activities include camping, hiking, bicycling, fishing, swimming, waterskiing, snowmobiling, ice fishing, and summer programs. *Nearby:* Neil Armstrong Museum in Wapakoneta.

34. INDEPENDENCE DAM STATE PARK. The park's hiking trail near Defiance has 7 miles of NCT, including 3 miles of towpath along the historic Miami-Wabash-Erie Canal. Activities include camping, hiking, fishing, riverboating, cross-country skiing, sledding, ice skating, and ice fishing. At Defiance, Au Glaize Village presents restored late-nineteenth-century buildings;

Flowing Rivers Festival is held in late June to early July at the site of the original Fort Defiance, constructed in 1794 during a campaign against the American Indians.

35. HARRISON LAKE STATE PARK. The lake park, near Fayette, has tent and trailer sites, a swimming beach, and boat ramps. Activities include camping, hiking, fishing, swimming, canoeing, sailing, boating, and sledding. In Archbold, the Sauder Farm and Craft Village demonstrates early craft activity in a restored village. Near Toledo, the NCT will follow one leg of the 17-mile loop trail in the Toledo–Oak Openings Park.

MICHIGAN

(1 , 1 5 0   M I L E S)

36. LOST NATIONS LAKE HUDSON STATE RECREATION AREA. The 500-acre man-made lake, southeast of Hudson, has camping, fishing, and swimming. *Other attractions:* At Tipton, Walter J. Hayes State Park has additional camping, boating, and a train trip into a forest of dinosaurs; Hidden Lake Gardens has hiking and a scenic drive; St. Joseph's Shrine is the site of a late 1790s religious settlement. Near Cambridge Junction, Cambridge State Historic Park features the Walker Tavern Historic Complex. *Nearby:* At Osseo, the NCT follows the Baw Beese Trail to Hillsdale. In Battle Creek, the NCT follows the Battle Creek Linear Parkway. Also in Battle Creek, Leila Arboretum and

Kingman Museum of Natural History; Kellogg Bird Sanctuary; Sojourner Truth Grave at Oak Creek Cemetery; Team U.S. Nationals Hot Air Balloon Championship and Air Show in July. Near Augusta, Fort Custer State Recreation Area, with camping and cabins; Fort Custer National Cemetery.

37. YANKEE SPRINGS STATE RECREATION AREA. The recreation area, adjacent to the 13,000-acre Barry State Game Area near Middleville, has a completed segment of NCT that passes through forest with more than seventy species of native trees, cabins, a boat launch, beach house, and two outdoor centers. Activities include camping (rustic/modern), hiking, horseback riding, fishing, swimming, cross-country skiing, snowshoeing, and snowmobiling. *Nearby:* In Grand Rapids, Blandford Nature Center, with hiking and a wildlife center; Frederik Meijer Gardens; Michigan Botanic Garden; Fish Ladder, where salmon leap rapids during spawning season on the Grand River. Grand Haven State Park has campsites on Lake Michigan, and Muskegon State Park near North Muskegon has the Muskegon Winter Sports Complex.

38. MANISTEE NATIONAL FOREST. Rolling hills in the south are connected to the steep hillsides in the north by approximately 120 miles of sandy-bottom trail that make up the NCT here. The NCT offers very pleasant trailside camping,

hiking, and snowshoeing. Other forest activities include swimming at Lake Michigan and canoeing on the beautiful Pere Marquette and Pine Rivers. Trout fishing is good at most of the forest's lakes and streams. In the spring, the forest attracts morel mushroom hunters. Forest Service offices are in Baldwin, Cadillac, Manistee, and White Cloud. *Other attractions:* Nordhouse Dunes Wilderness along Lake Michigan; Croton and Hardy Dams and Newaygo State Park near Oxbow; White Cloud County Park near White Cloud; Shrine of the Pines, a memorial to the white pine, near Baldwin; Charles W. Tippy and Stronach Dams near Wellston; William Mitchell State Park near Boon. *Nearby:* In Manistee, the municipal marina in the historic downtown; the Riverwalk for boat watching; scenic cruises; salmon fishing charters; Water Works Building with marine and logging exhibits; Orchard Beach State Park, with camping; and Ludington State Park, with camping and sand dunes.

39. INTERLOCHEN STATE PARK. The state park, south of Interlochen and adjacent to the National Music Camp, lies within the Pere Marquette State Forest. It contains one of the few remaining stands of virgin pine in the state and has tent and tepee rental, a boat launch, and a beach house. Activities include camping (rustic/modern), hiking, fishing, boating, and swimming. *Other attractions:* Concerts at Interlochen Summer Theatre. In Traverse City, the tall ship *Malabar* sails the beautiful West Grand Traverse Bay; Clinch Park offers a beach and the docked schooner *Madeline* (1845); the North American VASA Race is a cross-country ski competition held in February; Cherry Festival in July; Traverse City State Park. *Nearby:* Near Empire, Sleeping Bear Dunes National Lakeshore offers a diverse landscape with massive sand dunes, birch-lined streams, white sand beaches, dense beech-maple forests, clear lakes, and rugged bluffs towering as high as 460 feet above Lake Michigan; the western terminus of the Michigan Shore-to-Shore Riding-Hiking Trail (STS) to Tawas City on Lake Huron. In Charlevoix, the Beaver Island Boat Company takes passengers to Beaver Island, 30 miles off the coast; Fisherman's Island State Park has camping, fishing, and swimming; Mackinaw State Forest; Burt Lake State Park, on the southeast end of Burt Lake has additional camping.

40. PETOSKEY STATE PARK. The state park, located northeast of Petoskey on Little Traverse Bay, is a popular spot to camp, hike, fish, swim, cross-country ski, and hunt for Petoskey stones. *Other attractions:* Little Traverse Historical Museum. *Nearby:* Wilderness State Park, with camping and cabins, west of Mackinaw City and just south of the Straits of Mackinaw, has an 11-mile completed segment of NCNST that crosses varied topography.

41. COLONIAL MICHILIMACKINAC STATE PARK. This day-use park, near Mackinaw City, has a reconstructed eighteenth-century French fort, costumed guides, and craft demonstrations. A museum at the base of Old Mackinac Point Lighthouse tells the maritime history of the Straits of Mackinac, and affords excellent views of the straits, Mackinac Bridge, and Great Lakes shipping. *Other attractions:* At Mackinaw City, Mackinac Bridge serves as the gateway from the Lower Peninsula to the Upper Peninsula. Foot traffic is not allowed on the bridge, but a shuttle bus will transport NCNST hikers for a nominal fee. Mackinac Bridge Museum, at the base of the bridge, offers information on the bridge's history and construction. *Nearby:* Old Mill Creek State Historic Park, southeast of Mackinaw City, has a working water-powered sawmill, demonstrations, a visitor center, and hiking through natural forest.

42. MACKINAC ISLAND STATE PARK. The state's second state park (1895) was the nation's second national park (1875) before it was turned over to the state. The day-use park is reached by ferries from Mackinaw City and Saint Ignace. Special features include guided tours of the national historic landmark Fort Mackinac (1780–1895) and the visitor center. As an alternate route, the NCT traveler can proceed by ferry to Saint Ignace, thereby missing the bridge crossing. *Other attractions:* British Landing Nature Center; the shoreline road for hiking and biking (no motorized vehicles are allowed on the island); Skull Cave and Arch Rock, glacial rock formations; Fort Holmes, the island's highest point; Grand Hotel; Lilac Festival in mid-June.

43. STRAITS STATE PARK. The park, near Mackinac Bridge in the Upper Peninsula at Saint Ignace, houses the Father Marquette National Memorial and Museum. The Jesuit priest established a community at the Mission of Saint Ignace among the Huron, Ojibwa, Ottawa, and French people in 1671. Two years later, Father Jacques Marquette and Louis Joliet became the first Europeans to map the Mississippi River. The 52-acre park and museum overlooks the bridge and straits and offers over three hundred campsites. Activities include camping, hiking, fishing, cross-country skiing, and snowmobiling. *Other attractions:* Marquette Mission Park and Museum of Objibwa Culture contains the burial site of Father Marquette and a museum interpreting the French fur trade; Fort De Buade Museum has exhibits on the French and Indians at the original fort site; Mackinac Bridge Walk, in which more than seventy thousand people participate. Views of Lake Michigan and Huron are to the west and east, respectively; Castle Rock, located 4 miles to the north, was an ancient lookout for the Algonkin Indians. *Nearby:* Lake Superior

State Forest; Brimley State Park, near Brimley, with a view of the Canadian hills across Saint Marys River. At Sault Saint Marie, Soo Locks (NHS)—the two longest locks in the world—have been in operation since 1855; Parkland has observation platforms and a Corps of Engineers information center; Locks Park Historic Walkway; Tower of History, with a view of the locks and Saint Marys River.

44. HIAWATHA NATIONAL FOREST. Eighty-seven miles of trail are found in this forest. The eastern unit extends from Saint Ignace to Whitefish Bay, and the western unit stretches from the Bays de Noc to Munising to cover over 893,000 acres of woodland. With shoreline on Lake Huron, Lake Michigan, and Lake Superior, water recreation abounds. There are three historic lighthouses. Round Island Lighthouse, the most famous, guided ships between the islands in the Straits of Mackinac. Whitefish Bay is a major migratory gateway for numerous species of birds, including the hawk migration each spring. Frigid water temperatures have preserved shipwrecks that are accessible to divers at Whitefish Point, the Straits of Marquette, and Alger Underwater Preserve near Munising. Little Bay de Noc attracts anglers for its large walleyes, and fishing for bass, coho salmon, pike, and trout is also popular. Canoeing is a heritage of the North Woods, but noteworthy spots are the Big

Island Lake canoeing area southeast of Munising; Indian River canoe trail south of Munising; and the Flowing Well canoeing area on the Sturgeon River. Other activities include camping, hiking, bicycling, and winter activities. Wildlife includes deer, grouse, and black bears. Additional information is available at forest offices in Escanaba, Rapid River, Manistique, Munising, Sault Saint Marie, and Saint Ignace.

45. TAHQUAMENON FALLS STATE PARK. A highlight of the 22 miles of trail in this park is pausing at the 50-foot Tahquamenon Fall, over which water flows at a massive 50,000 gallons per second, then continues downstream to the Lower Tahquamenon Falls. Rowboats can be rented to view the Lower Falls, or a riverboat or train excursion is available. In the winter, huge icicles on the walls of the Tahquamenon Gorge create prisms that produce a rainbow of color. The park's Rivermouth unit is located 4.5 miles south of Paradise at the mouth of the Tahquamenon River on Whitefish Bay. Activities include camping, canoeing, boating, hiking, rock hunting, fishing, cross-country skiing, and snowmobiling. Nearby: In Whitefish Point, Whitefish Point Lighthouse; Shipwreck Historical Museum.

46. MUSKALLONGE LAKE STATE PARK. The park, at the village of Deer Park on Lake Superior and Muskallonge Lake, is a treasure trove for hunting semiprecious gems. Located in the middle of Lake Superior State Forest, the park and forest combined have more than 51 miles of NCT, with panoramic views of the lakefront and the surrounding wooded sand dunes, sandy beach on Lake Michigan, frontage on Muskegon Lake and on Muskegon channel, a beach house, a boat launch, and interpretive center. In July and August wild blueberries and raspberries are found along the trail. Activities include camping (rustic/electrical hookup), hiking, rock hunting, fishing, boating, swimming, and cross-country skiing. *Nearby:* In Grand Marais, Grand Marais Maritime Museum; the Grand Marais Historical Museum.

47. PICTURED ROCKS NATIONAL LAKESHORE. Permits to hike this 44-mile segment of the NCT can be obtained at visitor centers in Munising and Grand Marais on either end of the trail or at the Sand Point National Lakeshore headquarters. Designated the first national lakeshore and declared a biosphere reserve in 1980, Pictured Rocks is composed of multicolored sandstone cliffs, broad beaches, sand bars, dunes, waterfalls, inland lakes, ponds, marshes, hardwood and coniferous forests, and numerous birds and animals. About ten thousand years ago the last glacier left debris to form the banks at Grand Sable Banks and Dunes at the park's eastern end (see IANST). Activities include camping at the park's three campgrounds or thirteen backcountry campgrounds; hiking and backpacking; fishing in Lake Superior, Munising Bay, or the inland lakes and streams; boat tours from Munising; canoeing on Beaver and Grand Sable Lakes, boating and kayaking in the waters of Lake Superior; swimming; scuba diving at the Alger Underwater Preserve; winter camping, cross-country skiing, snowshoeing, snowmobiling, and ice fishing. The Grand Sable Visitor Center is open during the summer. *Other activities:* In Munising, the Gwinn-Munising Sled Dog Race in January; the Marquette County Winter Festival highlights winter activities for two months; the eastern terminus of popular lakeshore drive to Marquette. *Nearby:* Grand Island Recreation Area.

48. LAUGHING WHITEFISH FALLS STATE PARK. The day-use park, between Munising and Marquette, features the caramel-colored Laughing Whitefish Falls. *Nearby:* In Marquette, the Marquette Maritime Museum; Marquette Underwater Preserve; Presque Isle Park, with an inland forest that is preserved in its natural state. At Negaunee, the Michigan Iron Industry Museum tells the story of the state's three iron ranges. Escanaba River State Forest; Van Riper State Park near Champion has evidence of early mining, camping, and a scenic boat ride on the lake.

49. OTTAWA NATIONAL FOREST. More than 500 lakes, 2,000 miles of rivers and streams, and 50,000 acres of McCormick

Wilderness with old-growth forest and waterfalls attract recreationists to this 986,518-acre forest. Eight of the 90 miles of NCT in the forest cross the McCormick Wilderness. Activities include camping, hiking, fishing, swimming, boating, canoeing, and winter sports. Scenic Lake Gogebic State Park is located north of Marenisco. The forest supervisor is in Ironwood. *Nearby:* Houghton offers seasonal float plane and ferry service to Isle Royale National Park from June to Labor Day; A. E. Seaman Mineralogical Museum. The area's copper-bearing geological formations are thought to be the oldest rock formations in the world. The Portage Lake Vertical Lift Bridge joins the city to Hancock. Hancock, Quincy Mine Steam Hoist has underground tours; Fort F. J. McLain State Park offers camping. Near Calumet, Keweenaw National Historical Park preserves the first significant copper mining in the United States. Copper Harbor, a boat tour leads to Lighthouse Point; Fort Wilkins State Park has a historic fort; Brockway Mountain Drive off SR M-26 to Eagle Harbor offers a panoramic view of Lake Superior.

50. CRAIG LAKE STATE PARK. North of Three Lakes, Craig Lake State Park offers cabins, camping, hiking, fishing, and over 7 miles of NCT. *Nearby:* Copper County State Forest. In Republic, the Open Pit Iron Mine can be toured at no charge. In Baraga, the Hanka Homestead

Museum has unaltered examples of pioneer handwork; Baraga State Park, located on the scenic Keweenaw Bay, has camping. At Pequaming, Curwood Park is the site of an 1840 American fur trading Post; L'Anse Indian Reservation.

51. PORCUPINE WILDERNESS STATE PARK. This beautiful 63,000-acre wilderness park on Lake Superior, 3 miles west of Silver City, has 22 miles of NCT. The park has cabins, Adirondack shelters, a visitor center, a boat launch, and an observation tower on Summit Peak that offers a magnificent view from the Lake of the Clouds overlook. The trail passes secluded lakes, rivers, large tracts of forest wilderness, towering virgin timber, rugged shoreline, and the Porcupine Mountains, known as the "Porkies." The Presque Isle River unit features virgin timber on the scenic drive along the river and views of Iagoo, Nowadama, Manido, and Presque Isle Falls. Activities include camping, hiking, fishing, cross-country skiing, and snowshoeing. *Nearby:* Black River County Park; Lake Superior County Park; Mountain River County Park. At Ironwood, the Depot Museum; Hiawatha, a 52-foot statue, looks to Gitchee Gummee, also known as Lake Superior.

WISCONSIN (220 MILES)

52. COPPER FALLS STATE PARK. The park, north of Mellen, composed of ancient lava flows,

deep gorges, streams, and spectaular waterfalls, is surrounded by the wooded hills of the Penokee Range. The Copper Falls are formed by the Bad River, which flows into a 65-foot gorge. Traveling the 4.4-mile segment of the NCT offers up-close views of several inspiring waterfalls. Activities include camping, (rustic/electric hookup), hiking, bicycling, fishing, swimming, boating, waterskiing, canoeing, cross-country skiing, snowshoeing, and seasonal naturalist programs. An observation tower offers scenic views. *Other attractions:* Mellen, a 2.2-mile certified segment of the NCT, continues from the park to the western edge of town. Mellen has bears and is the gateway to Chequamegon National Forest. *Nearby:* The Bad and Tyler Rivers are fished for bass, northern pike, and trout; Bad River Indian Reservation; Red Cliff Indian Reservation; Apostle Islands National Lakeshore, with a visitor center in Bayfield.

53. CHEQUAMEGON NATIONAL FOREST. This 60-mile segment of the NCT begins 2 miles west of Mellen and continues to Iron River. Along the way it passes through the Penokee Range and the North Woods in the 4,500-acre Porcupine Lake Wilderness and 6,600-acre Rainbow Lake Wilderness. There are plentiful opportunities to fish in the numerous small lakes and streams. Wildlife includes the white-tailed deer, black bear, timber wolf, and some unusual birds. Elk are being reestablished in the forest and the herd is growing. Drummond Woods has an interpretive loop, and the Virgin Pine Trail runs through a section of old growth. Activities include hiking, bicycling, horseback riding, Great Divide Scenic Byway, fishing, swimming, boating, canoeing, cross-country skiing, snowshoeing, wildlife viewing, and naturalist programs. *Other activities:* In Drummond, the Drummond Museum offers displays on logging. *Nearby:* At Cable, the visitor center has campsite information; Cable Natural History Museum; the Birkebeiner is the largest and most important cross-country ski race in North America; the Fall Chequamegon Fat Tire Festival follows most of the 40-mile Birkebeiner Trail; Namekagon River.

54. BRULE RIVER STATE FOREST. This forest near Solon Springs has 7 miles of certified NCT, and more trail is under construction. This part of the trail is considered to be especially beautiful. Two miles of the segment near Douglas County Highway follow historic portage that has been marked with eight commemorative stones that name early explorers, traders, American Indians, and others who passed through this area. Brule River, fished by four U.S. presidents, offers invigorating white-water canoeing and kayaking. Activities include camping (rustic/electric hookup), hiking, bicycling, fishing, boating, cross-country skiing, snowshoeing, and snowmobiling.

55. SAINT CROIX NATIONAL SCENIC RIVERWAY. The Upper Saint Croix River and its Namekagon tributary make up one of the initial 1968 components of the National Wild and Scenic Rivers System. The Namekagon, an Indian name meaning "place of the sturgeon," begins at Namekagon Lake Dam near Cable and flows for 98 miles to join the Saint Croix River near Danbury. The source of the Saint Croix River is a small tamarack bog around upper Saint Croix Lake. The river is narrow and shallow until it is joined by the Namekagon. The Upper Saint Croix and Namekagon portion of the riverway offer 200 miles of varied canoe, camping, fishing, and wildlife viewing opportunities. The best canoeing is in April and May, and camping is generally by canoe access, although state parks and private campgrounds are located near the riverway. The Namekagon is known for trout and bass; muskie and walleye are caught in the Saint Croix. There is a visitor center and headquarters in Saint Croix Falls, which is also a site along the Ice Age National Scenic Trail, and seasonal information stations near Grantsburg and Trego. The lower segment, added to the system in 1972, covers a narrow river and shoreline corridor for 52 miles before it converges with the Mississippi River. The Lower Saint Croix has canoeing, fishing, power boating, waterskiing, and sailboarding. Boat rides are offered at Interstate Park near Taylor Falls, Minnesota (IANST). *Nearby:* Governor Knowles State Forest has rustic river and backpack camping by permit in the wilderness area along the Saint Croix River.

MINNESOTA (375 MILES)

56. JAY COOKE STATE PARK. The 8,800-acre preserve near Carlton has forests and scenic vistas along 3.1 miles of NCT. At the Saint Louis River rapids kayakers and rafters plunge through a rugged rocky gorge. Other activities include camping (rustic/electrical hookup), hiking, bicycling, horseback riding, Jay Cooke State Park Drive, fishing, cross-country skiing, skate skiing, snowmobiling, and naturalist programs. The park has a visitor center, a historic site, and a warming house. *Other attractions:* Raft rentals are available at Thomson Reservoir; the Willard Munger Trail offers 15 miles of paved trail from Carlton to Duluth.

57. SUPERIOR HIKING TRAIL. Following the ridge of the Sawtooth Mountains, this 200-mile wooded path offers lodge-to-lodge hiking with overlooks of the northwest shore of Lake Superior. Ranked among the top twelve trails in the national forests, this jewel skirts the western shore of Lake Superior. When complete, it will stretch from Duluth to Canada. Additional information is available from the Superior Hiking Trail Association, which became a partner of the

North Country Trail Association in 1998. *Other attractions:* In Duluth, the 5-mile Western Waterfront Trail used by hikers and cyclists follows the Saint Louis River; Canal Park has a visitor center, a boardwalk, the Corps of Engineers Marine Museum on shipping, and the unique Aerial Lift Bridge; the lake walk extends from Canal Park eastward to the Rose Gardens; Bayfront Festival Park offers seasonal outdoor concerts; Lake Superior Center has exhibits on the largest lake in the world; Tweed Museum of Art; Marshall W. Alworth Planetarium; Minnesota Point is a popular spot for hiking, bicycling, canoeing, kayaking, and birding; Hawk Ridge along Skyline Drive, for watching hawks during their migration south; North Shore Drive passes seven state parks on the way to Canada; Old Highway 61 follows the lake north of Two Harbors State Park. Fond du Lac, Vermillion Lake, and Nett Lake Indian Reservations; Fond du Lac, Cloquet Valley, White Face River, Bear Island, Sturgeon, Kabetogama State Forests; McCarthy Beach State Memorial Park; Bear Head Lake and Soudan Underground Mine State Parks; Superior National Forest; Boundary Waters Canoe Area Wilderness; Voyageurs National Park, near International Falls.

58. SAVANNA PORTAGE STATE PARK. The scenic park with a North Woods mix offers boat and canoe rental, a warming house, a historic site, the Historic Savanna Portage Trail, and the Continental Divide Trail (not related to the national trail by the same name), where the water flows in one direction to the Mississippi River and in the other to Lake Superior. Activities include camping (rustic/electrical hookup), hiking, fishing, boating, cross-country skiing, snowmobiling, and seasonal naturalist programs. *Nearby:* Sandy Lake Indian Reservation; Rice Lake National Wildlife Refuge; Moose Willow Wildlife Area; Hill River and Golden Anniversary State Forests.

59. CHIPPEWA NATIONAL FOREST. The 663,000-acre national forest is noted for its spectacular natural beauty, lakes, and big pines. The NCT passes many of these lakes as it weaves its way through the forest's beautiful glaciated terrain. From east of Remer to Leech Lake near Walker, the NCT extends through the forest's southern portion for 60 miles, passing diverse terrain that offers views of wetlands, lakes, and streams. Remer is one of the prime areas in the country to see bald eagles, and Leech Lake, the state's third-largest, is a favorite for fishing and sailing. There is a forest visitor information center on the shores of the lake. Activities include camping, hiking, bicycling, fishing, swimming, boating, canoeing, cross-country skiing, snowshoeing, and nature programs. *Other activities:* From Walker, the blacktopped Heartland Trail travels through woods and farmland to Park

Rapids, where an unpaved portion continues to Cass Lake, the forest headquarters. The popular Cut Foot Sioux Trail travels to Turtle Mound, an Indian effigy, and Farley Tower; Camp Rabideau is a Civilian Conservation Corps camp of the 1930s; Lost Forty is a stand of virgin pine with a short trail; Avenue of the Pines is a scenic drive through the middle of the forest; Edge of the Wilderness National Scenic Byway travels from Effie through the national forest to Grand Rapids. *Nearby:* Deep Portage Conservation Reserve, near Hackensack, details the plant and wildlife of the North Woods. Remer, Land O'Lakes, Battle Ground, Badoura, and Paul Bunyan State Forests; White Oak Point and Leech Lake Indian Reservations; Mud Goose Wildlife Area; Schoolcraft State Park, located within the boundaries of the Chippewa National Forest, offers additional camping.

60. ITASCA STATE PARK. Minnesota's oldest and second-largest state park, near the town of Lake Itasca, features the headwaters of the mighty Mississippi and 13 miles of NCNST that passes many small beautiful lakes, some with walk-in campsites. Hikers can cross the world's third-longest river at a small stream that flows from Lake Itasca. Facilities include a historic lodge and cabins, a lookout tower, a warming house, and a seasonal visitor center. Activities include camping, hiking, bicycling, scenic drive, fishing, boat excursions,

cross-country skiing, snowmobiling, and naturalist programs. *Other attractions:* Bohall Trail leads into the park's wilderness sanctuary; Wilderness Drive through old-growth forest; cruises aboard the *Chester Charles* to the headwaters; Itasca Indian Mounds; Bison Kill Site; Peace Pipe Vista; Preacher's Grove; Wegmann Cabin; Great River Road along the Mississippi River to Bemidji. Nearby: Clearwater County Forest has nearly 3 miles of certified NCT that continues west of Itasca State Park and ends at Gardiner Lake. White Earth Indian Reservation has a powwow in June; Headwaters, White Earth, Two Inlets, and Smoky Hills State Forests. At Bemidji, Paul Bunyan and Babe the Blue Ox are giant statues on the lakefront; Paul Bunyan Information Building houses a historical and wildlife museum; Lake Bemidji State Park features a spruce-tamarack bog.

61. TAMARAC NATIONAL WILDLIFE REFUGE. Black bears, coyotes, and whitetail deer roam the refuge, located north of Detroit Lakes. Bald eagles, loons, trumpeter swans, dozens of waterfowl, and thousands of songbirds bring birders to the area, especially during fall and spring. Nonmotorized watercraft are allowed in the refuge. *Nearby:* Detroit Lakes holds one of the largest country music festivals in the world each August; Becker County Historical Society Museum.

62. MAPLEWOOD STATE PARK. This wooded area with

eight major lakes, near Pelican Rapids, is surrounded by farmland. The region's largest park attracts white-tailed deer, beavers, and herons and other wading birds. The lakes offer excellent opportunities to fish for northern pike, walleyes, and panfish. Facilities include cabins and boat and canoe rentals. Activities include camping, hiking, horseback riding, fishing, swimming, boating, cross-country skiing, and snowmobiling. *Nearby:* Rothsay and Barnesville wildlife areas. The town of Fergus Falls has nineteenth-century architecture, archaeological ruins, and over 500 acres of parkland. The Otter Tail County Museum is one of the best local museums in the state; Otter Tail River with walkway. Pipestone National Monument is located near Pipestone.

NORTH DAKOTA (475 MILES)

63. SHEYENNE NATIONAL GRASSLAND. This 70,000-acre area, east of Lisbon, lies in the heart of Ransom County along the Sheyenne River. Its prairie, forests, and sand hills are home to some of the state's rarer plant species, such as the prairie-fringed orchid. The grassland also has booming grounds for the largest greater prairie chicken population in the state. Each spring and fall, millions of waterfowl travel overhead along the biggest migratory bird flyway in North America. Markers lead hikers through 25 miles of trail, although most take this segment of the NCT on horseback with compass in hand as the trail blends in with its prairie surroundings. Activities include camping, hiking, horseback riding, and cross-country skiing. The Custer National Forest Sheyenne Ranger District in Lisbon administers the grassland. *Nearby:* Dead Cott Creek Recreation Area, located about 5 miles south, has additional camping; Sheyenne State Forest, 14 miles northwest, offers camping, hiking, fishing, canoeing, cross-country skiing, snowshoeing, and snowmobiling; Storm Lake and Tewaukon national wildlife refuges; Fort Abercrombie State Historic Site, near the Minnesota border, north of Wahpeton, offers summer interpretive programs about the fort that served as a gateway to the Dakota frontier from 1857 to 1878.

64. FORT RANSOM STATE PARK. Two and a half miles of NCT with panoramic views are found at this state park. During Sodbuster Days in July and September, there are early farm equipment demonstrations and live entertainment. A demonstration farm near Fort Ransom represents a late-nineteenth-century farming operation. The Memorial Cavalry Performance, a reenactment of typical activities of the Seventh Cavalry, is held in late September. Activities include camping, hiking, horseback riding, fishing, canoeing, cross-country skiing, snowshoeing, and snowmobiling. *Other activities:* At Fort Ranson, the seasonal Fort

Ranson County Museum has pioneer exhibits; Fort Ransom State Historic Site marks the site of the military post that was used from 1867 to 1872. *Nearby:* Little Yellowstone State Park offers camping along a sheltered portion of the Sheyenne River; Clausen Springs Recreation Area features a 400-acre park with a 50-acre lake with camping (rustic/electric hookups); Baldhill Dam and Lake Ashtabula for fishing; Valley City National Fish Hatchery; Valley City's North Dakota Winter Show features a rodeo and livestock and horse show in March.

65. FORT TOTTEN STATE HISTORIC SITE. The historic site, located on the east edge of Fort Totten, was established in 1867 as a frontier military post during the Indian Wars era. After it was decommissioned in 1890, it became a school for Indian children. The site retains many of its original buildings and is considered one of the finest preserved forts of the period. A musical is held in summer, the Pioneer Daughter Museum is open seasonally, and an interpretive center offers displays. *Nearby:* Devil's Lake, named Bad Spirit Lake by the Sioux, is the state's largest natural lake. Walleye, white bass, and perch fishing are abundant. Ice fishing for yellow perch draws national attention to the lake, and in fall and spring, migrating birds darken the skies. Devil's Lake Sioux Indian Reservation; Sully's Hill National Game Preserve on the NCT offers an auto tour and nature trail; Johnson Lake, Silver Lake, Lake Alice, and Buffalo Lake National Wildlife Refuges; International Peace Garden at the Canadian border near Dunseith.

66. LONETREE WILDLIFE MANAGEMENT AREA. A 147-mile segment of the NCT follows the New Rockford and McCluskey Canal corridors and passes through the Wildlife Management Area near Harvey. It begins one mile east of Highway 281 near New Rockford and ends at the eastern shore of Lake Audubon. One can see native grasses and forbs and great migrating flocks of geese, ducks, and sandhill cranes. The trail through Lonetree, where cattle grazing is not permitted, offers views of pristine prairie. As much as 70 percent of the 30,000-acre management area may be restored to native prairies. Booming grounds for prairie chicken and sharptail grouse are near the trail. Guidelines for observation during mating season are available from the North Dakota Game and Fish Department, Lonetree Wildlife Management Area, RR 2, Box 32, Harvey, ND 58341. *Nearby:* At Rugby, 40 miles north near the intersection of Highways 2 and 3, is a marker for the geographical center of North America and the Geographical Center Pioneer Village and Museum.

67. LAKE SAKAKAWEA STATE PARK. The 1.1 miles of trail in this park anchor the western terminus of the NCT. Located just north of Pick City on the south

shore of Lake Sakakawea, the park offers campsites, an amphitheater, hiking trails, a beach, a marina, and boat rentals. Activities include camping, hiking, fishing, swimming, boating, cross-country skiing, snowmobiling, and ice fishing. *Nearby:* Garrison Dam, which creates Lake Sakakawea, is one of the largest rolled earth-fill dams in the world; Garrison National Fish Hatchery produces chinook salmon, northern pike, paddlefish, rainbow trout, and walleye; Audubon, Nettie Lake, and Camp Lake National Wildlife Refuges; Fort Berthold Indian Reservation. Lewis and Clark National Historic Trail sites include Knife River Indian Villages National Historic Site, near Stanton, Fort Clark State Historic Site, near Fort Clark; and Fort Mandan Historic Site, near Washburn (see LCNHT in *America's National Historic Trails*). Theodore Roosevelt National Park, near Watford City and Medora, is surrounded by Little Missouri National Grassland.

**WILD-
FLOWERS**

Trailside
wildflowers
offer a
rainbow of
delicate
colors along
turquoise
and sky blue
alpine lakes
and lush
green
mountain
meadows.

Pacific Crest National Scenic Trail

Climb the mountains and get their good tidings. Nature's peace will flow into you as sunshine flows into trees. The winds will blow their own freshness into you and the storms their energy, while cares will drop off like autumn leaves.

JOHN MUIR

The 2,650-mile Pacific Crest National Scenic Trail runs north-south near the crests of the mountains in the western United States. Trailside scenic beauty is found in the understated high desert chaparral at the Mexican border, along the alpine lakes and meadows of the high-altitude Sierra Nevada in California, in the mixed conifer forests of the volcanic Cascade Range in Oregon and Washington, along the awe-inspiring views of majestic snowcapped peaks, and through the Pasayten Wilderness at the Canadian border, home to gray wolves, mountain goats, and grizzly bears. Sections of the modern trail were once used by Indians, pioneers, trappers, and shepherds. An abundance of switchbacks lead to unbroken mountain views, ridgetop climbs, blankets of windblown wildflowers, and wildlife. Virtually no artificial shelters exist along the path, which lies mainly on public lands; instead, travelers discover mountain-high solitude, refreshment, and the challenge and delight of a lifetime.

ADMINISTERING AGENCY
USDA Forest Service
Pacific Northwest Region
333 SW First Avenue
P.O Box 3623
Portland, OR 97208-3623
503-808-2443

USDA Forest Service
Pacific Southwest Region
630 Sansome Street
San Francisco, CA 94111
415-705-2874

FURTHER INFORMATION
Pacific Crest Trail Association
5325 Elkhorn Boulevard, Suite 256
Sacramento, CA 95842
888-728-7245   888-PCTRAIL
www.pcta.org

DESIGNATED
1968

APPROXIMATE MILEAGE
2,650 miles (4,240 kilometers)

STATES
California, Oregon, Washington

219

The History of the Trail

Catherine Montgomery's vision of a "high trail winding down the heights of our western mountains" appeared in Joseph T. Hazard's book, *Pacific Crest Trails,* published in 1926. It was not an unreachable dream. In fact, portions of what became the Pacific Crest National Scenic Trail (PCT) were already under construction, including the John Muir Trail in California, the Oregon Skyline Trail, and the Cascade Crest Trail in Washington. Woven together with newer trails, the crest trail network became the realization of her vision.

Clinton C. Clark, co-founder of the celebrated Pasadena Playhouse in California and chairman of the executive committee of the Mountain League of Los Angeles County, was galvanized by the idea of a mountain-crest trail, made a plan, and promoted it. In 1932 he organized the various western hiking and riding clubs into the Pacific Crest Trail System Conference, became its president, and dedicated the rest of his life to the Pacific Crest Trail. The world-renowned photographer Ansel Adams served on the conference executive committee. Warren Lee Rogers, an outdoorsman, served as the executive secretary. A realist, Clark took the approach that the crest trail system could be composed of existing trails interconnected with new trail. He wrote that the final project would extend from Mexico to Canada as a scenic crest trail along the summit divides across California, Oregon, and Washington.

California's Desert Crest Trail, John Muir Trail, Tahoe-Yosemite Trail, and Lava Crest Trail; Oregon's Skyline Trail; and Washington's Cascade Crest Trail were already complete by 1932, and the California Conservation Corps, in conjunction with the USDA Forest Service, started to lay down the connector trails. Three years later the Oregon Skyline and Cascade Crest routes were connected in both Oregon and Washington to form the Pacific Crest Trail. Diamond-shaped signs stamped with "Pacific Crest Trail System" marked the route. That same year, Clark wanted to test his proposed border-to-border route and generate publicity at the same time. He devised a plan for a YMCA relay on the route. Rogers served as guide for all but two of the forty teams of boys that carried out the plan. June 15, 1935, marked the start in Campo, California, and the relay was finished three years later, on August 5, 1938, at the Canadian border 6 miles north of Three Fools Creek, Washington. It took four summers to prove it could be done. Along the way the teams of fourteen- to eighteen-year-olds recorded valuable trail observations. Portions of the relay trail are used today; other segments succumbed to private land exchanges, or were moved to avoid wet areas and steep inclines or to be closer to the crest. Modifications were also made to selected areas of old standbys such as the Oregon Skyline and the Cascade Crest.

During World War II, the trail's condition deteriorated, and after the war it was still difficult to maintain. Clark died in 1957 at the age of eighty-four, and with his death the twenty-five-year-old PCT System Conference disbanded. But Rogers rejuvenated the quest when he founded he

Pacific Crest Trail Conference and the Pacific Crest Club. Momentum increased when proponents of the Appalachian Trail (see AT) began to lobby for national trail status. With the passage of the National Trail System Act of 1968, the Pacific Crest Trail along with the Appalachian Trail were named America's first two national scenic trails.

ACTIVE VOLCANOES IN THE CASCADES

The volcanic Cascade Range stretches over 1,000 winding trail miles from northern California to southern British Columbia. Snow-clad peaks and other volcanic formations in the range can be grouped into five classifications, and all five are found along the PCT. Mount Shasta, Mount Hood, and Mount Rainier, for example, are composite stratovolcanoes. Conspicuous and beautiful mountains, composites usually have steep-sided, symmetrical cones that may rise more than 10,000 feet above their bases. The more simplistic cinder cone volcanoes are oval and circular cone-shaped hills that rarely rise more than 1,000 feet above their surroundings. Four hundred such cones exist near the Newberry Caldera in Oregon. Some are visible from the PCT, while Crater Butte in central Lassen Volcanic National Park (LVNP) and Collier Cone at the north base of North Sister in Oregon, are trailside examples. A third type, shield

MOUNT BAKER

Along with Mount Baker in northwestern Washington, seven volcanoes in the Cascades have erupted since the first Independence Day in the United States. Far to the east of the peak, the PCT passes through Mount Baker–Snoqualmie National Forest's best-known wildernesses, Alpine Lakes and the Henry M. Jackson (shared with Wenatche National Forest), crossing a variety of volcanic terrain.

volcanoes, have gently sloping domelike cones built almost entirely by lava flows. Shields in northern California and Oregon, such as Prospect Peak, whose southwest base skirts the PCT in northern LVNP, are relatively small examples of this type, achieving heights of 1,500 to 2,000 feet and diameters that typically measure 3 or 4 miles. A few miles east of the PCT where it traverses north through southern Oregon's Sky Lakes Wilderness is a classic example of a large, continental shield volcano (oceanic ones are much larger). Lying just east of the wilderness, this volcano stands about 3,900 feet above Upper Klamath Lake and measures about 6 miles in diameter. A fourth classification is the lava dome, which often forms within the crater of another volcano or on the flanks of a large composite volcano. Lassen Peak, near the PCT, is the largest lava dome in the Cascade Range. Although often not thought of as volcanoes because of their shape, a fifth type is referred to as a flood basalt province. These are regions of rock that are the result of massive lava flows. Potato Butte and Little Potato Butte, a few miles north of the LVNP, are two cinder cones from which emanated great volumes of lava to create the youthful Hat Creek lava flow, over 20 miles long. Another huge lava flow is visible along the PCT in Oregon near McKenzie Pass.

While volcanic eruptions in the Northwest are not a part of our everyday experience, evidence of their occurrence is certainly abundant. A powerful and vivid reminder of this potential was the eruption of Mount Saint Helens in 1980. It unleashed an explosive force in southern Washington equal to a 400-megaton hydrogen bomb, destroying millions of 200-year-old fir trees, clogging rivers, devastating the land north of the collapsed cone, and killing fifty-seven people. In the last two hundred years, seven eruptions have occurred, and USGS scientists found that in the last four thousand years eruptions in the Cascades occurred at a rate of one to two per century. When the next eruption will occur is not known, but eruptions are certain to happen in the future.

The Trail Today

Secretary of the Interior Bruce Babbitt drove a golden spike into the ground along the Pacific Crest Trail in the San Gabriel Mountains in 1993, an action reminiscent of the completion of the nation's first transcontinental railroad a century earlier. Although declared "complete," the PCT still needs improvement. As the chief nonprofit advocate for the trail, the Pacific Crest Trail Association (PCTA) has urged government officials to use federal money from the Land and Water Conservation Fund to relocate segments off public highways or away from private lands subject to sale. Aware of the threat of suburban and resort encroachment, the

PCTA plans to increase its nearly membership of approximately three thousand to strengthen the impact of its collective voice.

As specified in the National Trails System Act of 1968, the secretary of agriculture administers the trail in consultation with the secretary of the interior, who has delegated primary responsibility to the Forest Service in coordination with other agencies. Much of the trail lies on public lands. Stretching from the Mexican border in the south to the Canadian border in the north, the PCT follows the Pacific mountain system, principally the Sierra Nevada and the Cascade ranges, where average elevation is 6,000 feet in California, 5,000 feet in Oregon, and 4,000 feet in Washington. Just north of California's Mount Whitney, at Forester Pass, the trail reaches 13,200 feet, its highest elevation. Oregon's highest point is Tipso Pass, at 7,560 feet, and Washington's highest is Old Snowy Mountain, at 7,930 feet, where hikers take in spectacular views of 14,411-foot Mount Rainier. Awe-inspiring views of other high mountain peaks, such as Mount Whitney in California (14,494 feet) and Mount Hood (11,239 feet) grace the trail.

Outings on the PCT are for the most part day hikes, supplemented by legendary backpacking trips and horse, mule, and llama packing getaways. Each year a few through-hikers traverse the trail from end-to-end in one continuous journey. It takes most

WRANGLERS PACK UP

While outings on the PCT are for the most part day hikes, horse, mule, and llama packing trips are attractive alternatives. Through-hikers on foot take five to seven months to complete the arduous trek from end to end.

through-hikers five to seven months to trek the entire trail. The common strategy, dictated primarily by weather, is to leave the Mexican border by mid-April, maintain a pace of roughly 15 to 20 miles per day, and reach the Canadian border by mid-October, before the winter storms render the route impassable. Elite power hikers Ray and Jenny Jardine wrote a book about their travel-light techniques, which helped them to complete the trek in an amazing three months and three weeks in 1991. PCTA members who finish the trek in one season are awarded a special certificate. As an alternate to the fast pace, some undertake the journey over two summers. Other devotees complete the trek in one-month intervals over five summers, taking three summers just to pass through California.

BORDER NEAR CAMPO

The PCT begins near the high desert outpost of Campo, about 50 miles east of the seaside metropolis of San Diego.

Hardy individuals who go the distance delight in some of the nation's most spectacular scenery. En route one encounters twenty-four national forests, seven national parks, one national recreation area, one national monument, four Bureau of Land Management sites, thirty-three federally designated wilderness areas, and five state or provincial parks.

In California, the PCT begins near the high desert outpost of Campo, about 50 miles to the east of the seaside metropolis of San Diego. Elevation here is approximately 2,600 feet as the trail heads north through desert chaparral along mountains and through Anza-Borrego Desert State Park. Named for the eighteenth-century Spanish explorer Juan Bautista de Anza, the park marks his original route through the area with a party of colonists on an overland trek from Mexico to San Francisco (see JBANHT in *America's National Historic Trails*). After crossing through Mount San Jacinto State Park, the San Bernardino and San Gabriel Mountains, and a portion of the Mohave Desert, the trail climbs the southern Sierra Nevada, which in Spanish means "snow-covered mountain range."

Amid high mountain alpine terrain, west of Mount Whitney the PCT joins the spectacular 211-mile John Muir Trail (JMT) for 175 miles. Reaching its highest point at Forester Pass, the JMT passes through the John Muir and Ansel Adams Wildernesses; Sequoia and Kings Canyon National Parks, Devils Postpile National Monument, and Yosemite National Park. Both the John Muir Trail and the wilderness were named after the renowned naturalist John Muir, who wrote, shortly after his first sight of the Sierras in 1868, "I am hopelessly and forever a mountaineer." Muir later founded the Sierra Club, became an advocate for the protection of the Sierra Nevada and the creation of various national parks, and brought attention to the area's glacial topography.

Departing from the JMT in Yosemite National Park's Tuolumne Meadows, the trail proceeds to the heavily used Lake Tahoe basin and the Mother Lode

BRIDGE OF THE GODS

At an elevation of 140 feet just south of the Columbia River, the PCT reaches its lowest elevation near the Bridge of the Gods. In the gorge the PCT intersects with the Oregon National Historic Trail and the Lewis and Clark National Historic Trail. The 80-mile-long Columbia River gorge is the only route near sea level through the Cascade Range. A massive slide blocked the Columbia River here in 1250, perhaps forming a natural bridge that vanished long ago. American Indians referred to it as the "Bridge of the Gods."

THE SOUTH SIDE OF LASSEN PEAK

In northern California the southernmost volcano in the Cascade Range towers above high desert sage, manzanita, and geothermal features such as fumaroles, hot springs, and mudpots. Mount Lassen last erupted in 1914–15, surprising many emigrants who had passed by the active volcano on the Nobles Emigrant Trail of the California National Historic Trail that crosses the PCT terrain.

Country, where it begins several crossings of the California National Historic Trail and the Pony Express National Historic Trail (CNHT, PENHT; see *America's National Historic Trails*). The final encounter with the CNHT in California occurs in Lassen Volcanic National Park at the Nobles Emigrant Trail, where early settlers wrongly assumed the volcanic Lassen Peak was extinct. Devastating eruptions in 1914–15 proved otherwise. After a westward turn to the Klamath Mountains, the PCT returns to its northward course to pass through the Marble Mountains.

Moving across the Siskiyou Range, the trail enters Oregon and penetrates BLM land at the southern end of the Cascade Range. Through the Sky Lakes Wilderness to 7,320-foot Devils Pass, a steep spur track can be taken to Devils Peak, a 7,582-foot summit. At Crater Lake National Park, new trail leads directly to the 2,000-foot-deep lake, which emits a striking cobalt appearance

ON THE PCT IN WASHINGTON

As the PCT weaves on and off the William O. Douglas Wilderness and the Wenatchee National Forest, 3 miles of trail cross the eastern boundary of Mount Rainier National Park. Spectacular views of the massive and majestic volcano unfold, although the trail approaches no closer than 12 miles to Mount Rainier.

on a clear day. Only six lakes in the world are deeper than this jewel, which lies in the caldera of Mount Mazama, Spanish for "mountain goat." Before the collapse of its cone, it stood out as a giant of the Cascade Range at 12,000 feet. Other striking volcanic peaks are Shasta, Hood, Adams, Rainier, and Baker. Headed to Mount Hood, the PCT traverses the Mount Thielsen, Diamond Peak, Three Sisters, Mount Washington, and Mount Jefferson Wilderness Areas. In the Mount Hood National Forest, the trail crosses a segment of the Oregon Trail known as Barlow Road (see ONHT in *America's National Historic Trails*), where, for a toll Sam Barlow offered pioneers this difficult land route

in lieu of rafting down the untamed waters of the mighty Columbia River. Once around Mount Hood, the trail crosses the Columbia River near its lowest point, 140 feet, by way of the Bridge of the Gods.

In Washington, the trail intersects the auto route of the Lewis & Clark National Historic Trail (LCNHT; see *America's National Historic Trails*) and begins its ascent through the Gifford Pinchot National Forest. En route to Mount Rainier National Park, the PCT offers magnificent views of Mount Adams and Mount Saint Helens in the midst of colorful avalanche lilies, lupine, Indian paintbrush, pasque, and other wildflowers. Awe-inspiring views of the magnificent 3-mile-high Mount Rainier unfold as the trail keeps its distance of at least 12 miles, perhaps out of respect. This massive volcanic mountain has been quiet for twenty-five hundred years but is still very much alive. From here, the PCT progresses through wilderness areas in the Mount Baker–Snoqualmie and Wenatchee National Forests and weaves over the border of North Cascades National Park. As grizzlies attempt to make a comeback in the park complex, alpine fir forests, flower-graced ridgetop meadows, and glaciered peaks keep them company. Before reaching the Canadian border, the trail enters the Okanogan National Forest, crosses the North Cascades National Scenic Byway, and traverses the Pasayten

Wilderness. Mountain goats, gray wolves, and grizzly bears claim residency in the remote wilderness that spreads out to Canada. As a welcome change, the land traversed along the trail north of Rainy Pass receives less rain due to the mountain ranges to the west.

If planning a stay of three days or less in Canada, hikers may continue into Manning Provincial Park north of the border without reporting to Customs. PCT travelers are required to carry a special form, Entry to Canada via the Pacific Crest Trail, and a driver's license, passport, or birth certificate. The form should be requested from the Immigration Centre in Huntington, British Columbia, at least two months before leaving. Those who are ready to do a little more exploring in Canada can take a convenient bus from the Manning Park Lodge to Vancouver, British Columbia. If staying for a longer time, check in at the closest Canadian Customs Office or with the Royal Canadian Mounted Police. Those traveling with a dog or a horse will need additional information for Customs. After a longer stay, reentry to the United States requires clearance from the nearest Customhouse.

Whether planning a day hike or a long-distance trek, certain precautions need to be taken, the most important of which is checking on weather conditions. In general, the trail is usually snow-free from August to

MOUNT HOOD

After leaving the Mount Jefferson Wilderness, the PCT enters and reenters Mount Hood National Forest and proceeds to the base of the 11,239-foot volcanic Mount Hood near historic Timberline Lodge.

September and passable from July to mid-October. Weather in southern California can range from extremely hot in the desert to well below freezing at the higher elevations. Temperatures in the Mojave Desert may surpass a scorching 100 degrees, and in the high country, freezing temperatures occur suddenly, with extreme drops of 80 to 90 degrees possible. These conditions demand preparation and proper clothing to shield against cold, high winds, rain, and snow. Altitude sickness is more apt to affect short-term hikers than long-distance hikers, who gradually acclimate. Other conditions to prevent are hypothermia, dehydration, and giardiasis from untreated water. Wearing appropriate clothing, lotions, and insect repellent help to ward against sunburn, tick bites, and

VIEW FROM THE ROCKS NEAR LAGUNA SUMMIT

These hikers take a peek at the dry desert chaparral in the 105-mile segment in the Cleveland National Forest. In the southern reaches of the PCT corridor, temperatures range from extremely hot to below freezing in the nearby Laguna Mountains.

LLAMA PACKING

Once obscure, llama packing tours make great getaways on the PCT. Is this one posing?

mosquitoes. Some llama packers declare that bears will not enter a camp when their companion is present, but bears and other wildlife are a fact of life when traveling in the backcountry, and unnecessary chances should never be taken. When in bear country, food needs to be hung from a tree while in camp or, if this is impossible, placed in bear-resistant canisters.

Stock on the trail is a sensitive issue. Historically, equestrian use has been a part of the PCT, and recently the use of llamas as pack animals has gained popularity.

Llamas are native to high mountain terrain and have softer foot pads that make less of an impact than the hoofs of mules and horses. Established trail etiquette calls for hikers to step aside to allow pack animals to pass, which reduces impact on the terrain. Horses and large pack animals do not yield to anyone because they must stay on the well-worn path. Most packers are dedicated outdoors people who demonstrate responsible attitudes toward the environment. Any improper or careless handling of stock can damage riparian areas, meadows, and trees. Packers carry special feed, follow stock regulations, and make substantial preparations ahead of time. Regulations differ on trail

PCT THROUGH-RIDER BEN YORK

Avid PCT packer and through-rider Ben York is an active member of Backcountry Horsemen of America. A retired veterinarian, Ben and his wife wrote about their personal experiences on the trail in *PCT by 2*.

GROUP OF BACKPACKERS PREPARE TO HIT THE TRAIL

Clinton C. Clark took the approach that the crest trail system could be composed of existing trails interconnected with new trail construction. To test his route, forty teams of YMCA boys participated in summer relay teams that began in Campo on June 15, 1935, and finished three years later, on August 5, 1938, at the Canadian border 6 miles north of Three Fools Creek in Washington. Youth groups still enjoy backpacking on today's PCT, especially as a profusion of wildflowers bloom.

segments; some require picketing, hobbling, and special feed. Backcountry Horsemen of California offers clinics that emphasize low-impact trail use, Montana-based Back Country Horsemen of America has a general guide that offers insight into low-impact techniques, and the PCTA offers a list of equestrian advisers on request.

Long-distance hikers need to replenish their provisions and other supplies at several points during their marathon treks, which requires an extra hike into town or arrangements in advance for a friend to bring supplies to the trail. Many hikers send self-addressed supply packages to outposts along the way. On request, the helpful PCTA will provide a list that includes many mail drops that will hold packages free of charge. Any water that is available along the trail must be purified; in dry years, on occasion hikers leave the trail just to find water.

Staying well informed about trail conditions, weather, and the terrain is the best preparation for a successful journey. Excellent guidebooks are available to help plan an excursion, and trail information is available at the PCTA's

Web site and from the toll-free number. Topographic and quad maps are available from the PCTA, map stores, camping suppliers, and the USGS Distribution Branch in Denver. Permits are necessary to pass through numerous locations, and need to be requested well in advance. Consult guidebooks and the PCTA about permits and how to go about getting them. While the PCT is fairly well marked, a small compass and a watch altimeter or light pocket altimeter can keep you on the trail. Maps and other helpful information about the trail are available at local Forest Service offices. Whether on a short day hike or a long-distance journey, knowing the way makes the PCT a lot safer and shorter and a whole lot more fun.

Cascade Eruptions During the Last 4,000 Years

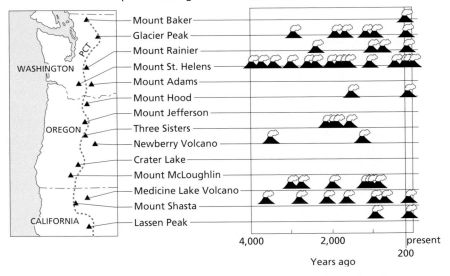

VOLCANIC ERUPTIONS IN THE CASCADES DURING THE LAST 4,000 YEARS

The map on the left shows the approximate locations of many of the Cascade volcanoes found along the Pacific Crest Trail. On the right, miniatrue volcanoes represent the number of eruptions that have occured during the past 4,000 years. Mount St. Helens has been the most active with fourteen eruptions, and Mount Shasta and Medicine Lake volcano follow with seven each. Source: U.S. Department of the Interior U.S. Geological Survey Cascades Volcano Observatory, USGS Open File 94-585, p. 2; and Robert I. Tilling, *Volcanoes* (Washington, D.C.: U.S. Government Printing Office, 1996).

1. CLEVELAND NATIONAL FOREST. The 105-mile Cleveland segment of the PCT begins in dry desert chaparral at the Mexican border near Campo, travels through the Laguna Mountain Recreation Area, and proceeds to the San Diego–Riverside County line. Primary access points for the trail are Campo, Morena Village, Mount Laguna, and Warner Springs. California's southernmost national forest has a warm, dry Mediterranean climate with hot summers and mild winters. Snowstorms in the Laguna Mountains surprise some hikers as they begin the trek north in April and May. A haven for wildlife, vegetation in the lower elevations is fire-prone chaparral, coastal sage, chamise, manzanita, and ceanothus. Live and black oaks grow in canyons and streambeds, Jeffrey pines and mountain mahogany at higher elevations. Near route S1, the Sunrise Scenic Highway, the trail passes over the historic Pioneer Mail Trail, where expansive views extend to the desert floor below. *Other activities:* Camping, hiking, bicycling, horseback riding, offroading, fishing, cross-country skiing, nature programs, and the Palomar Observatory. *Nearby:* In Campo, the San Diego Railroad Museum at the old depot has a collection of classic locomotives and offers a 16-mile round-trip to Tecate, Mexico; Motor Transport Museum; Gaskill Stone Store

Museum has exhibits about the history of San Diego County's mountainous backcountry. Campo can be reached from downtown San Diego via train or Greyhound bus.

2. ANZA-BORREGO DESERT STATE PARK. The PCT traverses the western perimeter of California's first and largest state park, where access is possible from State Highway 78 and S22 at Scissors Crossing. Park headquarters is located in low desert near Borrego Springs. Anza-Borrego has more than six hundred species of plants and three hundred fifty species of reptiles, mammals, and birds. Peninsular bighorn sheep and the nearly extinct desert pupfish are the most notable. Desert wildflowers and cactus flowers add brilliant color to the desert floor in spring, particularly when rainfall and weather conditions have been just right. The Juan Bautista de Anza National Historic Trail (JBNHT; see *America's National Historic Trails*) passes through the park and offers a walk along the route of the historic overland migration from Mexico to San Francisco Bay. *Other activities:* Camping (rustic/electrical hookup), hiking, horseback riding, and a visitor center.

3. LOS COYOTES INDIAN RESERVATION. The PCT crosses reservation land near Warner Springs between Cleveland National Forest and Anza-Borrego Desert State Park. The reservation is home to about two hundred members of the Los

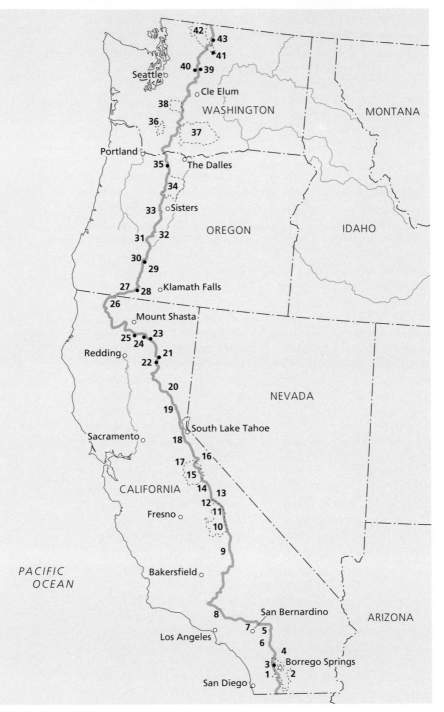

42
43
41
40 39
Seattle
Cle Elum
38
WASHINGTON
MONTANA
36
37
Portland
35
The Dalles
34
33 Sisters
31 32
OREGON
IDAHO
30
29
27 28 Klamath Falls
26
Mount Shasta
25 23
24
Redding
21
22
20
NEVADA
19
South Lake Tahoe
Sacramento
18
17 16
15
CALIFORNIA
14 13
12
Fresno
11
10
9
PACIFIC
OCEAN
Bakersfield
8
San Bernardino
7 5
Los Angeles
6
ARIZONA
4
3 Borrego Springs
1 2
San Diego

PACIFIC CREST NATIONAL SCENIC TRAIL

Coyotes Band of Mission Indians whose tribal affiliation is with the Cahuilla Indians. At Warner Springs, just outside the reservation, geologic faults create hot springs, perhaps the reason the town was a stop on the Butterfield Stagecoach Line from 1858 to 1861. *Other activities:* Camping, jeep trips, and touring geologic formations on the reservation.

4. SANTA ROSA INDIAN RESERVATION. Crossed by the PCT, this rancheria in the San Joaquin Valley is just outside Lemoore. Surrounded by the San Bernardino National Forest, the Tache, Tachik, and Yokut bands make up the Santa Rosa Indian community. Roundhouse sweat ceremonies are held on the last day of February and the first day of March. No photography is allowed at the all-night dance.

5. SAN BERNARDINO NATIONAL FOREST. Nearly 200 miles of the PCT pass through the forest, which offers rocky terrain and chest-high chaparral. In contrast, the first of the truly high mountain elevations is reached amid desert and alpine flora and fauna in the San Jacinto Wilderness. An occasional late spring snowstorm may greet the long-distance hiker amid the pines and incense cedar in the San Bernardino Mountains, where a glimpse of rare bighorn sheep is possible. Primary access points to the trail are at Cabazon, Big Bear City, and Summit. As the hiker leaves the beautiful San Jacintos, the PCT descends nearly 8,000 feet to San Gorgonio Pass, where earthquake faults flank either side. Mount San Jacinto and Mount San Gorgonio tower some 9,000 feet above. San Gorgonio is the highest point in the forest at 11,502 feet. From here, the trail crosses the mighty San Andreas Fault and ascends the east-west aligned mountains. Reaching alternating Jeffrey pine and pinyon forests near Big Bear Lake resort, the area draws visitors for fishing, boating, waterskiing, swimming, cross-country and downhill skiing, sledding, snowshoeing, and snowmobiling, as does Lake Arrowhead, another water reservoir resort near the trail. *Other activities:* Camping, hiking, bicycling, horseback riding, Rim of the World Scenic Byway, off-roading, rock climbing, cross-country and downhill skiing, snowshoeing, snowmobiling, and nature programs.

6. MOUNT SAN JACINTO STATE PARK. Unusual access via the Palm Springs Aerial Tramway is available at the western edge of the San Bernardino National Forest. Visitors are lifted 6,000 feet from the desert floor in Chino Canyon to Mount San Jacinto State Park. The PCT reaches an elevation of 9,030 feet in the San Jacintos. With three mountain peaks higher than 10,000 feet, the park is a mountain retreat often blanketed in snow. Bighorn sheep can be seen on the steep eastern slopes. *Other activities:* Camping, hiking the PCT and other trails, birding, horseback riding, cross-country skiing, and snowshoeing.

7. Silverwood Lake State Recreation Area. Along the PCT near Cajon Pass, the hiker can observe almost 130 species of birds, as well as black bears, bobcats, and coyotes. This recreation area is located near Perris between the desert and the mountains on the eastern side of the San Bernardino National Forest. An occasional bald eagle fishes in the lake, which is planted with bluegill, catfish, largemouth bass, and trout. *Other activities:* Camping, hiking, birding (tours to view bald eagles begin in December), bicycling, fishing, boating, waterskiing, and swimming.

8. Angeles National Forest. Trail elevations along this 185-mile segment of PCT range from an arid chaparral at 3,200 feet to subalpine terrain at 9,400 feet. The trail approaches the Sheep Mountain Wilderness, where Mount Baldy, the highest peak in the San Gabriel Mountains (10,064 feet), and Mount Baden-Powell (9,399 feet) come into view. The route skirts the San Gabriel Wilderness, where bears, coyotes, deer, mountain lions, and Nelson bighorn sheep may be seen. At higher elevations, the vegetation is typically Jeffrey pine, incense cedar, sugar pine, black oak, white fir, and white alder. Primary access points for the trail are Wrightwood, Palmdale, and Gorman. Some 15 million people are attracted to the Angeles and San Gabriel Mountains each year to enjoy activities such as camping, hiking, bicycling, horseback riding (rental), scenic driving, off-roading, fishing, boating, waterskiing, swimming programs, cross-country and downhill skiing, sledding, snowshoeing, snowmobiling, and nature programs. *Nearby:* At Lancaster, the Antelope Valley California Poppy Reserve; hot air balloon rides. Near Gorman, at Fort Tejon State Historic Park, the U.S. Army's First Dragoons established a post in 1854 to protect American Indians living on the Sebastian Indian Reservation.

9. Sequoia National Forest. The Sequoia segment of trail extends 160 miles from below Highway 58 to the vicinity of 12,123-foot Olanch Peak in the Golden Trout Wilderness. Solitude and panoramic views to the east are available as the PCT passes through three wildernesses: Dome Land, South Sierra, and Golden Trout. Dome Land offers granite domes, rock outcrops, scattered Jeffrey pine, sagebrush, mixed conifer forests, and wet meadows. South Sierra overlaps the Inyo National Forest and straddles the Sierra Nevada crest at the southern end of the range. Here the South Fork of the Kern River crosses the trail amid lodgepole and Jeffrey pine and red and white fir. The Golden Trout Wilderness has extensive forest and meadows. Glimpses of the rare and endangered Sierra Nevada bighorn sheep are possible on the eastern slopes and crest. Access to the trail is at

Tehachapi Pass, Walker Pass, and Kennedy Meadows. In the forest there are thirty-eight Sequoia groves, including one where the notable Boole Tree still stands. Named after the forester who saved it, Boole is the largest tree in any national forest. Assets of the area are the South Fork Kings Wild and Scenic River, Kings River Special Management Area, North Fork Kern Wild and Scenic River, South Fork Kern Wild and Scenic River, and Isabella Lake, which is a good distance from the trail. *Other activities:* Camping, hiking, bicycling, horseback riding (rental), scenic drives, off-roading, rock climbing, fishing, boating, river running on the Kern and Kings Rivers, swimming, cross-country and downhill skiing, snowshoeing, snowmobiling, and nature programs. *Nearby:* South of Dome Land Wilderness is the BLM's Owens Peak segment, a 41-mile stretch of PCT with spectacular mountain views.

10. SEQUOIA NATIONAL PARK. Mount Whitney, 14,494 feet, is the highest point in the coterminous United States and marks the southern terminus of the famous John Muir Trail, a large segment of the PCT. If the hiker is not already on the PCT, access is possible by taking State Route 180 east to Cedar Grove and then hiking in the rest of the way. In the park, the trail leads into a long segment offering some of the finest mountain scenery in the United States. The trail is very popular in this area, although hikers can still find solitude in the high mountain terrain where mild, sunny days are typical in this best of mountain climates. Even in late May, however, the long-distance through-hiker is often greeted with snow on the trail. The second-oldest national park in the United States, the park has groves of giant sequoias, the largest living things on earth; the General Sherman tree, the largest sequoia; and Mineral King Valley, a silver-mining area that is now a peaceful retreat. *Other activities:* Camping, hiking, horseback riding, fishing, cross-country skiing, snowshoeing, nature programs, and a visitor center.

11. KINGS CANYON NATIONAL PARK. This park is adjacent to the north side of Sequoia National Park. Here the PCT continues to follow along the John Muir Trail past mountain peaks and alpine lakes and meadows. Giant sequoias are found in the park, along with crystal-clear lakes, waterfalls, wildflowers, and mountain meadows framed by the sheer granite cliffs of one of the nation's deepest canyons. This and another canyon of Kings River and the summit peaks of the High Sierra dominate the mountain wilderness. Access to this area is via Highway 180. *Other activities:* Camping, hiking, horseback riding, fishing, cross-country skiing, snowshoeing, nature programs, and a visitor center.

12. SIERRA NATIONAL FOREST. Sierra National Forest,

bounded by the Inyo National Forest on the east, lies between Kings Canyon and Yosemite National Parks. As the trail leaves Kings Canyon National Park and the headwaters of the San Joaquin River, it passes through the forest's high lake basin to Edison Lakes, where a large stretch of trail on granite leads to Silver Pass. Primary trail access is at Florence Lake and Lake Thomas A. Edison. Almost half of the forest is dedicated to five wildernesses, and of these, the PCT traverses two: the John Muir and the Ansel Adams. Hundreds of alpine lakes and streams add to the beauty of the snowcapped mountains found in the John Muir Wilderness, which is the largest and most visited in California. The Ansel Adams Wilderness, formerly called Minarets, has the high country east of the Sierra crest. Besides spectacular alpine scenery, it boasts deep granite-walled gorges, small plateaus, streams and lakes, and the North, Middle, and Lower South Forks of the San Joaquin River. The PCT crosses by way of the John Muir Trail amid blankets of wildflowers that begin to bloom after the first snowmelt and finally fade with the first snowfall. The forest has rolling hills near the San Joaquin Valley, craggy peaks of the High Sierra, deep canyons and gorges, lakes, and sequoia groves. Besides the giant sequoias, there are incense cedars, sugar pines, white firs, and carpenteria. *Other activities:* Camping, horseback riding, Sierra

Vista Scenic Byway, off-roading, fishing, boating, waterskiing, river running, cross-country and downhill skiing, snowshoeing, snowmobiling, and nature programs.

13. INYO NATIONAL FOREST. The state's longest national forest stretches from Owens Lake to Mono Lake. The PCT on the Inyo starts from the South Fork of the Kern River and continues north to Siberian Pass. It reenters at Silver Pass and continues northward to Donohue Pass, where it exits the forest. Primary PCT access points are at Lone Pine, Independence, Bishop, Mammoth Lakes, and Reds Meadow. The Inyo has Mount Whitney (14,494 feet), the highest peak in the coterminous United States; the Hoover, Boundary Peak, South Sierra, Golden Trout, John Muir, and Ansel Adams Wildernesses; Devils Postpile National Monument; and Mammoth Lakes. A separate unit in the White Mountains protects an ancient bristlecone pine forest. Believed to be the oldest living things on earth, bristlecone pines there have lived over four thousand years. Mono Lake, at the northern end, was the first national forest scenic area created by Congress in 1984. Forest headquarters is located in Bishop. *Other activities:* Camping, hiking, birding, bicycling, horseback riding, scenic drives, fishing, boating, waterskiing, cross-country and downhill skiing, snowmobiling, nature programs, and visitor centers. *Nearby:* Lone Pine is a jumping-

off point for Death Valley National Monument, which contains the lowest point in the Western Hemisphere. At Independence, Manzanar National Historic Site in the Owens Valley commemorates the internment of ten thousand Japanese Americans during World War II.

14. DEVILS POSTPILE NATIONAL MONUMENT. The PCT follows the John Muir Trail through the monument where a side trail leads to a linear rock formation created some nine million years ago. Hot lava cooled and cracked to form 40- to 60-foot-high basalt columns that ancient glaciers later polished to a shine. The main route of the PCT skirts this area to minimize the impact that stock would have on the monument's most visited site. PCT hikers generally avoid the less exciting, but practical, stock route and opt for the side trail. Located near Mammoth Lakes, Devils Postpile is surrounded by the Inyo National Forest. *Other activities:* Camping, hiking, and interpretive programs.

15. YOSEMITE NATIONAL PARK. Spectacular alpine scenery unfolds as the PCT follows the John Muir Trail from Donohue Pass to Tuolumne Meadows. Here, the John Muir Trail splits off and heads for Yosemite Valley, while the PCT heads north on a route below timberline that descends and ascends one glaciated canyon after another and crosses rivers in the canyon bottoms before leaving the park at Dorothy Lakes. Side trails lead to waterfalls, which are especially beautiful during spring runoff. Yosemite National Park was created to preserve a portion of the Sierra Nevada with alpine wilderness, unusual rock formations, and beautiful cataracts. Groves of giant sequoias, mountain lakes, streams, and rivers, and the sublime Yosemite Valley draw millions of visitors each year. Access is by car or bus; a permit program limits visitors in the wilderness as well as in the park during the busiest times. *Other activities:* Camping, hiking, bicycling, horseback riding, Tioga Road/Big Oak Flat National Scenic Byway and other scenic drives, rock climbing, fishing, swimming, cross-country skiing, snowshoeing, interpretive programs, and visitor centers.

16. TOIYABE NATIONAL FOREST. The PCT traverses 74 miles of this forest as it loops along the East Fork of the Carson River. As the trail crosses the Sonora Pass, the terrain changes from alpine meadows to desert with notable amounts of volcanic rock. Trail access points for the Toiyabe-Stanislaus- Eldorado segment of the PCT are located on Highway 108 at Sonora Pass, Highway 4 at Ebbetts Pass, and Carson Pass. Toiyabe is the largest national forest in the contiguous United States and is composed of land in California as well as Nevada. In eastern California, the Toiyabe has the eastern slopes of the Sierra Nevada with a number

of crystal-clear lakes. Like much of the Sierra Nevada, the forest is black bear country. Bobcats, coyotes, mule deer, and mountain lions can be spotted too. Hoover Wilderness, shared with the Inyo National Forest, is found along the Sierra Nevada crest and has glacial lakes with good fishing. Peaks exceed 12,000 feet in the Carson-Iceberg Wilderness, shared with Stanislaus National Forest, where rivers such as the Clark Fork, Stanislaus, Mokelumne, and the headwaters of the East Fork of the Carson run. *Other activities:* Camping, hiking, horseback riding, scenic drives, off-roading, fishing, canoeing, cross-country skiing, snowshoeing, and snow-mobiling. *Nearby:* At Markleeville, Grover Hot Springs State Park has a hot springs mineral pool that is open all year and offers camping, hiking, swimming, and cross-country skiing.

17. STANISLAUS NATIONAL FOREST. In the 900,000-acre Stanislaus National Forest, on the western slopes of the Sierra Nevada in gold rush country (CNHT, in *America's National Historic Trails*), 32 miles of the PCT run through unusual rock formations. The trail generally follows the boundary of the Toiyabe National Forest through Emigrant, Carson-Iceberg, and Mokelumne Wilderness Areas. Miwuk Village, an American Indian town, the Tuolumne Wild and Scenic River, and Lake Alpine and Pinecrest Recreation Areas lie within the boundaries of Stanislaus National Forest. *Other*

activities: Camping, hiking, bicycling, horseback riding, scenic drive to the Sonora Pass, off-roading, fishing, canoeing, boating, river running, cross-country and downhill skiing, snowshoeing, snowmobiling, and nature programs. If accessing the trail in this area by car, the famous hotel in historic Groveland is a good overnight stop.

18. ELDORADO NATIONAL FOREST. Segments of the PCT pass through the Eldorado, which has Echo Summit, numerous lakes in the Sierra Nevada, and forests. The area lies between Mother Lode Country (CNHT) on the west and Lake Tahoe on the east. The PCT crosses two wildernesses here: the Mokelumne and the Desolation. Belying its name, Desolation is one of the most popular roadless areas in California, despite the glacier-carved valleys, with a notable absence of trees due to the rocky terrain, very little soil, and flooding from a nearby reservoir. The area is easily accessed from Highway 50. *Other activities:* Camping, hiking, bicycling, horseback riding, driving the scenic Carson Pass Highway, fishing, swimming, boating, waterskiing, river running, cross-country and downhill skiing, snowshoeing, snowmobiling, nature programs, and a visitor center. *Nearby:* At South Lake Tahoe, Emerald Bay State Park has seasonal tours of Vikings-holm, which is a reproduction of a Norse fortress from A.D. 800, camping, hiking, swimming,

boating, and a visitor center; D. L. Bliss State Park has one of Lake Tahoe's best beaches between Meeks and Emerald Bays, camping, hiking, fishing, swimming, boating, cross-country skiing, snowshoeing, and interpretive programs; the Heavenly Tram ride offers a panoramic view of Lake Tahoe; Tallac Historic Site offers visits to the turn-of-the-century summer estates built on the lake's shore; Eastshore Drive National Scenic Byway offers a 29-mile scenic drive along the Nevada side of Lake Tahoe.

19. TAHOE NATIONAL FOREST. The PCT passes through this popular section of Mother Lode Country (CNHT), which has Emigrant Pass, Donner Summit, the Sierra Buttes, and the Granite Chief Wilderness located at the headwaters of the American River. A side trail up Granite Chief offers the climber panoramic views of the Lake Tahoe basin and, farther down the trail, even more expansive views from Tinker Knob. Trail access points are at Highway 80 near Soda Spring and Highway 49 at Sierra City. Steep-walled river canyons, remnants of mining camps from the gold rush era, and American Indian sites that date back some eight thousand years are diverse resources found in the forest. *Other activities:* Camping, hiking, bicycling, horseback riding, scenic drive, off-roading, swimming, fishing, canoeing, river running, boating, waterskiing, cross-country and downhill skiing, snowshoeing,

snowmobiling, nature programs, and a visitor center. *Nearby:* At Truckee, Donner Memorial State Park memorializes the tragic events that befell the Donner Party's westward journey during the brutal winter of 1846–47 (CNHT). *Other activities:* Emigrant Trail Museum, camping, hiking, fishing, boating (rental), swimming, cross-country skiing, and snowshoeing. *Nearby:* At North Bloomfield, Malakoff Diggins State Historic Park interprets gold rush mining and offers cabins, camping, hiking, bicycling, horseback riding, fishing, swimming, and seasonal guided tours.

20. PLUMAS NATIONAL FOREST. More than 70 miles of PCT cross the Plumas from Gold Lake, north of Sierra City, to the North Fork of the Feather River. The trail in Bucks Lake Wilderness offers expansive views from the top of the escarpment. Primary access points are found near Quincy and Belden. The Plumas, also part of California's Mother Lode Country, sits on a transition zone between the Sierra Nevada and the younger, volcanic Cascades and offers the visitor Feather Falls Scenic Area, impressive Feather Falls, the wild and scenic Middle Fork of the Feather River, and historic gold mining areas. *Other activities:* Camping, hiking, bicycling, horseback riding, scenic drive, off-roading, swimming, canoeing, river running, tubing, boating, waterskiing, cross-country skiing, snowshoeing, snowmobiling,

touring the visitor center. *Nearby:* At Graeagle, Plumas Eureka State Park protects the remains of Mohawk Stamp Mill where gold was processed. Activities include a visit to the museum with exhibits on mining and pioneer life, camping, hiking, bicycling, horseback riding, fishing, cross-country and downhill skiing, and snowshoeing.

21. LASSEN NATIONAL FOREST. As the PCT leaves the Sierra Nevada, it heads for the Cascade Range, dominated by volcanic landscape. The Lassen segment of the trail departs the Feather River Canyon to pass through Lassen Volcanic National Park before reaching McArthur Burney Falls Memorial State Park on the Pit River. Lassen National Forest has lakes formed by volcanic action; human-made Lake Almanor; volcanic lava flow tubes; the world's largest plug-dome volcano; American Indian pictographs; and Ishi, Caribou, and Thousand Lakes Wilderness Areas. Trail access is from Routes 39, 44, and 299. *Other activities:* Camping, hiking, bicycling, horseback riding, scenic drives, off-roading, fishing, boating (rental), swimming, cave exploring, cross-country and downhill skiing, snowshoeing, snowmobiling, nature programs, and a visitor center.

22. LASSEN VOLCANIC NATIONAL PARK. The trail enters at Little Willow Lake on its approach to the southernmost volcano in the Cascade Range and then passes Boiling Springs Lake,

Corral Meadow, Lower Twin Lake, Nobles Emigrant Trail (CNHT), and Badger Flat before reentering Lassen National Forest. Views of Lassen Peak are the highlight of the trail in this area. Side trails to geothermal areas, where mud bubbles and water boils in hot springs, steaming fumaroles, mudpots, and sulfurous vents, are fascinating. Mount Lassen is an active volcano and last erupted in 1921. Park headquarters is located in Mineral. *Other activities:* Camping, hiking, birding, wildlife viewing, bicycling, horseback riding (no overnight stays with stock in the backcountry), scenic drives, fishing, swimming, canoeing, kayaking, rowing, naturalist programs, and the Loomis Museum at Manzanita Lake.

23. MCARTHUR–BURNEY FALLS MEMORIAL STATE PARK. The PCT passes through the otherwise arid land near Burney Falls to face the thundering 129-foot cateract that turns over an impressive flow of 200 million gallons of water each day. Springs in the vicinity provide gushing water all year to the mist-filled basin's lush vegetation. Black swifts nest in the lava-faced cliff walls behind the falls. A 40-foot bridge crosses over typically dry Burney Creek and leads to a large backpackers' camp that also hosts equestrian groups. *Other activities:* Camping, hiking, and horseback riding on the PCT and other trails, fishing, swimming, boating, waterskiing, and a visitor center.

24. SHASTA-TRINITY NATIONAL FOREST. This 154-mile segment of the PCT passes through densely wooded areas of ponderosa pine, Douglas fir, incense cedars, and Oregon oaks. Seldom far from the sounds of civilization, the trail meanders past Mount Shasta, Castle Lake, and the Trinity Alps. Access is possible near Interstate 5 north of Castella at the Soda Creek crossing and at Interstate 5 at Castle Crags State Park. In 1954 two separate forests, Shasta and Trinity, were combined to form one large administrative unit. The trail in this area as well as in California's largest national forest is dominated by Mount Shasta, a 14,162-foot volcano draped with five living glaciers. Towering above the surrounding 4,000-foot terrain, Shasta serves as a training ground for mountaineering, with about ten thousand summit attempts each year, mostly by novices. In the forest, a dramatic change occurs in the trail terrain, from relatively young volcanic rock to rock estimated to be over 400 million years old. The forest has 131 natural lakes; rivers, waterfalls, spectacular sheer granite cliffs and spires, Whiskey-town-Shasta-Trinity National Recreation Area, and portions of the Castle Crags, Chanchelulla, Mount Shasta, Trinity Alps, and Yolla Bolly–Middle Eel Wilderness Areas. *Other activities:* Camping, hiking, bicycling, horseback riding, scenic drives, off-roading, fishing, swimming, river running, boating, waterski-ing, cross-country and downhill skiing, snowshoeing, snow-mobiling, gold panning, interpretive programs, and a visitor center.

25. CASTLE CRAGS STATE PARK. Landmark granite spires, known as crags, date back some 140 million years and tower more than 4,000 feet above the upper reaches of the nearby Sacramento River. Easily accessible from Interstate 5, the park offers striking views of Mount Shasta and access to Castle Crags Wilderness and a section of the PCT. *Other activities:* Camping, hiking, horseback riding, fishing, swimming, boating, and a visitor center. *Nearby:* Off State Route 97, Lava Beds National Monument contains the remains of volcanic activity that spewed molten rock and lava, creating rugged terrain with lava caves and lava tubes. The Modoc Indians used this area as a fortress in the 1872 Modoc Indian War. Adjacent to the monument is Tule Lake National Wildlife Refuge.

26. KLAMATH NATIONAL FOREST. The Klamath segment of the PCT stretches for nearly 120 miles from the Scott Mountains, with a summit at 5,401 feet, to the Oregon border. It has 200 miles of designated scenic rivers and five wilderness areas. Elevation along the trail ranges from 1,400 feet at the Klamath River to above 7,000 feet near Smith Lake. Kings Castle and Black Marble Mountain are highlights along the trail. Hikers encounter numerous lakes in the

Russian Wilderness and the meadows, high country lakes, and streams with steelhead trout and salmon in the Marble Mountain Wilderness. Old-growth forests, Douglas fir, incense cedar, ponderosa pine, and twenty other pine-bearing trees are found in the forest. *Other activities:* Camping, hiking, bicycling, horseback riding, scenic drives, off-roading, fishing, river running, boating, swimming, cave exploring, cross-country and downhill skiing, snowshoeing, snowmobiling, interpretive programs, and a visitor center.

OREGON (430 MILES)

27. ROGUE RIVER NATIONAL FOREST. The PCT follows the Siskiyou and southern Oregon Cascades and stretches all the way to Crater Lake. En route, it enters the western unit of the Rogue River National Forest, with 7,523-foot Mount Ashland high atop the Siskiyou range. Interstate 5 provides access to this part of the trail. The eastern unit of the forest embraces the Sky Lakes Wilderness, the upper reaches of the Rogue River, and the 9,495-foot Mount McLoughlin. The PCT's Sky Lakes Wilderness, with its white fir forest, is accessible from Route 140. The hiker is rewarded with views of more lakes here than anywhere else along the PCT. A three-hour side trail up Mount McLoughlin offers some of the best views along the PCT. *Other activities:* Camping, hiking, bicycling, horseback riding, scenic drives, off-roading,

mountain climbing, swimming, fishing, boating, cross-country and downhill skiing, snowshoeing, sledding, and snowmobiling. *Nearby:* At Cave Junction, Oregon Caves National Monument contains a rare marble cave filled with stalactites, stalagmites, flowstone, and other beautiful formations. Near Klamath Agency Junction, eagles can be spotted in the Upper Klamath National Wildlife Refuge.

28. HYATT LAKE. Sandwiched between the Rogue River National Forest units, the PCT ascends the Siskiyou ridge to Soda Mountain before coming to the Hyatt Lake Recreation Site. This segment, managed by the BLM, has outstanding high Cascade Mountains landscape: Hobart Peak and Hobart Lake, scenic vistas, and segments of the California National Historic Trail. California pioneers watched for Pilot Rock, an ancient volcanic plug and famous landmark found on this segment. Route 66 provides access to the trail at Hyatt Lake, 18 miles east of Ashland. *Other activities:* Camping, hiking, bicycling, horseback riding, fishing, boating, cross-country skiing, snowshoeing, and snowmobiling.

29. WINEMA NATIONAL FOREST. The PCT touches on the western edge of Winema and the Sky Lakes and Mount Thielsen Wildernesses. Goose Nest and Goose Egg are two cones that stand among unusual volcanic peaks that protrude from pine and fir forest amid lakes and

streams. More than two hundred bird species have been cataloged along the Pacific Flyway in this area. *Other activities:* Camping, hiking, birding, bicycling, horseback riding, rock hunting, mountain climbing, fishing, boating, cross-country and downhill skiing, snowshoeing, snowmobiling, and a visitor center.

30. CRATER LAKE NATIONAL PARK. Crater Lake National Park, surrounded by the Winema, Rogue River, and Umpqua National Forests, boasts the deepest lake in the United States and the seventh deepest in the world at 1,932 feet. Renowned for its rich cobalt color on a clear sunny day, this natural wonder fills the caldera of Mount Mazama, a volcano of the Cascade Range that erupted and collapsed about seven thousand years ago. Wizard Island is actually a smaller volcano that formed in the lake. The PCT traverses the park on a north-south axis and is easily accessible via Highway 62. A new route of the trail passes alongside the rim of the lake; the older segment west of the lake takes parties with stock animals through viewless subalpine forests with pumice fields. Highlights of the park are the restored Crater Lake Lodge, Castle Crest Wildflower Trail, the Pinnacles, adorned with volcanic spires, Annie Creek Canyon, Pumice Desert, and Wizard Island. *Other activities:* Camping, hiking, bicycling, horseback riding, Rim Drive, fishing, boat tours, climbing

inside the caldera rim, cross-country skiing along the rim, snowshoeing, snowmobiling (only on the north entrance road), ranger-led activities, and a visitor center.

31. UMPQUA NATIONAL FOREST. The nearly one-million-acre forest, named for the Umpqua Indians, encompasses three wilderness areas, numerous waterfalls, and high-country trails. Here the PCT leaves Crater Lake behind as it heads for Windigo Pass and travels through the Mount Thielsen Wilderness. Mount Thielsen Wilderness, shared with the Winema National Forest, is part of the Oregon Cascade Recreation Area. The PCT reaches its highest point in Oregon at 7,560 feet on an unnamed saddle just north of Mount Thielsen. Access to the mostly lakeless trail is via SR 230 and SR 138. The forest has bedrock gorges, volcanic arches, Umpqua River canyon, Diamond and Toketee Lakes, and the world's tallest sugar pine. *Other activities:* Camping, hiking, bicycling, horseback riding, scenic drives, mountain climbing, swimming, fishing, canoeing, rafting, boating, cross-country skiing, snowshoeing, snowmobiling, and a visitor center.

32. DESCHUTES NATIONAL FOREST. Skirting along the slopes of towering volcanic peaks, the PCT pushes on through this popular 1.6-million-acre national forest as it crosses the Diamond Peak, Three Sisters, Mount Washington, and Mount Jefferson

Wildernesses, all shared with the Willamette National Forest. Trail access points are located at SR 58 at Ordell Lake and the seasonal McKenzie-Santiam Pass Loop at McKenzie Pass on SR 242. With small lakes and ponds, the Mount Jefferson Wilderness and adjacent Olallie Lake Scenic Area have some of the most striking scenery along the PCT. The heavily forested Deschutes, named for the river that descends the east slope of the Oregon Cascades, is dominated by the sweet smell of ponderosa pine. The forest has five wilderness areas, mountain lakes, rivers, alpine meadows, peaks, volcanic remnants, and caves. *Other activities:* Camping, hiking, bicycling, horseback riding, scenic drives, off-roading, mountain climbing, spelunking, swimming, fishing, river running, boating, cross-country and downhill skiing, snowshoeing, snowmobiling, nature programs, and a visitor center.

33. WILLAMETTE NATIONAL FOREST. The PCT traverses areas along the summit of the Cascades in the 1.7-million-acre Willamette National Forest, which is covered with Douglas fir. The forest has eight wildernesses; lava caves and extended volcanic formations; McKenzie River; and waterfalls, lakes, and streams. Three lakes are standouts: Translucent Clear Lake; disappearing and reappearing Fish Lake; and Waldo Lake, one of the world's purest bodies of water. The Three Sisters Wilderness, with glacier-clad mountains and trailside lava

flows, is regarded as the most scenic in the area. Exacting a fee of sorts from the hiker, the numerous scenic lakes and ponds in this wilderness produce an abundance of mosquitoes. Access points are at McKenzie Pass and Santiam Pass. *Other activities:* Camping, hiking, bicycling, horseback riding, scenic drives, off-roading, mountain climbing, spelunking, swimming, fishing, boating, cross-country and downhill skiing, snowshoeing, and snowmobiling. *Nearby:* Near Sisters, Elliott R. Corbett II State Memorial Park has additional hiking.

34. WARM SPRINGS INDIAN RESERVATION. The PCT weaves on and off the reservation as it proceeds north through the Mount Hood National Forest. Three tribes, the Wasco, Warm Springs, and Paiute, live on the reservation. They offer the Root Feast and Root Feast Rodeo in April, the Pi Ume Sha Treaty Days Celebration (inquire about dates), the All-Indian Rodeo in June, and the Huckleberry Feast in August. *Other activities:* Camping, fishing, and dances at Kah-Nee-Ta Resort in summer.

35. MOUNT HOOD NATIONAL FOREST. The one-million-acre national forest is named for Oregon's highest peak—the 11,239-foot volcanic Mount Hood. Access to the PCT is available at SR 35 at Barlow Pass. After leaving the Mount Jefferson Wilderness, the PCT enters and reenters forestland and proceeds to the base of Mount

Hood near historic Timberline Lodge. In a western loop around the glacier-draped peak, the PCT traverses the Mount Hood and Columbia Wildernesses. It does not provide much of a view of the spectacular Columbia Gorge during the 3,160-foot descent to Interstate 84 and the Bridge of the Gods, which crosses into Washington. Just south of the Columbia River the trail reaches its lowest elevation, 140 feet. Significant to the history of both the Oregon and the Lewis and Clark National Historic Trails, the entire gorge area is fascinating. The forest has hot springs, glaciers, alpine meadows, four wilderness areas, rivers, streams, awe-inspiring waterfalls, Timberline Lodge (NRHP); Barlow Trail (see ONHT), Mount Hood Loop, Columbia River Gorge National Scenic Area, Historic Columbia River Gorge Highway (an All-American Road), Multnomah Falls, and the Columbine Gorge Hotel, a National Historic Building. *Other activities:* Camping, hiking, bicycling, horseback riding, scenic drives, off-roading, mountain climbing, swimming, fishing, boating, canoeing, windsailing, cross-country and downhill skiing, snowshoeing, snowmobiling, and a visitor center.

WASHINGTON

(5 0 0   M I L E S)

36. GIFFORD PINCHOT NATIONAL FOREST. From the Columbia River, the PCT begins its dramatic ascent of nearly 8,000 feet in Washington as it passes through Indian Heaven Wilderness, noted for beautiful summer flowers, subalpine forests, meadows, stunning fall color displays, and more than one hundred fifty lakes and ponds, and Mount Adams Wilderness, with alpine meadows and a 12,326-foot volcano draped with impressive glaciers. Trail access points are found at the Bridge of the Gods and at Highway 12 at White Pass. Originally named the Columbia National Forest, it was renamed in 1946 to honor the first chief of the Forest Service, Gifford Pinchot (1865–1946), who later became governor of Pennsylvania. The 1.3-million-acre forest covers most of the southern Cascades from the Columbia River to towering Mount Rainier. Marked by Mount Saint Helens to the west and Mount Adams to the east, the forest encompasses seven wilderness areas, meadows, streams, caves, canyons, a lava tube at Ice Cave; unusual formations at Big Lava Beds, an area that is easy to get lost in without a compass; Packwood Lake; and Bear Meadow. *Other activities:* Camping, hiking, huckleberry picking, bicycling, horseback riding (rental), llama packing (rental at Llama Tree Ranch), scenic drives, off-roading, mountain climbing, spelunking, swimming, fishing, canoeing, river running, boating, cross-country and downhill skiing, snowshoeing, snowmobiling, nature programs, and a visitor

center. *Nearby:* At Silver Lake, Mount Saint Helens National Volcanic Monument encompassed the once most perfect of the Cascade peaks until it erupted on May 18, 1980.

37. YAKIMA INDIAN RESERVATION. The trail follows the border of Goat Rocks Wilderness as it proceeds through northern areas of the reservation along streams, alpine lakes, and volcanic lava flows that are reminiscent of the high Sierra. At elevations above 6,000 feet, snow is present most of the summer. Except for the PCT corridor, this portion of the reservation is closed to the public. Access is possible from White Pass. The Reservation, on the eastern slopes of the Cascade Range, is home to several tribes and bands of the Yakima Nation. At Toppenish, the Yakima Nation Cultural Heritage Center has a museum. Annual powwows are held each month from February to September, and there are rodeos in June and July.

38. MOUNT RAINIER NATIONAL PARK. Three miles of the PCT pass through parklands near the eastern boundary, as it weaves on and off the William O. Douglas Wilderness and the Wenatchee National Forest. Passing over subalpine terrain with many lakes, meadows, and forests and then a series of saddles on the crest, the route comes within 12 miles of Mount Rainier. Clear views of the monarch of the Cascades are possible from the trail, unless it is obscured by poor air quality from the many autos in the park. Access is at Chinook Pass on State Highway 410. The park is named for this majestic peak, which reaches 14,411 feet. Highlights are Longmire, the park's oldest developed area, with Longmire Museum and the National Park Inn; Carbon River, named for coal deposits found in the area; Ohanapecosh, a lowland forest; Paradise, a region of meadows and forests that is a winter wonderland; and Sunrise, an excellent spot to view Emmons Glacier on Mount Rainier. *Other activities:* Camping, hiking, horseback riding, scenic drives, mountain climbing, fishing, nonmotorized boating, cross-country skiing, snowshoeing, sledding, tubing, snowmobiling, nature programs, museum, visitor centers.

39. WENATCHEE NATIONAL FOREST. The 2.1-million-acre forest is one of the largest in the United States and derives its name from an Indian word that means "water pouring out." It encompasses seven wilderness areas: Goat Rocks (shared with the Gifford Pinchot), William O. Douglas, Norse Peak, Alpine Lakes , Henry M. Jackson, and Glacier Peak. The latter three are shared with Mount Baker–Snowqualmie National Forest. William O. Douglas Wilderness, on the eastern border of Mount Rainier National Park, honors the late Supreme Court justice and local resident. From the trail in Norse Peak Wilderness, there are excellent views of Mount Rainier

and opportunities to see mountain goats and elk. Glacier Peak Wilderness, as its name suggests, has dramatic glacier-crowned peaks. The rugged, switchbacked PCT is rendered even more challenging in the damp-wet-rainy climate, and ice axes are needed along the trail until the snow melts. Crossing streams may be more safely accomplished in the morning. Trail access is at White Pass and Snoqualmie Pass at Interstate 90. *Other activities:* Camping, hiking, bicycling, horseback riding, scenic drives, off-roading, mountain climbing, fishing, boating, cross-country and downhill skiing, snowshoeing, snowmobiling, and a visitor center. Unfortunately, the ravages of clear-cutting are visible on stretches of private land north of here.

40. MOUNT BAKER–SNOQUALMIE NATIONAL FOREST. Passing through the forest's best-known wildernesses, Alpine Lakes and the Henry M. Jackson (shared with Wenatche NF), the PCT covers varied Cascade terrain. Elevation ranges from 2,000 to 6,000 feet as the trail passes craggy crests, entire watersheds, alpine lakes, and mountains. Views are spectacular from Kodak Peak in the Henry M. Jackson Wilderness, where sections of the PCT are steep and rocky along the crest. As the trail crosses the Alpine Lakes Wilderness, many of its seven hundred lakes come into view. Weeklong backpacking trips are very popular. Access is from Snoqualmie Pass and Stevens Pass. The forest is composed of two sections on the western slopes of the Cascades. Snowqualmie is in west-central Washington, and Mount Baker is in the northwest. Special features of the national forest are Mount Baker, Baker Lake, Big Four Ice Caves, panoramic views of the northern Cascades, scenic byways and historic remnants of Snoqualmie Pass Wagon Road, eight wilder-nesses, and the Skagit Wild and Scenic River. *Other activities:* Camping, hiking, bicycling, horseback riding, scenic drives, off-roading, mountain climbing, fishing, white-water rafting, boating, cross-country and downhill skiing, snowshoeing, snowmobiling, and a visitor center.

41. LAKE CHELAN NATIONAL RECREATION AREA. The PCT enters the northwest corner of this popular outdoor playground, which is named for the fjordlike lake that rests in a glacially carved trough. This national recreation area in the beautiful Stehekin Valley adjoins the south unit of North Cascades National Park. *Other activities:* Camping, hiking, bicycling, horseback riding, fishing, boating, cross-country skiing, snowshoeing, and a visitor center. *Nearby:* At Chelan, uplake boat trips and floatplane service to Stehekin, the only town in Washington that cannot be reached by road; Lake Chelan Museum has American Indian, pioneer, and apple-box exhibits; Lake Chelan State Park has an

underwater park and is a mecca for water sports; Twenty-five Mile Creek State Park offers camping, hiking, fishing, and boating.

42. NORTH CASCADES NATIONAL PARK. North Cascades National Park is split into north and south units by Ross Lake National Recreation Area. The PCT passes through the southern portion of the south unit following the Bridge Creek Trail, which can be accessed at 4,840-foot Rainy Pass. The landscape is composed of high jagged peaks, mountain meadow slopes, countless waterfalls, and more than 750 perennial snowfields and small glaciers, accounting for half of all snowfields and glaciers in the contiguous United States. One of the wildest national parks in the lower forty-eight states, the park lies mostly in the Stephen Mather Wilderness, east of Sedro Wooley, although the PCT does not traverse this section. *Other activities:* Camping, hiking, horseback riding (rental), mule trekking (rental), mountain climbing, fishing, cross-country skiing, snowshoeing, and naturalist activities. Ross Lake National Recreation Area offers additional outdoor opportunities along the upper reaches of the Skagit River, where bald eagles soar near Bacon Creek and Newhalem. Cougars mark their boundaries with scrapes, mounds of dirt, urine, dung, and forest litter.

43. OKANOGAN NATIONAL FOREST. The PCT enters the Okanogan, meaning "rendezvous," after leaving North Cascades National Park. In the south, much of the trail follows river valleys well east of the craggy impassable crest. Before reaching the Canadian border, the trail traverses the remote Pasayten Wilderness for 63 miles, with spectacular scenery of high mountain spires. Along the way, the trail reaches Lakeview Ridge, at 7,100 feet one of the highest elevations in Washington. Only 50 percent clear of snow by early July, both snow and ice cover the trail much of the year. In the north, the trail returns to the crest as it approaches the Canadian border. Passing through Manning Provincial Park, the PCT reaches its northern terminus. Access is from scenic North Cascades Highway, State Highway 20 at Rainy Pass, or Forest Road 5400 at 6,100-foot Harts Pass. The Pasayten is one of the largest wildernesses in the lower forty-eight states and has deep canyons, high mountains, and an abundance of wildlife, including gray wolves and grizzly bears. Okanogan National Forest also contains the Sawtooth Wilderness, the young peaks of the North Cascades, and the rolling hills of the Okanogan highlands. *Other activities:* Camping, hiking, bicycling, horseback riding, scenic driving, off-roading, rock hunting, mountain climbing, swimming, fishing, river running, boating, cross-country and downhill skiing, snowshoeing, snowmobiling, nature programs, and a visitor center. *Nearby:* In Canada,

between Hope and Princeton, British Columbia, the nearly 163,000-acre Manning Provincial Park offers camping, hiking, bicycling, horseback riding, swimming, fishing, boating, winter sports, and a visitor center.

**STROLLING
IN OLD
TOWN
ALEXANDRIA**

City dwellers
regularly
stroll along
the Potomac
River on the
PHNST,
although the
route is not
yet marked
as a national
trail.

Potomac Heritage National Scenic Trail

. . . the River of Potowmack. Fish lying so thicke with their heads above water. For want of nets (our barge driving amongst them) we attempted to catch them with frying pan: . . . Neither better fish, nor more plenty, had any of us ever seen in any place so swimming in water.

CAPT. JOHN SMITH, SHIP'S LOG, JUNE 16, 1608

The Potomac Heritage National Scenic Trail (PHNST) will eventually extend some 700 miles from Chesapeake Bay to the Allegheny Mountain highlands along a corridor rich in natural scenic, historic, cultural, and recreational features. People, places, and stories that have made the Potomac River valley and the upper Ohio River basin such distinctive regions come to life along the trail: Pocahontas, John Smith, and George Washington; American Indian culture; early colonial families; tobacco and

ADMINISTERING AGENCY
National Park Service
Potomac Valley Field Office
P.O. Box B
Harpers Ferry, WV 25425
304-535-4014
www.nps.gov/pohe

FURTHER INFORMATION
Potomac Heritage Trail Coordinating
  Committee
c/o Potomac Heritage Partnership, Inc.
1623 28th Street NW
Washington, DC 20007
202-338-1118/6222

C&O Canal National Historical Park
P.O. Box 4
Sharpsburg, MD 21782
301-739-4200

Laurel Ridge State Park
Pennsylvania Department of
  Conservation/Recreation
R.D. 3 Box 246
Rockwood, PA 15557
412-455-3744

DESIGNATED
1983

APPROXIMATE MILEAGE
700 miles (1,129 km)*

STATES
Virginia, Maryland, Pennsylvania,
District of Columbia

*Some estimates suggest 775 miles.

plantation life in the Tidewater region; boatmen, emigrants, and commerce on the Chesapeake and Ohio (C&O) Canal; the Civil War and its impact; thriving Harpers Ferry; activities of the abolitionist John Brown; the building of the Baltimore and Ohio (B&O) Railroad; the riches of coal and the opening of the Appalachia; mining in western Maryland; and the emergence, splendor, and power of the U.S. capital.

While not yet marked, at least 271 miles of the trail in three large segments are currently in use: the Mount Vernon Trail, the C&O Canal Towpath, and the Laurel Highlands National Recreation Trail. In many respects, the identity and potential of the Potomac Heritage Trail is just emerging.

The History of the Trail

In total, the Potomac River basin encompasses 14,670 square miles and includes today's District of Columbia and parts of Maryland, Pennsylvania, Virginia, and West Virginia. Lands in the river basin vary; some provinces are hilly to mountainous, and others are open with scattered forests. Areas with metamorphic and igneous rock contrast with those of limestone, dolomite, sandstone, and shale. These lands in the river basin are crossed by completed segments of the PHNST such as the towpath of the C&O Canal, the Mount Vernon Trail, and the Laurel Highlands NRT. The Potomac River is approximately 400 miles long and was explored by Capt. John Smith in 1608. The banks were first settled by Europeans in 1634 in the colony of Maryland by the second Lord Baltimore, Cecil Calvert. Smith called the river Patawomeke after the Algonkian name that was used for the area that is now Washington, D.C. At that time, the river basin was inhabited by three American Indian tribes of the Algonkian family, the Pamunkey and Powhatan in what is now Virginia and the Nanticoke in present-day Maryland.

Early American commerce moved on rivers such as the great Potomac, but river trafficking had disadvantages (see NTNST). Water levels fluctuated, narrows and shallows obstructed passage, waterfalls were either impassable or created dangerous rapids, and it was often impossible to travel westward against the current. In the eighteenth and nineteenth centuries, canals were built that provided solutions to many of these difficulties. Thomas Hahn, the first president of the American Canal Society, explains that the canals built in the United States fell into three basic categories: "those to improve transportation between the up-country and tidewater along the Eastern seaboard; canals to connect the Ohio-Mississippi river systems with the Great Lakes; and canals to connect the Atlantic states with the Ohio River." This last category includes the C&O Canal. Its unique story begins with early efforts to connect the Eastern Seaboard with the rich Ohio

Valley, a goal not unlike that of today's PHNST project.

In 1747 a distinguished party of Virginians organized the Ohio Company with a twofold plan, to establish a trade route across the Appalachians and to acquire land for settlement in the Ohio Valley. Two years later the British granted the petition and provided the speculators with acreage west of the Monongahela River. This land, however, was also claimed by France and Pennsylvania. As the Ohio Company began to open an 80-mile wagon road to the river, the French advanced into the territory from Fort Niagara. Lt. Gov. Robert Dinwiddie, the highest resident Crown official in Virginia and a member of the Ohio Company, reacted swiftly by sending the younger brother of two company investors to the forks of the Ohio (now Pittsburgh) to warn the French that they were trespassing on Virginia territory. On young George Washington's return, he reported that the French had refused to withdraw. Earlier, in spring 1747, the newly commissioned Lt. Col. George Washington was sent back with a small force of Virginia militia to build a military road from Wills Creek (now Cumberland, Maryland) into the Ohio Valley and to seize the strategic junction of the Allegheny and Monongahela Rivers. It was on this assignment that Washington fought his first skirmishes. These would grow into the world struggle that became known in North America as the French and Indian

WINDOWS IN CUMBERLAND, MARYLAND

As a young surveyor, George Washington began to dream about a canal system that would make the Potomac River navigable, inspire trade with the Ohio Valley, and unite the country. The Patowmack Company, which Washington presided over, was formed in 1784 to construct a series of five canals. Today his image is depicted with good company as they look out over the Potomac River and the terminus of the Chesapeake and Ohio Canal in Cumberland, Maryland.

War and abroad as the Seven Years' War.

Washington received significant land claims in the Ohio Valley as a reward for his service in the war. He supplemented these lands with additional acreage purchased from other veterans. By the end of 1772 he had acquired more than 30,000 acres in the area. Already a major landholder in the Potomac Valley, Washington was convinced that a navigable Potomac River could provide a superior route west and a commercial link with tributaries of the Ohio. He began to pursue his vision, although the majority

KAYAKERS AT GREAT FALLS

Both kayaking and rock-climbing enthusiasts enjoy Maryland's Great Falls Gorge near Great Falls Tavern in Maryland. Here kayakers are often seen trekking with their kayaks slung over their backs on the Potomac Heritage Trail on the C&O towpath. Views from Amsted Bridge on the Maryland side and from overlooks on the Virginia side offer visitors bird's-eye views of the Falls of the Potomac, where only very skilled kayakers surf. Boating is not advisable for novices.

of his time was devoted to his Tidewater properties. Like his fellow planters, he felt exploited by British merchants and oppressed by British regulations. He voiced his resistance to the restrictions and advocated a boycott of English goods to protest the taxes that Parliament was attempting to impose on the colonies. These taxes were intended to remunerate the Crown for expenses related to the French and Indian War.

This, of course, led to the American Revolution, which distracted Washington from land development for more than a decade. After the revolution,

Washington's financial affairs were in such disorder that he decided to rent or sell his western properties. On returning to the Forks of the Ohio, Washington was struck by the fact that the immigrant settlers in the area held no particular allegiance to the United States. He concluded that a commercial tie to the east, such as the canal he had envisioned earlier, would provide the link to unification. With the encouragement of Thomas Jefferson, Washington agreed to take the leadership of the Potomac Canal project. In March 1784 he wrote to Jefferson, "Respecting the practicability of an easy, and short communication between the Waters of the Ohio and Potomac . . . I am satisfied that not a moment ought to be lost in recommencing this business."

Washington's name lured investors, and the Patowmack (sometimes spelled Potomack) Company was chartered by Maryland and Virginia in 1785. With postwar capital sparse, the severe physical challenges of the river channel would be difficult to alter. As the company's president, Washington and his directors decided to simply clear the river's channel and then provide canals around Little Falls, Great Falls, Seneca Falls, Shenandoah Falls at Harpers Ferry, and House Falls above Harpers Ferry. That same year, James Rumsey, an inventor and pioneer in steam navigation, was named the project's first superintendent. He convinced

Washington that locks were needed at Great Falls. The construction of these five locks presented such an engineering challenge for America's first canal system that the Great Falls area was not opened until 1802.

In the meantime, Washington had invited representatives from Maryland and Virginia to meet in Mount Vernon to discuss matters of free trade on the Potomac. Since Pennsylvania's cooperation would also be necessary if the canal was to eventually have connections with the Ohio River, the delegates discussed having another meeting in 1786 that would include Pennsylvania. Instead, however, they decided to invite all thirteen states "to consider how far a uniform system in their commercial regulations may be necessary to their common interest and their permanent harmony." The resulting Annapolis Convention succeeded in bringing representatives from only five states, but these delegates approved Alexander Hamilton's resolution for another convention in Philadelphia to consider constitutional reforms. As it turned out, Washington's canal project pointed the way to the Constitutional Convention.

When the Constitutional Convention opened on May 25, 1787, Washington was unanimously elected its president, and it would be less than two years later that he took the oath of office as the first president of the United States. During his presi-

MOUNT VERNON COUPLE IN PERIOD COSTUME

The Mount Vernon Trail stretches north along the Potomac River and the George Washington Memorial Parkway, connecting George Washington's home at Mount Vernon to downtown Washington, D.C. Attracting over one million visitors annually, the private site is managed by the Mount Vernon Ladies' Association, the first national historic preservation organization in the country.

dency, which lasted until 1797, his interest in the canal project never wavered. His presidency also influenced the development of two major Potomac River undertakings: the armory at Harpers Ferry and the nation's capital near Georgetown.

The Patowmack Canal— America's first canal system— operated at various levels of completion from 1788 to 1830 and played a role in bringing the western lands into the United States. Corn, flour, furs, iron ore, timber, tobacco, and whiskey were carried on flatboats from as far away as Cumberland, Maryland, to Georgetown. In Georgetown boatmen sold their boats for lumber

MILEPOST MARKER 184.5

Stretching 184.5 miles from Georgetown (Mile 0) to Cumberland, Maryland, the C&O Canal National Historical Park attracts hikers, cyclists, and, for most of the distance, horseback riders as well. At the Cumberland Terminus at milepost 184.5, the Western Maryland Railroad Station Center serves as a national park visitor center.

and walked home. Eventually, because of high operating costs and the lack of federal support, the Patowmack Company floundered. It served as the forerunner of the C&O Canal Company.

Construction on the C&O began with a ground-breaking ceremony on July 4, 1828, with the president of the United States bestowing his blessing on the great national project at Little Falls, 5 miles from Georgetown. Here the project got off to a rocky start, when it took a couple of attempts before President John

Quincy Adams could turn over a spadeful of earth and rock. Twenty-two years and seventy-four locks later, the 184.5-mile canal reached Cumberland at a cost of almost $12 million, not including interest on loans. According to the company's charter, the first 100 miles of usable canal had to be completed within five years. This goal was not met. It took two years just to complete the first 17-mile section from Little Falls to Seneca.

Canal construction problems included a scarcity of local labor. Workers were brought in from England, Wales, Ireland, and Germany, but unrest, desertions, and a cholera epidemic led to delays and increased financial difficulties. There were also material shortages, frequent flooding from the nearby Potomac, increased land costs, right-of-way disputes, and legal battles with the B&O Railroad. The project itself required the creation of seventy-four lift locks to overcome the 605-foot change in elevation from Georgetown and Cumberland. Hills had to be confronted by going around, over, or through them. Construction of the 3,118-foot Paw Paw Tunnel took approximately eight years at an average of one foot of tunnel completed per day. Intersecting roads, rivers, and streams presented additional obstacles. More than two hundred stone-arched culverts were built to carry the stream of water under the canal, and eleven aqueducts carried the canal and towpath over rivers. Seven dams were required to keep water in the canal, and 122 river and feeder locks were needed to let the water into the canal from the Potomac River.

By the time the canal reached Cumberland on October 10, 1850, excitement spawned rumors that the canal would extend to Pittsburgh and the Ohio River. This would not come to pass. The canal—the nation's deepest at 6 feet, widest at 60 to 80 feet, and sixth longest at 184.5 miles—was complete, save for one last, monumental, engineer-

HIGHWATER MARK

On the Virginia side of the Great Falls of the Potomac, footpaths lead to remnants of George Washington's Patowmack Canal at Great Falls Park where this highwater marker is seen. Because there is no direct connection from the Chesapeake and Ohio Canal National Historical Park, a side trip is typically made by automobile.

ing task. An incline plane was planned in Georgetown, which would allow boats that did not need to unload in Georgetown to transfer from the canal into the tidal Potomac River and avoid a wait at the Rock Creek outlet. The project started in 1872 and finished in 1876. Shortly thereafter the engineering marvel that had been recognized at the 1878 Paris Exposition was destroyed in the late spring flood of 1889. The flood caused so much damage on the canal that it was impossible for the C&O to recover from the financial disaster. Ownership shifted to its largest stockholder, the B&O Railroad. When another flood hit thirty years later, the C&O went out of business for good. The C&O's demise came just before the canal era in this country came to a close in the early 1930s. It is interesting to note that the first day of construction for the C&O Canal coincided with the day that a private corporation began to lay track for the B&O Railroad. Although America's first successful rail company would ultimately put the C&O out of business, on that Fourth of July in 1828 the interest in canals far overshadowed that in the railroad.

Canals rendered obsolete the roads of the time. The canal boat's hauling force, mules, could plod along a towpath at approximately three miles per hour pulling a 100-ton load and still make better time over a long distance than a team of horses pulling a single-ton load by wagon on the finest road.* There was simply less friction to overcome. There were, of course, trying moments. One canaler wrote, "When the boat entered a lock we came near having a bad accident. When the Capt. gave the word to stop I said 'Whoa' and stood still and expected the mules would do the same. Instead of stopping they laid back their long ears, rolled out their eyes and sprang into their harness and pulled as I never saw four mules pull before. 'Whoa' is not a part of the canal mules' language."

Construction of canal mileage burgeoned in the United States, from about 100 miles in 1816 to nearly 4,000 miles in the mid-1800s when the canal era reached its zenith. Although the canals were far more expensive than turnpikes and took far longer to build, industrialization was dependent on the internal transportation of raw materials and the distribution of manufactured goods. The C&O Canal was constructed to provide transportation by water for the commercial development of the Potomac River valley, and while it never reached Pittsburgh, its original intended terminus, its western end linked up with the National Road. This was an added boon to commerce.

The C&O's heyday began in 1865, when additional income allowed it to pay off debts, raise

wages, and make necessary repairs. Also, the Civil War was over and the mid-Atlantic states were rebuilding. The tonnage moved and tolls collected continued to climb. By the 1870s, five hundred boats annually were maneuvering through the canal carrying coal, grain, lumber, stone, flour, whiskey, and other products. During its peak year of operation in 1875, 973,805 tons were transported through the canal.

This cheap, easy means of transporting bulky products and heavy goods stimulated a more diverse economy in the mainly agricultural Potomac Valley. New jobs included milling, manufacturing, iron working, quarrying and stone cutting, and boat building. Grocery and feed stores opened, wharf owners prospered, and by far the biggest economic beneficiary was Cumberland coal. The C&O hired canal officials and construction and maintenance workers. At the peak of construction, approximately 4,700 workmen were employed by the Canal Company. Later, lock keepers were needed day and night to open and close the gates for canal boats. They would live in a house provided at the locks and would sometimes make extra cash by selling produce to boatmen. Finally, the canal created a way of life for the families who lived and worked on their own boats. The canalers,† in

---

*The mule became such an integral part of canal life that its legacy endured. When a small locomotive was used in later years to tow ships through a lock, it was referred to as a mule.

†In 1902 the canalers lost their livelihood when the canal company ended the era of independent boat owners by forming the Canal Towage Company.

turn, hired crews and young mule drivers. Before the canal froze over for the winter, they would all return to their homes in Cumberland, Georgetown, Williamsport, Alexandria, Washington, Hancock, Shepherdstown, or Antietam (Sharpsburg). Some tied up and stayed on their canal boats near these towns.

For nearly a century, the C&O served its region well. By 1938 a new era began when the B&O transferred ownership in the C&O to the federal government to help satisfy a debt. On September 23 of that same year, the canal was placed under the care and stewardship of the National Park Service. In the 1950s plans emerged to bulldoze the canal and replace it with a superhighway into Maryland. In 1954 Supreme Court Justice William O. Douglas invited editors of the Washington Post and others to join him on a walk along the towpath to garner their support for preserving the canal. As a result, the C&O Canal Association was formed, and by 1961 the canal was proclaimed a national monument. Ten years later, on January 8, 1971, the C&O was designated the Chesapeake and Ohio Canal National Historical Park, making it a public entity from terminus to terminus. In 1996 the canal suffered damage from its seventeenth major flood since ground breaking in 1828. Despite its devastating effects to man-made structures, flooding is largely

HARD HATS ON THE C&O CANAL TOWPATH

Flooding has occurred on the Potomac River for millions of years. The January 1996 flood became the seventeenth major flood during the life of the C&O Canal. It caused damage to canal structures and the surrounding areas that brought these workers and hundreds of volunteers to the trail. Although they bring exotics and alien weeds that crowd out native plants, floods help the natural system by creating rich soil that benefits the wildflowers that attract visitors in early spring.

responsible for the extraordinary biological diversity of the area.

In 1971 Douglas wrote of the C&O Canal Towpath: "Hiking or just sitting in the solitude of the woods and river has some magic. Why, I do not know. But exercise and quiet of cliffs, woods, and river generate powerful subconscious forces, and before I get home the seemingly insoluble problem has been solved." Today, the C&O draws three million to four million visitors each year.

Locks were identified by lock number, by mileage from the Georgetown Tide Lock, by towns, or by the name of the lock keeper. When the lock keeper heard the boatman's horn or cannon, he knew that the canal boat was close at hand. The lock's hand-operated miter gates (also known as swing gates), similar to those designed by Leonardo da Vinci's in 1485, consisted of two leaves that opened into the lock wall and closed on the lock axis into a V shape that pointed upstream. Though simple enough to use, they demanded a great deal of maintenance. Locking through, which took about eight to ten minutes, was also faster if another lock tender was on hand.

For the boatman, entering the lock was the most exacting part of canaling. If a loaded boat hit the lock walls, it could damage the walls and the load it carried. It could even sink. For protection, children were confined to their cabins when locking through, and mules were placed in the stable. Meanwhile, the boat—just 7 feet shorter than the lock—had to be stopped before it crashed into the gate at the far end. To do this, a crew member had to jump out and wind a line from the boat to a snubbing post near the towpath. If done right, this would break the momentum of the 93-foot craft. If the line was too tight, the boat's momentum could break the snubbing post, which was simply carried along as the boat crashed into the gates. According to one Williamsport lock tender, it was just not wise to drink in town before locking through:

That boat was flyin' comin' in there. The captain went to get the snubbin' post, but he couldn't get to it and fell on his face on the runnin' plank. . . . I seen he would knock the gates out if I didn't do sometun', so I run and got his bow line and got a couple of laps on there [on the snubbin post], but he still hit the lock gates and almost knocked them apart. I didn't even report it, 'cause he was a nice fellow when he was sober. . . . There wasn't many that drank anything.

The Trail Today

The Potomac Heritage National Scenic Trail (PHNST) was designated a component of the National Trails System by Congress in 1983 and a unit of the National Park System in 1985. As envisioned, the trail will trace diverse scenic, cultural, and recreational features of the Potomac River basin from Chesapeake Bay in Virginia to western Pennsylvania. To date, the National Park Service has recognized three official national trail segments. These ready-to-go sections are the 18-mile Mount Vernon Trail from

CRAB STAND

Vendors along the Potomac offer a tasty lunch to trail-goers on the 18-mile Mount Vernon Trail as it transitions to the C&O Canal Towpath near the national monuments of downtown Washington, D.C.

Mount Vernon, Virginia, to Washington, D.C.; the 184.5-mile C&O Canal Towpath from Georgetown to Cumberland, Maryland; and Pennsylvania's 70-mile Laurel Highlands National Recreation Trail stretching from the village of Ohiopyle to the Conemaugh Gorge near Johnstown. These segments are not yet marked or blazed. In 1998 the second annual caucus of the PHNST attracted approximately fifty trail officials who are pursuing partnerships and affiliations to strengthen corridor-wide coordination. Identification of additional routes is gaining momentum.

The trail offers travelers a rich experience: grandeur and sophistication of monuments in the U.S. capital, the natural beauty of bucolic pastoral countryside, the serenity of placid waters, and the exhilaration of white-water rapids. Landforms such as shorelands, marshes, stream valleys, gorges, scenic highlands, rugged bluffs, and forested mountainous areas are found along the trail, as well as wildlife, fish, and shellfish. The presence of the Potomac River, with its estuary, waterfalls, and tributaries, is abundantly evident. Some historic features date to precolonial times. Birthplaces, battlefields, once-thriving ports, former plantations, remains of American Indian civilizations, historic transportation routes, and official national heritage sites punctuate the trail route. Cultural features include dams, aqueducts, railroads, canals, lockhouses, tobacco barns, monuments, forts, churches, and both indoor and outdoor museums. Opportunities abound to sight-see, explore, hike, jog, bike, picnic, canoe, fish, horseback ride, cross-country ski, snowshoe, ice skate, and camp.

The hallmark of the Potomac National Scenic Trail is its diversity. The Mount Vernon Trail accommodates bikers, joggers, and hikers. The Rock Creek Park Horse Center offers horseback tours, and travel by horseback is allowed on the C&O Towpath in Maryland from Swains Lock to Cumberland. The C&O offers sites for tent camping every five miles between Horsepen Branch

JOGGER NEAR THE THOMAS JEFFERSON MEMORIAL

The Thomas Jefferson Memorial on the south bank of the Tidal Basin is breathtaking at night. At dusk, a jogger runs past cherry trees in bloom in mid-April as lights begin to shine on the Vermont white marble monument designed in the simple classical style admired by the president. Following Pierre-Charles L'Enfant's design, the memorial stands at the southern end of a cross whose other ends are marked by the Capitol, the Lincoln Memorial, and the White House. The cherry trees that surround the memorial and the Tidal Basin were gifts of the city of Tokyo in 1912.

and Evitts Creek; group campgrounds at Marsden Tract, where a permit is required; and primitive facilities on a first-come, first-served basis at McCoys Ferry, Fifteenmile Creek, and Spring Gap. Backpacking is popular on the Laurel Highlands Hiking Trail, where a string of eight overnight areas provide campsites every eight to ten miles. Each site contains five Adirondack-type shelters with fireplaces and spaces for thirty tents. Bicycles can be rented at

several locations along the Mount Vernon and C&O segments of the PHNST. The Washington Area Bicyclist Association and the American Youth Hostels Association offer maps and information on cycling in and around Washington, D.C. Additional information on cycling regulations can be obtained from the National Park Service at the addresses given at the beginning of this chapter.

Fishing is possible at several points along the trail. The Potomac is now a popular destination to fish for largemouth bass, striped bass, shade, and white and yellow perch. Anglers are cautioned that the river's edge can be dangerous: rocks can cause poor footing, and it is best to stay a body's length away from the water. The five-mile stretch south of Alexandria's Woodrow Wilson Bridge offers a great place to fish for largemouth bass. Along the C&O, the area around Fletcher's Boat House is well known for its perch; and the Youghiogheny River in Pennsylvania provides good wilderness trout fishing.

Canoeing, kayaking, sculling, sailing, and power boating are popular on the Potomac in the vicinity of Washington, D.C., and several establishments rent boats to the north and south of the city. Sculling classes are available at Thompson's Boat Center. Sailing is popular where the Potomac widens south of Alexandria, and the Chesapeake Bay offers one of the greatest sailing basins in the world.

Only experienced boat handlers should enter the Potomac, and boating should not be attempted when water levels are high. Muddy water indicates that conditions are especially dangerous. Canoeing and boating are generally safe along the C&O canal sections between Georgetown and Violettes Lock, and on short stretches above Violettes Lock at Big Pool, Little Pool, and from Town Creek to Oldtown. During the summer, at Georgetown and Great Falls, boat trips have been offered along the towpath using reconstructed mule-drawn canal boats, just like in the canal era. Motorized craft in these areas are generally prohibited. Outfitters rent canoes at various locations, and information on canoeing on the C&O can be obtained at Great Falls Tavern. Canoeing is discouraged and boating is hazardous along the C&O from Little Falls to Chain Bridge, at Great Falls, and between Dam 3 and U.S. 340. Above Great Falls the river funnels down to 200 feet, causing an alarming increase in the speed of the current. Only top-level white-water canoeists and kayakers should enter the waters below Great Falls in Mather Gorge, a canyon carved by the Potomac River, and even then good judgment is required. The swiftness of the water in this area can be particularly deceptive and dangerous. Ohiopyle State Park contains two segments on the Youghiogheny River that are used for white-water rafting and boat-

ing. Several outfitters are headquartered in the park.

THE MOUNT VERNON TRAIL SEGMENT

Administered and constructed by the National Park Service, the paved, 9-foot-wide, 18-mile-long multiuse Mount Vernon Trail stretches north along the Potomac River and the George Washington Memorial Parkway, connecting George Washington's home at Mount Vernon to downtown Washington, D.C. The route is rolling and wooded on its entire length, and interpretive pullouts are planned every two miles where information about directions will be available.

A mecca for visitors even in Washington's day, Mount Vernon now draws one million visitors annually thanks to the efforts of the Mount Vernon Ladies' Association, which has restored and operates the nation's most visited historic home. The first national historic preservation organization in the country, it is the nation's oldest women's patriotic society and has served as a model for many subsequent endeavors. Traveling upriver and north on the Virginia side of the Potomac, the trail leads to Alexandria's waterfront. Narrated cruises can be taken on the Potomac, and an array of museums, architecture, and special events draw more than 1.5 million visitors to Alexandria each year. Beyond Alexandria, Daingerfield Island is an attractive spot for bird-watching and

ALEXANDRIA'S GLASS MUSICIAN

The multiuse Mount Vernon Trail brings cyclists and other trail users through George Washington's hometown of Alexandria along the Potomac River at Old Town. Antique vessels, small river parks, historic architecture, and sidewalk entertainers, such as this glass musician, add to the charm of the trail.

sailboat watching. On the way to the 88-acre wilderness preserve at Theodore Roosevelt Island, views of Washington, D.C.'s skyline are available from Gravelly Point and Lyndon Baines Johnson Memorial Grove, and views of the downtown monuments and springtime floral displays, including cherry blossoms at the Tidal Basin in late March and early April, are possible.

Cottontails, foxes, muskrats, and turtles live in the swamp, marsh, and forest habitat at Theodore Roosevelt Island, dedicated to the twenty-sixth president, who signed the Antiquities

Act into law in 1906. The act greatly expanded the federal government's role in preserving the nation's resources by permitting presidents to establish national monuments. Roosevelt exercised this privilege eighteen times. Bicycles and camping are prohibited on the island, but fishing is permitted. On the west side of the river, a foot trail segment of the PHNST, maintained by the Potomac Appalachian Trail Club, continues along the river to just outside the Capital Beltway. Access by car to Roosevelt Island parking is via the northbound George Washington Parkway or the Roosevelt Bridge from downtown Washington, D.C.

THE CHESAPEAKE AND OHIO TOWPATH SEGMENT

The Chesapeake and Ohio Towpath, once used by mules to pull the canal barges, offers protection from the strong winds that come off the Potomac River during the fall, winter, and early spring. Sycamores, poplars, and oaks shade the path during summer months, although insect repellent and long pants are needed if going off-trail. The Chesapeake and Ohio Canal Historical Park, which hugs the northeast bank of the Potomac River from Georgetown to Cumberland, Maryland, offers glimpses of turkey vultures, great horned owls, beaver, raccoons, and white-tailed deer.

The canal officially begins at the tidewater lock at the mouth of

Rock Creek near the John F. Kennedy Center for the Performing Arts. Canal boats once used this lock to enter the Potomac River and bring goods, passengers, and building stone into downtown Washington, D.C. The C&O's Georgetown Visitor's Center is located in a little office on the canal between Thirtieth and Thomas Jefferson Streets. Near this site, NPS archaeologists have recently unearthed nine large storage pits and nearly sixty thousand artifacts that date to a.d. 1 to 200. This predates earlier finds by about one thousand years. The visitor's center will provide interpretation of this striking archaeological discovery. Rock Creek Park is one of the largest natural urban parks in the country, and offers 1,700 acres of hardwood forest with Civil War era historic sites. The bicycle trail here connects with the Mount Vernon Trail.

Heading northwest, the towpath enters Maryland. The next visitor center is found at Great Falls. Great Falls Tavern, once known as Crommelin House and dating to 1829, served as a lockhouse, a tavern, a hotel, and a private club before the structure became a National Park Service ranger station and an interpretive center. The aqueduct observation deck near the tavern is used to spot eagles and their nests on nearby Conn Island. Continuing in Maryland, the towpath passes many historic and archaeological features before reaching Brunswick. In 1890 the B&O

C&O TOWPATH, TAVERN, AND CANAL BOAT

Construction on the lockhouse began soon after the ground breaking of the C&O Canal in 1828 and eventually expanded into a hotel for canal traffic. After the 1924 flood ended canal operations, the Great Falls Tavern remained open for several years. Today the C&O Canal National Historic Park Museum and visitor center draws more than a million guests per year, including thousands of schoolchildren who benefit from educational tours on seasonal mule-drawn canal boat tours on a restored section of the canal.

Railroad moved its yard here from Martinsburg. At Weverton the Appalachian Trail merges with the towpath in Maryland. The AT can be followed over the Byron Memorial Footbridge for a detour into Harpers Ferry, West Virginia (see AT), at the confluence of the Potomac and Shenandoah Rivers. Thomas Jefferson wrote of the area, "The passage of the Patowmac through the Blue Ridge is perhaps one of the most stupendous scenes in Nature."

and full-size replica of a canal boat await the visitor at the last lift lock. The path leads on past the last aqueduct along Evitts Creek to its terminus at the old Western Maryland Railroad Station.

THE LAUREL HIGHLANDS HIKING TRAIL SEGMENT

LAUREL IN LAUREL HIGHLANDS

The 70-mile Laurel Highlands Hiking Trail travels along a scenic ridge of the Alleghenies where wildflowers make an appearance from mid-April to mid-May. Mountain laurel begins to bloom in June and rhododendrons follow later that month and in early July.

The towpath leads to the multiple-arched Antietam Creek Aqueduct near the site of the Civil War's bloodiest single-day battle, now Antietam National Battlefield. Continuing past the Four Locks Ranger Station and Fort Frederick State Park, the towpath makes its way to Hancock, the last large town before Cumberland. The first of a series of composite locks, partially built of wood, is found at lock 58. Now, adjacent to the Green Ridge State Forest, the towpath begins to weave its way toward the Paw Paw Tunnel, once a bottleneck for canal traffic. On the way to Cumberland, the towpath continues past Patterson Creek, the Potomac's south branch, and the picturesque Narrows, a gap between the river and Irons Mountain. A lockhouse

The Laurel Highlands Hiking Trail travels along a scenic ridge of the Alleghenies for 70 miles. Elevations along the trail range from approximately 1,300 to 2,900 feet, and portions of the route are rugged—particularly at the southern end. Two-by-five-inch yellow blazes mark the trail every 100 feet and make it relatively easy to follow. Mileage monuments are located every mile as the trail moves through state parks, state game lands, state forests, and some private land to reach its end at the Conemaugh Gorge near Johnstown. The trail is open all year. Fall brings brilliant color to the trail. The traveler should be alert to hunting season, which opens in the fall with bows and arrows and continues through March. Wildflowers in the Laurel Highlands make their appearance from mid-April to mid-May. Mountain laurel begins to bloom in June and rhododendrons follow in late June and early July.

FUTURE CONNECTIONS

The process of establishing and designating trail routes beyond and between the three established segments is dependent on local community interest. At present, the eastern and southern end of the trail beyond Mount Vernon has not been laid out, but potential sites may include Fredericksburg and Spotsylvania County Battlefields Memorial National Military Park, George Washington's Birthplace National Monument, and Robert E. Lee's Birthplace at Stratford Hall Plantation. The Northern Virginia Planning Commission has identified 48 miles of trail allignments in Prince William, Arlington, and Fairfax County. The U.S. Army has completed designs for a component of the trail in Fort Belvior in Virginia, and Alexandria, Virginia is preparing a guide for a bicycle route linking historic and prehistoric sites.

The abandoned Western Maryland Railroad corridor could serve as the route for the Allegheny Highlands Trail. The proposed trail would leave Cumberland and make its way across the Maryland panhandle to Frostburg, where it would begin a northerly route toward the Pennsylvania border. In Pennsylvania, the rail corridor would run through Somerset County, passing through small villages and boroughs including Deal, Myersdale, Garrett, Rockwood, Fort Hill, and Harnedsville to Confluence, where the Casselman and Youghiogheny Rivers join. The Allegheny Trail Alliance, a coalition of trail organizations in Pennsylvania and Maryland, completed a study for a trail network from Pittsburgh, Pennsylvania, and the Laurel Highlands Trail with the C&O Canal Towpath in Cumberland, Maryland. Trail and greenway connections are already being built to connect Confluence with the Pittsburgh area. From Confluence, the corridor heads northwest past Mount Davis, Pennsylvania's highest elevation at 3,213 feet. After passing through forest and Amish farms, the route follows a portion of the 67-mile Youghiogheny River Trail to Ohiopyle, the southern terminus of Pennsylvania's Laurel Highlands Hiking Trail.

In 1997 a new Potomac Heritage Trail Coordinating Committee was established at a summit meeting in Woodbridge, Virginia. The coordinating committee plans to keep the national trail project moving by developing and distributing public information about the trail and encouraging involvement. In 1996 disastrous flood waters washed away entire sections of the C&O Canal Towpath, the largest official section of the national trail. The restoration project led to major private donations, and Congress authorized emergency restoration funds. Congress also authorized a plan designed by the Clinton administration that allows a portion of visitors' fees at Great Falls Park to fund the restoration and maintenance of the towpath.

Points of Interest

1. MOUNT VERNON. George and Martha Washington's eighteenth-century plantation on the Potomac River, with botanical gardens, Mount Vernon Museum, and a seasonal hands-on history tent, is the country's oldest ongoing preservation project. The Mount Vernon Ladies' Association offers walk-through tours of the mansion, which they restored to its appearance during the last year of Washington's life. During the Christmas season, the decorated mansion's third floor is open to the public. Tours that focus on period slave life are offered from April through October, and during the summer there is a ceremonial wreath laying at Washington's tomb. Seasonal day cruises on the Potomac River can be taken from Washington, D.C., to Mount Vernon on the *Potomac Spirit. Other attractions:* George Washington Memorial Parkway contains nearly 40 miles of scenic roadways; George Washington's Grist Mill Historical State Park features a reconstruction of the mill built and operated by Washington; Woodlawn Plantation contains the Woodlawn Mansion (1806) and Frank Lloyd Wright's Pope-Leighey House (1940). *Nearby:* Washington's Birthplace is found nearby along the Potomac River at George Washington Birthplace National Monument. At Fredericksburg, Fredericksburg and Spotsylvania County Battlefields Memorial National Military Park. On the Mount Vernon Trail, Riverside Park and Fort Hunt Park; Fort Washington, across the river, is a nineteenth-century coastal defense fortification; Dyke Marsh, for birding and fishing; Belle Haven and Belle Haven Marina, for picnics, fishing, and boating.

2. JONES POINT LIGHTHOUSE. From 1836 to 1925 this lighthouse near Alexandria warned sailors of nearby sandbars. Jones Point, named for resident Cadwalder Jones, marks the southern tip of the District of Columbia. The forty boundary markers of the original District were surveyed from this point. Jones, a beaver trader, built a cabin here in 1692. The area is a popular spot for picnics and fishing.

3. ALEXANDRIA. George Washington helped to lay out the streets of the historic river city. He maintained a home here, served on the town council, and trained soldiers in Alexandria during the French and Indian War. During the Civil War, Union troops occupied the city to protect the Potomac River. Thus, Alexandria escaped the destruction that other southern towns suffered. Today, the Alexandria Convention and Visitors Bureau offers seasonal walking tours in the restored Old Town, and sightseeing cruises can be taken along the revitalized waterfront. The Visitors Bureau is located in Alexandria's oldest structure, the Ramsay House (1724). On Washington's Birthday Weekend, Alexandria celebrates with the

George Washington Birthday Parade, the George Washington Birthnight Banquet and Ball, and the Revolutionary War Encampment. *Other attractions:* Carlyle House (1753) served as a meeting place where royal governors planned strategies and funding for Gen. Edward Braddock's campaign against the French and Indians; Christ Church (1773) is where Washington and other leaders attended services; Gadsby's Tavern Museum, housed in the City Tavern (1770) and Hotel (1792), was visited by Washington; Stabler-Leadbeater Apothecary, founded in 1792, was patronized by Washington; Friendship Firehouse (Washington was a founding member of the Friendship Fire Company in 1774); Lee-Fendall House (1785), where "Light Horse" Harry Lee wrote a farewell address to Washington when he left Mount Vernon to become president; the Old Presbyterian Meeting House (1774) was the site of Washington's 1799 memorial services; George Washington Masonic National Memorial has a collection of Washington memorabilia, a striking portrait, the original Purple Heart decoration that Washington established, and a 17-foot-high bronze of the nation's first president; Lloyd House (1796) has one of the state's finest collections of genealogical and historical material; Boyhood Home of Robert E. Lee (1795); the Lyceum (1839) served as the city's first cultural center; the Atheneum was built around 1850 as a banking house; the Torpedo Factory, built by the U.S. Navy, serves as an art center and houses the Alexandria Archaeology Museum and Laboratory; the Alexandria Black History Resource Center documents Alexandria's African American heritage; Fort Ward Museum and Historic Site houses a Civil War collection. *Nearby:* On the Mount Vernon Trail, Daingerfield Island and Gravelly Point offer views of Washington, D.C.'s skyline; the Navy-Marine Memorial recognizes Americans who served at sea.

4. LYNDON BAINES JOHNSON MEMORIAL GROVE. South of the Arlington Memorial Bridge, this 15-acre grove in Lady Bird Johnson Park has azaleas, dogwood, rhododendrons, and white pines that surround a monolith of pink Texas granite that stands as a memorial to the nation's thirty-sixth president. From the shoreline of this 121-acre island park, President and Mrs. Johnson met to admire the nation's capital. President Johnson's vision of a nationwide system of trails led to the National Trails System Act in 1968 and the establishment of the PHNST.

5. ARLINGTON MEMORIAL BRIDGE. This neoclassical bridge, dedicated in 1932, symbolizes the union of the North and the South after the Civil War. *Other attractions:* At Arlington, Arlington House, the antebellum home of the Custis and Lee families overlooking the

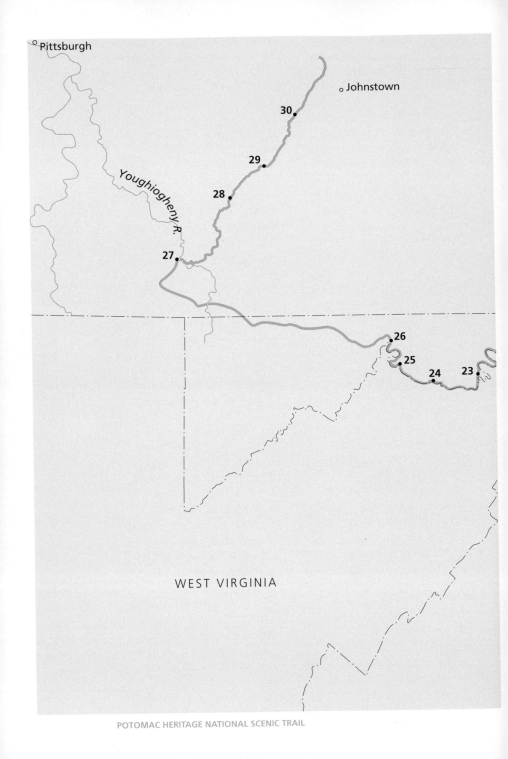

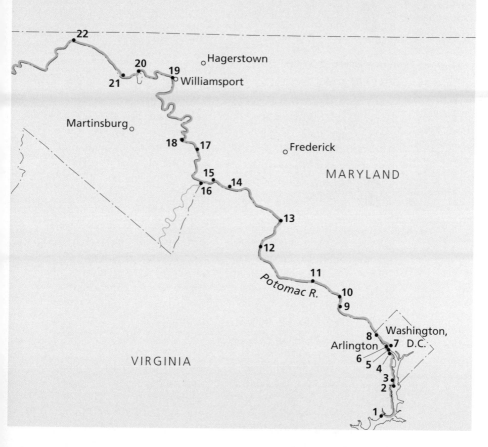

PENNSYLVANIA

22

20
21
19
Williamsport

Hagerstown

Martinsburg

18
17

15
16
14

Frederick

MARYLAND

13

12

11

Potomac R.

10
9

8
Arlington
6
5
4

Washington,
7 D.C.

VIRGINIA

3
2

1

Potomac River, became a permanent memorial to Robert E. Lee in 1955; the United States Marine Corps War Memorial, also known as the Iwo Jima Memorial, recognizes all Marines who died in defense of their country; the Netherlands Carillon, a gift from the Dutch to the Americans for aid during World War II, is tuned to the chromatic scale; the Pentagon is one of the largest buildings in the world. *Nearby:* In Washington, D.C.: the Arlington Memorial Bridge leads to the Lincoln Memorial, West Potomac Park, the Mall, and to memorials, museums, and government buildings.

DISTRICT OF COLUMBIA

6. THEODORE ROOSEVELT ISLAND. This island wilderness-preserve, surrounded by the Potomac River, bears the name of the conservationist president Theodore Roosevelt and honors him with a 17-foot bronze statue. Arrowarum, ash, cattails, maples, oaks, pickerelweed, and willows grow on the island. It is a popular spot to picnic, hike, and fish. Hikers can walk across Key Bridge and descend steps to the C&O Canal towpath. In 1933 Key Bridge replaced the Alexandria Aqueduct, which had carried canal boats across the Potomac River to a 7-mile branch canal whose tidelock lay in Alexandria. The aqueduct's remains are just upstream on the river side of the towpath near Mile 1 marker. A beautiful 10-mile trail, marked with blue blazes, starts on the island and proceeds northwest on the bluffs and banks of the Potomac past Turkey Run Park to Interstate 495. Many hikers make a return loop on the towpath.

7. GEORGETOWN. The tide lock at Virginia Avenue and Rock Creek Park is the zero milestone from which measurements on the C&O Canal are calculated. Locks 1–4 lift the canal from its tide lock for passage through Georgetown. Rubble from the inclined plane is seen near Mile 2. At Lock 3 there is a bust of Supreme Court Justice William O. Douglas, who spearheaded the movement to preserve the canal as a recreation area. The Georgetown Visitor's Center, at 1057 Thomas Jefferson Street N.W., sells tickets for seasonal mule-drawn barge trips down the canal on the *Georgetown.* Rowhouses along the towpath were built after the Civil War. The Abner Cloud House (1801) is the oldest existing structure on the canal. At Mile 0, Thompson's Boat Center rents canoes, kayaks, rowboats, sculls, and bicycles, and Fletcher's Boat House, just upriver from Georgetown at Mile 3, rents bicycles, canoes, and rowboats in the summer. *Other activities:* Concerts on the Canal from June to August; Foundry Mall, now a restaurant, once served as a veterinary hospital for canal mules; the Star-Spangled Banner Monument at Francis Scott Key Park is at the foot of Key Bridge; Alexandria Aqueduct at Mile 1; Old Stone House

(1765) is one of the oldest structures in Washington; Cox's Row is composed of five Federal houses on N Street; Smith Row includes an unbroken block of Federal rowhouses; Dumbarton House (1800) on Q Street serves as a house museum and the national headquarters for the National Society of the Colonial Dames of America; Dumbarton Oaks on 32d Street has 10 acres of formal gardens; St. John's Church (1809) is known as the Church of Presidents; the Customs House, built in 1858 to serve the port of Georgetown, now serves as a post office; the John F. Kennedy Center for the Performing Arts has tours; Rock Creek Park offers hiking, bicycling, horseback riding, and golf and features the nineteenth-century Pierce Mill and Civil War forts Reno, Bayard, Stevens, and DeRussy; the Capital Crescent Trail on the old railroad right-of-way travels along the Potomac River from Georgetown to Silver Springs, Maryland.

8. CHAIN BRIDGE. This bridge, near Mile 4, was named for the chains that held up the original structure. The Virginia side is known today for its fishing. During the Civil War, Union troops guarded the bridge on both ends. Fort Marcy and Fort Ethan Allen were built to guard the approach to the bridge. *Nearby:* In Glen Echo Park, Maryland, the Clara Barton National Historic Site is the former home of the founder of the American Red Cross; Glen Echo Park, administered by the National Park Service as a cultural arts park, was the site of the National Chautauqua Assembly in 1891 to promote liberal and practical education, especially among the masses, later a famous amusement park.

MARYLAND

9. GREAT FALLS TAVERN. Construction on the lockhouse near the Potomac River began soon after the ground breaking in 1828 and expanded into a hotel that opened in 1831. The 1924 flood ended canal operation, but the tavern remained open. When the National Park Service later acquired the property in 1938, it served as a restaurant, and today it serves as the C&O Canal National Historical Park Museum and visitor center. A mule-drawn canal boat, the *Canal Clipper,* offers seasonal rides on a restored section of the canal. Each year, in fall and spring, thousands of schoolchildren board the canal boat to be transported back to the nineteenth century by staff in period costume. The canal is home to an endangered species of freshwater mussels. Washington Aqueduct Observation Deck near the tavern is a great spot to watch for eagles; the eagle's nest on Conn Island is nearby. Trails near the visitor center lead to locks, gold mine remains, Civil War earthworks, and Olmsted Island—named in honor of Frederic Law Olmsted, Jr., a planner long active in shaping Washington, D.C.'s parks and monuments. Here, views unfold

of Mather Gorge, named for Stephen Mather, the first director of the National Park Service. Rock climbing and kayaking are popular in and around Great Falls Gorge. *Nearby:* Great Falls Park at Great Falls, Virginia, has excellent views of the Falls of the Potomac, Mather Gorge, and Patowmack Canal locks. The ruins of Matildaville, a 1790 town that declined in the 1820s when trade on the Patowmack Canal dwindled, are also on park grounds. Activities include bicycling, horseback riding, fishing, whitewater kayaking below the falls, rock climbing, and ranger-led programs. Wildflowers identified along the towpath include wild ginger, jack-in-the-pulpit, spring beauty, mayapple, trout lily, Dutchman's breeches, blue phlox, bloodroot, and violets.

10. SWAINS LOCK. Lock 21 near Mile 16 was built of red sandstone from Seneca, a stone that set the standard for elegant gaslight (1870–1910) townhouses in Washington, D.C. Lock 21 has a lockhouse, a campsite, and boat rentals. Horseback riding is permitted on the towpath below the lock.

11. SENECA CREEK AQUEDUCT. The aqueduct, lift lock, and lockhouse near Mile 23 were all built of Seneca red sandstone. *Nearby:* Near Seneca, Seneca Creek State Park has old mills, stone quarries, an old schoolhouse, hiking, bicycling, horseback riding, fishing, boating and canoeing rentals, cross-country skiing, snowshoeing,

sledding, ice skating, ice fishing, and campfire programs; McKee Beshers Wildlife Management Area is a good place for birdwatching.

12. WHITE'S FERRY. In earlier times, ferries crossed the Potomac at this spot, and they still do today. The *General Jubal A. Early* transports up to eight cars at a time across the Potomac and is the only remaining ferry on the river.

13. MONOCACY RIVER AQUEDUCT. At Mile 42.2 near Dickerson, this seven-arched aqueduct was saved from destruction when Union forces approached just as Confederates were about to blow it up. Constructed of pink quartzite from nearby Sugarloaf Mountain, the bridge was regarded as a paragon of the canal and is still a major attraction. *Nearby:* At Point of Rocks, the Calico Rocks Campsite near Mile 50 and the Victorian railroad station from the late 1800s. At Frederick, the Monocacy National Battlefield is the site of the battle that saved Washington, D.C.; Mount Olivet Cemetery has the graves of Francis Scott Key, Barbara Fritchie, and more than four hundred unknown Confederate soldiers of Monocacy and Antietam; the Barbara Fritchie House and Museum is the reconstructed home of the ninety-five-year-old woman who courageously waved the Union flag when Gen. Thomas "Stonewall" Jackson marched his confederate troops through town

and who was later immortalized in John Greenleaf Whittier's poem; the Schifferstadt Architectural Museum (1756) is the city's oldest standing structure; Rose Hill Manor Children's Museum offers tours of the 1790s house; Frederick County Historical Society Museum is located in a Federal-style landmark (1820); Frederick National Historic District offers guided walking tours; Roger Brooke Taney and Francis Scott Key Museum; Delaplaine Visual Arts Center; Sugarloaf Mountain, for picnicking and hiking.

14. WEVERTON. The C&O towpath and the Appalachian Trail merge near Weverton at Lock 31. Weverton was as an industrial community and the inspiration of Caspar Weaver, an engineer who worked on the National Road and later served as the superintendent of construction for the B&O Railroad. Town enterprises included a flour mill on the Virginia side of the Potomac, a sawmill, and the General Henderson Steel and File Manufacturing Company. Weaver held up C&O construction when he disputed the condemnation of a portion of his property. *Nearby:* Near Brownsville, Gathland State Park has the War Correspondents Memorial Arch honoring Civil War correspondents (see AT). Near Thurmont, Loy's Station Covered Bridge (1850–60) and Roddy Road Covered Bridge (1856) on Owen Creek; Catoctin Mountain Park, located on a spur that forms the eastern rampart of

the Appalachian Mountains in Maryland, has the restored Blue Blazes Whiskey Still and camping, hiking, horseback riding, fishing, cross-country skiing, snowshoeing, and interpretive programs. Administered by the National Park Service, the park adjoins Cunningham Falls State Park, which features Cunningham Falls and the Catoctin Iron Furnace (see AT), and the nearby presidential retreat, Camp David.

15. BRUNSWICK. In 1890 this railroad town at Mile 55 became the eastern switching yard for the B&O. Brunswick Railroad Museum has a scale model of the C&O Canal and the B&O Railroad from Union Station to Brunswick. Bridges in the area were destroyed by the Civil War and the flood of 1936. A boat launch provides convenient access here.

16. HARPERS FERRY NATIONAL HISTORIC PARK. The park is located where Maryland, Virginia, and West Virginia come together. Potomac Heritage travelers can reach the town from the Maryland side by following the Appalachian Trail over a footpath on the railroad bridge into West Virginia. Five themes run through the town's history: industry, environment, John Brown's attack on slavery, the Civil War, and African American history (see AT). George Washington selected the site of Harpers Ferry for the federal armory because of the area's natural water power and nearby ironworks. The abolitionist John

Brown led an attack on the armory in 1859 that influenced events leading up to the Civil War. A monument to the event is located by the B&O Railroad in town. Because of the town's strategic location at the confluence of the Potomac and Shenandoah Rivers, it would change hands eight times during the Civil War. Just across the river in Maryland, a few steps from the towpath, a trail leads to spectacular views of Harpers Ferry, the railroad bridge, and the confluence of the rivers. The popular cliff area—Maryland Heights—is made of Harper's shale. *Other attractions:* Amtrak's Capitol Limited serves Harpers Ferry station; Blue Ridge Outfitters offer river rapids excursions and enjoyable canoeing on the Potomac and Shenandoah Rivers; Appalachian Trail Conference Headquarters is on Washington and Jackson Streets. The NPS Office for the Potomac Heritage NST is in the Lower Town. *Nearby:* The Kennedy Farm in Maryland (NHL) has been renovated to match the period when John Brown and his raiders stayed there for weeks before launching their attack on the armory.

17. ANTIETAM CREEK AQUEDUCT. Just past Mile 69 near Sharpsburg, this three-arched aqueduct of blue-gray limestone was completed in 1834. The National Park Service has a canal information center at Antietam Creek. *Other activities:* At Sharpsburg, Antietam National Battlefield is the site of the bloodiest single-day

(September 17, 1862) battle of the Civil War. After twelve hours of fighting, some twenty-three thousand men were killed or wounded. Clara Barton, founder of the Red Cross nearly twenty years later, tended them. As a result of the battle, President Abraham Lincoln delivered the Emancipation Proclamation. Antietam National Cemetery holds the remains of 4,776 Union soldiers; Barron's C&O Canal Museum and Country Store has artifacts and pictures of the C&O Canal. *Nearby:* At Boonsboro, Boonsborough Museum of History; Washington Monument State Park holds the first monument (1827) to honor George Washington (see AT); Greenbrier State Park has a lake, a beach, camping, and many recreational activities (see AT); Crystal Grottoes Caverns offers tours from March through October.

18. FERRY HILL PLANTATION. Across from Shepherdstown, West Virginia, this historic structure served as a hospital for wounded officers after the Battle of Antietam and today has been adapted to serve as the headquarters of the C&O Canal National Historic Park. Built by Col. John Blackford around the War of 1812, Colonel Blackford later lost a legal battle with the C&O when he charged that a river lock would take business from his Shepherdstown ferry. His grandson Henry Kyd Douglas, aide to Stonewall Jackson during the Civil War, inherited the home, which even-

tually served as a restaurant for many years. Ferry Hill Trail passes the nearby restored Lock 38 with its arched culvert for the bypass flume. A short distance downstream is the Shepherdstown River Lock. *Nearby:* Shepherdstown (originally named Mecklenburg), in West Virginia, was once considered by George Washington as a site for the nation's capital. James Rumsey Historical Monument, at the site of the first successful public launching of a steamboat, commemorates the event and the inventor who was the first superintendent of the Patowmack Company; James Rumsey Steamboat Museum houses a half-size working replica of the first Rumsey Steamboat; Historic Shepherdstown Museum has artifacts that date to the 1700s; the Contemporary American Theatre Festival is held each year in July.

19. CONOCOCHEAGUE AQUEDUCT. Near Mile 100, the fifth of the canal's eleven stone aqueducts was finished in 1834. A shift in the type of masonry at the upper end of the three-arched bridge indicates where a blast occurred during the Civil War, and part of the masonry on the land side was lost in 1920 when a canal boat broke through. The nearby town of Williamsport was the site of a cholera epidemic in 1832, and a clash between Irish workers. During the Civil War, both Union and Confederate generals—including Robert E. Lee before and after the 1863 battle of Gettysburg—stayed in

Williamsport. The town, also accessible via the earlier Patowmack Canal, was considered by George Washington as the northern limit for siting a new capital city. At one time a racetrack ran between the canal and the Potomac River. The National Park Service is restoring canal features at Williamsport and has opened a visitor center there. *Nearby:* At Hagerstown, the Miller House (1820) exhibits C&O artifacts; Hagerstown Roundhouse Museum displays railroad memorabilia; Jonathan Hager House (1739) and Museum contains authentic period furnishings; South Prospect Street (NRHP) has homes dating to the early 1800s; Beaver Creek School is a turn-of-the-century schoolhouse and museum; Rose Hill Cemetery contains the Statue of Hope, which marks the burial place of more than two thousand Confederate soldiers who died in the Civil War battles of Antietam and South Mountain; Washington County Museum of Fine Arts.

20. FOUR LOCKS. The section of canal near Big Spring through Prather's Neck was begun in 1836 to avoid a four-mile loop that the Potomac River makes around the neck. Because four locks were needed to accommodate a 32-foot change in elevation, the shortcut was not opened for navigation until 1839. The river widens here, providing an excellent spot for boating and fishing. The area also has a hiker/biker campsite, a boat ramp, and Four Locks Ranger Station. The Four Locks Trail

leads to a restored mule barn, Lockhouse 49, locks 47–50, Charles Mill, and Dam 5. *Nearby:* Indian Springs Wildlife Management Area.

21. FORT FREDERICK STATE PARK. The country's finest pre–Revolutionary War stone fort is located near Big Pool at Mile 112. Fort Frederick, erected in 1756 during the French and Indian War, has costumed historians to interpret the fort's history. Popular activities are camping, hiking, bicycling, fishing, boating, canoeing, cross-country skiing, snowshoeing, sledding, ice fishing, and campfire programs. Special events include the Frederick Rendezvous in spring, Annual Military Field Days each summer, and Old Tyme Christmas in December. Big Pool at Mile 114 served as a turning basin for canal boats.

22. HANCOCK. This town at the foot of the Appalachian Mountains served as an important stop on the canal and the National Road. This center for taverns was home to many boatmen, and some boats wintered here. At the turn of the twentieth century, the *Oriole* provided boat and fish trips on the canal. The C&O Canal Museum and Visitors Center on Main Street has exhibits depicting canal life and a movie about the history of the canal. Area sites include locks 51 and 52, the ruins of a stone lock house, Tonoloway Creek Aqueduct, and the culvert for Little Tonoloway Creek, the remains of the Round Top Cement Mill, and Little Tonoloway Recreation Area.

23. PAW PAW TUNNEL. The C&O's longest tunnel (3,118 feet; (NHP) at the foot of the Green Ridge State Forest was designed as an alternative to the 6-mile stretch of the Potomac River known as Paw Paw Bends. The project was started in 1836, but it was not completed until 1850 due to laborers' unrest, financial difficulties, and outbreaks of cholera and other illnesses. On completion, the major engineering feat resulted in the largest and most impressive structure on the canal. Since the towpath inside the tunnel did not provide room for passing or turning, a bottleneck was created as boats lined up to wait for clearance to enter. Tunnel Hill Trail leads hikers to a deciduous forest on Tunnel Hill and back down to the canal. Those entering the tunnel should use care, take a flashlight, and use the guardrail as the towpath is uneven. Other canal features in the area are remains of a carpenter shop near lock 66; the Section House which served the canal's section superintendent; and Purslane Cemetery, where victims of the cholera epidemic were buried. There is a one-night canoe camp with a boat ramp for carry-in canoes near Mile 156 and Purslane Run campsite near Mile 160. *Other activities:* Green Ridge State Forest, adjacent to the canal, has a visitor center, campsites, a boat launch, a shooting range, and trails for hiking, bicycling, horseback riding, and snowmobiling.

24. OLDTOWN. Oldtown, at Mile 167, was settled by the Shawnee Indians in 1692. In 1741 frontiersman Thomas Cresap selected the abandoned site for a fortified settlement. When his son sued the canal company, the resulting 1848 compromise forced the C&O to accommodate his timber operation by financing a bridge across the canal. The Cresap House (NRHP, NHL, NHS), built in 1762, is the oldest structure in the county and may have housed Washington when he was in the area. The stone colonial home on Main Street can be toured by appointment.

25. THE NARROWS. The canal had to squeeze between the Potomac River and Irons Mountain between Spring Gap and North Branch near Mile 175. Just past Irons Mountain Campsite at lock 73, the B&O Railroad returns to Maryland from West Virginia for the first time since Harpers Ferry. *Other activities:* At lock 75, the C&O Canal Boat Replica, the *Cumberland,* offers tours from June to August. The single-arch Evitts Creek Aqueduct near Mile 180 is the smallest and last canal aqueduct.

26. CUMBERLAND TERMINUS. This important trading city was founded by the Ohio Company in 1749. The B&O Railroad beat the canal to Cumberland and eventually continued westward. The canal company abandoned its plans to continue west, but there was a great deal of excitement when the

canal opened all the way to Georgetown on October 10, 1850. In the meantime, the trip to the Ohio Valley could be continued by horse-drawn stagecoach at Cumberland via the National Road, replaced today with a new interstate highway. Many boatmen and their families wintered in Cumberland. Today the Western Maryland Railroad Station Center serves as a national park visitor center during the summer. The station also serves the Western Maryland Scenic Railroad, which offers excursions to Frostburg. *Other activities:* In Cumberland, the Transportation and Industrial Museum is located in the Western Maryland Station; Washington's Headquarters (1755) was used by George Washington during the French and Indian War; National Road and Narrows, the nation's first federally funded highway was rerouted through the Narrows in 1832; the stone-arched Clarysville Bridge (mid-1700s) is believed to be the last remaining on National Road U.S. 40 in Allegany County; LaVale Toll Gate House (1836), Maryland's only toll gate on National Road U.S. 40, has a historic plaque with fees for wagons, animals, and pedestrians (NRHP); Washington Street Historic District exhibits architectural styles from the last half of the nineteenth century; Emmanuel Episcopal Church (1849)/Fort Cumberland (1755) Earthworks, located under the church (NRHP, NHL, NHS); Turkey Flight Manor, originally a tavern, was used as a hospital for wounded soldiers during the Civil War; Cumberland City Hall (1911) has a mural of George Washington and General Braddock; Rocky Gap State Park, located in a natural saddle created by Evitts and Martin Mountains, has a lake, a visitor center, Country Bluegrass Festival each summer, camping, and many recreational activities as well as bicycle, canoe, paddleboat, and rowboat rentals.

PENNSYLVANIA

27. OHIOPYLE. The southern terminus of Pennsylvania's Laurel Highlands Hiking Trail begins in the village of Ohiopyle. The Delaware, Shawnee, and Iroquois Nations used this area as a hunting ground; "Ohiopehhle," meaning "white frothy water," refers to the Youghiogheny River. As a young man in 1754, George Washington was dismayed by the turbulent water and rough terrain of the Youghiogheny, which he had hoped would provide an easy transportation route. Today, the Youghiogheny River, affectionately known as "the Yock," is one of the best areas for white-water rafting in the eastern United States. Several outfitters offer rafting, canoeing, and kayaking trips, rentals, and clinics. The Laurel Highlands Information Center is located in the old train station at the trailhead, and the Ohiopyle State Park Campground is 3 miles away. The final 13.5 miles of the 67-mile Youghiogheny River Trail was just opened, connecting Boston and Confluence, Pennsylvania. This is part of a planned 400-mile-long trail that will link Pittsburgh and Washington, D.C. *Other activities:* Ohiopyle State Park has camping, hiking, bicycling, fishing, white-water boating, cross-country skiing, snowshoeing, snowmobiling, sledding, tobogganing, and environmental interpretation. Scenic tourist attractions include Ohiopyle Falls, Cucumber Falls, and Ferncliff Peninsula (NL). *Nearby:* At New Geneva, Friendship Hill National Historic Site tells the story of Albert Gallatin and Jeffersonian America. At Farmington, Fort Necessity National Battlefield commemorates Washington's first battles, which led to the start of the French and Indian War, and tells the story of the National Road; Mount Washington Tavern; Laurel Caverns offers tours and spelunking. At Chalk Hill, Braddock Grave memorializes the British major general who followed Washington's road in an attempt to capture French-held Fort Dusquesne. Near Mill Run, Fallingwater (1936) is one of Frank Lloyd Wright's most widely acclaimed architectural achievements; Bear Run Nature Reserve has hiking, cross-country skiing, and nature study.

28. SEVEN SPRINGS. Near Champion, the highest point on the trail reaches 2,950 feet. *Other activities:* At Champion, Seven Springs Ski Area offers golf and downhill skiing; the Roaring Run Natural Area has the Kooser Lookout Tower for scenic viewing.

Near Bakersville, the Hidden Valley Ski Area has downhill skiing; Kooser State Park offers camping, hiking, cross-country skiing, and fishing at a good trout stream. At Somerset, the Somerset Historical Center has exhibits on rural life; Laurel Hill State Park is where Washington's troops camped during the 1794 Whiskey Rebellion.

29. FORBES STATE FOREST. The 60,000-acre state forest near Jennerstown has camping, hiking, bicycling, horseback riding, fishing, cross-country skiing, snowshoeing, snowmobiling, and scenic views at Baldknob Tower. *Other activities:* Adjacent to the state forest are Linn Runn and Laurel Mountain State Parks; State Game Land Number 42. Laughlintown's Compass Inn Museum is a restored 1799 stagecoach stop. Ligonier has a reconstructed eighteenth-century British museum; Forbes Road Gun Museum.

30. LAUREL RIDGE STATE PARK. The trail's northern/western terminus ends at the state park's northernmost unit near the Big Spring Reservoir and the Conemaugh Gorge, cut by the Conemaugh River. A shelter area is located near Mile 57, Lower Yoder Fire Tower near Mile 66 may be used for scenic viewing, and views of the Conemaugh River and Johnstown are possible around Mile 67. *Other activities:* At Johnstown, the Johnstown

flood national memorial has ranger-guided activities and a visitor center that overlooks the ruins of the South Fork Dam, which broke in 1889, causing a disastrous flood that resulted in the deaths of 2,209 individuals and the first disaster relief effort of Clara Barton's Red Cross*; Johnstown Inclined Plane is the steepest vehicular inclined plane in the world; Amtrak's *Pennsylvanian* is the best way to see the route of the Johnstown flood and the Horseshoe Curve National Historic Landmark, an engineering marvel near Gallizin. The Ghost Town Trail begins in Dilltown and passes Eliza Iron Furnace (1905) and towns of the mining era. Windbur has the Coal Heritage Center and tours of Mine 40. At Jeanette, the Bushy Run Battlefield State Historical Site marks a British victory over the American Indians that was the turning point in Pontiac's Rebellion. The Path of Progress Heritage Route connects sites and attractions throughout the southwestern portion of Pennsylvania.

*The South Fork Fishing & Hunting Club Historic District was an exclusive resort built on the shores of an abandoned Pennsylvania canal reservoir. However, when their poorly maintained dam burst, it caused the nation's worst flood. The Johnstown Flood Museum offers a documentary film, photographs, and exhibits; Grandview Cemetery contains the remains of 777 unidentified flood victims.

Public Lands Information

Dept. of Agriculture

HEADQUARTERS

USDA Forest Service
Washington, DC 20013

REGIONAL OFFICES

Alaska Region
P.O. Box 21628
Juneau, AK 99802-1628

Eastern Region
310 W. Wisconsin Avenue,
   Room 500
Milwaukee, WI 53203

Intermountain Region
Federal Building
324 25th Street
Ogden, UT 84401

Northern Region
Federal Building
P.O. Box 7669
Missoula, MT 59807

Pacific Northwest Region
P.O. Box 3623
Portland, OR 97208

Pacific Southwest
630 Sansome Street
San Francisco, CA 94111

Rocky Mountain Region
P.O. Box 25127
Lakewood, CO 80225

Southern Region
1720 Peachtree Road NW
Atlanta, GA 30367

Southwestern Region
Federal Building
517 Gold Avenue
Albuquerque, NM 87102

U.S. Army Corps of Engineers
Office of the Chief Engineer
Pulaski Building
20 Massachusetts Avenue NW
Washington, DC 20314

Lower Mississippi Valley Division
Attn: CELMV-CO-R
P.O. Box 80
Vicksburg, MS 39181-0080

Missouri River Division
Attn: CEMRD-CO-R
P.O. Box 103, Downtown Station
Omaha, NE 68101-0103

New England Division
Attn: CENED-OD-P
424 Trapelo Road
Waltham, MA 02254-9149

North Atlantic Division
Attn: CENAD-CO-P
90 Church Street
New York, NY 10007-9998

North Central Division
Attn: CENAD-CO-OR
536 S. Clark Street
Chicago, IL 60605-1592

North Pacific Division
Attn: CENPD-CO-OR
P.O. Box 2870
Portland, OR 97208-2870

Ohio River Division
Attn: CEORD-CO-OR
P.O. Box 1159
Cincinnati, OH 45201-1159

South Atlantic Division
Attn: CESAD-CO-R
77 Forsyth Street SW, Room 313
Atlanta, GA 30335-6801

South Pacific Division
Attn: CESPD-CO-O
630 Sansome Street, Room 1216
San Francisco, CA 94111-2206

Southwestern Division
Attn: CESWD-CO-R
1114 Commerce Street
Dallas, TX 75242-0216

For information about recreational opportunities on military lands, write to:
Deputy Assistant Secretary of
   Defense
(Environment)
400 Army-Navy Drive, Room 206
Arlington, VA 22202-2884

Dept. of the Army

14th and E Streets NW
Washington, DC 20240

National Oceanic and
   Atmospheric Administration
   (NOAA)
National Marine Fisheries Service
1335 East-West Highway
Silver Spring, MD 20910

Dept. of Commerce

Dept. of the Interior

Office of Public Affairs
1849 C Street NW
Washington, DC 20240

Bureau of Indian Affairs (BIA)

HEADQUARTERS

Office of Trust and Economic
  Development
Department of the Interior
1849 C Street NW
Washington, DC 20240

BIA AREA OFFICES

Aberdeen Area Office
115 4th Avenue SE
Aberdeen, SD 57401

Albuqerque Area Office
615 First Street NW
P.O. Box 26567
Albuquerque, NM 87125

Anadarko Area Office
WCD—Office Complex
P.O. Box 368
Anadarko, OK 73005

Billings Area Office
316 N. 26th Street
Billings, MT 59101

Eastern Area Office
1951 Constitution Avenue NW
Washington, DC 20245

Juneau Area Office
Federal Building
P.O. Box 3-8000
Juneau, AK 99802

Minneapolis Area Office
Chamber of Commerce Building
15 S. Fifth Street, 6th Floor
Minneapolis, MN 55402

Muskogee Area Office
Old Federal Building
Muskogee, OK 74401

Navajo Area Office
P.O. Box M
Window Rock, AZ 86515

Phoenix Area Office
No. 1 North 1st Street
P.O. Box 10
Phoenix, AZ 85011

Bureau of Land Management

HEADQUARTERS

Office of Public Affairs
1849 C Street NW, Room 5600
Washington, DC 20240

STATE OFFICES

Alaska State Office
222 W. 7th Avenue, #13
Anchorage, AK 99513-7599

Arizona State Office
P.O. Box 16563
Phoenix, AZ 85011

California State Office
2800 Cottage Way, E-2841
Sacramento, CA 95825

Colorado State Office
2850 Youngfield Street
Lakewood, CO 80215-7076

New Mexico State Office
P.O. Box 27115
Santa Fe, NM 87502-7115

Eastern States Office
350 S. Pickett Street
Alexandria, VA 22304

Oregon State Office
P.O. Box 2965
Portland, OR 97208-2965

Idaho State Office
3380 Americana Terrace
Boise, ID 83706

Utah State Office
CFS Financial Center Building
324 S State Street, Suite 301
Salt Lake City, UT 84111-2303

Montana State Office
P.O. Box 36800
Billings, MT 59107

Wyoming State Office
P.O. Box 1828
Cheyenne, WY 82003

Nevada State Office
P.O. Box 12000
Reno, NV 89520-0006

HEADQUARTERS

Office of Public Affairs
1849 C Street NW, Room 7642
Washington, DC 20240

AREA OFFICES

Great Plains Region
P.O. Box 36900
Billings, MT 59107-6900

Lower Colorado Region
P.O. Box 61470
Boulder City, NV 89006-1470

Mid-Pacific Region
2800 Cottage Way
Sacramento, CA 95825

Pacific Northwest Region
P.O. Box 043
Boise, ID 83724

Upper Colorado Region
P.O. Box 11568
Salt Lake City, UT 84147

Bureau of Reclamation

HEADQUARTERS

Office of Public Inquiries
P.O. Box 37127
Washington, DC 20013-7127

REGIONAL OFFICES

Alaska Region
2525 Gambell Street
Anchorage, AK 99503-2893

Mid-Atlantic Region
143 S Third Street
Philadelphia, PA 19106

Midwest Region
1709 Jackson Street
Omaha, NE 68102

National Park Service

National Capitol Region
1100 Ohio Drive SW
Washington, DC 20242

Southeast Region
75 Spring Street SW
Atlanta, GA 30303

North Atlantic Region
15 State Street
Boxton, MA 02109-3572

Southwest Region
P.O. Box 728
Santa Fe, NM 87504-0728

Pacific Northwest Region
83 S King Street, Suite 212
Seattle, WA 981104

Western Region
600 Harrison Street, Suite 600
San Francisco, CA 94107-1372

Rocky Mountain Region
12795 W. Alameda Parkway
Denver, CO 80225-0287

U.S. Fish and Wildlife Service

HEADQUARTERS

Office of Public Affairs
1849 C Street NW, Room 3447
Washington, DC 20240

REGIONAL OFFICES

Alaska Regional Office
1011 E. Tudro Road
Anchorage, AK 99503

Mountain Prairie Regional Office
Box 25486, Denver Federal Center
Denver, CO 80225

North Central Regional Office
Federal Building, Fort Snelling
Twin Cities, MN 55111

Northeast Regional Office
1 Gateway Center, Suite 700
Newton Corner, MA 02158

Pacific Regional Office
911 NE 11th Avenue
Portland, OR 97232

Southeast Regional Office
75 Spring Street SW
Atlanta, GA 30303

Southwest Regional Office
P.O. Box 1306
Albuquerque, NM 87103

Independent Agencies

Land Between the Lakes
100 Van Morgan Drive
Golden Pond, KY 42211-9001

Tennessee Valley Authority
Communications and Employee
  Development
400 W. Summit Hill Drive
Knoxville, TN 37902

Although the U.S. Geological Survey does not manage federal lands, it does produce one of the principal tools for understanding and enjoying those lands: maps! The USGS has covered the country with the most detailed topographic maps available from any source, including special maps for national parks and monuments, which are available from many dealers all over the country. The maps and information about them, such as available scales and date of last revision, can also be obtained from the following USGS Earth Science Information Centers:

345 Middlefield Road
Mail Stop 532
Menlo Park, CA 94025-3591

P.O. Box 25046 Federal Center
Mail Stop 504
Denver, CO 80225-0046

507 National Center
Reston, VA 22092

U.S. Geological Survey (USGS)

State Lands
Information

Alabama Bureau of Tourism &
   Travel
P.O. Box 4309, Sept. TIA
Montgomery, AL 36103-4309
205-242-4169
1-800-ALABAMA

Alaska Division of Tourism
P.O. Box 110801, Dept. TIA
Juneau, AK 99811-0801
907-465-2010

Arizona Office of Tourism
1100 W. Washington
Phoenix, AZ 85007
888-520-3434

Arkansas Tourism Office
1 Capitol Mall, Dept. 7701
Little Rock, AR 72201
501-682-7777
1-800-NATURAL

California Office of Tourism
P.O. Box 9278, Dept. TIA
Van Nuys, CA 91409
916-322-2881
1-800-TO CALIF

Colorado Tourism Board
P.O. Box 38700
Denver, CO 80238

Connecticut Department of
   Economic Development,
   Tourism Division
865 Brook Street
Rocky Hill, CT 06067
203-258-4355
1-800-CT BOUND

Delaware Tourism Office
99 Kings Highway
P.O. Box 1401, Dept. TIA
Dover, DE 19903
302-739-4271
1-800-441-8846

Florida Division of Tourism
126 W. Van Buren Street, FLDA
Tallahassee, FL 32301
904-487-1462

Georgia Department of Industry,
   Trade, & Tourism
P.O. Box 1776, Dept. TIA
Atlanta, GA 30301
404-656-3590
1-800-VISIT GA

Hawaii Department of Business,
Economic Development, and
Tourism
P.O. Box 2359
Honolulu, HI 96804
808-586-2423

Idaho Division of Tourism
Development
700 W State Street, Dept C
Boise, ID 83720
208-334-2470
1-800-635-7820

Illinois Bureau of Tourism
100 W. Randolph, Suite 3-400
Chicago, IL 60601
312-814-4732
1-800-223-0121

Indiana Department of Commerce
Tourism and Film Development
Division
1 N. Capitol, Suite 700
Indianapolis, IN 46204-2288
317-232-8860
1-800-289-6646

Iowa Division of Tourism
200 E. Grand, Dept. TIA
Des Moines, IA 50309
515-242-4705
1-800-345-IOWA

Kansas Travel and Tourism
Division
400 W. 8th Street, 5th Floor, Dept.
DIS
Topeka, KS 66603-3957
913-296-3009
1-800-252-6727

Kentucky Department of Travel
Development
2200 Capitol Plaza Tower, Dept.
DA
Frankfort, KY 40601
502-564-4930
1-800-225-TRIP

Louisiana Office of Tourism
Attn: Inquiry Department
P.O. Box 94291, LOT
Baton Rouge, LA 70804-9291
504-342-8119
1-800-33-GUMBO

Maine Office of Tourism
189 State Street
August, ME 04333
207-289-5711
1-800-533-9595

Maryland Office of Travel and
Tourism
217 E. Redwood Street, 9th Floor
Baltimore, MD 21202
410-333-6611
1-800-543-1036

Massachusetts Office of Travel
and Tourism
100 Cambridge Street, 13th Floor
Boston, MA 02202
617-727-3201
1-800-447-MASS
(for ordering vacation kit only,
U.S. only)

Michigan Travel Bureau
P.O. Box 30226
Lansing, MI 48909
517-373-0670
1-800-5432-YES

Minnesota Office of Tourism
375 Jackson Street, 250 Skyway
    Level
St. Paul, MN 55101
612-296-5029
1-800-657-3700

Mississippi Division of Tourism
P.O. Box 22825
Jackson, MS 39205
601-359-3297
1-800-647-2290

Missouri Division of Tourism
P.O. Box 1055, Dept. TIA
Jefferson City, MO 65102
314-751-4133
1-800-877-1234

Travel Montana
Room 259
Deer Lodge, MT 59722
406-444-2654
1-800-541-1447

Nebraska Division of Travel and
    Tourism
301 Central Mall S., Room 88937
Lincoln, NE 68509
402-471-3796
1-800-228-4307

Nevada Commission of Tourism
Capitol Complex, Dept. TIA
Carson City, NV 89710
702-687-4322
1-800-NEVADA 8

New Hampshire Office of Travel
    and Tourism Development
P.O. Box 856, Dept. TIA
Concord, NH 03302
603-271-2343
800-386-4664

New Jersey Division of Travel and
    Tourism
20 W. State Street, CN 826,
    Dept. TIA
Trenton, NJ 08625
609-292-2470
1-800-JERSEY 7

New Mexico Department of
    Tourism
1100 St. Francis Drive
Joseph Montoya Building
Santa Fe, NM 87503
505-827-0291
1-800-545-2040

New York State Department of
    Economic Development
One Commerce Plaza
Albany, NY 12245
518-474-4116
1-800-CALL NYS

North Carolina Division of Travel
    and Tourism
430 N. Salisbury Street
Raleigh, NC 27603
919-733-4171
1-800-VISIT NC

North Dakota Tourism
    Promotion
Liberty Memorial Building
Capitol Grounds
Bismarck, ND 58505
701-224-2525
1-8090-HELLO ND

Ohio Division of Travel and
    Tourism
P.O.. Box 1001, Dept. TIA
Columbus, OH 43211-0101
614-466-8844
1-800-BUCKEYE

Oklahoma Tourism and
  Recreation Department
Travel and Tourism Division
500 Will Rogers Building, DA92
Oklahoma City, OK 73105-4492
405-521-3981
1-800-652-6552
(Information requests only)

Oregon Economic Development
  Department
Tourism Division
775 Dummer Street NE
Salem, OR 97310
503-373-1270
1-800-547-7842

Pennsylvania Bureau of Travel
  Marketing
130 Commonwealth Drive
Warrendale, PA 15086
717-787-5453
1-800-VISIT PA

Rhode Island Tourism Division
7 Jackson Walkway, Dept. TIA
Providence, RI 02903
401-277-2601
1-800-566-5404

South Carolina Division of
  Tourism
P.O. Box 71, Room 902
Columbia, SC 29202
803-734-0235
1-800-872-3505

South Dakota Department of
  Tourism
711 E. Wells Avenue
Pierre, SD 57501-3369
605-773-3301
1-800-843-1930

Tennessee Department of
  Tourism Development
P.O Box 23170, TNDA
Nashville, TN 37202
615-741-2158

Texas Department of Commerce,
  Tourism Division
P.O. Box 12728
Austin, TX 78711-2728
512-462-9191
1-800-888-8TEX

Utah Travel Council
P.O. Box 147420
Salt Lake City, UT 84114-7420
800-200-1160

Vermont Travel Division
134 State Street, Dept. TIA
Montpelier, VT 05602
802-828-3236

Virginia Division of Tourism
1021 E. Cary Street, Dept. VT
Richmond, VA 23219
804-786-4484
1-800-VISIT VA

Washington, D.C., Convention
  and Visitors Association
1212 New York Avenue NW
Washington, DC 20005
202-789-7000

Washington State Tourism
  Development Division
P.O. Box 42513
Olympia, WA 98504-2513
206-586-2088, 206-586-2012
1-800-544-1800

West Virginia Division of
Tourism & Parks
2102 Washington Street E.
Charleston, WV 25305
304-348-2286
1-800-CALL-WVA

Wisconsin Division of Tourism
P.O. Box 7606
Madison, WI 53707
608-266-2161
In state: 1-800-372-2737
Out of state: 1-800-432-TRIP

Wyoming Divison of Tourism
I-25 at College Drive, Dept. WY
Cheyenne, WY 82002
307-777-7777
1-800-225-5996

Puerto Rico Tourism Company
P.O. Box 5268, Dept. TH
Miami, FL 33102
1-800-866-STAR, Ext. 17

U.S. Virgin Islands Division of
Tourism
P.O. Box 6400, VITIA
Charlotte Amalie, St. Thomas
USVI 00801
809-774-8784
1-800-372-8784

Bibliography

Appalachian National Scenic Trail

Appalachian Long Distance Hikers Association. *Appalachian Trail Thru-hikers' Companion.* 7th ed. Harpers Ferry, W.Va.: Appalachian Trail Conference, 2000.

Appalachian Trail Conference. *Long Distance Hiking on the Trail.* Appalachian Trail Conference, 1998. www@atconf.org.

———. *Member Handbook.* Harpers Ferry, W.Va.: Appalachian Trail Conference, 1988.

———. *Walking the Appalachian Trail Step by Step.* Harpers Ferry, W.Va.: Appalachian Trail Conference, 1993.

Adkins, Leonard M. *Walking the Blue Ridge: A Guide to the Trails of the Blue Ridge Parkway.* Chapel Hill: University of North Carolina Press, 1996.

Austin, Phyllis. "Paradise or Private Club?" *Backpacker* 24 (September 1996): 52–58, 136.

Berger, Karen. *Hiking and Backpacking: A Complete Guide.* New York: Norton, 1995.

———. "The Over the Hill Gang." *Backpacker* 25 (April 1997): 86–90.

Chazin, Daniel. *Appalachian Trail Data Book.* Harpers Ferry, W.Va.: Appalachian Trail Conference, 1999.

Clark, Wendy Mitman. "Discovering Life." *National Parks* 72, nos. 11–12 (November-December 1998): 22–25.

Edwards, Henry, ed. *Appalachian Trail Thru-Hikers' Companion 1999.* Harpers Ferry, W.Va.: Appalachian Trail Conference, 1999.

Elkinton, Steve. "How the National Trails System Came to Be." *Pathways Across America* 2 (Winter 1998): 3–6.

Ellison, George. "Exploring Old-Growth Forests." *Discovering the Smokies* 1, no. 1 (1997): 3–5. Gatlinburg: Great Smoky Mountains Natural History Association.

Fisher, Ronald M. *The Appalachian Trail.* Washington, D.C.: National Geographic Society, 1972.

———. *Mountain Adventure: Yesterday's Vision, Today's Trail.* Washington, D.C.: National Geographic Society, 1988.

Great Smoky Mountains Natural History Association. "Forests and Wildflowers in the Great Smoky Mountains National Park," ed. Steve Kemp. Gatlinburg: Great Smoky Mountains Natural History Association, 1994.

Green Mountain Club. *A Decade of Protecting Vermont's Mountain Lands, 1986–1996.* Waterbury Center, Vt.: Green Mountain Club, 1997.

———. *The Long Trail: A Footpath in the Wilderness.* Waterbury Center, Vt.: Green Mountain Club, 1996.

Grove, Noel. "A Tunnel through Time." *National Geographic* 171 (February 1987): 216–40.

Logue, Victoria, and Frank Logue. *The Best of the Appalachian Trail Day Hikes.* Birmingham, Ala.: Menasha Ridge Press; Harpers Ferry, W.Va.: Appalachian Trail Conference, 1994.

———. *The Best of the Appalachian Trail Overnight Hikes.* Birmingham, Ala.: Menasha Ridge Press; Harpers Ferry, W.Va.: Appalachian Trail Conference, 1994.

Lord, William G. *Blue Ridge Parkway Guide: Grandfather Mountain to Great Smoky Mountain NP.* Birmingham, Ala.: Menasha Ridge Press, 1997.

———. *Blue Ridge Parkway Guide: Rockfish Gap to Grandfather Mountain.* Birmingham, Ala.: Menasha Ridge Press, 1998.

Luck, John. "The Name of the Game." *Backpacker* 26 (December 1996): 126–27.

Luxenberg, Larry. *Walking the Appalachian Trail.* Mechanicsburg, Pa.: Stackpole Books, 1994.

Mann, Paul. "The Province of Dreamers." *Backpacker* 26 (October 1998): 49–54, 102–3.

National Park Service. *Appalachian Trail.* Washington, D.C.: U.S. Government Printing Office, 1996.

———. *Appalachian Trail Comprehensive Plan.* Washington, D.C.: U.S. Government Printing Office, 1987.

Thoreau, Henry David. *The Maine Woods.* Boston: Houghton Mifflin, 1893.

Continental Divide National Scenic Trail

American Hiking Society. "A Trail Along the Great Divide." *American Hiker* 20 (December 1995): 14–15, 19.

Berger, Karen, and Daniel Smith. *Where the Waters Divide.* New York: Harmony Books, 1993.

Carrier, Jim. "Bear Mauling Expert Offers New Strategy to Survive." *Continental Divide Trail News* 1 (Fall 1996): 4–5.

Continental Divide Trail Alliance. "CDTA Position Statement on Motorized Use of the Continental Divide Trail." *Continental Divide Trail News* 2 (Spring 1997): 1–2.

———. "Continental Divide National Scenic Trail State of the Trail Report." November 1998. Produced in cooperation with USDA Forest Service, National Park Service, and Bureau of Land Management.

Continental Divide Trail Society. "Continental Divide Trail

Society Border-to-Border."
www.gorp.com/edts/.

Davis, Lora, and Scott T. Smith (photographer). *Wyoming's Continental Divide Trail: The Official Guide.* Englewood, Colo.: Westcliffe, 1999.

Edwards, Mike. "Along the Great Divide." *National Geographic* 30 (October 1979): 483–511.

Fielder, John (photographer), and M. John Fayhee. *Along Colorado's Continental Divide Trail.* Englewood, Colo.: Westcliffe, 1997.

Howard, Lynna, and Leland Howard (photographer). *Montana and Idaho's Continental Divide Trail: The Official Guide.* Englewood, Colo.: Westcliffe, 1999.

Jones, Tom, with John Fielder (photographer). *Colorado's Continental Divide Trail: The Official Guide.* Englewood, Colo.: Westcliffe, 1997.

Julyan, Bob, and Tom Till (photographer). *New Mexico's Continental Divide Trail: The Official Guide.* Englewood, Colo.: Westcliffe, 1999–2000.

Krautwurst, Terry. "Grizzly Encounters." *Backpacker* 161 (August 1997): 61–63, 114–15.

Mangum, Neil. *In the Land of Frozen Fires: El Malpaís.* Washington, D.C.: U.S. Government Printing Office, 1990.

Muir, John. *Our National Parks.* Reprint, Madison: University of Wisconsin Press, 1981.

Oswald, Mark. "Stumbling Block." *Continental Divide Trail News* 1 (Fall 1996): 1, 5.

Richardson, Bill. "Why Northern New Mexico Is Different." *Continental Divide Trail News* 2 (Winter 1997): 2.

Ruhoff, Ron. *Colorado's Continental Divide.* Evergreen, Colo.: Cordillera Press, 1988.

Sprung, Gary, and Dennis Hall. "The Great Trails Debate: Two Views on Recreation and Wildlife." *High Country Citizens Alliance* (Spring 1997): 10.

USDA Forest Service, Northern Region. *The Continental Divide National Scenic Trail in Montana and Idaho.* Washington, D.C.: U.S. Government Printing Office, 1989.

USDA Forest Service, Rocky Mountain Region. *Continental Divide National Scenic Trail Comprehensive Plan.* Washington, D.C.: U.S. Government Printing Office, 1985.

———. *Final Environmental Impact Statement for the Continental Divide National Scenic Trail in Colorado and Wyoming.* Washington, D.C.: U.S. Government Printing Office, 1993.

Ward, Paula. "United Along the Divide: A Historic Event for CDT." *Pathways Across America* 10 (Fall 1997): 5, 9.

Whittlesey, Lee H. *Death in Yellowstone.* Boulder, Colo.: Roberts Rinehart, 1995.

Wilkinson, Todd. "Grizzly Fate." *National Parks* (November-December 1998): 30–33.

Wolf, James. *Guide to the Continental Divide Trail, Volumes I–VI.* Baltimore: Continental Divide Trail Society, 1982–1998.

Florida National Scenic Trail

American Hiking Society. "Surf's Up: Coast through Summer with these Oceanside Hikes."

American Hiker 11 (August 1998): 10–11.

Berlin, B. "Hiking the Florida National Scenic Trail." *American Hiker* (December 1996): 21–24.

Department of Environmental Protection Park Information. *Florida State Parks . . . the Real Florida.* Tallahassee: Florida Department of Environmental Protection, n.d.

Douglas, Marjory Stoneman. *The Everglades: River of Grass.* St. Simons Island, Ga.: Mockingbird Books, [1947] 1991.

Florida Department of Commerce. *Florida Trails.* Tallahassee: Florida Division of Tourism, n.d.

Florida Division of Forestry. *Your Guide to Florida's State Forests.* Tallahassee: Florida Department of Agriculture and Consumer Services, n.d. Brochure.

Ibrahim, Hilmi, and Kathleen A. Cordes. *Outdoor Recreation.* Dubuque: WCB Brown & Benchmark, 1993.

Keller, Jane, and E. Baldini. *Walking the Florida Trail.* Gainesville: Florida Trail Association, 1985.

McGivney, Annette. "Mother Nature's Theme Park." *Backpacker* 22, no. 3 (April 1994): 52–57.

National Geographic Society. *Pathways to Discovery.* Washington, D.C.: National Geographic Society, 1991.

U.S. Department of Agriculture, Department of Natural Resources, Florida Trail Association, and Forest Service Southern Region. *A Guide to Your Florida National Scenic Trail.* Washington, D.C.: U.S. Government Printing Office, April 1993.

U.S. Department of the Interior, National Park Service. *Wetlands in the National Parks.* Washington, D.C.: U.S. Government Printing Office, n.d.

U.S. Forest Service. *National Forests in Florida Recreation Area Directory.* Washington, D.C.: U.S. Government Printing Office, 1993.

———. *The Sunshine Connection.* Washington, D.C.: U.S. Government Printing Office, Winter 1997.

U.S. Fish and Wildlife Service. *America's Endangered Wetlands.* Washington, D.C.: U.S. Government Printing Office, 1990.

Ice Age National Scenic Trail

Black, Robert. *Geology of Ice Age National Scientific Reserve of Wisconsin.* Washington, D.C.: National Park Service, 1974.

Clayton, Lee, and John Attig. *Pleistocene Geology of Dane County, Wisconsin.* Madison: Wisconsin Geological and Natural History Survey, 1997.

Cvancara, A. *A Field Manual for the Amateur Geologist.* New York: John Wiley, 1995.

Department of Natural Resources, State of Wisconsin. *Interstate Park Visitor.* Saint Croix Falls: Wisconsin Department of Natural Resources, 1992.

Department of Natural Resources, State of Wisconsin, and National Park Service. *Ice Age.* Washington, D.C.: U.S. Government Printing Office, 1983. Brochure.

Division of Parks and Recreation. *The Geology of Interstate Park.* Minneapolis: Minnesota

Department of Natural Resources, June 1994.

Ham, Nelson, and John Attig. *Pleistocene Geology of Lincoln County, Wisconsin.* Madison: Wisconsin Geological and Natural History Survey, 1997.

Harrington, J. *Dance of the Continents.* Los Angeles: J. P. Tarcher, 1983.

Imbrie, John, and Katherine Palmer Imbrie. *Ice Ages: Solving the Mystery.* Cambridge, Mass.: Harvard University Press, 1979.

LaBastille, A. "On the Trail of Wisconsin's Ice Age." *National Geographic* 152 (August 1997): 182–205.

Leopold, Aldo. *A Sand County Almanac.* New York: Oxford University Press, 1949.

National Park Service. *Ice Age National Scientific Reserve: A Proposal for Cooperative Conservation.* Washington, D.C.: National Park Service.

National Park Service and State of Wisconsin Department of Natural Resources. *Ice Age National Scenic Trail Comprehensive Plan for Management and Use.* Denver: National Park Service, September 1983.

———. *Ice Age Trail.* Washington, D.C.: U.S. Government Printing Office, 1993. Brochure.

———. *A Master Plan Ice Age National Scientific Reserve Wisconsin.* Denver: National Park Service, July 1973.

Reuss, Henry. *On the Trail of the Ice Age.* Sheboygan, Wis.: Ice Age Park and Trail Foundation, 1990.

Trepanowski, Sally. "Visit Wisconsin's Ice Age on Foot." *American Hiker* 10 (February 1997): 14–17.

U.S. Department of the Interior U.S. Geological Survey. *The Great Ice Age,* by Louis L. Ray. Washington, D.C.: U.S. Government Printing Office, 1992. Brochure.

U.S. Forest Service. *Ice Age National Scenic Trail: Chequamegon National Forest.* Washington, D.C.: U.S. Government Printing Office, 1992. Brochure.

Wolfe, Linnie M. *Son of the Wilderness: John Muir.* Madison: University of Wisconsin Press, 1945.

Natchez Trace National Scenic Trail

Clemons, Samuel Langhorne [Mark Twain]. *Life on the Mississippi.* Reprint, New York: Penguin Books, 1984.

Daniels, Jonathan. *The Devil's Backbone: The Story of the Natchez Trace.* New York: McGraw-Hill, 1962.

Davis, Edwin, and W. Ranson. *The Barber of Natchez.* Baton Rouge: Louisiana State University Press, 1954.

Davis, William C. *A Way Through the Wilderness.* New York: HarperCollins, 1995.

Finley, Lori. *Traveling the Natchez Trace.* Winston-Salem, N.C.: John F. Blair, 1995.

Jekel, Pamela. *Natchez.* New York: Kensington Books, 1995.

Keating, Bern. "Today Along the Natchez Trace." *National Geographic* 134 (November 1968): 641–67.

National Park Service. *Comprehensive Trail Plan Natchez Trace.* Denver: National Park Service, 1987.

———. *Natchez Trace National Scenic Trail*. Washington, D.C.: U.S. Government Printing Office, November 1996.

———. *Natchez Trace Parkway*. Washington, D.C.: U.S. Government Printing Office, 1997.

———. *National Scenic Byway and All American Roads*. Denver: National Park Service, 1996.

Nicholas, W. "History Repeats in Old Natchez." *National Geographic* 95 (February 1949): 181–208.

Public Radio Mississippi. "Natchez Trace: A Road Through the Wilderness." Thomas Films, Inc, serial aired throughout 1996–97.

Thomas, David Hurst, Jay Miller, Richard White, Peter Nabokov, and P. Deloria. *The Native Americans: An Illustrated History*. Atlanta: Turner Publishing, 1993.

Silverberg, R. *The Mound Builders*. Athens: Ohio University Press, 1970.

Summerlin, C., and V. Summerlin. *Traveling the Trace*. Nashville: Rutledge Hill Press, 1995.

Trepanowski, S. "The Natchez Trace: A Scenic Trail through America's Past." *American Hiker* (April 1996): 10–14.

North Country National Scenic Trail

American Hiking Society. "Hike the North Country Trail State by State." *American Hiker* 9 (August 1996): 23.

Boyd, Wes. "Following the North Country National Scenic Trail." www.northcountrytrail.org.

Menke, Bill. "A Report from New York." *North Star* 16 (August-September 1997): 11–13.

Miller, Arthur P., and Marjorie L. Miller. *Trails Across America*. Golden, Colo.: Fulcrum, 1996.

National Park Service. *Comprehensive Plan for Management and Use*. Washington, D.C.: National Park Service, September 1982.

———. *North Country Trail*. Brochure.

Reimers, Tom. "North Country Trail New York to North Dakota." *Backpacker* 7 (October 1989): 64.

Seher, Jennifer. "Natural Passages." *National Parks* 65 (September-October 1991): 42–44.

USDA Forest Service. *Why Leaves Change Color*. October 1990. Brochure.

Pacific Crest National Scenic Trail

Bureau of Land Management. *Beyond the National Parks: A Recreation Guide to Public Lands in the West*. Edited by Mary E. Tisdale and Bibi Booth. Washington, D.C.: Smithsonian Institution Press, 1998.

Cash, David L. *A Brief History of the Pacific Crest National Scenic Trail*. Eugene, Ore.: Pacific Crest Trail Conference, 1988.

Elkinton, Steve. "How the National Trails System Came to Be." *Pathways Across America* (Winter 1998): 3–6.

Jardine, Ray. *The PCT's Hiker Handbook*. Berkeley, Calif.: Wilderness Press.

Johnson, Verna R. *Sierra Nevada: The Naturalist's Companion*. Berkeley: University of California Press, 1998.

La Pierre, Yvette. "Hot Spots." *National Parks* 69, nos. 1–2 (January-February 1995): 38.

Schaffer, Jeffrey P., Ben Schifrin, Thomas Winnett, and Ruby Johnson Jenkins. *The Pacific Crest Trail*. Vol. 1: *California*. Berkeley, Calif.: Wilderness Press, 1995.

Schaffer, Jeffrey P., and Andy Selters. *The Pacific Crest Trail, Volume 2: Oregon & Washington*. Berkeley, CA: Wilderness Press, 2000.

Tilling, Robert I. *Volcanoes*. Washington, D.C.: U.S. Government Printing Office, 1996.

USDA Forest Service. *Comprehensive Management Plan for the Pacific Crest National Scenic Trail*. Portland, Ore.: Pacific Northwest Region, USDA Forest Service, January 1982.

———. *Find Yourself . . . on the Pacific Crest Trail*. Pacific Crest Trail Association and USDA Forest Service, December 1993.

———. *National Parks and National Forest in the Pacific Northwest*. Washington, D.C.: U.S. Government Printing Office, 1986.

———. *Pacific Crest Trail: Washington, Oregon, California*. USDA Forest Service, National Park Service, Bureau of Land Management, and California Department of Parks and Recreation, July 1988.

Potomac Heritage National Scenic Trail

American Hiking Society. "Potomac Heritage Trail Committee to Meet." *American Hiker* 10 (October 1997): 24.

———. "Potomac Heritage Trail Update." *American Hiker* 10 (August 1997): 21.

Flexner, James Thomas. *Washington the Indispensable Man*. Boston: Little, Brown, 1974.

Garrett, William. "Waterway That Led to the Constitution: George Washington Patowmack Canal." *National Geographic* 171 (June 1987): 716–53.

Gore, Al. "Restoring Our Links to America's Heritage." *American Hiker* 10 (June 1997): 1, 17.

Hahn, T. F. *The Chesapeake & Ohio Canal: Pathway to the Nation's Capital*. Metuchen, N.J.: Scarecrow Press, 1984.

High, Mike. *The C&O Canal Companion*. Baltimore: Johns Hopkins University Press, 1997.

National Park Service. *Chesapeake and Ohio Canal*. Washington, D.C.: U.S. Government Printing Office, 1997.

———. *Fort Necessity*. Washington, D.C.: U.S. Government Printing Office, 1996. Brochure.

Pierce, D., ed. "Waterways West." *The Guide to Historic Virginia* 5 (July-August 1996): 1, 27.

Reed, John C., Jr. et al, Robert S. Sigafoos, and George W. Fisher. *The River and the Rocks*. U.S. Geological Survey Bulletin 1471. Washington, D.C.: U.S. Government Printing Office, 1980.

Shank, William H. *Towpaths to Tugboats: A History of American Canal Engineering*. York, Pa.: American Canal and Transportation Center, 1998.

U. S. Department of the Interior/U.S. Geological Survey. *River Basins of the United States: The Potomac*. Washington, D.C.: U.S. Government Printing Office, 1991.

Index